PATRIOTS, ROYALISTS, AND TERRORISTS
IN THE WEST INDIES

The French Revolution in Martinique and Guadeloupe,
1789–1802

WILLIAM S. CORMACK

Patriots, Royalists, and Terrorists in the West Indies

The French Revolution in Martinique and Guadeloupe, 1789–1802

UNIVERSITY OF TORONTO PRESS
Toronto Buffalo London

© University of Toronto Press 2019
Toronto Buffalo London
utorontopress.com

ISBN 978-1-4875-0395-6

Library and Archives Canada Cataloguing in Publication

Cormack, William Stewart, 1961–, author
Patriots, royalists, and terrorists in the West Indies : the French Revolution
in Martinique and Guadeloupe, 1789–1802 / William S. Cormack.

Includes bibliographical references and index.
ISBN 978-1-4875-0395-6 (hardcover)

1. Slave insurrections – West Indies, French.   2. West Indies, French –
History – 18th century.   3. France – History – Revolution, 1789–1799.   I. Title.

F2151.C67 2019   972.97'6   C2018-904039-4

This book has been published with the help of a grant from the Federation
for the Humanities and Social Sciences, through the Awards to Scholarly
Publications Program, using funds provided by the Social Sciences and
Humanities Research Council of Canada.

University of Toronto Press acknowledges the financial assistance to its
publishing program of the Canada Council for the Arts and the Ontario Arts
Council, an agency of the Government of Ontario.

Canada Council   Conseil des Arts
for the Arts   du Canada

Funded by the   Financé par le
Government   gouvernement
of Canada   du Canada

ONTARIO ARTS COUNCIL
CONSEIL DES ARTS DE L'ONTARIO
an Ontario government agency
un organisme du gouvernement de l'Ontario

Canadä

Table of Contents

vi   Contents

Illustrations and Maps

Illustrations

Maps

Acknowledgments

This book would never have been completed, let alone published, without help from many people, to whom I owe an enormous debt of gratitude. First and foremost, I want to express my profound thanks to my wife, Penny, and my daughter, Meg, for all of their love and support at every stage of this project.

I would like to thank the anonymous readers appointed by the University of Toronto Press for their careful reading of my manuscript, their thoughtful comments, and their excellent suggestions for revision: their constructive criticism helped to improve the final text immensely. I am also very grateful to three other people who read earlier versions of the manuscript. David Murray provided helpful advice and unflagging encouragement. Jeremy Popkin gave me the invaluable benefit of his expertise on the revolution in the French colonies and reassured me that this project was a valid one. Bette Oliver's sound editorial suggestions helped me to reduce the manuscript's length and to sharpen its focus. I also wish to acknowledge the kindness, assistance, and guidance I received from editors Stephen Shapiro and Richard Ratzlaff. All errors or flaws that remain in the book are, of course, entirely my responsibility.

The research for this project was supported financially by a standard research grant from the Social Sciences and Humanities Research Council of Canada. This research was only possible with assistance from the staff of the *Archives nationales* in Paris, the *Centre des archives d'Outre-Mer* in Aix-en-Provence, the *Archives départementales de la Martinique* in Fort-de-France, the *Archives départementales de la Guadeloupe* in Basse-Terre, the *Archives départementales de la Gironde* in Bordeaux, and the *Archives municipales de Bordeaux*. In metropolitan France and in the Caribbean, these busy people were always patient and helpful.

I also wish to express my appreciation to Marie Puddister, cartographer in the department of geography at the University of Guelph, who created the superb maps, and to Dr Katy Barrett, curator of art at the National Maritime Museum, Greenwich, who graciously gave me a personal viewing of the images used to illustrate this book.

Finally, I would like to thank my faculty colleagues and friends, for their support in various forms, and the students I have taught for their interest and enthusiasm that constantly reaffirmed the value of teaching and studying history.

PATRIOTS, ROYALISTS, AND TERRORISTS
IN THE WEST INDIES

The French Revolution in Martinique and Guadeloupe,
1789–1802

Introduction

In September 1789, two months after crowds stormed the Bastille in Paris, merchant ships from Bordeaux arrived at the colonies of Martinique and Guadeloupe in the eastern Caribbean bringing news of the French Revolution. The effect of this news, and of the tricolour cockades worn by the ships' passengers and crews as symbols of revolutionary liberty and national sovereignty, was dramatic. The colonial governors' efforts to prevent the wearing of such cockades sparked riots in the ports of Saint-Pierre in Martinique and Pointe-à-Pitre in Guadeloupe, and these riots began a protracted and convoluted revolutionary struggle in the Lesser Antilles or, as French contemporaries referred to them, the *Îles du Vent* or the Windward Islands. While smaller than the colony of Saint-Domingue, their sugar and coffee production made the Windward Islands valuable components of France's commercial economy. This production depended on slave labour, and the black slaves who worked the plantations vastly outnumbered the free population, which was itself divided along racial, economic, and social fault lines. The grievances and agency of the colonial population shaped the ensuing struggle but so did metropolitan influences. This study provides a history of the French Revolution in Martinique and Guadeloupe.

The arrival of news, ideas, and language from France provided a script for revolutionary action in the Windward Islands, a script that was revised periodically by new metropolitan communications. Rumours of emancipation sparked an abortive slave revolt in Martinique at the end of August 1789 and revealed the depth of white fears regarding the fragility of the slave system. Revolutionary symbols and rhetoric encouraged white resistance to colonial elites and provided new political identities: *petit-Blanc*, or poor white, and merchant supporters of the revolution called themselves "patriots," while referring to the governors as "despots" and to their planter enemies as "aristocrats." Travellers' accounts and newspaper reports, as well as official announcements, undermined royal authority in the colonies and provoked local claims to national or popular authority. While planters used existing colonial assemblies to arrogate legislative authority, defying metropolitan regulation of trade, a popular committee in Saint-Pierre claimed to speak for "the people" and denied the legitimacy of both the colonial assembly and the governor general. The colonial revolution, however, was deeply ambiguous. White colonists demanded freedom for themselves but also wanted the maintenance of black slavery. White insistence on strict racial hierarchy poisoned debates on citizenship for the *gens de couleur*, the colonies' free people of colour, whose aspirations for equality were clear before 1789. Planters sought greater colonial autonomy yet backed governors against popular challenges to the islands' elites.

The revolution's ambiguity in the Windward Islands continued after 1789, as did competition between rival claims to legitimate authority. A bitter factional struggle escalated to civil war in 1790, and the representatives from France sent to end the conflict failed to reconcile the two sides or to impose principles of the liberal revolution. In 1792 planter-controlled colonial assemblies in Martinique and Guadeloupe rebelled against metropolitan authority under the banner of the old monarchy. A single frigate captain defeated this counter-revolution by both undermining its legitimacy and by promising equality to free people of colour, all the while reassuring masters that the French Republic would not threaten slavery. The tensions and contradictions within the republican regimes subsequently established in Martinique and Guadeloupe diminished the colonies' ability to resist British conquest in 1794. In the context of international war, new agents of metropolitan France regained control of Guadeloupe and delivered the most radical of revolutionary scripts: the abolition of slavery and the Jacobin Terror. Yet racial and political ambiguity also characterized this radical regime. At the same time, planters in Martinique collaborated with the British occupation to maintain slavery and to isolate the colony from all notions of liberty and equality.

Developments in the colonies were not part of the traditional history of the French Revolution.[1] Yet since 1989 the study of upheaval in the Caribbean, along with the colonial questions facing metropolitan legislators, has shifted from the specialized field of colonial history to become part of mainstream revolutionary scholarship.[2] Growing historical interest in slavery and its abolition, however, has focused almost exclusively on developments in Saint-Domingue. This concentration reflects the reality that in 1789 Saint-Domingue was the richest colonial possession in the world. Moreover, the colony was the site of a massive slave revolt in 1791 that threatened French control. After representatives of the metropolitan government proclaimed freedom for Saint-Domingue's slaves in the summer of 1793, the National Convention voted the decree of 16 *Pluviôse* in February 1794 that abolished slavery throughout the French empire. Subsequent revolt against Napoleon Bonaparte's attempt to reintroduce slavery in 1802 led to the declaration of the independent Republic of Haiti in 1804. Given the world-historical importance of the events in Saint-Domingue, many historians now refer to the entire period as the Age of the French *and* Haitian Revolutions.[3]

Revolution in the Windward Islands has not been neglected entirely. The recent historical literature on the interaction of slavery and revolution in the French Caribbean includes two important studies of developments in Guadeloupe. In *Esclavage, métissage, liberté: La révolution française en Guadeloupe 1789–1802*, Frédéric Régent emphasized the limits of revolution and emancipation in the colony since racial distinctions and forced labour continued after the formal abolition of slavery in 1794. People of colour in Guadeloupe who were free before 1789 enjoyed relative prestige and prosperity under the new republican regime, while the newly freed slaves continued to work the colony's plantations as "cultivators." Régent argued that this reflected limited free-coloured militancy before 1789, as well as complex ties of solidarity and clientage between whites and free-coloured people that persisted after 1794.[4] Rather than social structures, Laurent Dubois's *A Colony of Citizens: Revolution and Slave Emancipation in the French Caribbean 1787–1804* centred on revolutionary conflict in Guadeloupe. He argued that slave insurgents at Trois-Rivières in 1793 succeeded in integrating themselves into the Republic by claiming to be "citizens" and that Guadeloupe's revolt against Bonaparte's new administration in 1802 influenced Haiti's War of Independence by exposing the French state's intention to restore slavery. Thus the study placed events in Guadeloupe in the context of a larger struggle for liberation. Moreover, if the French Declaration of the Rights of Man and Citizen of 1789 provoked debates on whether freedom and equality were possible in the colonies, Dubois contended that it was slave and free-coloured insurrection in the Caribbean that gave these revolutionary principles universal meaning.[5]

This assertion that colonial revolution influenced European ideology fits into a larger trend within the historical literature that emphasizes globalization.[6] While investigating the French Revolution's origins in the context of global trade and finance in the eighteenth century represents a promising research subject, the "global turn" risks exaggerating the colonies' importance to the debates and decisions of revolutionary assemblies.[7] Moreover, it could minimize or downplay the extent to which the metropolitan revolutionary dynamic shaped colonial upheaval. In his recent book, *You Are All Free: The Haitian Revolution and the Abolition of Slavery*, Jeremy Popkin argued that the radical and completely unauthorized decision of metropolitan commissioners in Saint-Domingue to proclaim freedom in June 1793 for slaves who would fight for the Republic was not the direct outcome of the slave uprising. Rather, it was taken in response to a crisis in the town of Cap Français arising from conflict among the colony's free population. Popkin argued that a further series of contingencies, rather than any inevitable logic of revolutionary ideology, caused the deputies of the National Convention to condone the granting of general liberty in Saint-Domingue and to vote the decree of 16 *Pluviôse* in February 1794.[8] Beyond its emphasis on contingency, Popkin's study demonstrated that the complex revolution in Saint-Domingue cannot be reduced to a struggle between masters and slaves. Destabilizing conflict among free colonists also played a critical role.

This was even more the case in the Windward Islands, which did not experience a slave uprising on the same scale as that which occurred in Saint-Domingue. If the importance of political struggles between rival white factions has been downplayed in recent literature, these clashes were crucial to the revolution in Martinique and Guadeloupe. Fear of slave revolt was always present, as was the tension between white resistance to racial equality and desire for allies among the *gens de couleur*. Central to the factional conflict, however, were revolutionary ideas, language, symbols, and practices from metropolitan France. These were the elements of a new political culture, through which power could be exercised or contested. This new political culture undermined the authority of Old Regime administrators, but it also generated a struggle between competing claims to a new legitimacy based on the nation's or the people's will.[9]

The role and impact of revolutionary political culture in Martinique and Guadeloupe can be clarified by consideration of the transmission and reception of news and information from France and of its circulation and interpretation within the colonies. A recent history of France's colonial empire between the Treaty of Utrecht and the end of the Seven Years' War suggests the value of applying aspects of communications theory. Kenneth J. Banks's *Chasing Empire across the Sea: Communications and the State in the French Atlantic, 1713–1763* provides a comparative study of Canada, Louisiana, and the Windward Islands, as well as an Atlantic-world revision of the understanding of absolutism and its relationship to empire. Banks broadly defined "communications" as the gathering, analysing, displaying, storing, and disseminating of information and representations of authority, suggesting that communications should be understood to encompass shipping patterns and public celebrations as well as official correspondence and merchants' letters. He argued that while the absolutist state was relatively successful in monopolizing communications in metropolitan France, it faced serious difficulties in obtaining, analysing, and controlling information in the colonies as part of its effort to shape the social order and to maintain metropolitan control.[10]

Three of Banks's themes regarding the problems encountered by the metropolitan state in reinforcing its authority and shaping colonial society have direct relevance to revolutionary struggles over political culture. First, he examined the significance of delays in the transmission of important news from France to the colonies, and of confusion regarding its implications, using the announcement of peace in 1713 as a case study.[11] News of the outbreak of revolution in 1789 had an even bigger impact in the colonies, while the nature of its dissemination, and how it was received, was even more threatening to colonial authorities. Second, he contended that the French state sought to control marginal groups in colonial society by curtailing their freedom of communication. He refers to convicts, soldiers, and slaves, arguing that the *Code Noir* represented an attempt to encode and control slaves by circumscribing their learning, travel, and assembly.[12] The colonial administration's inability to control the communication of revolutionary ideas and symbols after 1789 threatened not only its domination of slaves but also free people of colour and *petits Blancs*. The republican authorities who superseded governors and colonial assemblies associated with the Old Regime, as well as the royalists who returned to power in Martinique under British occupation and Victor Hugues's Jacobin-inspired regime in Guadeloupe, also sought to control the communications of slaves and *gens de couleur* with limited success. In discussing the absolutist state's reliance on merchant networks to carry dispatches and to gather news in the colonies, Banks developed a third theme that might be applied to the revolutionary struggle. He argued that local elites became "culture brokers," who mediated between the state and colonial society, and that competition and conflicting interpretations among these colonial elites weakened metropolitan administration in the French Atlantic.[13] Arguably the French Revolution divided colonial elites even more than the Seven Years' War. Different representatives of the state, sent by successive metropolitan regimes after 1789, introduced different variants of revolutionary political culture and, with the support of local allies, these culture brokers sought to enforce compliance in the colonies.

This study of Martinique and Guadeloupe is less concerned with the mode or logistics of sending information across the Atlantic, however, than with how the contents of communications helped to influence colonists' political action and understanding. Such a hermeneutic approach fits with the notion of the "revolutionary script" that Keith Michael Baker and Dan Edelstein suggest can be applied to the comparative study of revolutions. Revolutionaries have been intensely self-conscious of previous revolutions, which offered frameworks to define situations, suggest actions, and project narratives. They did not merely follow existing scripts but adapted, revised, and transformed them.[14] The modern revolutionary script was written during the French Revolution of 1789, according to Baker, because this was the historical moment when the idea of revolution as descriptive fact was replaced by a conceptualization of revolution as self-conscious act. French revolutionaries, unlike previous rebels acting against established authority, perceived themselves to be seeking to achieve universal values that were at risk in an uncertain political drama.[15]

A possible criticism of this concept, however, might be that it implies that historical actors, like those in a theatre, follow scripts that dictate their actions: it could suggest that they have no volition or free agency. To be clear, the concept of the "revolutionary script" is not used here to deny historical agency or to imply that the actions of colonial actors were ideologically determined by metropolitan patterns. Rather, the notion of scripting is applied to the revolution in Martinique and Guadeloupe to argue that such patterns were more influential than recent studies suggest. News from France provided different groups in colonial society with a cause to justify resistance to metropolitan control, to the domination of colonial elites, to racial inequality, and even to the continuation of slavery. The revolutionary script did not play out in the colonial setting without tensions and contradictions, of course, and successive representatives of the metropolitan state brought revised versions that altered the narrative. Opponents of the revolution in the colonies also found inspiration and direction in metropolitan scripts of counter-revolution or conservative reaction. Concepts, symbols, and language provided roles to be played, rhetorical lines to be delivered, and ideological understanding of a struggle that linked the colonies to France and beyond.

This study examines the revolution in the Windward Islands from 1789 to 1802. It considers developments in Martinique and Guadeloupe within a single geographical setting, given the important commercial, administrative, and political links between the two colonies. The international context of war and great power politics reinforced these links. Beyond addressing the relative neglect of this archipelago in the historical literature, the study argues that the metropolitan revolutionary dynamic helped to shape developments in the colonies. Its focus is on the political struggle to apply or implement revolutionary principles in the Windward Islands but also to qualify or resist them. Thus it considers the words and actions of "patriots" and "aristocrats," republicans and royalists, radicals and moderates. This study involves an exploration of the role of political culture, emphasizing the power of revolutionary ideas and language to provide a script for political action, as well as their ambiguity in the colonial setting. These political actors sought to control the transmission and circulation of news, rhetoric, and symbols, and they tried to monopolize the interpretation of this information. The questions of whether liberty applied to slaves and whether equality applied to *gens de couleur* were crucial to the revolution in Martinique and Guadeloupe. Conflict over these questions occurred within a larger struggle for power among different factions; however, it was a struggle shaped by conflicting conceptions of authority and driven by competing claims to legitimacy. Given the crucial interaction between colonial upheaval and metropolitan political culture, therefore, what follows is a history of the French Revolution in the Windward Islands.

Dramatis Personae

The Old-Regime Administrators:
Charles-Joseph Hyacinthe du Houx, comte de Vioménil (governor general, 1789–90)

Pierre-Xavier-François Foullon d'Écotier (intendant, Martinique)
Baron de Clugny (governor of Guadeloupe, 1786–92)
René-Marie d'Arrot (second in command, then governor of Guadeloupe,
    1792–3)
Claude-Charles, vicomte de Damas (governor general, 1783–9, 1790–1)

The "Patriots":
Ruste (Martinique)
Crassous de Médeuil (Martinique)
Thoumazeau (Martinique)
Jacques Coquille Dugommier (Guadeloupe)
Thyrus Pautrizel (Guadeloupe)

The "Royalists":
Louis-François Dubuc (Martinique)
Louis De Curt (Guadeloupe)
Bellevue-Blanchetière (Martinique)
Baron de Clairfontaine (Martinique)
Romain Lacaze (Guadeloupe)

The Representatives of Metropolitan France (1791–4):
Jean-Pierre-Antoine, comte de Béhague de Villeneuve (governor
    general, 1791–3)
Jean de Lacoste (king's commissioner 1791; Minister of Marine 1792)
Louis-Maurice Magnytôt (king's commissioner, 1791)
Antoine Eu de Montdenoix (king's commissioner, 1791)
Jacques Linger (king's commissioner, 1791)
Donatien-Marie-Joseph de Vimeur Rochambeau (governor general,
    1793–4)
Georges-Henri-Victor Collot (governor of Guadeloupe, 1793–4)

The Officers of the French Navy:
Henri-Jean-Baptiste, vicomte Pontevès-Gien (captain, *Illustre*;
    commander Windward Islands Station, 1788–90)
Chevalier de Rivière (captain, *Ferme*; commander Windward Islands
    Station, 1790–2)
Vicomte d'Orléans (captain, *Embuscade*)
Louis Mallevault de Vaumorant (captain, *Calypso*)
Jean-Baptiste-Raymond Lacrosse (captain, *Félicité*; commander
    Windward Islands Station, 1793–4; captain general, Guadeloupe, 1801)

Corentin-Urbain de Leissègues (captain, *Picque*; rear admiral,
    commander Windward Islands Station, 1793–9)

The "Terrorists":
Victor Hugues (civil commissioner, 1794–6; agent of Directory, 1796–8)
Pierre Chrétien (civil commissioner, 1794)
Goyrand (civil commissioner, 1795–6; agent of Directory, 1796–8)
Lebas (civil commissioner, 1795–6; agent of Directory, 1796–8)
Pierre Villegégu (administrator, Guadeloupe)

Victor Hugues's Critics:
Mathieu Pelardy
Hapel de La Channie
Thouluyre Mahé

The Republicans of Colour:
Bellegarde (Martinique)
Julien Fédon (Grenada)
Chatoyer (St Vincent)
Marinier (St Vincent)
Jean Kina (royalist, Martinique)

The British:
Lieutenant General Sir Charles Grey
Vice Admiral Sir John Jervis
Major General Thomas Dundas
Brigadier General Colin Graham
Lieutenant General Robert Prescott
Lieutenant General Sir John Vaughan
Governor Robert Shore Milnes
Governor William Keppel

1 The Windward Islands on the Eve of Revolution

On the eve of the revolution France's Caribbean colonies were sources of tremendous national wealth, but these overseas possessions were neither secure nor stable. The colonies were the basis of a commercial network that had developed since the seventeenth century around the production and marketing of colonial products such as cotton, indigo, coffee, and, above all, sugar. By the mid-eighteenth century the dramatic expansion of sugar consumption drove a thriving industry that accounted for sixty million *livres'* worth of French exports to Europe in 1785 alone.[1] This rich trade depended on the fertile plantations of the West Indies. Saint-Domingue was the most important French possession: by 1789 the annual revenue from its production had reached an estimated 180 million *livres.*[2] This was almost seven times that of Martinique or Guadeloupe, but these smaller colonies in the Windward Islands remained extremely valuable. The French decision to retain Guadeloupe rather than Canada in the Treaty of Paris of 1763 reflected the disproportionate wealth generated by the small island.[3] Yet if the colonies were valuable, they were also vulnerable. War cut communications and disrupted trade. The British capture of Guadeloupe during the Seven Years' War, along with Martinique and the other French islands in the Lesser Antilles, demonstrated the threat posed by France's imperial rivals to its colonies. Despite the return of Guadeloupe and Martinique to French control after 1763, and France's success in the American War of Independence, this threat remained in 1789. Beyond the external threat of war, Martinique and Guadeloupe were also highly vulnerable to dangers intrinsic to the colonial system. In keeping with the mercantilism of the age, the French Crown sought to prevent its colonies from trading with rival powers and to limit their commerce to French shipping. Planters deeply resented these restrictions, embodied in the regulations of the *Exclusif*, and such resentment fuelled demands for autonomy from metropolitan control. News of revolution in France undermined the authority of royal administrators, thus opening the door to greater independence. Yet it was the bitter tensions within colonial society that made the Windward Islands a powder keg. White colonists were socially and economically divided between the *grands Blancs*, consisting of government administrators, rich merchants, and the owners of large sugar plantations, and the *petits Blancs*, who included minor merchants and small planters, as well as the rootless population of artisans and seamen in colonial ports. This crucial division was overshadowed by the brutal disproportion between free minority and enslaved mass: the black slaves who worked the plantations made up 80 per cent of the colonies' population. If slave labour was the basis of the colonial economy, it was also a source of fear and instability: vastly outnumbered, the white population was preoccupied with maintaining control over the blacks. Socially and legally inferior to all whites, although sometimes the owners of substantial property, was a heterogeneous class of free blacks and people of mixed race known as the *gens de couleur*. This group's aspirations to civil equality with whites before 1789 challenged the racial hierarchy upon which colonial society was based. The other, even more radical challenge was the call for slavery's abolition. A small but vocal number of metropolitan liberals insisted that slavery was abominable and incompatible with the principles of reason and humanity associated with the Enlightenment. The communication of these ideological threats to the colonial system inspired fears and hopes that exacerbated the economic, social, and racial tensions in the colonies. Therefore, if the Windward Islands represented precious sources of commercial wealth in 1789, the French Revolution would expose the precarious nature of their internal regimes.

I France's Colonies in the Eastern Caribbean

Eighteenth-century Frenchmen knew the Lesser Antilles, the archipelago of small islands curving north from Trinidad and separating the Atlantic Ocean from the Caribbean Sea, as the *Îles du Vent* or the Windward Islands. This designation was based on the direction of the prevailing trade winds, which blow from east to west, and distinguished them from the *Îles sous le Vent* or the Leeward Islands. These large islands to the west, now referred to as the Greater Antilles, include Puerto Rico, Jamaica, Cuba, and Hispaniola, which was divided between the Spanish colony of Santo Domingo and French Saint-Domingue. On the eve of the revolution, France's colonies in the Windward Islands included Tobago; Sainte-Lucie (Saint Lucia); Martinique; Guadeloupe and its small dependencies of Marie-Galante, Desirade, and the Saints, as well as the northern part of Saint-Martin.[4] The division of the West Indies into different colonial domains was based in part on initial settlement but also on war. Some French influence remained on the British colonies of Dominica, St Vincent, and Grenada, which had been under France's control until they were granted definitively to Great Britain in 1763. The largest and most important of the French Windward Islands were Guadeloupe and Martinique. Two linked islands made up the colony of Guadeloupe, with Grande-Terre to the north-east separated from Basse-Terre by the Rivière Salée. Mountainous Basse-Terre was topped by the volcanic summit of La Soufrière, rising 1,464 metres above the sea, which overlooked the major town and administrative capital also called Basse-Terre. In contrast, the flat limestone island of Grande-Terre had no elevation above 200 metres. The town of Pointe-à-Pitre on Grande-Terre was the colony's principal commercial port.[5] If Guadeloupe's plantations had become more prosperous, Martinique had vital strategic importance: the superb natural harbour of Fort-Royal on the island's west side was France's principal naval base in the West Indies. To the north of Fort-Royal, with its fortifications and administrative headquarters, was the flourishing commercial port of Saint-Pierre. With a population of between twenty thousand and twenty-five thousand people, many of them living in imposing stone houses, Saint-Pierre was the largest town in the Windward Islands. Northern Martinique was characterized by dense forest and volcanic mountains, the highest being Mont Pelée at 1,397 metres, whereas the south featured lower summits and somewhat sparser vegetation.[6] The colonies' tropical climate made them ideal for growing crops like sugar and coffee. For all of the Windward Islands the year was divided between two basic seasons: the dry season, *le carême*, from January to May, and the wet season, *l'hivernage*, from June to December. It was during the latter that hurricanes could sweep across the islands, devastating crops and sinking any vessels outside sheltered harbours.[7]

French colonization of the Lesser Antilles began in the seventeenth century under the auspices of trading companies with royal sponsorship.[8] After the foundation of a French colony on Saint-Christophe

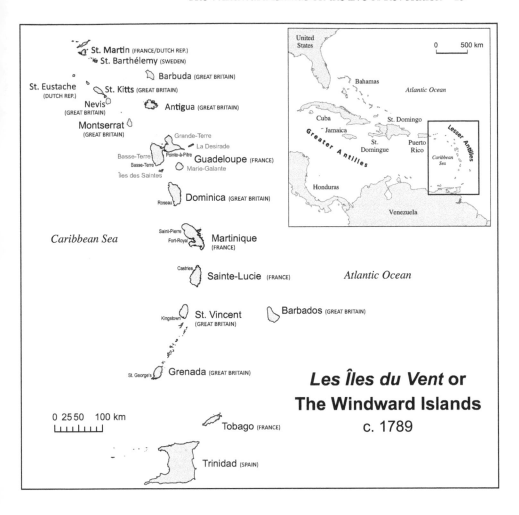

St. Martin (FRANCE/DUTCH REP.)
St. Barthélemy (SWEDEN)
Barbuda (GREAT BRITAIN)
St. Eustache (DUTCH REP.)
St. Kitts (GREAT BRITAIN)
Nevis (GREAT BRITAIN)
Antigua (GREAT BRITAIN)
Montserrat (GREAT BRITAIN)
Grande-Terre
La Desirade
Basse-Terre
Pointe-à-Pitre
Basse-Terre
Guadeloupe (FRANCE)
Marie-Galante
Îles des Saintes
Roseau
Dominica (GREAT BRITAIN)

Caribbean Sea

Saint-Pierre
Fort-Royal
Martinique (FRANCE)

Castries
Sainte-Lucie (FRANCE)

Atlantic Ocean

Kingstown
St. Vincent (GREAT BRITAIN)
Barbados (GREAT BRITAIN)

St. George's
Grenada (GREAT BRITAIN)

Les Îles du Vent or
The Windward Islands
c. 1789

0 25 50   100 km

Tobago (FRANCE)

Trinidad (SPAIN)

United States
0   500 km
Bahamas
Atlantic Ocean
Cuba
St. Domingo
Greater Antilles
Jamaica
St. Domingue
Puerto Rico
Lesser Antilles
Caribbean Sea
Honduras
Venezuela

Map 1 *"Les Îles du Vent* or The Windward Islands, circa 1789." Map by Marie Puddister of the Department of Geography, University of Guelph.

(St Kitts) in 1625, the *Compagnie des Îles d'Amérique* established small settlements on both Guadeloupe and Martinique in 1635. Initial friendly relations between European settlers and the indigenous inhabitants were short-lived. The Caribs resisted French colonization and the ensuing warfare only came to an end in 1660, when the Caribs had been driven from both colonies and confined to the islands of St Vincent and Dominica.[9] In 1648 the *Compagnie des Îles d'Amérique* went bankrupt and the governors of Guadeloupe and Martinique become independent governor-proprietors. Jean-Baptiste Colbert, Louis XIV's great minister, was determined that the colonies should increase France's power and expand its economy. In 1664 he created the *Compagnie des Indes Occidentales*; gave it a monopoly on all West Indian trade; and sent Alexander Prouville, seigneur de Tracy, with warships and soldiers to return the islands to the French empire. Planters resented the West India Company's monopoly, and the outbreak of war with England devastated the company's profits. Colbert's vision prevailed, however, and he strengthened the commercial links between France and the Antilles. In 1674 Colbert dissolved the West India Company, placing the colonies under the direct authority of royal government.[10]

The structures established under Colbert laid the basis for colonial administration in the eighteenth century. A governor, who was a high-ranking military officer and thus a noble, represented the king in each colony. He commanded its military forces, the militia as well as regular troops, and had authority over commerce and general administration. After 1714 the French possessions in the Leeward and Windward Islands were administered separately. Saint-Domingue's governor general resided in Port-au-Prince, while the governor general of the Windward Islands was based at Fort-Royal in Martinique. Therefore, except for a brief period following the Seven Years' War, the governors of Guadeloupe and the other Windward Islands were subordinate to that of Martinique. An *intendant*, also appointed by metropolitan government, although from the ranks of the sometimes non-noble officers of the pen, assisted each governor. *Intendants* were responsible for public works, the administration of justice, the registration of royal laws, supervision of accounts for the navy and merchant marine, and above all for finances and collection of the *impôt*, a head tax on colonists and on their slaves, the only direct tax paid in the islands. While in theory there would be complete harmony between them, governors and *intendants* were sometimes rivals rather than allies.[11] The two agents of royal authority shared a number of powers in common, the most important being the power to assemble the colony's sovereign council.[12] Created in 1645, these councils were composed of the principal administrators as well as a number of the richest planters nominated by the governor. The sovereign council was somewhat analogous to a *parlement* in metropolitan France: it functioned as the colony's high court of justice, but it also had the right to examine ordinances introduced by the governor or *intendant* and to submit remonstrances to the king. Members of the councils exercised various police powers and enjoyed a number of jealously guarded privileges.[13] If the sovereign councils demonstrated the influence of the colonies' elite, Colbert and his successors wanted colonial administration to remain independent from the planters; governors were to uphold royal will and metropolitan interests, particularly with regard to trade.

Parallel to the transition from governor-proprietors to royal administration, the colonies' economy changed from one of small-scale agriculture with a mixed labour force to a plantation system dependent on black slavery. Early settlers in Guadeloupe and Martinique grew cash crops of cotton, indigo, cocoa, ginger, and especially tobacco. Producing tobacco on small estates using white indentured servants, or *engagés*, was profitable as long as the demand in Europe was high.[14] After 1630, however, the market was saturated and prices slumped. It was then that the Dutch, who controlled trans-Atlantic trade, introduced the growing of sugar cane to the English and French Caribbean colonies. During the seventeenth century most of Europe's sugar had come from Brazil, where the Portuguese had developed a system of large plantations. The Portuguese first enslaved native Indians, but when this proved unsatisfactory they began to import slaves from Africa to work in the sugar fields.[15] English Barbados was the first colony in the Lesser Antilles to switch fully from tobacco to sugar in the 1640s.[16] By 1680 Barbados was beginning to experience soil exhaustion, but it had already provided a successful model for the rest of the Caribbean. After 1654 Dutch merchants and Portuguese Jews expelled from Brazil brought expertise in sugar growing to Martinique and Guadeloupe.[17] Sugar production required major capital investment in land but also in mills to extract the juice from the canes and in boiling houses to transform the juice into crude sugar and molasses. The planting, weeding, manuring, and especially harvesting of sugar cane were very labour intensive activities. *Engagés* were neither available in sufficient numbers nor economical to employ. Therefore, like the Portuguese before them, the French colonists imported increasing numbers of African slaves beginning in the

1660s. Guadeloupe moved first from tobacco farms to sugar plantations, but Martinique's many small holdings were also giving way to
fewer large sugar estates by 1670, when the West Indies faced a crisis of
overproduction. The European market was oversupplied with sugar
and prices plummeted. This did not end production, however, but ac-
celerated its concentration into the hands of fewer but richer planters.
By the time prices recovered in 1690, a sugar economy had been established in Saint-Domingue and the Windward Islands had been transformed. In 1661 there were only 3,000 slaves in Guadeloupe, and even
fewer in Martinique. By 1700 Guadeloupe had 73 sugar plantations and
6,700 slaves, while Martinique had 183 plantations with 14,200 slaves.[18]

Colonial trade boomed in the period of peace after 1715. Its contribution to France's economy rose rapidly in the first half of the eighteenth
century and continued to grow until the revolution.[19] A high demand
for sugar rewarded large investments of capital in the West Indies and,
consequently, as much land as possible was put into sugar. Other tropical products remained important as well, and colonists first planted
coffee in Martinique in 1720. While some food for the slaves was grown
in the colonies, everything else was imported. Therefore, metropolitan
merchants shipped, unloaded, and processed commodities imported
from the islands, and they also exported food and all other goods demanded by the colonists. Almost as important as the direct trade between France and the colonies was the re-export of colonial products to
the rest of Europe, which accounted for 32 per cent of all French exports
in 1787.[20] The trade in slaves became a crucial and lucrative adjunct of
the trade in colonial commodities. The demand for slaves in the French
colonies rose in proportion to the expansion of sugar cultivation. Originally royal government gave chartered companies such as the *Compagnie
du Sénégal* a monopoly on the slave trade, but they proved unable to
meet the growing demand. In 1716 the trade was opened to *négriers*
from five French ports; by 1741 this had been extended to merchants
from virtually all French ports. Even when it was placed in the hands of
private slavers, the trade received important fiscal concessions from the
state. Goods traded for slaves in Africa were exempt from export duties, and sugar and other products purchased from the sale of slaves in
the colonies received a 50 per cent reduction on entry duties to France.
In 1784 the crown abolished the exemptions, which cost millions of
livres in lost tax revenue, replacing them with a subsidy based on the
tonnage of each slave ship.[21] The French slave trade expanded rapidly
between 1713 and 1744, then stagnated during the middle decades of

the eighteenth century largely because of the maritime struggles with Great Britain, before growing again from 1778 to the French Republic's declaration of war against Britain in 1793.[22] Nantes became the centre of the French slave trade, and that city's merchants outfitted more than 1,400 slaving expeditions in the eighteenth century, accounting for 45 per cent of the national total.[23] Nantes prospered because of the slave trade, but all of France's great seaports and their hinterlands benefitted from thriving colonial trade and the production it stimulated: the colonies were a captive market for metropolitan flour, wine, codfish, salt beef, textiles, and many other products. Bordeaux was the most important of these port cities; its West Indian trade in 1789 had a value of 112 million *livres*.[24] The wealth generated by all of this commerce was reflected in Bordeaux's grand *Place de la Bourse*, its busy warehouses and impressive merchants' residences. Thus the Caribbean colonies, including Guadeloupe and Martinique, were crucial to the most dynamic segment of the French economy at the end of the Old Regime.

The colonies were also central to the intense imperial rivalry between France and Great Britain during the eighteenth century.[25] War revealed the close connection between colonies, trade, and sea power. Major military expeditions from Great Britain conquered the French Windward Islands during the Seven Years' War (1756–63).[26] Prime Minister William Pitt the Elder guided British strategy, advocating aggressive colonial and naval warfare to destroy the bases of French commercial and maritime strength.[27] Yet concessions to France at the peace table, principally the return of Guadeloupe and Martinique, foiled his plans. The subsequent recovery of the French Navy, which had suffered shattering defeats at sea in 1759, vindicated Pitt's insistence that the roots of French power had not been pulled out. In 1778 France declared war on Great Britain in support of the American rebels. The French Navy's victory at Chesapeake Bay contributed directly to the British surrender at Yorktown in 1781, thus assuring the independence of the United States.[28] In the Caribbean, French forces captured St Kitts, Dominica, Grenada, and St Vincent, but naval defeat at the Battle of the Saints in 1782 thwarted French plans to conquer Jamaica. In the Treaty of Versailles of 1783 ending the war, France ceded all its conquests in exchange for Sainte-Lucie and the former British colony of Tobago. French commerce expanded in the final decade of the Old Regime as sugar and coffee production boomed. For both France and Great Britain the Caribbean colonies had become the biggest depositories of overseas investment, but they were also the most vulnerable. Statesmen on both sides of the Channel perceived that colonial trade was vital to French shipping and naval strength. Therefore when war came again in 1793, conquest of the French sugar islands was a major element of British strategy for ruining France's commercial and sea power.[29]

Wars in the eighteenth century threatened the French Windward Islands with conquest, but they also disrupted the patterns of trade dictated by metropolitan government. The French Navy's weakness enabled the British enemy to stop French merchant ships from reaching the colonies. As a result, wartime saw trade between the French islands and foreign merchants increase significantly. Such illegal trade was a direct threat to the colonial system where the colonies were the domain of the crown, and all their trade had to be conducted with metropolitan France using French ships only. Planters in the Caribbean resented this system, which benefitted metropolitan commercial interests at their expense, and they resented the colonial administrators who sought to enforce it.

II Regulation of Trade and Resentment of Colonial Administration

Episodes of conflict at the beginning of Louis XV's reign revealed the early strength of this resentment and the weakness of colonial authority. In 1715 the crown attempted to impose an *octroi*, an additional tax to help pay for colonial defence, on the Windward Islands. After initial acceptance by assemblies of notables in Martinique and Guadeloupe, noisy popular protests forced colonial administrators to abandon the project. Poor white colonists took part in demonstrations, but resistance to the *octroi* was coordinated by rich planters in the islands' sovereign councils.[30] This resistance was minor compared to *la Gaoulé*, a revolt in Martinique two years later, which was the first serious conflict of the eighteenth century between the Caribbean colonies and the French state.[31] While the revolt was essentially a protest against restrictions on trade and constraints on the expansion of sugar production, the rebels claimed a colonial identity and colonial interests distinct from those of metropolitan France in order to legitimize their challenge to the authority of royal administrators. The mild repression following the revolt's collapse provided further evidence of the weakness of this authority. Developments similar to *la Gaoulé* followed in Saint-Domingue, where colonists revolted in 1722.

The crown crushed the rebellion in Saint-Domingue but also moved to codify its control of colonial trade clearly and rigorously in a series of regulations known collectively as the *Exclusif*. These regulations were contained specifically in the *Lettres Patentes* of 1717 and of 1727. Those of 1717 addressed metropolitan commerce with the colonies and required ships destined for the colonies to return to their port of departure, exempted outbound cargoes from all duties save those of the *Ferme générale des Aides et Domaines*, and insisted that colonial imports be charged only 3 per cent *Domaine d'Occident* on their value. The 1717 text also regulated the re-export of colonial merchandise as well as the slave trade.[32] The *Lettres Patentes* of 1727 addressed foreign commerce in the colonies. They strictly forbade importing from or exporting to the colonies any slaves, effects, or produce from or for foreign countries. Foreign ships could neither land nor navigate within a league of French colonies, and all merchandise of foreign origin would be confiscated.[33] While these regulations clarified the royal government's intentions regarding colonial trade, the repressive edicts proved difficult to enforce. The practice of illegal or contraband trade, known to contemporaries as *le commerce interlope*, posed a constant challenge to the *Exclusif* throughout the eighteenth century. In some cases illegal trade occurred openly with the complicity of corrupt administrators, while in others it involved fraudulent claims of French ownership or of storm damage, which allowed foreign vessels to enter French colonial ports. Given the general complicity of the colonies' inhabitants, administrators and naval officers acknowledged the impossibility of stopping this traffic.[34] The French colonists' participation in illegal trade reflected a tradition of defying authority going back to the pirates who had helped to found the colonies. Fundamentally, however, *le commerce interlope* demonstrated both the failure of metropolitan suppliers to meet colonial demands and the colonists' perception that unrestricted trade better served their interests.[35]

War opened breeches in the *Exclusif*, making it even more difficult to enforce when peace returned. Even colonial administrators admitted that trade with foreigners was often necessary in wartime to maintain the colonies and to feed their slaves. During the Seven Years' War there was a de facto suspension of the *Exclusif*. Yet metropolitan chambers of commerce, representing the interests of merchants and ship owners, were powerful enough to prevent the royal government from permitting the complete opening of colonial ports to neutral vessels that the inhabitants wanted. Colonial dissatisfaction with the compromise adopted helps to explain the tepid resistance offered to British forces, particularly in the conquest of Guadeloupe.[36] Metropolitan government perceived that the influence of colonial proprietors on its administrators had become dangerous, and the royal ordinance of December 1759, increasing the pay of governors and *intendants* but forbidding their marriage to Creole women, was an attempt to reduce this influence.[37] French planters in the Windward Islands thrived under British occupation, and they were even more inclined to engage in contraband trade when the *Exclusif* was reimposed in 1763 at war's end. Moreover, the Treaty of Paris created conditions encouraging this tendency, particularly the cessation of Dominica, directly between Martinique and Guadeloupe, to Great Britain.[38] Resentment of the *Exclusif* and the return of full metropolitan control was dramatic in Saint-Domingue, where colonists revolted against the administration of the governor general, the comte d'Estaing, in 1768–9. Poor whites opposed reforms to the militia placing them on the same level as free-coloured troops. The rebellion's leaders in the sovereign council and the *Chambre d'Agriculture*, however, had more fundamental grievances. Their challenge to the political power of royal administration and the economic power of metropolitan commerce demonstrated the existence of an autonomist spirit in Saint-Domingue.[39] Royal administrators believed that such a spirit also existed in the Windward Islands. The new governor general and the *intendant* of Martinique strongly distrusted the Dubuc brothers, planter grandsons of the *Gaoulé* revolt's leader, who had arranged the colony's surrender to the British in 1762. They accused the Dubuc clan of being "republicans" and being devoted to the system of "English government."[40] Such charges may have been exaggerated, but many planters in the Windward Islands saw the existing relationship between France and its colonies as harmful to their interests.

Following the Seven Years' War metropolitan government introduced a series of reforms to modify the *Exclusif*. Initial measures reflected the influence of Jean-Baptiste Dubuc, member of the family of Martinique planters, whom the duc de Choiseul appointed head of the *Bureau des Colonies* within the ministry of marine.[41] In 1767 the new secretary of state for the marine, the duc de Praslin, opened two *entrepôts* to enable the colonies to acquire needed provisions (but not slaves) from foreign suppliers in exchange for rum and sugar syrup: the one for Saint Domingue was located at Môle Saint-Nicolas, and the other for the Windward Islands was established at le Carénage in Sainte-Lucie.[42] This marked the beginning of the *"Exclusif mitigé,"* a trade regime in which colonial administrators permitted an increasing number of exceptions to the original restrictions of the *Lettres Patentes* while also claiming to police contraband trade, which provoked protests from metropolitan commerce.[43] The American Revolution transformed the situation. Ships from New England, no longer able to trade with British Caribbean colonies, converged on the French islands in even greater numbers than before. Yet metropolitan merchants ceased to demand full restoration of the *Exclusif*, because the rebel British colonies were now opened to them.[44] This changed in 1778 with the outbreak of war between France and Great Britain. Metropolitan chambers of commerce again called for restrictions, but British sea power prevented supplies from France reaching the colonies. Therefore, as in previous conflicts, application of the *Exclusif* was suspended during the War of American Independence.[45] French colonists in the Windward Islands supported the American rebels and fought under their governor general, the marquis de Bouillé, to capture Dominica, St Vincent, and Grenada. The very different spirit in the islands than that which had prevailed during the Seven Years' War reflected the belief by some colonists that this war was a struggle for economic liberty and greater colonial autonomy.[46]

Such attitudes, as well as the new situation created by France's treaty with the United States, made it impossible for metropolitan government to reimpose the strict principles of the *Exclusif* when the war ended in 1783. The energetic Charles-Eugène de La Croix, marquis de Castries, who had been minister of marine since October 1780, was determined to reform colonial economic policy definitively in order to achieve a balance between the interests of metropolitan merchants and ship owners, and those of colonists. This was the objective of the royal government's *Arrêt* of 30 August 1784, which introduced an expanded but clarified version of the *Exclusif mitigé*. It designated a new *entrepôt* for every colony in the Windward Islands (Saint-Pierre for Martinique, Pointe-à-Pitre for Guadeloupe,[47] le Carénage renamed Castries for Sainte-Lucie, and Scarborough for Tobago) and one for each region of Saint-Domingue, into which foreign vessels could import a range of necessities, subject to a special 1 per cent duty, in exchange for sugar syrup or rum.[48] Colonial policy in the final years of the Old Regime, however, was markedly different from the loose, often corrupt, toleration that had characterized the *Exclusif mitigé* before the American War. Castries intended that the regulation of colonial trade be enforced rigorously to preserve the monopolies of metropolitan commerce. The minister took firm measures to suppress contraband trade, including the replacement of the ineffective customs patrols with permanent naval stations in the Leeward and Windward Islands.[49] Castries resigned in 1787, having quarrelled repeatedly with the controller-general of royal finances, Charles Alexandre de Calonne, but his policy continued under his successor, César-Henri, comte de La Luzerne, who had been governor general of Saint-Domingue. Thus royal government made significant reforms to the *Exclusif*, yet the vigorous efforts by administrators to stamp out illegal commerce and to uphold metropolitan trade privileges aroused anger in the colonies on the eve of the revolution. If this anger was more pronounced in Saint-Domingue, planters in the Windward Islands also resented the remaining restrictions on their access to foreign commerce. This resentment, expressed as opposition to "despotism," shaped their responses to 1789.

In the same context of reform in which the *Exclusif* was modified, the royal ordinance of 17 June 1787 created colonial assemblies in Martinique and Guadeloupe.[50] They replaced the *Chambres d'Agriculture*, formed following the Seven Years' War, and they were intended to give colonists a more formal role in the colonies' fiscal and economic administration to placate the autonomist spirit in the islands. The colonial assemblies were composed of the governor, the *intendant*, the *commandant en second*, the *commissaire général de la marine*, and a number of deputies. Governors and *intendants* were to convoke the assemblies annually, while between sessions a *Comité intermédiaire* of six members was to execute the assembly's *arrêtés* and prepare material for its deliberations. The colonial assemblies were not legislatures, but they were to advise the administrators on matters pertaining to commerce and agriculture, public works, and, most important, taxation. Composed almost exclusively of planters, Martinique's colonial assembly pushed in its first sessions for the burden of taxation to be shifted on to the shoulders of the commercial community in the island's ports. The assembly also called for the *impôt* to weigh more heavily on free-coloured proprietors than on white ones.[51] The colonial assembly in Guadeloupe was more concerned in 1788 to press the government to make both Pointe-à-Pitre and Basse-Terre *entrepôts*. *Intendant* Foullon d'Écotier reported to the minister that the "particular interests" of planters dominated the assembly, which he characterized as hostile to both local merchants and national commerce.[52] The sessions of the colonial assemblies in Martinique and Guadeloupe on the eve of the Revolution, therefore, point to a fundamental economic conflict in colonial society.

III Hierarchy and Conflict in Colonial Society

Following the outbreak of civil war in Martinique in 1790, Antoine-Pierre-Joseph-Marie Barnave reported to the National Assembly that division in the colony was based on an old hatred between the planters and the merchants of Saint-Pierre to whom they were in debt.[53] Under the conditions of the *Exclusif*, or the *Exclusif mitigé*, planters in the Windward Islands had to market their produce through merchants in the colonies' ports, who they hoped would sell to metropolitan commerce at the highest possible price. These merchants extended credit for the commodities they received or were promised and dispersed the provisions and other goods they had purchased from French ships to the planters. The need for supplies, and hence credit, was constant, but colonial harvests could be reduced by poor weather or devastated completely by hurricanes. Under these conditions, planters quickly went into debt and profits had to be turned over to these local agents of commerce. Colonial debt mounted in the late eighteenth century as plantation size and the need for slaves and provisions grew. Mutual suspicion and animosity also intensified: planters accused merchants of selling their products at low prices, while buying provisions at exorbitant prices, and merchants accused planters of being careless and dishonest and of pursuing luxury rather than attempting to pay their debts. Contrasting attitudes towards the *Exclusif* accompanied these sentiments. Planters wanted free access to foreign commerce, even if this meant resorting to contraband trade. Colonial merchants, on the other hand, vigorously supported the monopoly of metropolitan commerce to force repayment of the credit they had extended.[54]

The principal objects of the planters' hostility were the commissioners of Saint-Pierre. This mercantile elite had controlled the commerce not only of Martinique but also of all the Windward Islands since 1720.[55] Their wealth enabled them to buy entire cargos from ship captains and to advance credit to planters for potential harvests. Moreover, they acted as intermediaries between the colonies and metropolitan merchant houses, many of which had permanent representatives based in Saint-Pierre who negotiated directly with the commissioners. Guadeloupe's colonists were even more dependent upon Saint-Pierre's commissioners than were those of Martinique. Because few French ships stopped at Guadeloupe, the colony relied on the coasting trade with Martinique for its provisions and to export its products.[56] This dependence decreased somewhat following the Seven Years' War, but Guadeloupe's planters remained indebted to the merchants of Saint-Pierre. In 1788 the commissioners responded to the colonial assembly's changes to the assessment of the *impôt* and to the import/export duties for Martinique with outraged protests. When these brought no satisfaction, they refused to pay any taxes. Governor General the vicomte de Damas and *Intendant* Foulquier appealed to the minister to rule on the issue that had created a financial crisis in the colony.[57] La Luzerne had also received numerous statements of support for Saint-Pierre's commissioners from French seaports, and he ordered the administrators in Martinique to lower the duties.[58] The ministerial decision represented a victory for the merchants, but it also stiffened the resolve of the colonial assembly to assert the interests of Martinique's planters in 1789 and beyond.

Just as important as the economic conflict between planters and merchants was the social division between the *grands Blancs* and the *petits Blancs* in the Windward Islands. Royal administrators and the wealthiest merchants were among those who dominated colonial society, but most *grands Blancs* were rich planters. A wide spectrum of French society had settled the colonies in the seventeenth and early eighteenth centuries: nobles, members of the merchant bourgeoisie, peasants, and urban artisans, as well as deserters, exiles, mutinous sailors, buccaneers, and filibusters.[59] If early settlers, of whatever background, farmed small holdings using *engagés*, the shift from tobacco growing to sugar production demanded increasing investments of capital and slave labour. Land became concentrated in fewer hands, small proprietors were squeezed out, and a planter class emerged. The planter elite in the Windward Islands was not exclusively of noble origin, and it was different than that which developed later in Saint-Domingue. By the late eighteenth century the *grands Blancs* of Saint-Domingue controlled enormous wealth, but most were absentee owners of estates who were not embedded in colonial society. The *grands Blancs* of the Windward Islands, in contrast, constituted a truly colonial aristocracy. In these older colonies the plantations were smaller than in Saint-Domingue, there were fewer slaves and the planters' fortunes were more modest. Yet these resident *grands Blancs* enjoyed immense local prestige and preponderance, not only economic and social sway but also political influence exercised through the colonies' sovereign councils. A number of family clans dominated Martinique, like the Dubucs, some of which had their origins at the beginning of colonization while others had arrived early in the eighteenth century. Some colonists of modest social background rose into the planter class by marriage or through the assistance of a powerful patron, but family alliances were crucial to the success of all Martinique's *grand Blancs* who saw themselves as a unified elite.[60]

A vast social gulf separated the Windward Islands' planter aristocracy from the colonies' *petits Blancs*. In his description of Martinique following the Seven Years' War, the *abbé* Raynal identified categories or classes of *habitants* beneath the rich sugar planters, including those who grew "less important crops" such as coffee or cotton on their estates using fewer slaves and those whose plantations had simply failed.[61] Many French immigrated to the West Indies hoping to make their fortune as planters. Few succeeded. Many of those who managed to purchase a small holding were forced to abandon it because of a lack of capital, crop failure, or other misfortune. Those who did not secure work as an overseer on someone else's plantation ended up in the colonial port towns where they joined floating populations of minor merchants, clerks, artisans, innkeepers, soldiers, sailors, and foreign adventurers. Together these constituted the *petits Blancs*, who formed a turbulent underworld that colonial elites regarded as dissolute, vice-ridden, and dangerous.[62] Retailers and craftsmen might aspire to buy enough land to become *habitants* themselves,[63] but most poor whites were deeply hostile towards the planters. *Petits Blancs* were numerous in the port towns of the Windward Islands in 1789: their concentration in the commercial quarter of Saint-Pierre made it, for contemporaries and historians, the "foyer of revolution" in these colonies.[64] The colonial ports were important windows on to the wider world of the greater Caribbean and the Atlantic. Sailors were a highly visible element of port society, one that often ran afoul of colonial authority, and their reputation for rebellion fit with the image of all poor whites as unruly and violent. As migrant and often multilingual workers who criss-crossed different colonial empires in their voyages, sailors were also a vital source of news regarding developments in other colonies and overseas.[65] The spread of such information, and its reception among *petits Blancs*, was crucial to the revolution in the Windward Islands.

Yet it was the institution of slavery that made the Caribbean colonies so unstable. Black slaves made up the vast majority of the islands' population. The disproportion on the eve of the revolution was most dramatic in Saint Domingue, which had over 500,000 slaves and fewer than 36,000 whites.[66] The smaller colonies had grown much less than Saint-Domingue during the second half of the eighteenth century, but their populations were also lopsided. In 1789 Guadeloupe's population numbered 106,293, of which 89,523 were slaves and only 13,712 were white. Martinique's population in 1789 was slightly smaller at 96,158 people, including 83,414 slaves and 10,636 whites.[67] Because the slave trade had neglected these colonies, the nature of their enslaved majorities was also somewhat different than that of Saint-Domingue. Fewer of the Africans were from the Congo, and more of them were from the regions of Biafra and Sierra Leone, while the proportion of women and children among the slaves of Guadeloupe and Martinique was higher. There were also proportionally more Creoles, or slaves born in the colonies, than *bossales*, African-born slaves.[68] These demographic differences, however, did not eliminate the tensions associated with slavery from the Windward Islands, where the free population was overshadowed by the enslaved mass.

Slave labour was fundamental to the colonies' economy and had been since the sugar revolution of the seventeenth century. Slaves represented the planters' major capital investment and the number of slaves determined a plantation's value. Figures for 1790 suggest that 112 slaves worked an average sugar plantation on Guadeloupe. Abbé Raynal's assessment of Martinique in 1770 claimed that the 100 large, self-sufficient sugar plantations had 120 slaves each, while the remaining 186 estates had sixty slaves apiece.[69] Masters organized their slaves into *ateliers*, or gangs, to carry out collective labour under tight discipline and close supervision. On most plantations slaves were divided between three gangs. Adults of both sexes, chosen for their strength and ability, were assigned to the *grand atelier*, or great gang, which performed the most difficult, labour-intensive tasks. The *petit atelier*, or second gang, was composed of those slaves not physically capable of working in the great gang and worked either in conjunction with the great gang or independently at lighter tasks. Younger children were initiated to the discipline of collective labour under the supervision of an old slave woman in the weeding gang.[70] The slaves' working day on the plantations began with prayers at sunrise, and aside from pauses for breakfast and another for a meal at noon, they toiled until sunset. At harvest time this was extended late into the night.[71] The division between planting and harvest defined the agricultural year, but masters sought to minimize the natural season break and kept their slaves working continuously.[72] Work was less intensive, and surveillance of slaves less exact, on the coffee estates because coffee plants required less care than sugar cane and the production process was more fragmented.[73]

A hierarchy existed within slavery, resulting in more privileges for the skilled slaves and fewer for the *esclaves de jardin*, or field slaves, in the gangs. On sugar plantations, the most important slaves were the master of the mill, who managed ten to twenty other slaves, and the head refiner, who supervised the boiling, skimming, and transfer of the cane juice and decided when the sugar was ready to strike.[74] In addition to these skilled slaves and the field hands, others were needed to perform various tasks, including herdsmen and mule drivers, and artisans, such as carpenters and barrel makers.[75] The residence also needed slaves to clean, cook, and drive coaches for the white master and his family.[76] The domestic slaves enjoyed better food, clothing, and lodging than the field slaves, just as conditions for town slaves were preferable to those of plantation slaves. Many urban slaves were owned by rural masters; merchants, administrators, and military officers often rented slaves instead of buying them. Once the contracted sum for their labour was given to the master, these rented slaves could sometimes work for wages in town, thus saving money to buy their freedom.[77]

The status and treatment of all slaves in the French colonies was determined legally by the royal edict of 1685, known as the *Code Noir*. The *Code Noir* did not contain any philosophical justification for slavery but provided only a legal framework for its operation. Slaves had no legal or juridical identity; they were property.[78] The *Code Noir* did prescribe, however, that masters must fulfil various responsibilities towards their slaves. Slaves were to be baptized and instructed in the Catholic faith and be given rest on Sundays and on religious holidays. The *Code Noir* required masters to provide adequate provisions for their slaves.[79] To save on the expense of importing provisions, planters preferred to grow food for the slaves on their plantations. They set aside time during the work schedule for slaves to tend their own plots or to cultivate fields designated for provisions rather than commercial crops.[80] Various administrators tried in vain to curb this practice that, along with insufficient imports of provisions from France, created periodic shortages of food. If a hurricane destroyed local crops, shortages could threaten slaves with starvation. Such a hurricane struck Martinique in the summer of 1788, and the resulting provisioning crisis was an important context for slave reactions to the advent of the revolution.[81]

If the *Code Noir* required masters to baptize, feed, and house their slaves, it also insisted on the slaves' obedience to their masters. The planters' main concern was to make their slaves work. This required domination that, along with the limitations on the amount of labour available or on the effective division of labour possible under slavery, revealed the fundamental weakness and danger of the slave system.[82] A hierarchy of authority on the plantation was responsible for the discipline and control of the field slaves.[83] The master was at the summit. In the case of absentee owners or masters uninterested in the administration of their estates, however, a *gérant*, or manager, was in charge of the plantation's operations. Beneath the manager was the *économe*, or overseer, who supervised the slaves and was responsible for maintaining order. Traditionally overseers were *petits Blancs*, but as sugar production expanded in the eighteenth century free-coloured overseers became more common. Immediate control of the field hands lay with the *commandeurs*, or drivers, who were slaves themselves. This hierarchy of domination sought to motivate slaves with small rewards, but above all it relied on fear of punishment. Slaves were subject to the lash, to being placed in irons, to imprisonment, or to even more brutal treatment. The *Code Noir* placed limitations on punishment and even allowed for slaves to inform royal prosecutors in the case of inhumane treatment.[84] Economic self-interest was more important in limiting excessive cruelty: to kill or mutilate slaves was to destroy capital investment. In 1784–5 Castries, the reform-minded minister of marine sought to force masters to respect the tenets of the *Code Noir* regarding adequate food and humane treatment of slaves.[85] These reforms proved impossible to enforce and planters resented them as restrictions on their property. The punishment and treatment of slaves was appalling.[86]

The slaves' response to their enslavement was not passive, and their resistance posed a constant threat to the prosperity and security of the French colonies. Slaves worked neither willingly nor enthusiastically, but their resistance could be much more dangerous. Some slaves, newly arrived from Africa, committed suicide rather than submit to enslavement. White colonists often feared that slaves were trying to poison livestock, or even their masters, and believed that this was linked to the practice of voodoo religion or witchcraft.[87] The most important form of slave resistance, however, was *marronage*, or the flight of slaves from the plantations. French colonists recognized two different forms of this phenomenon. *Petit marronage* involved individual absenteeism for limited periods. *Grand marronage*, in contrast, involved the flight of slaves, often in groups, for long periods with no intention of returning. The latter also implied the commission of a crime, requiring the intervention of royal justice.[88] *Marronage* represented flight from work or from harsh treatment, but it was often linked to the food supply problem. Hunger drove slaves to steal, an act for which they were punished, and many fled to avoid further punishment.[89] While Saint-Domingue's larger areas of uninhabited forest and its border with Spanish territory gave *marrons*, or runaway slaves, more chance of eluding capture, *marronage* was also a serious problem in Guadeloupe and Martinique in the eighteenth century.[90] *Marronage* deprived plantations of labour, but colonial administrators also believed that it could lead to something much more dangerous: slave revolt. Runaways sometimes formed armed bands that raided estates, and governors feared that these bands encouraged rebellion.[91] In 1789 Governor General Vioménil emphasized this link in his assessment of developments in Martinique.

The *Code Noir* prescribed harsh punishment for runaway slaves,[92] but this was neither an effective deterrent nor widely used in the eighteenth century. Colonial administration relied on armed forces to hunt down *marrons*.[93] Regular troops sometimes participated in sweeps for runaway slaves, but internal security was primarily the responsibility of the colonial militia. In theory all free men belonged to the militia, but white colonists avoided military service whenever possible. Therefore during the eighteenth century the mainstay of the militia were free men of colour. These were the troops who rounded up *marrons* and who provided the colonies' primary defence against slave revolt.[94]

The *gens de couleur*, or free people of colour, were an intermediate group within colonial society between the mass of black slaves and the white minority. Comprised of freed slaves and the offspring of black slaves and white masters, this group's legal and social status was complicated by the terminology for the different patterns of miscegenation (*mestizo, mulatre* or mulatto, *quateron*) and of manumission (*affranchis, nègre libre*).[95] Beyond the differences in origins implied by all of these terms, the free people of colour were not a unified class but rather a socially and economically heterogeneous group: some lived on the margins of colonial society as subsistence farmers or poor labourers, while others were planters or urban property owners. None of them, however, were considered to be the equals of whites.

Changes in the status of free people of colour in the Windward Islands were linked to an increase in their numbers. The free-coloured population rose from the late seventeenth century, reflecting increased manumissions, and then declined in the 1730s before rising strongly after the Seven Years' War.[96] On the eve of the revolution there were 5,235 *gens de couleur* in Martinique and 3,149 in Guadeloupe, constituting 5 and

3 per cent respectively of the populations of these colonies.[97] The free-coloured percentage of Saint-Domingue's population was much higher: that colony's 21,813 free people of colour constituted almost half of its total free population in 1788.[98] Nonetheless, colonial administration in the Windward Islands sought to control and limit manumission from the early eighteenth century in order to limit the numbers of free people of colour.[99] In the seventeenth century slave owners could free their slaves at will, but after 1713 manumission required the permission of the governor general and was to be awarded only for long service or acts of devotion. In 1767 a local statute in Martinique forbade notaries to accept deeds of manumission unless they were accompanied by the explicit permission of colonial authority. Other measures were also taken to undermine the tenets of the *Code Noir*, which declared that a slave who married her master was free, as were her children.[100] The most important means to limit manumission, however, was taxation. In 1745 colonial authority imposed a duty of 1,000 *livres* for the enfranchisement of a single male slave and 600 *livres* for a female slave. The duty was subsequently reduced, then abandoned in 1766, before being re-established in 1775. Masters resented this tax on liberty as an infringement on their private property and found ways to get around it.[101] Manumissions multiplied, as did the number of children born to white fathers and coloured mothers, and the colonies' free-coloured population continued to rise.

White concern at this increase was manifested in a broadening range of racially restrictive legislation.[102] In 1763 a royal decree forbidding free people of colour to adopt the names of whites was promulgated in Guadeloupe; in 1773 it was extended to Martinique and Saint-Domingue. In 1765 Martinique's sovereign council ruled that it was improper to employ *gens de couleur* in notaries' offices – the year before they had been forbidden to practice medicine, surgery, or pharmacy. In 1781 notaries were forbidden from designating *gens de couleur* as *Monsieur* or *Madame* in official deeds, and in 1788 a decree compelled free coloureds to apply for permits to carry on any other trade than farming. Despite the lower numbers of free people of colour, racist legislation was more discriminatory in the Windward Islands than it was in Saint-Domingue.[103]

This tide of legislative discrimination reflected the expanding free-coloured role in the colonial economy, perceived by whites as a competitive threat.[104] There were free-coloured landowners in Guadeloupe and Martinique during the eighteenth century, mostly peasant farmers growing foodstuffs, but after 1730 free people of colour moved into coffee or cotton production on small estates. In Saint-Domingue a significant number of *gens de couleur* became prosperous planters during the coffee boom following the Seven Years' War, but the limited amount of cheap, new land in the Windward Islands meant that fewer free-coloured farmers achieved such success.[105] Free people of colour did find opportunities for economic success in the port towns. They were active in the coasting trade between colonies; they became tavern keepers; and many were successful craftsmen, artisans, and small merchants.[106] Whether as small planters or as urban proprietors, *gens de couleur* in Martinique and Guadeloupe owned slaves; they seem to have felt little solidarity with the enslaved blacks despite their own origins.[107]

Their role as slave holders, like the role they played in the militia, reflects the ambiguous position of free people of colour in colonial society. Not only were *affranchis* admitted into the militia, but after 1768 slaves attempting to purchase their liberty could bypass the tax in Guadeloupe and Martinique through several years of loyal service in the militia.[108] Agents of royal government and members of the planter aristocracy in the Windward Islands praised the efforts of free-coloured militia in rounding up *marrons* and valued their role in providing colonial security.[109] Moreover, white society appealed to the *gens de couleur* – as owners of property and slaves – to defend colonial interests and the institution of slavery. Yet this group was expected to accept and acknowledge its inferiority based on race: beyond the tax to be paid for liberty or the certificates of proof required, free people of colour were obliged to show respect not only to their former master but to all whites.[110] If the *gens de couleur* adhered to the values of colonial society, by the end of the Old Regime their frustration was apparent.

IV Challenges to the Colonial System at the End of the Old Regime

On the eve of the revolution free people of colour in the French colonies had begun to demand equality with whites. Such demands reflected both specific grievances and the general climate of opinion in the late eighteenth century. *Gens de couleur* in the Windward Islands were frustrated by legal and social discrimination and by restricted economic opportunities.[111] When Martinique's colonial assembly raised the *capitation*, or the *impôt*, on free-coloured proprietors in 1788, fifty of them left Saint-Pierre to seek their fortunes in the Spanish colony of Trinidad.[112] The free-coloured elite, many of whom had travelled to metropolitan

France, were aware of the liberal currents in the Enlightenment criticizing privilege based on birth and calling instead for status to be based on merit. Some eighteenth-century writers opposed racial inequality specifically, and in 1779 a European observer informed the minister of marine that Martinique's free men of colour knew the work of Abbé Guillaume Thomas Raynal, author of the anti-colonial *Histoire philosophique et politique des établissements et du commerce des Européens dans les deux Indes* (1770), by heart.[113] Arguably more important to the Windward Islands' *gens de couleur* than the impact of certain intellectual texts, however, were the political activities of free-coloured notables from Saint-Domingue who had begun to petition metropolitan authority directly for equality with whites.

In 1785 the wealthy coloured planter Julien Raimond met with the marquis de Castries to seek the repeal of discriminatory laws and to end the exclusion of his "fellow citizens" in Saint-Domingue from public life. Raimond argued that free men of colour had proven their virtue: they had demonstrated economic virtue in the successful operation of plantations and in owning slaves, they had shown social virtue as good husbands and fathers, they had displayed civic virtue through loyal service in the militia.[114] It should be noted, however, that Raimond advocated equality with whites for the wealthy light-skinned elite and not for all *gens de couleur*.[115] Castries was impressed with Raimond's appeals and in 1786 asked the new governor general of Saint-Domingue, La Luzerne, to consult the colony's prominent inhabitants about the feasibility of raising free men of colour to the same status as whites.[116]

The coming of the revolution in France presented a new opportunity to those campaigning for free-coloured rights. On 26 August 1789 Raimond and another wealthy free man of colour, Vincent Ogé, approached the *Société correspondante des colons français de Saint Domingue*, or the Club Massiac, in Paris to seek support for making an appeal to the National Assembly. The Club Massiac had been formed by absentee planters to lobby for colonial interests. A text Ogé prepared for submission to the club suggests that Saint Domingue's free-coloured elite hoped to gain the support of white colonists by convincing them that they could help to prevent a slave revolt, which the revolution in France might trigger.[117] Ogé's text showed the extent to which wealthy *gens de couleur* identified themselves with white planters in terms of common interests. The Club Massiac refused to admit Ogé and Raimond, however, and instead lobbied to thwart the extension of rights to free men of colour.[118] Raimond and Ogé turned for support to metropolitan liberals.

Étienne-Louis-Hector De Joly, a barrister and member of the Parisian municipality, agreed to act as their legal counsel. He presented the free-coloured demands, which included the right to be represented by six deputies, to the National Assembly on 22 October 1789.[119]

This campaign also received substantial support from the journalists, intellectuals, and philanthropists of the *Société des Amis des Noirs*. The Abbé Baptiste Henri Grégoire, a prominent member of this group and a deputy to the National Assembly, published a *Mémoire en faveur des gens de couleur ou sang-mêlés de St Domingue* in December 1789. This text denounced the continuation of racial discrimination in the colonies and demanded that free men of colour be granted equality before the law and representation in the National Assembly. It also suggested that granting rights to the *gens de couleur* would head off the violence of slave rebellion.[120] Grégoire and the *Amis des Noirs* had a much more radical agenda than obtaining equality for free men of colour: they advocated the abolition of slavery itself.

This anti-slavery campaign fit within the climate of reform opinion at the end of the Old Regime, and it also grew out of the intellectual critique of slavery within the Enlightenment.[121] Eighteenth-century thinkers were not unanimously opposed to colonial slavery, but a significant number of French writers condemned it. The Baron de Montesquieu criticized slavery in the *Lettres persanes* (1721), and in Book 15 of *De l'Esprit des Lois* (1748) he refuted the historical justifications for slavery. Montesquieu later declared that "slavery is against the Natural Law by which all men are born free and independent."[122] Voltaire and Diderot denounced the cruelty and hypocrisy of European Christians' enslavement of Africans and praised the contrasting charitable concern for black slaves shown by American Quakers.[123] D'Alembert and Diderot's *Encyclopédie* (1751–72) included various articles challenging slavery's legitimacy and attacking its inhumanity.[124] In 1756 Victor Riqueti, marquis de Mirabeau, argued that the importation of black slaves had hampered the economic development of the colonies and that free labour was more efficient than slavery. Du Pont de Nemours also presented an economic critique of slavery in the volumes of the *Ephémérides du citoyen, ou bibliothèque raisonnée des sciences morales et politiques* (1767–72).[125]

The most scathing condemnation of colonial slavery came from Abbé Raynal's *Histoire des deux Indes*, which went through seventeen editions between 1772 and 1780. Raynal appealed to reason as well as to moral principle in his indictment of slavery's denial of liberty in the service of greed.[126] Raynal denounced slavery as wicked, as well as contrary to reason, but he did not advocate its immediate abolition. He demanded an end to the slave trade and he called on colonial powers to improve conditions for their slaves while preparing them to become free workers. Yet the *Histoire des deux Indes* also contained a radical warning that if Europeans did not act, a black Spartacus would emerge to lead the slaves in revolt against their oppressors.[127]

Beyond Raynal, the clearest demand for slavery's abolition associated with the Enlightenment came from the brilliant mathematician and political theorist Marie-Jean-Antoine-Nicolas de Caritat, marquis de Condorcet. His advocacy of reform and his belief in natural rights led him to condemn the system of colonial slavery in a 1781 pamphlet and to call for its abolition.[128] Condorcet joined the *Société des Amis des Noirs* early in 1789.

While growing out of Enlightenment ideology, the anti-slavery campaign of the *Amis des Noirs* drew direct inspiration from the Anglo-American abolitionist movement. Jacques-Pierre Brissot, an aspiring journalist and enthusiastic admirer of the United States, founded the group in May 1788 in collaboration with Etienne Clavière and Honoré-Gabriel Riquetti, comte de Mirabeau. Within a year it had 141 members, including not only Condorcet and Grégoire but also other future revolutionaries such as the marquis de Lafayette and Jérôme Pétion. The charter members hoped to imitate the London Society for the Abolition of the Slave Trade, an amalgamation of anti-slavery groups organized by Thomas Clarkson to lobby Parliament. While lacking the grass-roots provincial organization that had mobilized public opinion in Britain, the *Société des Amis des Noirs* was an ideologically defined group that represented a model for the revolutionary clubs that formed in France after 1789. Its members hoped to advance their cause through existing institutions, but their demand that laws conform to natural rights was radical.[129] The calling of the Estates General appeared to present a glorious opportunity. In February 1789 Condorcet wrote addresses on behalf of the *Amis des Noirs* to all the electoral assemblies in the kingdom charged with selecting deputies to the Estates General, urging them to abolish slavery in keeping with their determination to end despotism.[130] Forty-nine of the six hundred general *cahiers de doléances* drafted by these assemblies called for abolition of the slave trade or for eventual emancipation. The *Société des Amis des Noirs* believed that a common Anglo-French abolition of slavery was imminent, and its members threw themselves behind the cause of free-coloured rights, which they thought could clear the way for gradual abolition.[131]

The *Amis des Noirs* demanded the abolition of the slave trade, not of slavery itself, yet this failed to strengthen the campaign or limit opposition to it. Brissot and his colleagues hoped that ending the trade would force masters to improve conditions for their slaves and that it would lead to gradual emancipation. They believed that they could persuade the royal government to cancel the subsidies for the slave trade, and they sent an open letter to Finance Minster Jacques Necker with this demand on 6 June 1789, after the opening of the Estates General at Versailles but before the declaration of the National Assembly.[132] The campaign against the slave trade, however, suffered from serious flaws. The Society lacked a broad-based organization, relying exclusively on pamphlets and newspaper articles. The evidence used to condemn slavery's evils was drawn from English examples, because the *Amis des Noirs* had not undertaken their own detailed investigation of French participation in the slave trade. The group's arguments were almost entirely moral and humanitarian, and its members made little attempt to present an economic case against slavery.[133] Moreover, by insisting on the distinction between ending the slave trade and abolishing slavery, the *Amis des Noirs* compromised their position, appearing to confirm the need to maintain slavery and its importance to the economy.[134] The rhetorical and political difficulty of defending a moderate attack on colonial slavery was evident in the Society's 5 February 1790 address to the National Assembly, which denied accusations that its members sought immediate abolition.[135]

Although the *Amis des Noirs* failed to mobilize substantial public support for gradual emancipation, they aroused hostile and ferocious opposition. Port chambers of commerce and the Club Massiac instigated petitions supporting the slave trade and circulated letters claiming that the *Amis des Noirs* were English agents who sought to provoke slave revolt in the colonies. Colonial and commercial interests also used the beginning of debate on rights for free men of colour as an opportunity to attack the abolitionists.[136] These attacks demonstrate that in 1789, despite the actual weakness of the campaign against the slave trade, many people believed that strong support existed for slavery's abolition within the National Assembly. Merchants, slavers, and colonists genuinely feared that it might become a reality if it was not opposed.[137] Just as the authority of royal government was crumbling, metropolitan liberals announced their intention to overturn the bases of the colonies' society and economy: slavery and racial hierarchy. As news of this radical challenge to the colonial system reached the Caribbean, it raised fears and hopes that shaped the responses to the revolution in the Windward Islands.

The anti-slavery campaign of the *Société des Amis des Noirs* exposed deep fears because it reflected crucial tensions in the Windward Islands on the eve of the revolution. Since the introduction of sugar production, colonial agriculture depended on slave labour that had to be controlled for the economic success and personal security of the white plantation owners. At the same time, the frustrations of a growing free-coloured population threatened racial hierarchy in the colonies. Alongside this racial tension, social and economic conflict between white colonists smouldered. The rootless *petits Blancs* not only loathed the *gens de couleur* but also despised the colonial elite who regarded them as inferior and dangerous. This elite was itself divided between planters, whose debts were mounting, and colonial merchants, who extended them credit. These merchants vigorously defended the *Exclusif*, while planters bitterly resented these restrictions on trade and defied them in smuggling and illegal commerce. If these smouldering tensions threatened the stability of the colonies' internal regimes, it was the communication of new political forms, radical concepts, and subversive language from France that set them ablaze. The crown's creation of colonial assemblies for Martinique and Guadeloupe in 1787 provided the planters – unintentionally – with potential instruments to seek greater autonomy from metropolitan control. The revolution of 1789 presented the colonial assemblies with the opportunity to claim some degree of legislative independence in the context of opposition to "despotism." Yet the revolutionary script from metropolitan France also provided the means and justification for attacking the existing social and racial hierarchy. At the same time as it undermined the authority of colonial administration in the Windward Islands, the French Revolution unleashed the aspirations and anger of the colonies' *petits Blancs*, *gens de couleur*, and slaves.

2 Rumours of Revolution: The Impact of 1789 in Martinique and Guadeloupe

The revolution of 1789 had a profound impact in the Windward Islands. The collapse of royal authority in metropolitan France undermined that of colonial governors. Moreover, the ideals of liberty and equality associated with 1789 challenged the social and racial hierarchies in the Caribbean and encouraged the participation of groups previously excluded from political activity: *petits Blancs*, free people of colour, and, most radically, black slaves. News of the revolution in France, however, reached Martinique and Guadeloupe in the form of rumours. Given the limitations of communications in the age of sail, information on developments at Versailles and Paris took several weeks to cross the Atlantic, so that news from Europe lagged significantly behind events. More important, unofficial, incomplete, and even utterly false rumours preceded the arrival of official accounts. This was not unique to the colonies. Rumours were integral elements to the unfolding of the revolution in France, as Georges Lefebvre demonstrated in his classic examination of the Great Fear of 1789.[1] More recently, Bronislaw Baczko emphasized the importance of revolutionary rumours that reflected a primarily oral culture and that, even when completely inaccurate, revealed real concerns and insecurities of eighteenth-century society. Inseparable from the revolutionary imagination and its obsession with plots and hidden enemies, "rumours reappear throughout the Revolution, mobilizing people's minds, channeling their fervour, orienting their fears."[2] In 1789 rumours played just such a role in the Windward Islands: they exposed the bitter divisions within colonial society, and they unleashed and shaped fierce political conflict.

News of the metropolitan revolution provoked conflicting reactions in Martinique and Guadeloupe in 1789 and triggered conflict over the control of information and the interpretation of information arriving from Europe. Rumours of emancipation, associated with the meeting of the Estates General and the beginning of the National Assembly, inspired a slave revolt in Martinique at the end of August 1789. Beyond the power of rumour to mobilize black resistance, the revolt revealed the depth of white fear regarding the fragility of the slave system and the white obsession with the threat posed by the propaganda of metropolitan abolitionists. In September the first news of the revolution reached Guadeloupe and Martinique, inciting riotous enthusiasm among *petits Blancs* who, in alliance with port merchants, challenged the authority of the colonies' governors. These colonial revolutionaries defied orders forbidding the national cockade and demanded the convocation of general assemblies in their colonies. Their words and actions revealed the powerful influence of the opening scenes of the revolutionary script from France, yet this script was not without ambiguity for the colonies. If Frenchmen were now free and equal citizens, was citizenship restricted to whites? Not even ardent supporters of the revolution, the "patriots," would accept that free men of colour could be equal to whites, yet most of colonial society feared (or, in the case of the slaves themselves, perhaps hoped) that revolutionary ideals were antithetical to slavery. Just as important as the problem of citizenship, however, was the dynamic of popular sovereignty. The revolution of 1789 challenged the authority of royal government by asserting the nation, rather than the king, as the source of sovereignty. While revolutionaries in France did not clearly establish the new location or nature of legitimate authority, popular sovereignty undermined royal executive power explicitly. In the colonies this script provided an opportunity and a justification to attack representatives of the metropolitan state. A popular committee in the town of Saint-Pierre, which inspired the formation of municipalities elsewhere in the colonies, claimed to speak for "the people" and denied the legitimacy of both the governor general and the existing colonial assembly. Thus the revolutionary struggle in the Windward Islands that began in 1789 included not only contestation over the control of communications but also the assertion of competing claims to legitimate authority.

I. Slave Revolt in Martinique (August 1789)

The French Revolution resulted from the collapse of the old order,[3] not from the agitation of any revolutionary movement, and the crisis of the Old Regime in metropolitan France reached Martinique and Guadeloupe. The royal government's creation of the colonial assemblies in 1787 had occurred in the context of sweeping reform proposals to address the growing financial crisis facing the French state. The crisis became political when the Assembly of Notables and then the *Parlements* refused to accept the royal reform package, insisting that only the Estates General could authorize such constitutional innovations. Bankruptcy forced Louis XVI to concede to demands and to summon the Estates General for May 1789. The public consensus against "despotism" shattered when the *Parlement* of Paris ruled in September 1788 that the Estates General would meet according to traditional forms, implying the predominance of the clergy and nobility. This was unacceptable to non-noble men of property who, in alliance with liberal nobles, lobbied for the doubling of representatives of the third estate and for voting by head in the Estates General. Aware that elections and the drafting of *cahiers de doléance* were proceeding in France, in February 1789 the colonial assemblies in Martinique and Guadeloupe asked the minister of marine to authorize them to send deputies to represent their colonies in the Estates General.[4] Members of the planter elite hoped to advance their interests, but they had only limited understanding of the resentment of privilege sweeping France or of the emerging conviction that sovereignty lay with the nation rather than the king. On 17 June 1789 deputies of the third estate at Versailles, supported by "patriots" in the other two orders, declared themselves to be the National Assembly. This revolutionary defiance succeeded because the popular uprising in Paris, culminating with the fall of the Bastille on 14 July, ended the threat of a possible *coup d'état* by royal troops. The National Assembly subsequently abolished "feudalism" and all forms of privilege, and it proclaimed the revolution's universal principles in the Declaration of the Rights of Man and Citizen on 26 August.[5]

During the first eight months of 1789, however, royal administrators and the colonial elite in the Windward Islands were preoccupied with a crisis of their own. On 14 August 1788 a hurricane had swept through the eastern Caribbean and battered Martinique. In March 1789 Governor General Claude-Charles, vicomte de Damas referred to the situation as a "disaster" and informed the minister that given the colony's devastation it would be impossible to collect the taxes for 1788; even worse, he reported, the colony could hardly feed its slaves.[6] Martinique's sovereign council described the state of the colony in dramatic terms: "The current existence of our Negroes is a miracle of Providence; our less industrious slaves, and that is the greatest number, die in misery," warning that black suffering could lead to dangerous unrest.[7] Given this troubling prospect, Damas agreed in May to the council's request to open at least one of the colony's ports to foreign ships so that inhabitants could buy cheap flour and other provisions for their slaves.[8]

Although Damas justified this concession in terms of extraordinary circumstances, it represented a victory for those colonists who aspired to greater freedom from metropolitan restrictions on trade and, as such, it created conflict among colonial administrators. *Intendant* Pierre-Xavier-François Foullon d'Écotier co-signed the governor general's ordinance of 10 May 1789 permitting the importation of foreign provisions, but he expressed opposition to this course of action and claimed that it was not necessary.[9] He told the minister that there had been a "schism" between Martinique's planters and merchants since the convocation of the colonial assembly in 1788. He alleged that planters exaggerated the extent of hurricane damage and that he opposed opening the colony's ports as being prejudicial to metropolitan interests, but he had been forced to acquiesce to Damas who favoured planters to the detriment of commercial interests.[10] Foullon's opposition to the opening of Martinique's ports continued a pattern of both support for colonial merchants and conflict with governors that he had established previously as the *intendant* in Guadeloupe. He had been highly critical of Guadeloupe's colonial assembly in January 1788, claiming that it failed to consider the colony's deficit seriously and that it privileged planters over merchants.[11]

In December 1788 Foullon requested a leave from his duties as *intendant* so that he could return to France and attend to family matters, but Clugny and Guadeloupe's sovereign council denied his request. Martinique's *intendant*, Foulquier, had fallen gravely ill and the minister of marine had ordered Foullon to replace him.[12] Foulquier died in February 1789; Foullon arrived in March, nursing a sense of grievance, to take up his new post in Martinique.[13] The colony also received a new governor general in 1789. When Damas sailed for France in July to recover from poor health, his interim replacement was Charles-Joseph Hyacinthe du Houx, comte de Vioménil. A *maréchal du camp* and professional soldier, he had served with distinction in the French conquest of Corsica in 1768–9 and during the War of American Independence in the comte de Rochambeau's expeditionary force.[14] He was sympathetic to colonists in the Windward Islands, but his perspective was that of a metropolitan aristocrat and servant of the crown. Vioménil had been

Map 2 "Martinique, circa 1789." Map by Marie Puddister of the Department of Geography, University of Guelph.

governor general for less than two months when Martinique was confronted with the most terrifying of colonial crises: slave revolt.

On 30 August 1789 half a dozen slaves, including the jail warden Marc, met furtively in a carpenter's workshop near Saint-Pierre's waterfront. At sundown they led many of the town's slaves into the countryside, where perhaps as many as eight hundred field slaves from gangs in at least two parishes had gathered. The sound of gunshots, signalling the arrival of militia from Saint-Pierre, caused the crowd to scatter. At least one member of the original group from Saint-Pierre, Jean Dominique, roused the slaves of the neighbouring Valmenière plantation: proclaiming that they were now free and that he would lead them to demand their freedom from the governor general, he persuaded them to abandon their quarters and to flee into the night. The following day slaves on other estates in the vicinity of Saint-Pierre refused to work, but, in fact, suppression of the revolt was already underway.[15] The comte de Vioménil arrived from Fort-Royal with regular troops of the Martinique Regiment and more detachments of free-coloured militia. The soldiers rounded up the runaways, returning them to their masters, and arrested those identified as ringleaders. On 2 September they delivered two supposed conspirators, Fouta and Honoré, to Martinique's sovereign council. The council ordered them tortured to make them reveal their accomplices, despite a recent royal ordinance outlawing the practice, and then sentenced them to death. The *procureur général du roi*, or king's attorney, told the councillors that only the example of punishment would create salutary fear and restore subordination.[16] On 10 September Fouta was broken on the wheel and Honoré was hanged.

Three days before these first executions, the sovereign council had authorized the *Sénéchal de Saint-Pierre* to interrogate prisoners and to act as a special commission to investigate the cause of the uprising. Under interrogation by the lower court's judges, plantation slaves claimed that they had been incited to revolt by "Negro doctors" from Saint-Pierre, who assured them that newspapers from France revealed that their "friends of distinction in Paris" had obtained slaves' liberty from Louis XVI: the instigators told the field hands that because their masters opposed their liberation, the masters must be massacred.[17] The investigation identified the slave Marc as the chief conspirator and the sovereign council put a price of his head. On 18 September the court condemned six more prisoners to death, sentencing others to be lashed, branded, or sent to the galleys. In describing the plot, which supposedly included plans for murder, arson, and poison against white men, while sparing white women to become concubines for the blacks, and in fulminating against the abolitionist propaganda of the *Société des Amis des Noirs* in France, the council expressed long-standing colonial obsessions.[18]

In his report on the revolt to the minister, Governor General Vioménil emphasized his efforts not only to break up the slave gatherings but also to prevent the junction of these rebels with the bands of *marrons*, or runaways, in Martinique's mountainous interior. He also sought to stop all communication between slaves who had deserted their plantations and the town slaves of Saint-Pierre. He had ordered the general mobilization of the militia to carry out a sweep of the colony and to hunt down all runaways who, Vioménil claimed, represented the greatest threat to security.[19] The number of these *marrons* was increasing and, according to the governor general, they frequented the colony's markets and public places with impunity, encouraging other slaves to flee their masters. If the solution to this problem was the establishment of a well organized mounted police force, Vioménil also believed it was necessary to distinguish between legitimate freedmen and runaways. On 10 September he issued an ordinance requiring the registration of all titles of liberty: "so-called *libres*" who did not submit to this formality would be considered *marrons* and therefore would be sold.[20] The governor general's report went beyond security measures, however, and stated that certain priests had instigated the revolt. In particular, he accused Father Jean-Baptiste, a former *Directeur des Nègres* for the parish of du Fort in Saint-Pierre, of spreading "seditious insinuations." This Capuchin had fled to Dominica, where he carried on a "guilty correspondence" with several whites. Other priests, entrusted to minister to the slaves, had also preached rebellion. Vioménil asked the minister "to reflect on the indiscretion of the publicity given today to certain political ideas, the discussion of which brings the greatest danger. Because of this the colonies find themselves surrounded by the most frightful peril: the slave is no longer ignorant that his revolt has found those who approve, who would not dispute his choice of means."[21] In the *intendant*'s version of events, written a month after the governor general's report, Foullon d'Écotier was even more emphatic that the origins of the revolt lay in dangerous ideas imported from France. He blamed Vioménil for encouraging black aspirations with his public reproaches of masters who treated their slaves harshly, which was suggestive of the governor general's humane inclinations. More important, Foullon reported that the slaves had acted on the belief that they were now free: they claimed that Louis XVI had granted their emancipation, but that the planters had persuaded the governor general to conceal the royal order.[22]

Foullon's report and the judicial investigation suggest that, beyond the influence of abolitionist rhetoric, the slave revolt in Martinique was connected to rumours of the political drama unfolding across the Atlantic. Neither the king nor the National Assembly actually proposed the abolition of slavery in 1789, but there is significant evidence that such rumours did have an impact in Martinique. Following the revolt's suppression, but while the hunt for runaways continued, Vioménil received reports from militia captains across the colony. Several of these confirmed that the slaves spoke of being free, that they believed the king had given them freedom but that their masters refused to acknowledge it, and even that they were affected by announcements of "the first decrees of the nation."[23] Letters written by slaves themselves on the eve of the revolt reinforce this suggestion. A letter delivered to planter Pierre-Auguste de Mollerat, dated 28 August and signed "*Nous, Nègres*," states that, "we know that we are free and that you allow these rebel people to resist the King's orders." These slaves claimed their liberty whatever the price, stated that they were willing to die for it, and if it were denied, the letter warned, the streets would run with "torrents of blood."[24] A second letter was sent to the governor general from the slaves of Martinique, identifying themselves as the "entire Nation of Black Slaves," who demanded freedom: "This is no longer a Nation blinded by ignorance or which trembles at the prospect of the lightest of punishments; its sufferings have clarified and given it determination to spill its blood to the last drop rather than endure any longer the shameful yoke of slavery, a frightful yoke condemned by the law, by humanity, by the entire nation, by the Divinity and by our good King Louis XVI. We want to believe that it will be condemned by the illustrious Vioménil. Your response alone, great General, will decide our fate and that of the entire colony."[25] Beyond the reference to the king's supposed sympathy with the slaves' plight, the letter's rhetoric certainly suggests some familiarity with the language of the political crisis in France. Furthermore, the letter also referred to the free-coloured campaign for equal rights in which Julien Raimond and Vincent Ogé sought to influence the deputies at Versailles. If incorrect in their assumption that such lobbying had been successful, the slaves were well aware that it had not questioned the continuation of slavery.[26] If this document provides evidence of the rivalry between black slaves and free people of colour, it also demonstrates that slaves had picked up on more than the themes of abolitionist literature denounced by the sovereign council. Rumours of liberty, associated with the meeting of the Estates General in France, had incited slave resistance in Martinique in 1789.

II The Cockade Arrives in Guadeloupe (September–November 1789)

In September the first definite news of revolution in France reached the Windward Islands, but this information should also be classified as rumour: it was unofficial, incomplete, and its implications were ambiguous. On 18 September the merchant vessel *La Jeune Bayonnaise* from Bordeaux dropped anchor at Pointe-à-Pitre, Guadeloupe. Her crew announced that Louis XVI had entered Paris and donned the tricolour cockade presented to him by the people, the same cockade worn by the sailors. The distribution of cockades at Pointe-à-Pitre culminated in a riot. More than two hundred people wearing the revolutionary symbol forced the port's commandant, Captain de Michon, to accept a cockade after they had already roughed up a number of foreigners for resisting one. Three days later a larger crowd at Sainte-Anne demanded that Guadeloupe's governor, the baron de Clugny, also don a cockade. In his account of these events, Clugny stated that he refused because of the group's "heated spirits" and lack of respect. But when the crowd returned the following day, the governor conceded: "I then responded to them that I would accept it voluntarily as His Majesty had from the hands of his people as witness of the obedience, respect and love they had shown him, that this cockade was nothing but the emblem of the union of all Frenchmen and their loyalty to their sovereign."[27] Clugny gave the same speech in Pointe-à-Pitre, claiming that it inspired the same loyalty and orderly enthusiasm. His denial that the tricolour was a symbolic challenge to royal authority reflected the governor's anxiety regarding the unclear situation in France, its ramifications for his administration, and how his actions would be judged by metropolitan government. His account stressed that while it was the inhabitants of Guadeloupe's towns who had taken up the cockade, rather than the planters, the colony's "notable inhabitants" approved of his measures of compromise to preserve order.

Order and stability, however, proved elusive. Describing the period following the cockade's arrival in Guadeloupe to the minister, Clugny and *Intendant* Viévigne stated: "Every day was marked by a new insurrection."[28] On 1 October the merchants of Pointe-à-Pitre requested that the port be opened to foreign commerce. The governor and *intendant*

Map 3 "Guadeloupe, circa 1789." Map by Marie Puddister of the Department of Geography, University of Guelph.

refused. The next day they faced a noisy demonstration by two hundred carpenters and caulkers demanding the freedom to careen vessels anywhere in Pointe-à-Pitre's roadstead. Again the administrators stood firm. But on 6 October a much more dangerous mob threatened the town with violence and arson, and residents told Clugny that his refusal to open the port had provoked popular anger. He restored calm by promising to convoke Guadeloupe's colonial assembly to consider the matter.[29] This suggests the concession that legitimate authority lay, at least in part, with a quasi-representative body. Of greater concern to the governor, however, were violent clashes at Basse-Terre in early October between the town's young men and junior officers of the Guadeloupe Regiment. If Clugny attributed the maintenance of order to the prudent conduct of the *intendant* and Basse-Terre's commandant, he deemed the punishment of a number of the Regiment's *sous-lieutenants* necessary to appease the "bourgeoisie." Above all, Clugny and Viévigne worried that the disorder in Guadeloupe's towns could lead to slave revolt.[30]

In the final months of 1789, however, the threat to Guadeloupe's royal administrators came from the increasingly politicized white population. Clugny convoked the colonial assembly on 19 October, but rather than dampening spirits, this provoked even more unrest. This body, nominated from members of the colonial elite, was unacceptable to the *petits Blancs* of Pointe-à-Pitre and Basse-Terre who insisted that only an elected assembly could decide which of the colony's ports might admit foreign ships. The colonial assembly hurriedly announced that Guadeloupe's parishes were to elect deputies to a new general assembly of the colony, which would meet on 1 December at Petit Bourg. It chose this location, in the island of Basse-Terre but just across the bay from Pointe-à-Pitre, to avoid offending the population of either principal town. Rivalry over which should be designated as the *entrepôt* for foreign trade created what the governor called a "schism" in the colony. Parish assemblies would also draft *cahiers* and the new assembly's first duty would be to name the colony's representatives to the National Assembly in France.[31] The atmosphere in which these decisions were made was reflected in the sovereign council's general order of 22 October. *Intendant* Viévigne addressed the court, and having expressed astonishment that the troubles that agitated France had caused such distress in Guadeloupe, he called for a closer alliance between judicial authority and the government to prevent the complete breakdown of law and order. In response, the judges declared that they would remain in permanent session and issued a warning to the people: "that all tumultuous gatherings, seditious signs, posters and writings, and any particular or public violence, excesses or crimes would render those guilty unworthy of this legitimate and precious liberty, to which all virtues and hopes tend; and that the tribunals, guardians of the laws which assure this liberty, will be forced to punish according to the rigour of these same laws."[32]

The communication of revolutionary news and symbols from France continued to inspire challenges to the governor's authority in Guadeloupe. In November Basse-Terre's commissioners of commerce, on behalf of the town's "citizens," approached Clugny to request the singing of a *Te Deum* to rejoice at the union of the three estates in France, marked by the formation of the National Assembly and the benediction of a national flag. Clugny agreed to and participated in these revolutionary celebrations, as did contingents of militia and soldiers from the Guadeloupe Regiment. The hymns, parades, and salutes did not satisfy all inhabitants, however, and a number of persons demanded that the troops take the new oath of loyalty decreed by the National Assembly. According to the governor, colonists had learned of the oath only through a newspaper account; thus he refused to authorize something for which he had no official notification of royal assent.[33] The clash of opposing definitions of legitimate authority was evident in an orator's response to Clugny: he insisted that the citizens would be reassured only after hearing the oath pronounced and told the governor not to delay, given the people's impatience. Once again Clugny gave in to pressure and promised that the regiment would swear the oath. In the days leading up to this ceremony, residents of Basse-Terre distributed barrels of wine to the soldiers and encouraged drunken insubordination towards their officers. On 22 November troops of the Guadeloupe Regiment, as well as militia companies, assembled in the presence of magistrates of the sovereign council and the king's attorney to swear the oath of loyalty to "Nation, Law and King" alongside their governor. Afterwards, crowds mixed freely with the soldiers and orators delivered what Clugny described as the "most dangerous speeches." Reporting on these events to the minister, he despaired of the state of his authority and his inability to control communications: "Anarchy has established itself under the name of liberty, and the administration is the object of all tirades."[34]

III The Revolution Comes to Martinique (September–November 1789)

News of metropolitan revolution produced similar developments in Martinique. Until mid-September the colony received only vague rumours, based on English newspaper accounts, of what had occurred in France during the month of July. Attending the theatre at Saint-Pierre, the comte de Vioménil encountered a man wearing the tricolour cockade who told him that this was the "standard of liberty"; the governor general asked him to remove it. It was not so easy, however, to control the arrival or reception of information. On 15 September the merchant ship *La Jeune Cecile* arrived at Saint-Pierre from Bordeaux, bringing both news and more cockades. The ship's passengers announced that these cockades were the same as that which the king had received from

the hands of his people and which "all of France was wearing in cel-
ebration of a revolution accomplished in favour of national liberty."[35]
Without official confirmation of the king's acceptance, Vioménil forbade colonists from wearing the cockade until the situation in France
could be verified. For Saint-Pierre's self-styled "patriots," however, the
testimony of merchant captains, their crews and passengers, was sufficient proof of the glorious events in Paris. Moreover, there was no
need for the minister of marine to authorize the cockade. As a pamphlet
printed in Saint-Pierre would soon declare: "The cockade was chosen
and adopted by the nation, which presented it to the king, his ministers cannot prescribe to the people on this subject."[36] In keeping with
this conception of popular sovereignty, patriots claimed that Vioménil's
opposition to the cockade revealed his hostility to the revolution. The
pamphlet reported enthusiasm in Saint-Pierre for news that the French
Guards had not fired on the people, a reference to the military unit that
had joined the insurgents attacking the Bastille in Paris on 14 July. In
this context, patriots claimed that Vioménil's order that Martinique's
regular troops swear an oath of loyalty to the king had sinister connota-
tions and was further evidence of his "despotism."[37]

Yet the governor general's report to the minister suggests that his
primary concern was the possible effect that the cockade might have
on the slaves. The judicial investigation, still underway, had already
indicated that belief in their imminent emancipation had inspired the
slaves to revolt. In the aftermath of this insurrection, Vioménil told the
minister, it was dangerous to permit the display of a symbol associated with "the idea of liberty, which the Negroes had already imbued
from the troubles which agitate France and which they could take as
a mark of independence, all the more indefinite since it is not known
whether the question of their status occupies the National Assembly."[38]
Vioménil recognized, even if the patriots did not, the ambiguity of revolutionary ideals.

It proved impossible for the governor general to ban the cockade in
Martinique or, more important, to control revolutionary communications. When Vioménil spoke to leading merchants and inhabitants of
Saint-Pierre on 18 September, warning them of the cockade's potential
dangers, he promised that with the first authentic news of the king's
acceptance he would set an example by wearing one. Such news arrived in the form of the printed *Gazette de Sainte-Lucie*. Informed of
this newspaper account, Vioménil wrote to Saint-Pierre's commissioners of commerce and gave his authorization for the town's inhabitants to

don the cockade, portraying it as a sign of union and concord.[39] They did not wait for permission. A riotous crowd converged on the residence of Commandant Jean-Baptiste-Joseph de Laumoy, who had ordered the arrest of a young man for wearing the symbol, and forced him to release the prisoner and to accept a cockade.[40] On 26 September Saint-Pierre celebrated the revolution in France with a *Te Deum*, which Laumoy approved under pressure. Patriots displayed not only national flags but also "those of our allies the Americans."[41] Vioménil travelled to Saint-Pierre from Fort-Royal that evening, demanding an apology for the affront to Laumoy's authority but instead accepted a cockade himself upon entering the town.[42] He received applause at the theatre when he appeared wearing the tricolour.

As at Guadeloupe, however, concessions to popular enthusiasm marked not the end but the beginning of conflict in Martinique generated by the revolutionary script. After returning to his headquarters at Fort-Royal, the governor general authorized the residents of that town to wear the cockade. A delegation of leading inhabitants asked him to give permission as well for celebrations of the revolution modelled on descriptions of those at Bordeaux. Initially he resisted requests for a *Te Deum*, which required royal approval, and for the town to give a banquet for the troops of Fort-Royal's garrison, but eventually he acquiesced to the first and satisfied the second by pledging to provide the refreshments himself so that soldiers could share in the festivities. On 28 September the governor general and the Martinique Regiment staged a military parade, and the following day Vioménil allowed soldiers to participate with civilians in other celebrations. At first these were orderly. Commenting on a dinner he hosted for sixty of the most qualified representatives of the three estates in Fort-Royal, Vioménil told the minister that this was a happy occasion of peace and tranquility, "at a time when astonishment and diverse interpretations of the events in France have agitated spirits in different ways."[43] Peace and tranquility vanished when members of the coloured militia asked to participate.

Planters had praised these *gens de couleur* for their contribution to suppressing the slave revolt and presented them with the national cockade, but revellers at Fort-Royal refused to admit them to their celebrations. According to the governor general's account of events, a number of free men of colour entered the dining hall to inform him of their exclusion and mistreatment. He responded: "I showed my displeasure and I exhorted the citizens to treat them with gentleness and good will."[44] Governor Clugny faced a similar dilemma in Guadeloupe when free men of colour asked to wear the cockade and whites demanded that he refuse: while he approved of the former's request, he equivocated by ordering that any slave donning the tricolour would be punished.[45] In Martinique, Vioménil's public support for the *gens de couleur* touched off a riot. As shouting and fighting erupted in the dining hall, with a coloured man struck down beside him, the governor general stood, drew his sword, and tried to make his orders heard above the din. He acknowledged that some free men of colour had cried "To Arms!" and he ordered their arrest. But his report to the minister made clear that whites were at least equally responsible for the brawl and that afterwards they dispersed to spread alarm and accusations against him.[46] Specifically, they accused Vioménil of loving the free coloureds, giving them preference over white troops and inhabitants, and of aspiring to erect a despotic power: this was an ironic but potent mix of revolutionary rhetoric and colonial racism. Disorder reigned in Fort-Royal for the next two days, and insubordinate soldiers mixed freely with civilian mobs. The governor general claimed that during this time he was in constant danger, not only of insult but also of assassination or of being forced aboard a ship bound for France.

The turmoil at Fort-Royal led directly to the emergence of an alternate authority in Martinique, which not only denounced Vioménil but also challenged the legitimacy of executive power in the colony. News of events in the colony's capital reached Saint-Pierre on 30 September. According to the *Journal de Saint-Pierre – Martinique*, an individual identified as M. Tannais arrived from Fort-Royal at three o'clock in the morning and reported the disorder to the commissioners of commerce and to Commandant Laumoy. Tannais claimed that the governor general, drunk on wine, had berated two of his officers for not allowing the mulattos to enter the celebrations and then enjoined the troops to recognize the coloured militiamen as good citizens with whom they should socialize. Puffed up by this treatment, the mulattos delivered themselves to such excesses that the whites were obliged to take up arms to defend themselves.[47] The effect of this report was electrifying. "The people," according to the *Journal de Saint-Pierre – Martinique*, "animated only by patriotism," gathered en masse at the church of Du Fort. Along with calls for action to help their brother whites came the proposal to form a municipal committee in Saint-Pierre. Subsequent messengers qualified the first report and contradicted each other. Rumours continued to shape developments in the colony. The popular assembly eventually decided to send thirteen deputies to Fort-Royal to facilitate the return to peace and to gather exact information on the actions imputed to the governor general.[48] Early on the morning of 1 October, residents of Saint-Pierre gathered again, this time at the theatre. In a much more orderly meeting they named M. Ruste president of the assembly, M. Thore vice president, and M. Crassous de Médeuil secretary, then chose 101 electors from the town's notable citizens and charged them with the formation of an eighteen-member committee.

This committee, as described by the *Journal de Saint-Pierre – Martinique*, imitated the revolutionary municipalities, which had emerged in Paris and throughout France during the summer of 1789, both in terms of its determination to establish civilian militia to keep order and of its self-justification as an emanation of popular sovereignty: "This committee was to be uniquely the organ and council of the people."[49] The new political culture also resonated in the townsfolk's decisions that afternoon that committee members must swear an oath and that their deliberations would only have effect when sanctioned by the people in public session.[50]

Although he disapproved of the disorder and popular effervescence surrounding its formation, Vioménil told the minister that he hoped Saint-Pierre's committee would assist him in re-establishing civil peace. He attributed the worsening situation to Saint-Pierre's rootless and dangerous population. As the colony's commercial centre, the town was full of vagabonds and debtors, foreigners and stateless men, seamen and pirates: "This portion of the population, without manners or restraint, whose interest and desire is to enter into trouble and to profit from disorder, must be distinguished from the merchants and property owners who make up the other, but weaker part."[51] The *petits Blancs* certainly had enormous influence on Saint-Pierre's politics, but the patriots also included members of the urban elite. Twelve of the eighteen original members of the committee were merchants; four of these, including the president, Ruste, were commissioners of commerce. Three members were *Chevaliers de Saint-Louis*, and two of these were former infantry officers. The secretary, Crassous de Médeuil, was a lawyer.[52] The emerging struggle in the colony was driven by more than conflict between social classes and by more than *petit-Blanc* resentment of the *gens de couleur*. The opposing factions came to embody competing conceptions of legitimate authority.

The Saint-Pierre committee's campaign against Governor General Vioménil reflected the revolutionary concept of popular sovereignty and was soon linked to demands for the democratic reconstitution of the colonial assembly.[53] Patriots reacted with suspicion and hostility to the governor general's letter to Ruste, in which he congratulated Ruste on being named head of the assembly to elect a municipal committee. Confident that this group would use its wisdom to calm and contain the people, "who would never have strayed if they had not been misled," Vioménil offered to come to Saint-Pierre, once order was restored, and meet with Ruste to explain his conduct.[54] This attempt at reconciliation failed utterly.[55] On 2 October Ruste and the committee, in public session, prepared a response in which they reminded the governor general, given the news from France, of the new order of things. The people were not to be contained; rather their will was the source of authority.[56] Vioménil's subsequent offer to convoke Martinique's colonial assembly, even with new representation for Saint-Pierre more proportional to the size of its population, failed to satisfy this new conception of political legitimacy. In asking Ruste to recommend commissioners of commerce and principal citizens from the town, he was still thinking in terms of a nominated rather than an elected assembly.[57]

Over the next few days the patriots articulated their demands for a new assembly. On 3 October the deputies sent to Fort-Royal returned to Saint-Pierre; their report strengthened the patriot conviction that Vioménil had compromised the garrison, the citizens, and the entire colony by indulging free men of colour.[58] To restrain angry demands for punishment, Arnaud de Corio, in the name of the committee, moved that the governor general, as the king's representative, be under the safeguard of the people and the colony; therefore, only a general assembly of the colony could judge his conduct.[59] The demand for such an assembly soon appeared in correspondence from the committee to parish militia captains.[60] The following day the committee presented a tableau of Vioménil's conduct, emphasizing his words as much as his actions. The offences attributed to the governor general included: his opposition to the cockade and his "vehement speech" in that regard; his initial refusal of a *Te Deum* at Fort-Royal and his resistance to citizens mixing with the troops; his insistence that soldiers swear an oath of loyalty to the king; his statement, overheard at the dinner on 29 September, that the colony was full of men with "branded shoulders," or criminals; his chastisement of his officers for failing to admit the mulattos to the celebrations and his subsequent order, sword in hand, that they be treated as good citizens; his statement that he esteemed mulattos as much as white officers; his denial, in the aftermath of the riot, of these words and acts; and finally, in response to demands that the mulattos be punished, his statement that he first wanted to know who was the aggressor. These charges amount to disdain and distrust for the *petits Blancs* and, worse, a failure to uphold strict racial hierarchy. As the committee observed, some of these were "offenses toward the nation, others are toward the colony in particular."[61] If it claimed that these offences were easy to prove, the committee insisted that they could only be verified in a general assembly of the colony; meanwhile, the person of the comte de Vioménil was sacrosanct. The crowd watching over the meeting accepted this, but its members demanded that the committee work to achieve this general assembly and to prepare a formal indictment of the governor general's conduct to be submitted to the National Assembly.[62]

Competing claims to legitimacy were at the heart of the struggle. Vioménil prepared to convoke Martinique's existing colonial assembly. He informed the *intendant* that he believed that it was necessary to do this as soon as possible, and that he hoped to confer with Ruste on the best means to do so.[63] The two then wrote to the parish commandants authorizing the inhabitants to send deputies to the assembly, with special instructions to those of Saint-Pierre to send extra deputies for each of the two parishes.[64] Vioménil told Foullon that it was indispensable to convoke the colonial assembly to limit the effervescence that had produced unrest at Saint-Pierre and also to convoke the colony's sovereign council to advise them on the means to end it: "It is necessary to prevent by this convocation any kind of illegal enterprise."[65] Learning of Vioménil's plan to convoke the colonial assembly, Ruste and Crassous de Médeuil issued an ultimatum to the *intendant* and Commandant de Laumoy. They informed these administrators that the governor general had promised Ruste he would convoke a general assembly, not as it existed to assess taxes but in a form that the current state of affairs demanded. But he could not be permitted to convoke a body that would judge his crimes.[66] As to the formation of this general assembly, Ruste and Crassous insisted that it should not distinguish between planters and merchants, agriculture and industry. All colonists had an equal interest in the colony and all must be represented equally in an assembly that "needs men from part of the French nation which must raise it to the same dignity which the nation has raised itself."[67] Furthermore, the general assembly must not meet at Fort-Royal, the colony's military headquarters, but at Saint-Pierre: "This assembly of citizens must be free, above all from the military apparatus that M. de Vioménil is accused of wanting to employ."[68] Ruste and Crassous declared in conclusion that Saint-Pierre would refuse to participate if Vioménil convoked the colonial assembly and that an assembly convoked according to the ordinance of 1787 was not competent for the current object. This assertion was a direct challenge to the governor general, who responded with a clear pronouncement of the legitimacy of his authority and the illegality of his enemies' position. In a letter to Laumoy, also dated 5 October, Vioménil reminded the commandant that only the governor general and *intendant*, together, had the right to convoke the colonial assembly and that they had the obligation to instruct it on the means to re-establish order. As for the number of deputies, his consent that Saint-Pierre could send twelve adjunct deputies to the assembly, as compared to six from Fort-Royal and one from each of the other parishes, demonstrated his desire that representation be complete. "The dispositions of the ordinance of 17 June 1787 on the creation of the colonial assembly are decisive," declared Vioménil, "and destroy the doubt proposed by the Saint-Pierre committee."[69] The king had neglected nothing that could procure the well-being of colonists and, in any case, only the colonial assembly created by the 1787 ordinance had any basis in law. But, as Vioménil reported to the minister, members of the committee had arrogated to themselves the right to convoke a general assembly and sought to cover this illegal act with the appearance of regularity: "They do not recognize the legitimate authority confided in me."[70]

The communication of opposing interpretations of the governor general's actions demonstrated competing claims to legitimate authority. Vioménil was aware that the Saint-Pierre committee was preparing a detailed denunciation of his conduct; he understood the necessity of defending himself to the minister of marine and, potentially, to public opinion in France. To document his actions, and to provide evidence that he had fulfilled his duties correctly and honourably, he compiled a thick dossier to be sent with his detailed report of 17 October. These documents included the testimonials of various military officers in Martinique, who declared that the governor general never ordered the use of force against citizens of the colony; he was determined to uphold law and order but had acted always in the spirit of moderation.[71] If these show that he still enjoyed the army's loyalty, they also suggest what Vioménil thought was the most dangerous of the accusations he faced. While he refuted the allegations of despotism and contempt for the nation imputed to his words and actions, Vioménil did not deny that he told soldiers at Fort-Royal to treat the *gens de couleur* as good servants of the king. The Saint-Pierre Committee regarded this support for "those who must be maintained in an inferior class" as perhaps his most serious crime.[72] Vioménil told the minister that the committee spread calumnies against him to perpetuate the popular insurrection that caused all work to cease and commerce to be abandoned in Saint-Pierre.[73] Evidence that Vioménil's life had been threatened came from a letter to him from the committee; it provides further indications that the revolutionary concept of popular sovereignty was crucial to the campaign against him. Informing the governor general that it had collected accusations against him, the committee insisted that only a general assembly could pronounce upon them. The committee spoke for the people and thus it must be satisfied: "It is to the committee, *M. le comte*, that the colony owes the tranquility that it again enjoys; you owe it your security, perhaps your life: you still owe it the justification which is necessary for you."[74]

Vioménil convoked the colonial assembly at Fort-Royal on 9 October. He exhorted the deputies on the urgent need to end the threat to the colony posed by the insurrection in Saint-Pierre, and he pressed them to rule on the committee's incendiary charges against him that compromised his authority.[75] Following his opening address, however, deputies from Saint-Pierre protested that the present assembly was insufficient to deliberate on the governor general's conduct, and they demanded that a general assembly of the colony, formed according to the respective population of each parish, be convoked at Saint-Pierre.[76] The colonial assembly attempted first to achieve reconciliation between Vioménil and Saint-Pierre, and it sent deputies to the town. The deputies reported calm and tranquility there, but also that the townspeople continued to demand a general assembly.[77] On 15 October, after debating the demands of the Saint-Pierre Committee, the colonial assembly declared that it could pronounce neither on the accusations against the governor general nor on his defence of his conduct.[78] That same day Martinique's sovereign council ruled that it was not competent to make a judgment on the complaints against the governor general submitted to the *procureur général* by the Saint-Pierre Committee. Instead, the court invited "all classes of citizens to await in peaceful silence the orders of the National Assembly sanctioned by the King for the new constitution."[79] These decisions represented a defeat for Vioménil. Although military officers, magistrates, parish commandants, and various prominent planters submitted testimonials defending his conduct, neither the sovereign council nor the colonial assembly would back his resistance to the assertion of popular sovereignty.[80]

Martinique's *intendant* also undermined Vioménil's hope for a united front against the Saint-Pierre Committee. In response to the ultimatum sent to Laumoy and himself, Foullon d'Écotier informed the committee of the governor general's decision to convoke the colonial assembly. His message concluded, however, with an indication that he was sympathetic to the patriots' position.[81] Foullon was not present when the colonial assembly opened at Fort-Royal on 9 October. Vioménil was furious and accused the *intendant* of deliberately abandoning him. Foullon claimed that rough seas had prevented him from embarking for the voyage to Fort-Royal and that subsequent poor health had kept him in Saint-Pierre. He also told the minister, however, that he thought he had served the colony better by remaining in Saint-Pierre, "where I flatter myself to have many friends," than by attending the sessions of the colonial assembly, "from which I would have been forced to distance myself."[82] While suggesting that he had supported the governor general, his report corroborated the patriots' version of events since news of the revolution had reached Martinique. In contrast to Vioménil's opposition to the national cockade, Foullon had accepted one happily from the people of Saint-Pierre. Proof of their recognition of his patriotism, he claimed, was the kindness they showed him at the "first news of my unhappiness."[83]

Martinique's *intendant* had a direct family connection to the violence of the revolution in Paris. On 22 July a crowd had murdered his father, Joseph-François Foullon, along with his brother-in-law Bertier de Sauvigny, *intendant* of Paris, whom popular militants suspected of trying to starve the city. While this savagery appalled most educated witnesses, some deputies in the National Assembly tried to justify the killings.[84] The shock of his father's death may have weakened the *intendant*'s health, but it did not affect his positive interpretation of the Saint-Pierre Committee's actions in contrast to those of the governor general.[85] Vioménil, for his part, informed the minister that Foullon d'Écotier's ability to carry out his functions was compromised by a name that was now "anathema to the nation." Since the *intendant* had not offered his resignation, however, Vioménil requested that the minister replace him.[86] The conflict between these two men may have been personal, although both denied it, and Foullon's record as *intendant* in Guadeloupe suggests his affinity with colonial merchants in opposition to planters and governors. Yet the division between the two administrators went beyond these issues and was tied to the emerging revolutionary struggle in the colonies: Foullon backed the Saint-Pierre

Committee's claim to popular sovereignty in opposition to Vioménil's defence of executive authority.

On 17 October members of Martinique's colonial assembly spelled out the conditions under which a general assembly might be convoked. Any man "Creole and European" (i.e., white) bearing arms since he was sixteen years old, would have the right to vote in his parish on the militia role. Any man not on the militia role would be held, in order to vote for an elector, to prove that he was a taxpayer. This presumably would exclude the rootless and transient elements that Vioménil saw behind the disorder at Saint-Pierre. Furthermore, only the prefects and superiors of religious orders could vote, and thus not the junior priests suspected of inciting the slave revolt, and they could only become deputies to the general assembly as citizens, not as deputies of their order. The number of deputies per parish was to be proportional to their white population, with one deputy for every fifty voters. These deputies chosen in the parishes would be given unlimited powers; that is, they were not to be bound by mandates from their constituents. The date of the general assembly's convocation was fixed for 16 November and its object was defined: it would name the colony's representatives to the National Assembly in France, draft the colony's *cahiers de doléances*, and consider other objects of public utility. These tasks were to be its only purpose; while making no reference to the governor general's conduct, the order stated explicitly that this convocation did not interfere with the interests of the colonial assembly created by the ordinance of 1787. Just as significantly, deputies to the existing colonial assembly would be eligible to become members of the new general assembly.[87] Rather than being the instrument of the Saint-Pierre Committee, this new assembly would become its rival and the voice of Martinique's planter elite. This was not yet clear, of course, and the ordinance of 22 October by which the governor general and the *intendant* gave their formal sanction to the convocation of a general assembly represented another defeat for Vioménil.[88]

Even before the colonial assembly's order received sanction, the Saint-Pierre Committee had taken steps to formalize its power. The governor general informed the minister on 18 October that the committee intended to give itself a mayor and to create a general commander of militia. "This undertaking, without precedent and destructive of the established order," wrote Vioménil, "is due particularly to the fiery genius of Ruste, president of the committee that nothing will stop unless this leader is removed from the colony."[89] The decision to establish a municipality was in keeping with the revolutionary script from France, where committees of electors had formed spontaneously in July 1789 and organized bourgeois militia to keep order; these committees became the basis for new municipal authorities.[90] In Martinique, the question of municipalities arose during the sessions of the colonial assembly.[91] On 13 October, the deputies considered the National Assembly's decree of 10 August, which required military officers to swear the new oath and insisted that armed force could be used only at the requisition of municipal officers. This went against the established pattern for mobilizing the militia. Since parish commandants only repeated the orders they received from the colony's military commanders, the deputies decided that municipal officers would need to be established in the parishes with authority to call out the militia.[92] Thus the colonial assembly may have endorsed the formation of municipalities, but the radical rhetoric that accompanied this development in Saint-Pierre could only increase the governor general's fear of anarchy. A public address in praise of the committee, delivered on 20 October and signed "Your Fellow Citizens, the People of Saint-Pierre," was printed and distributed in the colony. It heralded the triumph of the French Revolution that inspired the establishment of a municipality in Saint-Pierre: "The unexpected and salutary revolution which has come to pass in France, the tribunals created by the French people to reestablish public tranquility have by their success excited the admiration of the entire universe."[93] If the address disputed claims of disorder at Saint-Pierre, its guarantee of safety to visitors was linked to a threat against the committee's opponents.[94]

Martinique's general assembly opened on 16 November at Fort-Royal and Governor General Vioménil delivered the opening address. He appealed to the deputies to help unite the colony as a whole and to remind it of the importance of obedience to the law. The colony could enjoy the benefits of the "regeneration of the state," he said, without the violence and upheaval that had occurred in France. Calm and tranquility were vital because the colony was in danger not only from an uncertain international situation but also more urgently from the colony's slaves. Despite this peril, which demonstrated the need for strong and respected authority, Vioménil reported that the Saint-Pierre Committee spread libels against him, even in the midst of this assembly. This would not deter him from his duties, he assured the deputies, and no part of the island would escape his vigilance.[95] Yet not even the colony's administrators were united in this defence of executive authority. Following Vioménil's speech, Foullon recommended to the general assembly that it elect Levassor as president. This man had championed the demands from Saint-Pierre in the previous colonial assembly and Foullon's intervention sparked an angry exchange between himself and the governor general in sight of the deputies. "I cannot hide from you that if you indicate that it is my duty to conserve Foullon, the task will become too difficult and perilous for me," Vioménil wrote to the minister, "it is impossible for me to administer with him."[96] The Saint-Pierre Committee's response to Vioménil's accusations that the town's agitation was encouraging a slave uprising, however, demonstrated the more serious challenge to the governor general's authority. The committee affirmed that it would send representatives to the general assembly, as "depositories of authority," insisting that this body alone would determine the means to eliminate the danger.[97] For the patriots of Saint-Pierre, who had taken up the revolutionary script from France, legitimate authority resided only in the people's will.

Rumours of revolution proved impossible to control. The formation of the Saint-Pierre Committee inspired similar developments in Guadeloupe. Governor Clugny and *Intendant* Viévigne informed the Minister on 29 November that they had approved the establishment of a thirty-six-person committee for the town of Basse-Terre with jurisdiction over police and the authority to mobilize the militia. "The example of Martinique forced our hands, " they explained, "All that happens on that island warms heads here."[98] They fully expected that patriots would establish other committees elsewhere in Guadeloupe. While these could resolve immediate problems, the administrators worried that they could soon become dangerous. Should these nascent municipalities be maintained and, if so, what powers should they be given? Above all, Clugny and Viévigne wanted the minister to clarify the new colonial system the National Assembly intended to introduce and explain whether existing laws retained their authority until new ones arrived, "because the shadow in which this leaves the colonies throws them into anarchy, of which the effects become more and more to be feared every day."[99] This fear and uncertainty reflected the larger context of confusion and ambiguity that characterized 1789 in the Windward Islands. Even more than the slow speed of communications between Europe and the Caribbean, the arrival of unofficial, incomplete, and even utterly false news determined the initial impact of the French Revolution in Martinique and Guadeloupe. The slaves near Saint-Pierre rose up at the end of August because they believed, incorrectly, that Louis XVI had granted them freedom and that their masters refused to obey the royal order. Both the judicial investigation into the cause of the revolt and the letters written by slaves themselves suggest that this belief resulted more from rumours connected to the meeting of the Estates General and the beginning of the National Assembly in France than from older abolitionist propaganda. If the slave revolt demonstrated the colonial administrators' failure to control the exchange of information between the slaves and other elements of the population, the arrival at Guadeloupe and Martinique of the first news of the revolution in Paris revealed their inability to control the *petits Blancs'* communications. The governors could not prevent the arrival of the national cockade; it proved impossible to stop the disorderly residents of the colonies' ports from displaying it; and, worst of all, they could not control how it would be interpreted. Governor General Vioménil recognized the dangerous ambiguity of a symbol associated with "liberty" in a slave colony, but the principal effect of revolutionary news was to unleash white defiance of his authority and that of Governor Clugny.

If information arrived initially in the form of rumours, the French revolutionary script influenced developments in the Windward Islands directly. Supporters of the revolution soon adopted the metropolitan title of "patriots" for themselves, and they imbued the concept of revolutionary popular sovereignty from metropolitan news and rhetoric. Sovereignty lay only with the nation, or "the people," and royal executive power was suspect. Thus patriots challenged the authority of the king's representatives in the colonies, the governors. This revolutionary ideology was superimposed on a colonial context. Patriot rhetoric fit with *petit Blanc* hostility towards colonial elites and merchant resentment of planters, while patriots in both Fort-Royal and Saint-Pierre considered Vioménil's cardinal crime to be his metropolitan disregard for strict racial hierarchy. Colonial patriots could not see the irony in venerating revolutionary principles while simultaneously railing against the suggestion that free men of colour should be treated with respect. This was not the only ambiguity in the developments of 1789. Revolutionaries in France and in the colonies insisted that only authority derived from the nation's or people's will was legitimate, yet where that will was located was neither clear nor uncontested. In its struggle with the governor general, the Saint-Pierre Committee pushed for the creation of a general assembly of Martinique, but that assembly would soon become its bitter rival and would dispute its claim to speak for the colony.

3 Patriots versus Aristocrats: The Coming of Civil War, 1789–1790

In September 1790 Martinique descended into a state of civil war. Troops of the Martinique Regiment stationed in Fort-Bourbon, the colony's primary fortification above the town of Fort-Royal, mutinied against their officers and against the authority of the vicomte de Damas, governor general of the Windward Islands. Defiance spread to Fort-Royal itself, where soldiers released colonists awaiting deportation to France and declared their alliance with the town's patriots and, more ominously, those of Saint-Pierre. The governor general and members of the colonial assembly, along with most of the colony's military officers, retreated to Gros Morne in the island's interior, where white and free-coloured militia rallied to their support. This bitter factional struggle had simmered in Martinique since the convocation of the colony's general assembly in November 1789. The assembly's decrees on municipalities, on future colonial assemblies, and on the establishment of new *entrepôts* for foreign commerce provoked escalating conflict with Saint-Pierre. The patriots arranged their own municipal organization, boycotted the general assembly, and defended a riot protesting the possibility of martial law. This political strife overlapped with the erosion of military discipline. Provocations by captains of Saint-Pierre's garrison triggered a popular insurrection in March 1790. Volunteers from Guadeloupe, where similar conflict had emerged, came to Saint-Pierre to defend the patriot stronghold. While this confrontation ended without military action, a massacre of free men of colour at Saint-Pierre in June led Damas to march his troops against the town. Yet Saint-Pierre's occupation only intensified the struggle between "patriots" and "aristocrats."

The revolutionary script from metropolitan France helped to shape the coming of civil war in the Windward Islands. Both contemporaries and historians have recognized that the conflict between white colonists reflected deep economic and social divisions.[1] Rich planters controlled the general assemblies formed in Martinique and Guadeloupe late in 1789, while merchants found support from the *petits Blancs* of the colonies' ports who detested both the planters and the royal administrators. Yet class conflict provides only part of the explanation. If the revolt of 1789 had demonstrated that slaves were not isolated from rumours and revolutionary ideas, the events of 1790 showed that the colonial administration had also failed to curtail freedom of communications for other marginal groups. Soldiers' indiscipline and outright mutiny reflected the influence of revolutionary rhetoric, adopted and disseminated by colonial patriots. Yet the revolutionary script's performance in the colonies was deeply ambiguous. *Petits Blancs* saw no contradiction between commitment to an egalitarian revolution and a ferocious insistence on strict racial hierarchy. Given the patriots' hostility towards them, in 1790 free men of colour saw their interests aligned with those of planters and royal administrators, despite the fact that the former insisted they would refuse metropolitan reforms to the status of *gens de couleur*. The revolution's most central ambiguity, however, was common to both the colonies and metropolitan France: If the nation was now sovereign, who spoke for the nation? Patriots enthusiastically embraced popular sovereignty, embodied in the political form of the revolutionary commune, to challenge colonial governors, but their enemies in Martinique's colonial assembly also adopted the concept to usurp legislative power. Thus behind the outbreak of civil war in 1790 lay a revolutionary struggle between competing claims to legitimate authority.

I Martinique's Assembly and Saint-Pierre's Commune (November 1789–January 1790)

Martinique's general assembly opened at Fort-Royal on 16 November 1789 with the mandate to draft *cahiers* and to name the colony's representatives to the National Assembly. Its members soon discovered, however, that Creoles in France had beaten them to the punch. Meeting at the Paris residence of Dubuc-Duferret on 6 September, these self-appointed electors had chosen two prominent colonists, Moreau de Saint-Méry and the comte de Dillon, to be Martinique's deputies. The National Assembly admitted the two deputies, along with those from Guadeloupe, on 14 October.[2] This revelation cast doubt on the general assembly's mission, but the deputies' immediate concern was to unite the white population. After debating what should be the basis for representation in future assemblies: property or population;[3] the assembly attempted to resolve the conflict with the governor general. Vioménil and all of the deputies travelled to Saint-Pierre, where they gathered with the members of the Saint-Pierre committee on 21 November. "In the name of the people," Ruste expressed joy at the presence of the general assembly and, significantly, recognized the governor general. Vioménil gave a speech exhorting the people to forget the past and to embrace peace. Some spectators booed. But later, at a benediction of national flags at the church of the Mouillage, when the governor general swore to be loyal to the colony, he was rewarded with shouts of "*Vive le comte de Vioménil!*" Reporting to the minister on what he called "the happiest day of my life," Vioménil wrote that he had restored tranquility in the colony with the help of the general assembly and the "patriotic efforts of members of the Saint-Pierre Committee."[4] On this occasion the committee did want reconciliation.[5]

This unity was short-lived because in December the general assembly arrogated legislative authority for Martinique. The governor general informed the minister that the assembly had gone beyond drafting *cahiers*, or choosing deputies to the National Assembly, and had asked him to sanction its *arrêtés* concerning the colony's laws and administration.[6] This exceeded not only the mandate given to the general assembly in the ordinance of 22 October but also the powers given to the colonial assemblies in 1787. Between its return to Fort-Royal and its final session on 10 December, the assembly issued a series of decrees that strengthened colonial institutions in anticipation of possible metropolitan interference; cast aside restrictions on commerce in the name of present exigency but to the economic benefit of planters; and sought to control the political power of urban patriots. On 1 December the deputies proposed a new regulation for the colony's militia; this was intended to prevent the formation of a citizen's militia or national guard.[7]

The assembly also issued new regulations regarding enfranchisement and the status of *gens de couleur libres*. These regulations obliged all freedmen and their descendants to serve in the militia and promised liberty to any slave who rendered essential service to the colony. In all other cases, however, the regulations laid out the specific taxes to be paid for manumission. The assembly affirmed that free people of colour could seek judicial redress against whites who mistreated them; authorized them to practice all trades and forms of commerce; insisted that slaves must show freedmen respect; but also ordered notaries and clergy to indicate colour and status on all certificates of marriage, birth, and burial.[8] These regulations illustrate white colonists' ambivalence towards *gens de couleur*. On the one hand, planters saw them as reliable defenders of the slave system and useful intermediaries between whites and slaves. On the other hand, whites were adamant that their number not increase too much and that they remain subservient.[9] The assembly's regulation on the form of enfranchisements required the newly freed to swear, "before God to be all my life loyal, respectful, devoted to whites, my lords and patrons, to inform them of anything I learn to be against their interests."[10]

The assembly's decrees demonstrated the assertion of planters' interests, but they also revealed its claim to represent legitimate authority in opposition to disorderly expressions of popular will. Deputies representing Saint-Pierre protested all of the general assembly's acts and began to boycott its sessions. Given that the assembly's regulation of the militia had placed policing under the orders of municipalities, on 2 December it decreed the provisional establishment of a municipality for each town in the colony. The assembly gave considerable responsibility to these new bodies, but the colonial elite was determined that Saint-Pierre remain firmly under the authority of executive power. The regulation's final article stated that if municipal officers failed to uphold order and public tranquillity, the governor general would employ whatever means he deemed necessary, and the municipal officers would be held responsible for any disorder they could have prevented.[11]

More than the establishment of municipalities, the general assembly's *arrêté* of 3 December opening Martinique's ports to foreign ships signalled open conflict between the interests of agriculture and commerce. In blatant challenge to the restrictions of the old *Exclusif*, the decree called for not only the admission of American ships into Martinique's four principal ports but also for the creation of a fifth *entrepôt* for foreign commerce at François. The justification for these measures included the colony's slow recovery from the devastation of the previous year's hurricane and the shortage of food for the slave gangs. The assembly also referred to the injustice of Saint-Pierre's monopoly on foreign commerce, however, and the resulting price differentials and cornering of service and transport charges.[12] Despite the assembly's assurance that it would do all in its power to protect the fundamental law reserving colonial goods for French commerce, the decree fit with planters' longstanding desire for freer trade.

Perhaps the most striking demonstration of the general assembly's appropriation of legislative authority was its decree of 8 December setting out the rules and procedures for future colonial assemblies. It also provided further evidence of the assembly's intention to reduce the influence of port merchants and *petits Blancs*. The proposed regulation called for a new assembly of eighty-one members, of which Saint-Pierre would name only seven for the town and two for the surrounding countryside, while Fort-Royal would name four for the town and three for the country. The age, residency, and property qualifications to vote were also tilted in favour of planters.[13] Despite the serious implications of this regulation, it was the assembly's decree the following day that inflamed the colony's smouldering factional strife. That *arrêté* was linked to the establishment of municipalities in the colony; it also reflected news of the National Assembly's law of 21 October against tumults.[14] Above all, it revealed the general assembly's fear of popular upheaval at Saint-Pierre. The decree stated that all riotous assemblies were contrary to the law, that at their first appearance municipal officers must demand of the persons gathered the reason for their unlawful assembly, and then ask them to disperse. After this one and only summons, municipal officers were obliged to request military force be employed in all its energy against those who resisted.[15] On 10 December the general assembly adjourned, and the following day its permanent committee asked the governor general to sanction its decree on martial law. Vioménil and Foullon d'Écotier issued an ordinance – although the *intendant* would claim later that he had resisted doing so – and submitted it to the *sénéchaussée* of Saint-Pierre to be registered, printed, and posted. On 13 December an angry mob invaded the office of Arnaud de Corio, *sénéchal intermédiare* and member of the Saint-Pierre committee, telling him either to cross out the *arrêté* or be hanged. His clerk crossed out the offending lines, but the crowd deemed this insufficient and one of its members snatched the text of the ordinance and emptied an inkwell over it.[16] Rather than intimidating Saint-Pierre, the general assembly's martial law decree had provoked angry defiance.

The aftermath of this riot saw mutual recriminations among colonial administrators, magistrates, and the general assembly. According to Vioménil's account of events, on 12 December the *intendant* seized the ordinance from the printer to prevent its publication. This action encouraged the attack on the *sénéchaussée* the following day and confirmed the *intendant*'s alliance with "the mutinous portion of the people of Saint-Pierre." Because the *sénéchal* took no action, Vioménil convoked Martinique's sovereign council to register the martial law ordinance.[17] In Foullon's own report, he claimed that the people of Saint-Pierre approached him after they had invaded the office of the *sénéchal* and asked him not to publish the ordinance. He informed the minister that there was no justification for the martial law decree in the first place; that there was no parallel between Saint-Pierre's effervescence and the "brigands" against whom the law was aimed in France; and that the governor general's actions, "in time of general revolution, can only be regarded with severity."[18] The *intendant*'s principal concern was to alert the minister that Martinique's general assembly was not examining the colony's *cahiers* but investigating its administration: "It has persuaded itself that it is legislative."[19]

Yet the governor general's support for the assembly's assumption of legislative power was more reluctant than Foullon suggested. Vioménil had submitted a memorandum to the assembly at its last meeting on 10 December, giving only conditional support for its decrees. Any fundamental change to the enfranchisement of slaves, he suggested, required the National Assembly's approval. He stated that he could authorize the establishment of municipalities and the opening of the colony's ports provisionally, pending the sanction of king and National Assembly, and that he could also give conditional approval to the formation of annual colonial assemblies, but only if they did not derogate authority attributed to the colony's administration by the royal ordinance of June 1787.[20] Nevertheless, he issued ordinances giving sanction to all of the assembly's regulations – obtaining Foullon's signature for every one of them – and submitted them to the sovereign council for registration.[21] In its sessions of 19 and 26 December, the high court registered the ordinances, but not without reluctance and equivocation of its own.[22] The general assembly's arrogation of legislative authority was a revolutionary course of action, which shocked its allies among the colonial elite as much as it enraged its enemies among port merchants and *petits Blancs*.

Patriots had begun to see the "aristocrats" of the assembly as their principal enemies, and to assert their claim to popular sovereignty against them and not just against the governor general. According to Saint-Pierre's commissioners of commerce, a thousand citizens had gathered at the theatre on 17 December to demand that a municipality be established without delay.[23] The crowd acclaimed M. Thoumazeau mayor and M. Ruste his lieutenant and elected other municipal officers by the same means the following day. Even more of a challenge to the proposed regulation on municipalities, Saint-Pierre also elected a popular municipal assembly, or "commune," of sixty-one members. As anger grew over the decrees, Saint-Pierre not only refused to send deputies to the general assembly but also encouraged other parishes to do the same.[24] Thoumazeau wrote to the governor general on 28 December to insist that the cause of the troubles agitating the colony was not the withdrawal of Saint-Pierre's deputies, but the assembly itself that "has seized all authority, broken ties to society and crushed under its feet all general principles and particular rights." He accused the planters' deputies of seeking a "schism" between the town and the rest of Martinique as a pretext to default on twenty million *livres* of debt. Beyond berating Vioménil for convoking the general assembly, Thoumazeau announced that Saint-Pierre would not recognize its decrees: "The assembly claims to give laws to this country, but Saint-Pierre does not want to accept them or to be dictated to. No people will subscribe to laws to which it has not consented ... The people demand laws that the revolution authorizes."[25] This assertion of popular sovereignty, identified with the municipality and commune, was a direct challenge to the assembly's claim to legislative authority.

Two rival factions had emerged in Martinique, one associated with Saint-Pierre's municipality and the other with the general assembly, and the colony's administrators took sides. Foullon d'Écotier aligned himself with the patriots of Saint-Pierre, accused the general assembly of aspiring to pronounce a schism with the town, and identified its most dangerous members as "Vioménil's creatures."[26] Yet an alliance between Vioménil and the assembly was not automatic. Vioménil had opposed the formation of a general assembly. He was concerned by its assumption of legislative power, but he embraced its acknowledgment of his authority as legitimate. In his letter to the minister of 20 December, Vioménil reported that the sovereign council had begun to register his ordinances, thus vindicating his sanction of the assembly's decrees, "at a time when news from France inflames spirits by examples of the destruction of authority and when I've become convinced that enemies of the state are bribing agents of trouble and insurrection in the colony."[27]

Control of communications was central to the factional struggle. On 30 December Vioménil went to Saint-Pierre to try again to reconcile the town to the general assembly. He wrote to Thoumazeau asking him to persuade Saint-Pierre's deputies to unite with those from the rest of the colony, but he received only an "indecent reply" from the new

To. *Major Hare, of the 12ª Light Dragoons. This view of the Bay & Town of S.ᵗ Pierre is inscribed by his sincere & obliged Friend Cooper Willyams*

1 Cooper Willyams and S. Alken, "View of the Bay and Town of St Pierre, Martinique," 1796. PY3023/National Maritime Museum, Greenwich, London.

commune. This body prevented the general assembly's decrees from being printed, and Vioménil told the minister that the printer at Saint-Pierre had become a source of agitation only.[28] The patriots now controlled the most important communications media in the colony. On the eve of his departure from Saint-Pierre, the governor general received an anonymous letter containing a tirade against his short-lived reconciliation with the Saint-Pierre committee. This letter illustrated not only the violent animosity towards Vioménil in Saint-Pierre but also the degree to which colonial radicals had absorbed metropolitan discourses of revolutionary justice and popular sovereignty:

The threats you have made do not frighten us, but do not doubt those of a people justly aroused against you who would already have ended your life if not for the pathetic committee which deflected them with futile words of pacification. But there are limits which will be broken if you continue to vex us, we know how to defend ourselves … we have risen up to prove to you and to those who seduce you that it is in us alone that force and authority resides … Fear the fate of the great ones in Paris who paid on the gallows for the outrages they committed against the Nation, to whom they were denounced; you warrant it even more than they did, their vexation lasted only an instant, yours is continual; and in acting thus you have rendered yourself a traitor to *la Patrie*, subject consequently to the punishment for *lèse-Nation* … In a word, if you again dare to trouble us with new vexations or ordinances for which you have no right, the people have decided to hang you from the first lantern in Saint-Pierre the moment that you put a foot here.[29]

Despite this threat, the governor general returned to the town again on 10 January 1790 to suggest that if Saint-Pierre sent deputies to the colonial assembly, as the general assembly began to call itself, he could end the provisional opening of ports to the Americans. The municipality brushed this olive branch aside. Deputies pronounced a schism when Vioménil delivered the news to the assembly on 12 January, but he succeeded in preventing it from becoming formal. Vioménil informed the minister that because of Saint-Pierre's refusal, however, he was unable to stop the admission of American ships.[30] Commandant Laumoy summed up the difficult situation confronting royal administrators at the beginning of 1790. On the one side, the general assembly had assumed the functions of a legislature, while on the other side, Saint-Pierre had established a municipality and a commune. Clearly the king's wish that there be no changes in the colonies before the National Assembly had deliberated on them had not been followed.[31] Given this uncertainty regarding existing law and the colonies' future regime, and given the patriots' unrelenting hostility, Governor General Vioménil backed Martinique's assembly because it at least acknowledged the legitimacy of executive power.

II Insubordination, Provocations and Insurrections (December 1789–April 1790)

The general assembly in Guadeloupe also began to assume the role of a legislature. It opened at Petit-Bourg on 2 December, and Jacques Coquille Dugommier, one of the colony's leading patriots, raised the dreaded question of a "schism" between Basse-Terre and Pointe-à-Pitre over which one should be the *entrepôt* for foreign trade. The assembly responded: "There is no schism! We are all brothers!"[32] Despite the fraternal embraces and expressions of patriotic enthusiasm, Governor Clugny and *Intendant* Viévigne reported that nothing had been resolved in this opening session. They were certain, however, that if the schism persisted, the capital Basse-Terre would be ruined.[33] Thus they felt they had no choice but to provisionally concede to the general assembly's *arrêté* of 8 December, opening both Pointe-à-Pitre and Basse-Terre to foreign vessels. As the Clugny and Viévigne told the minister, the general assembly had decided it did not need to await confirmation from the National Assembly to reform laws governing colonial commerce.[34] Having named M. de La Charreière and M. Saintrac as the colony's deputies to the National Assembly, and elected a committee to draft *cahiers*, Guadeloupe's general assembly ended its sessions on 11 December and adjourned to Basse-Terre. When it reconvened on 15 January 1790, its members believed they had received new powers from the parishes. Clugny and Viévigne refused to sanction its members constituting themselves as the general colonial assembly and instead convoked the old colonial assembly based on the 1787 ordinance. Its members informed them, however, that the electors would never recognize their regulations. As a gesture of compromise with existing law, the governor and *intendant* united the members of the old assembly with those of the new and sanctioned this group as the general colonial assembly on 24 January. Their concession was rewarded when the assembly approved the year's taxation and acknowledged the need for the administrators to sanction its decrees.[35] When Clugny and Viévigne told the minister in their letter of 10 February that only a "shadow of authority" existed in Guadeloupe, they referred to the uneasy calm in the slave gangs and to the uncertain discipline of the colony's troops. But these words also described their own situation vis-à-vis a colonial assembly arrogating legislative powers.

Between 15 January and 1 April 1790 Guadeloupe's general assembly addressed the colony's internal regime. In particular, it established municipalities for the towns of Basse-Terre and Pointe-à-Pitre. Under this regulation Thyrus Pautrizel, one of the most fervent partisans of the revolution, was elected mayor of Basse-Terre, much to the governor's dismay.[36] The assembly intended to expand this system to the entire colony. It suspended the old militia led by parish commandants, replacing it with the kind of citizen's militia that Martinique's assembly had hoped to thwart.[37] At the beginning of May, Clugny and Viévigne informed the minister that the general assembly had attacked existing ordinances, principles, and administrative personnel, but that they were powerless to prevent the demolition of the Old Regime, given the effervescence of the people who insisted that they "end despotism."[38] Later in the month Clugny and Viévigne reported that the assembly had declared itself permanent, to be represented when not in session by a standing committee of its members. While it would have been preferable to wait for specific regulations from the National Assembly, they told the minister that it was neither prudent nor possible to oppose "liberty."[39]

If Guadeloupe's patriots appeared to support the general assembly's appropriation of legislative authority, an episode in January 1790, involving a key revolutionary symbol, revealed the tension between the *petit-Blanc* understanding of popular sovereignty and the colonial elite's desire for order. This incident also demonstrated that the colonies' military forces were not isolated from the revolutionary struggle. Angry residents of Point-à-Pitre invaded the barracks of the town's garrison to liberate a solider imprisoned for wearing a national cockade on his hat. They also demanded that his commanding officer be tried for treason, or "*lèse-Nation*."[40] A more dangerous episode in Martinique further demonstrated the erosion of discipline among the colonies' regular troops. In February three companies of royal artillery stationed at Fort-Royal – complaining that they had not received pay for work on the fortifications – seized control of the batteries and powder magazines. They demanded that the artillery commander, M. de Chappuis, be imprisoned. To calm the troops' fury, Vioménil ordered Chappuis to surrender himself aboard the battleship *Illustre* at anchor in Fort-Royal Bay; this was the flagship of Henri-Jean-Baptiste, vicomte de Pontevès-Gien, commander of the Windward Islands' naval station. Yet this action only escalated the rebellion. Armed soldiers marched on the governor general's headquarters and warned that if he did not surrender the artillery commander, they would sink the ship and bombard the town.[41]

After several days of disorder, colonial administrators resolved the crisis by conceding to the rebels' demands. Vioménil convoked an emergency council that ruled that 12,202 in *piastres* should be paid to artillery troops to compensate them for unpaid wages. It also pronounced that 72,000 should be paid to members of the Martinique Regiment for similar claims. Such a sum could only be paid using funds Foullon borrowed on the basis of his personal credit.[42] Yet if payment ended the soldiers' open defiance, the episode demonstrated that they had absorbed the language and spirit of the revolutionary script. It was impossible to keep them isolated from the growing factional strife.

Nevertheless, in the aftermath of this mutiny, both Vioménil and Clugny sought to limit their troops' communications in order to quarantine disciplined soldiers from the revolutionary contagion. The governor general proposed to the minister that a "foreign regiment" be sent to replace the Martinique Regiment. Presumably, he referred to one of the German-speaking units in the French army, possibly untouched by the revolution in France and thus less susceptible to the patriots' influence in the colonies.[43] More immediately, he planned to transfer some of the troublemakers in the artillery companies away from Martinique; but Clugny asked Vioménil not to send any of these troops to Guadeloupe. His request came too late and the frigate *Active* arrived at Basse-Terre with forty gunners from Fort-Royal, including twelve of the most mutinous. Once ashore they denounced the governor general and their officers and tried to forge alliances with the grenadiers of the Guadeloupe Regiment and with "bad subjects of the town." Clugny ordered the gunners from Martinique re-embarked – they would eventually be shipped to France aboard a merchant vessel – and informed the minister of his effort to maintain discipline.[44] It remained to be seen how long this would last.

If the colonies' troops had become increasingly insubordinate, their officers became dangerously provocative. Such a provocation in Saint-Pierre triggered a patriot insurrection. At issue again was the display of the key symbol of adherence to the revolution. Captain Du Boulay, commanding three companies of the Martinique Regiment in garrison at Saint-Pierre, refused to wear the national cockade. His appearance at the theatre wearing not a tricolour but a white cockade, the symbol of the Bourbon monarchy, caused indignation. When Du Boulay reappeared at the theatre without a national cockade on 21 February, he provoked such outrage that Commandant Laumoy ordered him to don one to prevent a riot. The captain complied, but this concession was followed by an ugly exchange between Du Boulay and Captain de Malherbe, on one side, and several townsfolk on the other. Du Boulay declared that the garrison's fourteen officers were ready and willing to meet an equal number of bourgeoisie in combat. This challenge aroused the fury of Saint-Pierre's populace. On 22 February the *tocsin* sounded and 1,500 armed men, including sailors from merchant ships in the roadstead, poured into the streets. Laumoy called out the garrison, but

Du Boulay and Malherbe surrendered themselves to the municipality. To appease the mob outside the *Hôtel de Ville*, which demanded that the captains be hanged, municipal officers stripped off their uniforms and threw them out the window. The crowd tore the uniforms to pieces, then seized the two captains, dragged them through the streets, and threw them into cells to await embarkation on a ship bound for France. The garrison's soldiers and remaining officers retreated to Fort-Royal, while *petits Blancs* took control of Saint-Pierre's batteries and powder magazines and posted guards throughout the town.[45]

Competing claims to legitimate authority and the circulation of rumours thwarted early attempts to resolve the crisis. The patriot account of these events, presented in a pamphlet printed on 25 February, claimed that Saint-Pierre rose up not merely in response to the captains' provocation but to counter the threat posed by the garrison. When the town's young men gathered to fight with the officers, armed soldiers marched out of their barracks and deployed as if to open fire on the civilians. The *intendant* intervened, throwing himself in front of the troops, and prevented a massacre. This action caused the tocsin to sound, and the people took up arms, seizing the batteries and fortifications.[46] For the patriots, the soldiers' actions were part of a sinister plot hatched by Vioménil. They accused the governor general of scheming for revenge against Saint-Pierre ever since the affair of the cockade in September 1789, and they charged him of hoping that his officers could provoke the people into violence, so that troops would shoot them down.[47]

Although the existence of such a conspiracy is highly unlikely, Vioménil's response to the crisis only increased tensions. When the governor general learned of the events in Saint-Pierre on 23 February,[48] he assembled a council of his military commanders, administrative officers, and the colonial assembly's permanent committee. The council resolved that the governor general should write to Saint-Pierre's municipality to demand that it surrender Du Boulay and Malherbe but also to reassure the people that they would be tried by court martial and punished appropriately. Vioménil's letter also suggested that if the captains were not given up, it would be difficult to stop the Martinique Regiment from marching on Saint-Pierre to avenge them.[49] Patriots interpreted this as a threat, and it made them even more adamant that the National Assembly judge the captains; thus, they embarked Du Boulay and Malherbe aboard the merchantman *Deux Cousines*. Patriots also increased their preparations to defend the town and welcomed offers of assistance from American sailors. "The Americans, these heroes of liberty," reported the *Gazette de la Martinique*, "have rallied to the cause of the people."[50] Even before receiving Vioménil's letter, the municipality and commune sealed and took possession of all papers in the headquarters of Commandant Laumoy. They also ordered residents to form a militia and to elect its officers.[51] Patriots would soon refer to this militia as the national guard. These acts, based on no existing law or regulations, were further assertions of popular sovereignty by Saint-Pierre's municipal authorities.

On 24 February the governor general received Saint-Pierre's reply to his letter. Beyond refusing to surrender the two captains and informing Vioménil that they had been embarked for transportation to France, the municipality made clear that it did not regard his authority as a manifestation of national sovereignty and that the nation's will must prevail over military orders.[52] The Martinique Regiment's officers were furious at Saint-Pierre's treatment of the two captains, and they insisted that a warship stop the merchantman on which the prisoners had been embarked and bring them back.[53] The frigate *Gracieuse* intercepted the *Deux Cousines*, removed Du Boulay and Malherbe, and returned them to Fort-Royal. Vioménil imprisoned them pending the departure of another frigate, which would take them to France to face justice from the minister; such punishment would challenge the legitimacy of neither military law nor executive authority in the colonies.[54] Yet according to Vioménil, this did not satisfy the soldiers of the Martinique Regiment.[55] The governor general wrote again to Saint-Pierre's municipality, demanding the return of the soldiers' remaining comrades and their arms. Beyond suggesting that this was necessary to appease the angry troops at Fort-Royal, Vioménil's letter challenged the municipality's claim to embody national sovereignty in Martinique: "Do the people of Saint-Pierre alone have the right to dispense justice, in the manner of the National Assembly, if the general assembly of the colony decreed that the two officers must be sent to France?"[56] Mayor Thoumazeau responded that Vioménil's threats of military vengeance justified the town's defensive measures: "As to whether the people are charged with the defense of this part of the colony, I write as one placed at the head of the people. The people, sir, charge themselves only with defending themselves against their enemies."[57] Other municipal officers also suggested that the people's will legitimized Saint-Pierre's insurrection.[58]

If Saint-Pierre's commune claimed to represent the people's will, Martinique's new assembly was equally implacable in asserting its claim to legislative authority in the colony. In the context of the dangerous standoff between patriots at Saint-Pierre and the regiment at Fort-Royal, elections took place according to the general assembly's regulation of 8 December. Some parishes refused to participate, but most sent deputies to the new assembly, which opened at Fort-Royal on 25 February. The members created a permanent committee, or directory, to oversee the colony between sessions, and appointed Louis-François Dubuc as its president. According to Henry Lémery, this son of the powerful planter clan was the real author of the colonial assembly's strategy.[59] On 10 March it adopted an elaborate set of instructions to be delivered to Martinique's deputies in the National Assembly by Bellevue-Blanchetière, who would remain in France to provide confidential reports of metropolitan developments. These instructions began with the statement that the colonies could not be considered provinces of France. If Martinique had the right to representatives in the National Assembly, these representatives also had the right to resist the imposition of laws contrary to the colonies' interests and basic nature.[60]

The colonial assembly was determined to defy metropolitan government if its legislation threatened the institution of slavery, or the colony's ability to decide on the status of free people of colour. Slaves were property that could not be usurped. Freedmen were slaves to whom colonists had voluntarily given their liberty. Therefore, Martinique's deputies were instructed to demand absolute legislative power for the colony in all matters concerning its internal regime.[61] The colonial assembly's adoption of this document did not merely demonstrate its intent to defend slavery and to serve the economic interests of agriculture in opposition to those of commerce. Foullon's angry characterization of the assembly as "planters who aspire only to throw off the yoke of metropolitan dependence"[62] was accurate. Yet this agenda of virtual independence made the colonial assembly's alliance with the embattled governor general ironic rather than natural.

The arrival at Saint-Pierre of patriot volunteers from other colonies on 6 March further demonstrated the power of the revolutionary script and the administration's inability to control communications in the Windward Islands. The Gazette de la Martinique reported that volunteers had come from Guadeloupe and Sainte-Lucie, as well as from all parts of the colony, to help defend the town from the Martinique Regiment. The patriot newspaper also included a message from "The People of Pointe-à-Pitre to the People of Saint-Pierre" denouncing intriguers who resisted equality and promising fraternal assistance against the enemies of the public good: the impact of metropolitan political culture had not been confined to Martinique.[63] The governor and four members of Guadeloupe's general assembly accompanied the detachment of volunteers from Basse-Terre.[64] Clugny's correspondence reveals, however, that he was a reluctant participant, who sympathized with executive power rather than with the patriots. Rumours spread in Guadeloupe at the beginning of March that the Martinique Regiment was about to attack Saint-Pierre but that its citizens were under arms. After trying in vain to dissuade Basse-Terre's patriots from embarking on a rescue mission, Clugny announced he would travel to Martinique to restore peace. Coquille Dugommier commanded the volunteers who accompanied the governor.[65] If Clugny believed that the movement at Saint-Pierre included "spiteful men and vagabonds," he also thought that the restoration of tranquility was vital. Every day saw the arrival at Saint-Pierre of new detachments of volunteers, or *confédérés* as patriots now called them, from other colonies. Clugny feared that the slaves of Guadeloupe, Marie-Galante, and Sainte-Lucie would take advantage of the colonists' absence to revolt.[66]

Mediation proved difficult. Saint-Pierre's municipality and commune rejected the regiment's first conciliatory message of 7 March as insufficient. They declared that the people of Saint-Pierre would await the National Assembly's judgment for a crime of "*lèse-nation*," demanded that the regiment repudiate guilty officers and men, and insisted that the citizens and *confédérés* would not abandon their defensive measures.[67] On 9 March, however, Clugny convinced the regiment's officers to acknowledge that the Saint-Pierre garrison had been at fault and to approve the dispatch of those whom the municipality deemed guilty to face judgment from the National Assembly.[68] The following day the commune accepted these concessions and declared that tranquility must reign among Martinique's citizens, although it attributed this outcome to the firmness of the people's defence and the support from the heroic volunteers.[69] On 13 March Governor Clugny and the Guadeloupe volunteers embarked for the return voyage to Basse-Terre.

Martinique's factions had not truly reconciled. Saint-Pierre's uprising had radicalized patriots in the rest of the colony who took up revolutionary political forms. Not only had volunteers from the parishes of Grande Anse, Macouba, Trinité, Robert, and Lamentin arrived at Saint-Pierre, but the *Gazette de la Martinique* also reported that the parish of Carbet had formed its own municipality and citizens' militia.[70] The establishment of a municipality at Fort-Royal pitted supporters of the colonial assembly against local patriots. Foullon reported: "The voice of the people has prevailed in the elections; while the party opposed to the people, that of the so-called assembly, has tried to destroy this establishment at birth."[71] Conflict in Fort-Royal was linked to that in rural parishes. On 25 March a force of whites and armed *gens de couleur* descended on the market town of Lamentin, where they intimidated an assembly of the residents into agreeing to accept municipal officers named by planters from the surrounding countryside and into signing a "confederation" against Saint-Pierre.[72] The planters and their allies then marched to Fort-Royal, where they effected a municipal coup and persuaded the colonial assembly to formally adopt a proposal on 28 March inviting all parishes to unite in a colony-wide confederation.[73] This project was in direct response to Saint-Pierre's own "confederation" with the patriots from other colonies and other parishes in Martinique. Both sides had adopted the language of the metropolitan revolution.

In the midst of this factional strife, Claude-Charles, vicomte de Damas, arrived at Fort-Royal on 26 March to resume his post as governor general of the Windward Islands. Patriots placed great hopes in him, assuming that he would put both the colonial assembly and the *gens de couleur* in their places, but almost immediately Damas fell seriously ill and could not take up his duties until June.[74] Nevertheless, on 6 April the comte de Vioménil sailed from Fort-Royal aboard the frigate *Gracieuse* bound for France. Although he was willing to serve longer, his departure continued his pattern of seeking to uphold the letter of the law: Damas's arrival ended his appointment and he stepped down, assuming that Clugny would succeed him until Damas recovered. While concerned for his reputation, and worried about the attacks against him that had been sent to France, he was grateful to leave such a vexatious post.[75] Vioménil's disapproval of the revolution reflected his understanding of its attack on executive power; but, in fact, patriots hated him as much for his metropolitan and more liberal attitude towards racial hierarchy as for his royalism. Bellevue-Blanchetière, bearing the assembly's instructions for Martinique's deputies in Paris, also sailed in *Gracieuse*. The same day that the frigate left Fort-Royal, Saint-Pierre dispatched vessels to Guadeloupe and Sainte-Lucie, asking patriots to again rally to its defence.

Detachments of patriot volunteers from different parts of Guadeloupe and from Saint-Lucie again converged on Saint-Pierre in April. Clugny accompanied the *confédérés*, but he was even more reluctant this time; he believed that there were signs of an impending slave revolt in several parts of Guadeloupe.[76] Saint-Pierre's renewed appeal to patriots from other colonies also exposed a major dilemma for Pontevès-Gien. Martinique's factional division made it increasingly difficult for him to maintain the stance of strict neutrality that he believed appropriate as naval commander in the Windward Islands. The colonial assembly tried to force him to take sides, asking that he deploy the king's ships to stop the arrival of patriots from other islands. "I do not know if the permanent committee of the colonial assembly, which is not recognized generally in the island, is truly authorized to make such a perilous request of executive power," he told the minister.[77] Pontevès-Gien tried to escape the dilemma by pledging to protect all citizens who acknowledged the governor general's authority. Clugny's mission to Martinique was based on a similar strategy of navigating between competing claims. Guadeloupe's governor and deputies went to Fort-Royal, where they joined Joseph de Gimat, governor of Sainte-Lucie, and members of that colony's assembly. On 12 April this group tried to convince Martinique's assembly to accept patriot demands that towns and parishes organize municipalities according to the will of their citizens, that the assembly be suspended until the National Assembly judged otherwise, and that the colony's *gens de couleur* be disarmed. The assembly rejected these demands, countering that all volunteers must return to their own colonies.[78]

More important than these formal negotiations were the factions' appeals to public opinion. The assembly had published a *Profession of Faith* that suggested the virtual impossibility of reconciliation, declaring that it had been the victim of calumnies initiated by spiteful men. Allegations that the assembly was "unconstitutional and illegal," and that its members were "aristocrats, instigators of despotism, oppressors of liberty," had been accepted because Saint-Pierre controlled the colony's only printing press. The *Profession* stated that the assembly could now disabuse citizens and declare its principles, because its permanent committee had acquired a small press of its own. The document emphasized the assembly's opposition to anarchy and its support for executive power. The colony's deputies respected the National Assembly, but they would not follow its principles if these could not be adapted to the colonies. Most important, the *Profession* insisted that the assembly's decrees represented legitimate authority: "It believes that it alone, with the assistance of the king's representative, can exercise provisional legislative power."[79] This assertion was not mere insistence on traditional prerogatives, because royal government had never bestowed such authority. The assembly's claim, like those of Saint-Pierre's patriots, was based in revolutionary political culture.

When Clugny returned to Saint-Pierre, angry crowds booed the announcement that the assembly had refused the patriots' demands and cried "To Arms!"[80] In response to rumours from the countryside that the assembly had sent *gens de couleur* to attack the plantations of those who supported Saint-Pierre, Dugommier led a contingent of volunteers into the hills to destroy these enemies. This force retreated to Saint-Pierre after inconclusive encounters with coloured troops.[81] On 15 April the deputations from Guadeloupe and Sainte-Lucie returned to Fort-Royal, but Clugny stayed behind to try to prevent Saint-Pierre's *petits Blancs* and the volunteers from marching on the capital. "Martinique is in the most violent state," he told the minister on 19 April, and one of the sources of division was the question of who should act as governor general. The committee of the colonial assembly recognized Louis-Armand Désiré, vicomte de Damoiseau, director of fortifications for the Windward Islands, as Martinique's interim governor.[82] Saint-Pierre, however, favoured Pierre-Auguste de Mollerat, whom the municipality had recognized as the town's military commandant. Clugny did not want the job; instead he asked the minister for a leave from his post as governor of Guadeloupe.[83] He sailed from Saint-Pierre on 24 April, summoned to deal with an even more urgent crisis there: Guadeloupe's slaves had revolted.

There had been fears of a slave revolt in Guadeloupe before Clugny left for Saint-Pierre on 6 April. The governor led a detachment of troops to the village of Capesterre, where it reduced the most mutinous of the area's slaves to silence and rounded up 150 runaways. Another detachment marched into the parish of Du Parc, just outside Basse-Terre. One of the parish's planters, La Salle, had captured a slave identified as the leader of revolt there.[84] According to *Intendant* Viévigne, under torture this slave revealed the existence of a plot and identified his accomplices. Commandant d'Arrot sent more troops into the parishes, but, in the absence of the governor and so many other colonists, fears of a general insurrection increased. Viévigne requested that Guadeloupe's sovereign council establish a special tribunal to investigate the revolt and to punish the guilty.[85] When Clugny returned to Basse-Terre on 25 April, he reported that the denunciation of ringleaders to this tribunal had deterred other slaves.[86] A month later five slaves had been executed and the details of the supposed plot were clearer. Domestic slaves in the vicinity of Capesterre, Goyave, and Petit-Bourg had believed themselves to be free, and they persuaded field slaves that they were also free and that whites were hiding the truth. They planned to set fire to plantations at Goyave on the night of 11–12 April, as a signal for a general uprising. Rebels at the Deceleron plantation were to cut their master's throat, gather the gangs, deploy flags, and follow two *marrons* to other villages, massacring all whites they encountered. Heavy rain that night impeded the project to set fires, and colonists discovered the plot the following day. Clugny claimed that talk of "liberty" in the colony's assemblies had inspired the domestic slaves, but he put more emphasis on the absence of over one thousand white men emboldening the rebels.[87] Viévigne, however, was adamant that the aborted insurrection was the result of metropolitan abolitionist propaganda.[88] The evidence is inconclusive regarding the extent of the plot or the degree to which it was motivated by either abolitionist ideas or revolutionary rhetoric. News of the slave uprising in Guadeloupe, however, increased both the determination of Martinique's assembly to resist metropolitan legislation and the patriots' hostility towards *gens de couleur*.

III Massacre of Coloured Militia and the Occupation of Saint-Pierre (June 1790)

The volunteers' departure from Saint-Pierre ended the crisis that began in February but not the bitter factional strife in Martinique. On 16 April Foullon wrote to the minister: "The colony is on the point of being delivered to all of the horrors of civil war."[89] This fear was justified but premature. Eleven days later, he reported that Clugny had restored calm in Saint-Pierre before returning to Guadeloupe. More accurately, Clugny had persuaded the volunteers to return to their colonies. Martinique was still divided, according to the *intendant*, between two parties: patriots, who comprised the majority of the white population, and secessionist planters, who supported the despotic colonial assembly.[90] On 14 April an American ship anchored at Saint-Pierre with a package addressed to the commissioners of commerce by Bordeaux's chamber of commerce. It announced the National Assembly's decree of 8 March 1790 on the formation and competence of colonial assemblies. News of the decree inspired rejoicing in Saint-Pierre.[91] Patriots assumed that it ended the existing assembly's claims to legitimacy, since it required citizens to freely elect colonial assemblies, and that a new assembly would restore Saint-Pierre's control of foreign trade. The decree was ambiguous, however, being the outcome of parliamentary compromise and equivocation.[92] It declared that the colonies were a part of the French empire, but that they would not be subjected to laws incompatible with their local situation. It stated that citizens would elect colonial assemblies, recognizing these assemblies as expressing the voice of the colony, and invited them to submit suggestions for modifying regulations governing trade between France and the colonies. Yet the decree did not define who were considered "citizens" in the colony.[93] The instructions to accompany the decree, voted by the National Assembly on 28 March, indicated that following the decree's proclamation in every parish, all persons twenty-five years or older, owners of landed property or residents of the parish for at least two years, as well as taxpayers, must form a parish assembly.[94] Did "persons" include free men of colour?

Before the arrival of these instructions, and patriots' horrified contemplation of the fact that many *gens de couleur* fit the criteria given to participate in colonial politics, Martinique's assembly interpreted the first news of the 8 March decree as a vindication rather than as a blow to its legitimacy. It continued to claim legislative authority despite the refusal of several parishes to send deputies and protests from Saint-Pierre.[95] When official dispatches reached Guadeloupe, containing the National Assembly's decree of 8 March and its instructions, Clugny asked the general assembly to deliberate on the organization of elections for a new assembly. He also sent the decree and instructions to Guadeloupe's justices of the peace and municipal committees. Inhabitants were enthusiastic at the prospect of voting for a new assembly, but Clugny told the minister that the duties and powers of different bodies remained unclear. This uncertainty made government difficult, "above all in a country where the king's name is almost unknown and his authority almost destroyed since the revolution."[96] The dilemma for Governor Clugny was not only how to ensure the execution of ambiguous legislation from France but also how to uphold state power in the context of competing revolutionary claims to local authority. Vioménil had struggled with this dilemma until Saint-Pierre's relentless hostility had pushed him into the arms of Martinique's assembly. A new and even more violent crisis at Saint-Pierre ended any hope that the new governor general could keep executive power from being drawn into the factional conflict.

Requests that free-coloured militia participate in celebrations of the *Fête Dieu* incited the massacre of fourteen coloured men and three white officers at Saint-Pierre on 3 June. The killings were a brutal demonstration of the racism of *petit-Blanc* patriots, and the competing accounts of the violence revealed very different interpretations of the revolution. According to the patriot *Gazette de la Martinique*, Saint-Pierre had been faced with a free-coloured insurrection; the mulattos' intention to carry arms in the religious procession was mere pretext and the outcome of previous seditious assemblies held only "to acquire rights of equality at any price." Companies of free-coloured militia had been guarding the town since the departure of the garrison of regular troops during the crisis in February, and Saint-Pierre viewed them with resentment and suspicion. On 2 June the white captains of two of these companies, Fournier and Dufau, asked the militia commander at Saint-Pierre to allow their troops to carry a flag in the procession the following day. He refused – and other officers declared that only "detachments of citizens" could participate. The ceremony on 3 June occurred without incident, but a large number of coloured men gathered at the Place du Fort. At the procession's conclusion, a coloured man confronted the black drummer boy who had led the parade and insisted that he remove his cockade. The resulting confrontation led to the sounding of the *tocsin* and a bloody mêlée in the streets. White townsfolk shot seven men of colour, hanged seven others, and threw sixty more in prison. They also shot Fournier and Richemont, another white militia captain found hiding in a barrel, and hanged and possibly hacked Dufau to death. The *Gazette de la Martinique* claimed these three were instigators and that the mulattos, inspired by false interpretations of the National Assembly's decrees, had long been conspiring to rise up: "It is evident that these rogues aspire to the quality of citizens."[97]

The vicomte de Damas, who had only just recovered his health and taken up his duties as governor general, travelled immediately to Saint-Pierre from Fort-Royal accompanied by a single aide. The atmosphere in Saint-Pierre shocked Damas. When he visited the municipality, he heard violent motions calling for the extermination of the *gens de couleur*. Desperate to prevent another massacre, Damas proposed the creation of a special commission to judge the prisoners. The governor general was reluctant to leave Saint-Pierre, with many *petits Blancs* threatening to storm the prisons, but he accepted Foullon's assurance that he would prevent the people from committing excesses, and Damas returned to Fort-Royal on the evening of 4 June. Before departing, Damas refused the municipality's request to establish the kind of commission he had proposed.[98]

Public opinion in Fort-Royal condemned the killings. Many *gens de couleur* had taken refuge in the capital and they denounced the atrocities at Saint-Pierre. According to Damas, however, the crowd gathered on 5 June demanding that he march his troops against the town included white as well as coloured inhabitants, all of whom supported the current colonial assembly. Damas also reported that Saint-Pierre's hatred made free men of colour firmly loyal to his government.[99] Thus there was a direct connection between portrayals of the violence at Saint-Pierre and factional loyalties. Saint-Pierre's municipal officers claimed that the town's heroic citizens had saved the colony from a coloured uprising, which they blamed in part on the mulattos' "revolting ambition."[100] The colonial assembly's interpretation of the episode was drastically different. Its *arrêté* of 7 June referred not only to the massacre of the white officers and the coloured troops but also to the many *gens de couleur libres* detained in prison. The assembly was concerned with the fate of these prisoners as well as the well-being of "all honest citizens of Saint-Pierre," who were in grave danger. Given the town's importance as a commercial *entrepôt*, the fortunes of all colonists were exposed to pillage and arson by these rogues. Thus the assembly suggested that the massacre of the coloured militiamen had been the culmination of crime and disorder at Saint-Pierre, linked to news of the revolution in France, and could not be allowed to continue.[101] If the assembly's denunciation of injustice towards the *gens de couleur* was ironic, given its determination to resist any metropolitan legislation altering their status, the alliance between planters and free men of colour against the urban patriots was a real consequence of Martinique's factional struggle. Since Vioménil's intervention at Fort-Royal in September 1789, *gens de couleur* had regarded royal authority as sympathetic, and since Saint-Pierre's uprising in February, the colonial assembly had begun to see free men of colour as valuable allies against the patriots. The assembly's *arrêté* asked the governor general to rescue the citizens of Saint-Pierre from the oppression of a gang of brigands.

The massacre of the coloured militiamen and their officers thus provided the colonial assembly with the justification to unleash military force against its patriot enemies. Although the killings alarmed Damas, he was equally appalled at the prospect of leading troops against Saint-Pierre.[102] Nonetheless, when the colonial assembly presented him with its *arrêté* on the evening of 7 June, Damas agreed to deploy his forces. Along with five hundred regular troops, the governor general mobilized over two thousand militia.[103] He also dispatched formal letters to Saint-Pierre's municipal officers, informing them that he intended to come at the head of his troops to restore order in the town.[104] As Damas's troops marched from Fort-Royal on 9 June, the battleship *Illustre* appeared outside Saint-Pierre's roadstead. Pontevès-Gien ordered all foreign ships to recall their crews and prepare to sail at his signal. He also ordered the captains of French merchantmen to keep their men aboard ship.[105] The sailors' departure discouraged the patriots, who abandoned their posts. Damas's soldiers entered Saint-Pierre without firing a shot. Some residents attempted to flee, but the militia had surrounded the town while *Ilustre* blocked escape by sea. Along with praising the conduct of the Martinique Regiment, the governor general also praised the loyalty and discipline of the free-coloured militia. "I believe I can assure you," Damas wrote to the minister, "that this operation will forever reestablish order in the colony."[106]

Members of the colonial assembly, who arrived in Saint-Pierre shortly after Damas's troops, wanted to eliminate their enemies rather than merely restore order. Military occupation, however, did not silence patriot communications. Although Saint-Pierre's municipal officers begged him not to confuse simple faults of opinion with true crimes, Damas ordered them to prepare lists of troublemakers.[107] On 13 June he ordered a general round-up of those named in these proscription lists. Troops occupied every corner of the town and went house to house to arrest over two hundred people. Pontevès-Gien sent armed naval crews in longboats to arrest some twenty merchant sailors from various vessels. A colonist from Guadeloupe described these events in a pamphlet printed to expose the arrests, to patriots in both France and the colonies, as despotic repression.[108]

Foullon's report to the minister echoed these views. Hatred motivated the arrests and rather than reassuring honest citizens or re-establishing order, they had only humiliated the residents of Saint-Pierre. Soldiers arrested all citizens on the proscription lists indiscriminately, including fathers and wealthy merchants. While they soon freed the majority, they put more than sixty aboard a ship to await trial or deportation to France. Foullon blamed these "violations of the Rights of Man" on Martinique's assembly, which had seized on the brawl between whites and mulattos as a pretext for striking at Saint-Pierre.[109] The day after the arrests, the assembly issued two decrees regarding the occupied town. The decrees ordered the creation of a special tribunal to annul trials of imprisoned men of colour initiated by the municipality's illegal commission and the release of those mulattos against whom there were no charges; they also asked Damas to suspend the municipality.[110] On 18 June Damas and his forces marched out of Saint-Pierre, leaving behind a garrison of five hundred troops. Accompanied by members of the assembly's permanent committee, the governor general passed through dissident parishes and suspended their municipalities before returning to Fort-Royal. Foullon insisted that these actions, the occupation of Saint-Pierre, and the subsequent arrests could only have disastrous consequences: "This expedition, far from returning calm in this part of the colony, seems to have excited new discontents and to have given birth here to new hatreds which, perhaps hidden, are only more dangerous and could have deadly results."[111]

IV Mutiny and Civil War (June–November 1790)

These discontents extended beyond Martinique – the occupation of Saint-Pierre provoked several days of riot and disorder in Guadeloupe. This episode also provided further evidence that the revolutionary script was undermining military discipline in the Windward Islands. Patriots in Basse-Terre considered Damas's entry into Saint-Pierre to be an act of despotism and denounced the arrests as barbaric. Disorder spread to the soldiers of the town's garrison. Clugny reported that "ill-intentioned men" had seduced the company of *chasseurs* posted on the seafront, where they were in close contact with sailors and other *petits Blancs*. The *chasseurs* planned to seize their colonel's flag on 27 June and demand justice for a stoppage in pay. With the support of loyal grenadiers, Clugny and the *chasseurs'* officers quelled this insubordination. The governor then ordered that three of the mutineers be sent to Martinique for transportation to France. While reporting that these measures brought the revolt to an end, Clugny insisted that the inspiration for insurrection had come from outside the Guadeloupe Regiment.[112] In his own report, Damas suggested that the uprising set a dangerous example for the Martinique Regiment and, as he told the minister, without military discipline the colonies were lost.[113]

In the weeks following the occupation of Saint-Pierre, Martinique's colonial assembly wielded what it now believed was unchallenged authority in the colony. Claiming that it was constituted according to the National Assembly's decrees of 8 and 28 March, the assembly established a new administrative structure for the colony modelled on that of the new departments in France. It also began to reform Martinique's finances. This represented a usurpation of the *intendant*'s authority and responsibility. On 13 July the assembly dismissed Foullon and, six days later, deported him from the colony along with Mayor Thoumazeau.[114] The assembly made these decisions despite opposition from the governor general.[115] In August Clugny learned of Foullon's precipitous departure and the seizure of the king's finances by Martinique's assembly. He also learned of the arrival at Martinique of a ship bearing 87,500 *piastres* from the royal treasury. Clugny reminded Damas of the king's order entrusting the administration of that part of these funds intended for Guadeloupe to *Intendant* Viévigne. The colony needed money desperately to pay its troops; yet the anticipated amount for Guadeloupe was not delivered. Clugny also informed the minister that Martinique's directory had invited Guadeloupe's assembly to follow its example and take over the administration of royal finances.[116]

Martinique's assembly did not only arrogate colonial administration and finance, it also sought to tighten its political control. On 6 August the assembly decreed that all municipalities in the colony would be suppressed until 1 September when the election of new ones would proceed according to a new regulation further reducing their power and independence.[117] The following day it suspended any reorganization of the militia until its next session. This prevented the formation of any citizens' militia and left public force in the parishes in the hands of coloured militiamen commanded by white officers.[118] The assembly also wanted those arrested following the occupation of Saint-Pierre to be tried by the sovereign council or deported to France, and it ordered the prisoners transferred to Fort-Royal. The legalities of these trials, and their political impact, worried Damas.[119] The governor general was also apprehensive about the prisoners' presence in Fort-Royal; certainly those held in the dungeons of Fort-Bourbon used any contact with the soldiers to communicate revolutionary news and to sow doubt regarding the legitimacy of their commanders' authority.[120]

The arrests and the suspension of Saint-Pierre's municipality had not suppressed patriot communications. While the occupation ended patriot control of the printing press in Saint-Pierre and shut down the *Gazette de la Martinique*, new political newspapers emerged elsewhere in the Windward Islands. The *Courrier des Petites Antilles* began publication on 15 July from Roseau in Dominica. The announcement of its launch made clear that this journal would be based on patriotic principles.[121] Seamen distributed free copies of the first issue, but the publishers intended subsequent issues to be sold at Basse-Terre, Pointe-à-Pitre, Castries in Sainte-Lucie, and at Saint-Pierre. Thus the journal's appearance demonstrated the existence of a patriot communications network throughout the Windward Islands. The journal's language and contents also provide further evidence that patriots perceived the conflict in the colonies in terms of a struggle between the "people," on one side, and "despotism" and "aristocracy," on the other. This language was faithful to the revolutionary script from metropolitan France. Colonial patriotism, however, included deep resentment of *gens de couleur* and bitter antipathy towards any whites who sympathized with them. The first full issue of *Courrier des Petites Antilles*, printed on 24 July, provided an account of Saint-Pierre's occupation. The origin of this tyrannical repression, it implied, went back to Vioménil's hostility towards symbols of the revolution: "Saint-Pierre raised the liberty cap and one man, justly hated, wanted revenge." While the journal made no direct reference to the massacre of coloured men on 3 June, it criticized Damas for being more concerned with seeking justice against a white man who had killed a coloured slave woman than with allowing Saint-Pierre to establish a tribunal in response to a mulatto insurrection. The issue denounced Damas for his occupation of the town and ended with a call for revenge.[122] The journal's second issue, dated 31 July, focused its tirade on Martinique's assembly. The suspension of Saint-Pierre's municipality, a body devoted to the people and the nation, had allowed the assembly, characterized by the journal as the repository of the Old Regime, to seize power.[123]

The *Courrier des Petites Antilles* illustrated not only the influence of metropolitan political culture but also the colonial patriots' conviction that they had the support of revolutionary France. The third issue, of 7 August, included petitions from Bordeaux's national guard to that city's municipal officers and from Bordeaux's Jacobin Club to the National Assembly. Both protested the treatment of Saint-Pierre, suggesting that metropolitan ports had received the patriot version of events. "The arrival of these two pieces from Bordeaux has produced two very different responses in Martinique," the journal reported. "It has restored the hope and courage of patriots in Saint-Pierre, and it has produced consternation and fear among the aristocrats of Fort-Royal."[124] The journal's next issue, of 14 August, focused on Guadeloupe, with a column addressed to "Dear Fellow Citizens of Guadeloupe," which reminded that colony that the *Courrier* was the rampart of patriotism and that colonists must be vigilant against aristocratic plots. The issue also featured an "Epistle to the Aristocrats of Martinique's Colonial Assembly by a citizen of Pointe-à-Pitre," which echoed metropolitan radicalism.[125] The issue of 21 August denounced the colonial assembly's secret manoeuvres and the sovereign council's establishment of a commission to investigate the events of 3 June: "The members, lacking witnesses, have accepted depositions from their domestics and a crowd of mulattos and *mulâtresses* acting against their masters or against individuals."[126] Assuming that people of colour were capable of giving evidence in court was, according to patriots, aristocratic. On 28 August the journal reported on how the arrival of new recruits from France thwarted efforts to suppress patriotism within the Martinique Regiment. The officers feared the recruits' spirit of liberty and feared above all the arrival of men who had aided the revolution's triumph by taking the Bastille.[127] The journal thus confirmed the fears of officers and administrators that revolutionary subversion posed a serious threat to military discipline in the colonies.

The seventh issue of the *Courrier des Petites Antilles*, dated 4 September, provided a detailed condemnation of the new decree by Martinique's assembly regarding the organization and functioning of municipalities. Along with reflecting the struggle in the colony, this condemnation mirrored the emerging challenge from radicals in France to the National Assembly's preparation of a liberal, rather than truly democratic, constitution.[128] The journal denounced the decree's article on the selection of Saint-Pierre's mayor by electors rather than by the citizens directly. It also condemned the article requiring municipalities to inspect arrivals to the colony as an infringement of citizens' freedom of movement, and it fulminated against members of the colonial assembly as wicked men who deserved to be hanged from the lantern. The final column in this issue, added just before publication, announced much more exciting, if unconfirmed news: Fort-Royal was in the hands of mutinous soldiers, while the assembly and governor general had fled to the hills.[129]

Unlike previous crises, this insurrection at Fort-Royal marked the beginning of civil war because insubordinate troops allied themselves with Martinique's patriots in defiance of their commanders' authority. On 1 September Fort-Bourbon's garrison seized control of the powder magazines, raised the drawbridges, and prevented their officers from leaving. The soldiers also released prisoners from Saint-Pierre held in the fort's dungeon and raised a tricolour flag made of handkerchiefs from the main bastion so that it was visible throughout the town of Fort-Royal below. Governor General Damas climbed to the entrance of Fort-Bourbon to meet with the soldiers. Fearing that they intended to take him prisoner, rather than negotiate or express grievances, he did not enter. While descending again to Fort-Royal, a fall down the steep steps left him seriously injured. At the urging of the assembly's directory, Damas recalled the garrison from Saint-Pierre and ordered guards to isolate Fort-Bourbon from the town. Meanwhile, Fort-Royal's municipal officers met with a delegation from Fort-Bourbon, which wanted the municipality to deliver a proper national flag and to come to the fort to swear a civic oath.

The mutiny expanded the following day. The garrison of Fort Saint-Louis and troops in Fort-Royal marched on the town's jail, liberated the patriots imprisoned there, and escorted them to Fort-Bourbon. The companies from Saint-Pierre arrived, but their soldiers also joined the rebels. Faced with the defection of nearly all the troops under his command, Damas left Fort-Royal during the night to join the members of the colonial assembly at Lamentin. The assembly's supporters, including both planters and free-coloured militia, rallied there. On 3 September an assembly at Fort-Royal, including municipal officers, the released prisoners, and delegates named by the mutinous soldiers, voted to coordinate its actions with those of Saint-Pierre and dispatched a deputation with an address for the people there. At Saint-Pierre a similar assembly had formed at the home of M. Molerat; it resolved to restore both the town's districts and the citizens' militia abolished by the colonial assembly. When Damas and the assembly learned of Fort-Royal's alliance with Saint-Pierre, they retreated to Gros Morne in the island's interior.[130] The marquis de Bouillé, governor general during the War of American Independence, had fortified this location with earthworks as the colony's final defensive position in case of British invasion. Damas sent some of his forces to occupy the small port of la Trinité through which Gros Morne could be supplied by sea. On 4 September the garrison of Fort-Bourbon demanded that the ships of the French Navy at anchor in Fort-Royal Bay enter the inner harbour, where they could be guarded more easily, and threatened to fire on them if they refused. On the orders of Captain Durand d'Ubraye, who had become naval station commander following Pontevès-Gien's death from fever on 23 July, the crews of *Illustre*, the frigate *Sensible*, and the corvette *Épervier* cut their cables and got under way. Rebel-controlled batteries opened fire, but the warships sailed out of the bay and set a course for France.[131] Sailing in *Sensible* to escape the outbreak of civil war, and to rejoin her husband in France, was a Creole destined to become Martinique's most famous daughter: Josephine Rose de Beauharnais.

While both factions claimed to want only peace, their military preparations continued and their rhetoric hardened. On 5 September the planters raised the national flag at Gros Morne; they swore to remain united and to make any sacrifice to defend their rights, liberty, property, and the constitution the National Assembly had given them (presumably, the decree of 8 March as interpreted by the colonial assembly). That same day commissioners from Saint-Pierre arrived at Fort-Royal where, in accord with the town's municipality and the troops, they wrote to Damas asking him to support the nomination of conciliators in all parishes to restore peace in the colony. These conciliators represented an alternative to the colonial assembly, which patriots did not recognize. The governor general convoked the assembly at the village of Gros Morne, however, and it issued a decree forbidding the parishes from naming such conciliators. Even as the colonial assembly issued its decrees, the patriot conciliators met and published a declaration on 10 September, inviting all colonists to unite in fraternity, forget past resentments, and rally to the constitution (presumably the national constitution still in preparation in France). The declaration also contained a threat: if these invitations were rejected, if hostilities were committed against patriots, or if the camp at Gros Morne thought of war, there would be reprisals and both the governor general and the assembly would answer to the nation.

As in March and April, contingents of volunteers from Guadeloupe, Marie-Galante, and Sainte-Lucie arrived at Saint-Pierre beginning on 17 September to join with patriots there, and some of these men then travelled to Fort-Royal. After a skirmish between troops and militia the day before, on 25 September an armed column led by Colonel Chabrol and Dugommier marched out of Fort-Royal, possibly on its way to attack the camp at Gros Morne, only to be ambushed in the deep gorge outside Lamentin. Many patriot troops were killed or wounded. Both factions accused the other of initiating hostilities, of treacherously appealing to the English for help against their fellow citizens, and of arming and inciting slaves against fellow whites.[132] After the fighting at Lamentin, patriots armed trading vessels as privateers at Saint-Pierre and sent them to patrol Martinique's coasts to prevent foreign ships from delivering supplies to their adversaries.[133] If this threatened to starve the planters' army – and the colony's slave gangs – forces loyal to the governor general regained command of the sea around Martinique in November. Two men-of-war, the 74-gun ship *Ferme* and the frigate *Embuscade*, arrived from France to reinforce the Windward Islands' naval station. Damas ordered the *Ferme*'s captain, the chevalier de Rivière, who unexpectedly found himself station commander, to blockade Saint-Pierre and Fort-Royal and to counter the privateers. Although Rivière told merchant captains that he had been sent to protect French trade, many of them accused him of complicity in an aristocratic plot. Rivière and the *Embuscade*'s captain, the vicomte d'Orléans, however, had sailed with orders to obey the governor general, and they saw themselves as strengthening metropolitan executive authority rather than siding with a local faction.[134] The warships' arrival ensured that there would be no quick end to the conflict. Both sides appealed to public opinion in France and awaited the nation's intervention to give them victory and to punish their enemies.[135]

This struggle was not confined to Martinique. Governor Clugny, who had tried to contain revolution in Guadeloupe and to mediate the conflict in Martinique, recognized that he could not shield his colony from the impact of civil war. In September patriots at Basse-Terre confined Clugny to his headquarters for over two weeks because they suspected he intended to aid Damas against their comrades at Saint-Pierre.[136] At the end of November the governor informed the minister not only that Guadeloupe's deputation to Martinique had failed to end the conflict but also that the mutiny had infected the Guadeloupe Regiment. Troops had seized control of the port and magazine at Basse-Terre to prevent the distribution of arms to planters, who feared the landing of "brigands" from Martinique. The soldiers also accused the planters of conspiring to arm blacks and mulattos against patriots.[137] The governor advised the minister not to send more troops or warships to the colonies, fearing that they would only perpetuate disorder.[138] Both factions appealed to the nation, both literally and rhetorically, and awaited the arrival of its forces to support their cause and punish their enemies. These factions reflected deep social and economic divisions in the colonies' white population, but civil war had emerged from the clash between competing claims to legitimate authority. This was an essential characteristic of the revolutionary script from France, and the making and refuting of such claims were part of a larger struggle to control the communication of revolutionary news, language, and symbols. It remained to be seen how metropolitan government would interpret the conflict in the Windward Islands, however, and whether colonists would accept its judgment.

4 "The Nation, the Law, the King": The Liberal Revolution's Failure in the Windward Islands, 1791

On 12 March 1791 a fleet of nineteen French ships appeared off Martinique. Along with six thousand regular troops, these ships brought Jean-Pierre-Antoine, comte de Béhague as new governor general, and four king's commissioners with a mandate to end the civil war and restore metropolitan control over the Windward Islands. The National Assembly's decision to send this major expedition reflected growing pressure from French seaports, concerned over the interruption of colonial commerce. Both factions in Martinique had sought metropolitan intervention, assuming that it would uphold their claim to be the true supporters of the nation. When the fleet arrived, Béhague and the commissioners deported the soldiers who had mutinied against Damas, sent the volunteers back to their home islands, and annulled the municipalities at Fort-Royal and Saint-Pierre. Patriots felt betrayed. Yet the commissioners also suspended Martinique's colonial assembly and established reconciliation committees to investigate the causes of the civil war. Reconciliation, however, proved elusive. The king's commissioners also became embroiled in Guadeloupe's bitter factional strife. Guadeloupe's assembly appeared to pose a more serious challenge to national authority than its patriot rivals, but Governor Clugny refused to sanction the commissioners' criticism of the assembly. Two of the commissioners demanded that Clugny be deported to explain his conduct in Paris, but the other two sided with Béhague in support of Guadeloupe's governor. Clugny's critics departed for France in November, denouncing the colonial assembly, the governor general, and their colleagues.

The king's commissioners had come to the Windward Islands not merely as agents of the metropolitan government but also as the bearers of a specific liberal revolutionary script. This script had been present since 1789, but moderate revolutionaries wanted its formal acceptance to prevail over more radical scripts. The National Assembly was in the process of completing the constitution of 1791, which embodied a "new ideal of the polity" based on political liberty and civic equality.[1] If the commissioners were unsympathetic to military insubordination and imposed controls on the communications of soldiers and *petits Blancs*, this was in keeping with the suspicion of popular revolution held by most deputies in the National Assembly. If they did not question the institution of slavery, this reflected the conviction of statesmen like Barnave that colonial commerce was crucial to the new liberal order.[2] In contrast to Old Regime administrators, however, the king's commissioners of 1791 believed that impartial enforcement of the law as the nation's will was the path to social peace. This strategy required all factions to submit to the commissioners' authority as representatives of "The Nation, the Law, the King," yet both sides continued to assert competing claims to legitimacy. In this context, the commissioners' unity and commitment to liberal principles broke down over fears that patriot-incited defiance posed a grave threat to colonial security. News of the massive slave revolt in Saint-Domingue suggested the kind of catastrophe to which such disorder could lead in Martinique and Guadeloupe. Ultimately colonial security meant maintaining control over the slaves and the *gens de couleur*; planters and governors believed that the communication of radical ideas and language threatened this control. Although they had allied with free men of colour against the patriots, planters opposed granting *gens de couleur* political rights, insisting that the colonies must determine free-coloured status without interference. This entrenched resistance to equality and reform, given the contested location of legitimate authority, thwarted the king's commissioners' attempt to bring the liberal revolution to the Windward Islands.

I Towards Metropolitan Intervention (June–November 1790)

The events of 1789–90 in Martinique and Guadeloupe demonstrated the metropolitan state's inability to control communications in the colonies, particularly in terms of the arrival of rumours and news from France. Similarly, news of the factional struggle in the Windward Islands reached France through the unofficial channels of commercial shipping. Evidence of the strong reaction of mercantile interests in French seaports to news of the troubles in Martinique can be found in the deliberations of Bordeaux's chamber of commerce. In 1789 members of the chamber expressed grave concern regarding proposals in France to abolish the slave trade, and they blamed Martinique's slave revolt on the influence of the *Amis des Noirs*.[3] Although colonists shared these attitudes, the merchants of Bordeaux opposed the admission of colonial representatives to the National Assembly, referring to them as "enemies of commerce."[4] This charge was linked to news that colonial ports had been admitting foreign ships. The chamber agreed in April 1790 to support Saint-Pierre's protests to the National Assembly against the opening of four new *entrepôts* in Martinique and vowed to oppose the "ambitious pretensions of the colony's inhabitants."[5] Communication between Saint-Pierre and Bordeaux was based on the two merchant communities' common interests, but it also established a sympathetic metropolitan audience for patriot accounts of the conflict in Martinique. Letters from Saint-Pierre's commissioners of commerce denounced the "unconstitutional [colonial] assembly" and informed the chamber that Saint-Pierre's municipality and commune had been forced to name two extraordinary deputies to defend the town's rights. These deputies were Corio and Ruste; the commissioners asked the chamber to assist them in putting Saint-Pierre's case before the National Assembly.[6] In response, the chamber wrote to Bordeaux's deputies asking them to support Ruste and Corio.

As it received news of escalating conflict in the colony, Bordeaux's merchant elite became even more willing to put pressure on the National Assembly to address the situation in Martinique. In a letter to Corio and Ruste, the chamber of commerce declared: "The disaster of Martinique has become the cause of all maritime and commercial towns of the kingdom."[7] More significant it approved an address to the National Assembly on 24 August, sending it not only to Bordeaux's deputies but also to all chambers of commerce in France. This address placed the colonial situation in a larger revolutionary context supporting the patriot outlook.[8] In November Bordeaux received further correspondence from the Windward Islands. Saint-Pierre's commissioners of commerce denounced the colonial assembly's continued admission of foreign ships, while French merchant captains at Saint-Pierre reported that citizens faced criminal proceedings resulting from the "Affair of 3 June." But the chamber also received word from Point-à-Pitre's municipal committee of a "happy event which inspires liberty to triumph anew."[9] What the Guadeloupe patriots referred to was the mutiny of the troops at Fort-Bourbon and the outbreak of civil war.

News of civil war in Martinique provoked French commerce to demand that the government act.[10] Even before some of the petitions reached Paris, however, revolutionary legislators had decided to intervene in the colonies. On 29 November 1790 the National Assembly decreed the suspension of Martinique's colonial assembly and the appointment of civil commissioners to re-establish order in the Windward Islands. Antoine-Pierre-Joseph-Marie Barnave proposed the decree on behalf of the Assembly's colonial committee. His report provided a balanced assessment of the situation in Martinique and the causes behind the outbreak of civil war. Barnave distinguished the troubles in Martinique from those in Saint-Domingue, where there were two parties: one attached to the mother country and the other being rebels "who put their own will in place of the law."[11] The rebels referred to the members of the general assembly of Saint-Marc, who had proclaimed a constitution on 28 May to make the colony virtually independent from France.[12] But Barnave insisted that both parties in Martinique considered themselves French and recognized the authority of the National Assembly. The division was based on an old hatred between the colony's planters and the merchants of Saint-Pierre, he suggested, due largely to the fact that the former were debtors to the latter. The colonial assembly had issued its own decrees and had established a provisional administrative corps, which Barnave insisted had not been authorized by the National Assembly's decree of 8 March. Therefore, Barnave introduced the proposed decree in terms of the need to clarify the limits and nature of colonial authority: "The old powers are without force, the new are yet to be established."[13]

The decree of 29 November began with the order for instructions to be sent to the Windward Islands, without delay, to speed their new organization. In the meantime, the National Assembly ordered Martinique's colonial assembly to suspend its sessions. Administrative officers were to remain at their posts provisionally, while the colonial assembly's acts creating the Directory and dismissing several of these officials were nullified. Even more important, the decree asked the king to name four commissioners to be sent to Martinique to investigate the causes of the troubles there: all decrees or judgments rendered as a result of these troubles were to be suspended. In order to provide temporarily for the colony's internal administration, the commissioners would receive all necessary powers. Regular troops, militia, and national guard were to be at their disposal. Thus the National Assembly invested these king's commissioners with its full authority. The commissioners were empowered to go to the other colonies in the Windward Islands, where they could exercise the same powers to suspend the colonial assemblies, if necessary, until the arrival of new instructions. To enable the commissioners to end the civil war and to assert national authority, the decree also asked the king to send six thousand soldiers and four ships of the line. The deployment of these forces would be determined by the officer appointed by the king as new governor general of the Windward Islands, "to whom he will give all necessary authority to concur with the commissioners for the duration of their commission."[14] Therefore, according to the decree, which with the king's sanction became the Law of 8 December 1790,[15] the governor general would command the armed forces in the colony but in support of the commissioners' authority.

Charles-Pierre Claret, comte de Fleurieu, the minister of marine, appointed the men who were to execute the Law of 8 December, and prepared instructions to guide them in carrying out their mission. The minister chose Jean-Pierre-Antoine, comte de Béhague de Villeneuve to become the new governor general of the Windward Islands. A *maréchal de camp* promoted to lieutenant general to command this expedition, Béhague's principal qualification for the post was his previous service as second in command to the governor in Cayenne and Guyana (1762–4). In March 1790, however, Béhague had defended the maintenance of colonial slavery in a memoir to the National Assembly.[16] As king's commissioners, the minister chose two officials from his *Bureau des Colonies*: Jean de Lacoste, who had been *premier commis* responsible for America and the African coast (1776–81), and Louis-Maurice Magnytôt. Fleurieu sought to balance these two bureaucrats with two colonial administrators. Therefore, he appointed Antoine Eu de Montdenoix, who had served as *commissaire général de la marine* and then *ordonnateur* in Martinique from 1775 to 1780,[17] along with Jacques Linger, who also had experience in the Windward Islands.[18]

The four commissioners' mission was to reassert the metropolitan state's authority, but they would also impose the principles of the liberal revolution. The minister's instructions for executing the Law of 8 December, presented to them on 24 January 1791, emphasized key themes. First, they must do everything possible to avoid resorting to the use of force: "His Majesty hopes that it will be sufficient to speak to Frenchmen in the name of the Nation, the Law and the King."[19] The commissioners must restore legitimate authority, but without violence if at all possible. It was in this context that the commissioners were to establish a reconciliation committee including members of both opposed parties. A second theme was the importance of legality. Upon the expedition's arrival, the governor general would issue a proclamation demanding that all judicial tribunals, administrative bodies, and military officers recognize the king's commissioners. The instructions reaffirmed that all decrees and judgments rendered because of the colony's disorder would remain suspended, and they ordered the commissioners to investigate all legal proceedings, as well as the fate of the accused, as part of their larger efforts to gather information on the causes of the troubles. All public functions and powers not based in law were to cease immediately. With power over the colonies' administration, they also had the right to maintain or replace agents, "but they will not displace a person without listening to him and without addressing an official report of the reasons, including the statements of those who complained."[20] With regard to the commissioners' power to suspend other colonial assemblies, the instructions advised them to act cautiously but suggested the possible benefits of such suspensions.

These instructions confirmed that the governor general commanded all military forces at the commissioners' requisition, but they also introduced confusion regarding the division of authority by identifying the occasions on which joint deliberations must be held. "His Majesty's intention is that the governor-general not intervene in the commissioners' deliberations," but they were to consult with him if armed force was to be employed; if troops were to be deported; or if any governor, commandant, or military officer was to be returned to France.[21] Did such consultations imply that the governor general could question the validity of the commissioners' decisions? The ambiguity in the relationship between civil commissioners and the governor general, like that between the National Assembly and the king, was intrinsic to the emerging constitutional order.

II Civil War and the Expedition's Arrival
(November 1790–March 1791)

As the expedition prepared to sail from Brest, Martinique remained in a state of civil war. Both sides recognized that only outside intervention would bring victory, so discrediting enemies and preparing self-justifications were as important as military dispositions. According to Damas, in the memoir he published after returning to France in 1791, the planters had not attacked Saint-Pierre, an action that would have inspired the slaves to violence, waiting instead to receive justice from the National Assembly.[22] Damas contrasted this moderation with the actions of their enemies who had treacherously appealed for foreign intervention. Specifically, he accused Saint-Pierre's municipality of approaching the British commander in Grenada.[23] This charge, like Damas's general characterization of the struggle, attacked the patriots' claims to legitimacy. Patriot accounts of the civil war represented the actions of the governor general and colonial assembly as counterrevolutionary. Crassous de Médeuil, secretary of the Saint-Pierre committee, published a narrative of events in Martinique that was a direct refutation of Damas's memoir. According to this account, troops of the Martinique Regiment rose up to defend patriots oppressed by the tyrannical colonial assembly, and it was the assembly that rejected all proposals for reconciliation, provoked the outbreak of hostilities, and asked the British for assistance. Crassous claimed that the army of Gros-Morne had spread terror throughout the colony, and he accused Damas and the assembly of arming slaves and encouraging them to revolt.[24]

On 22 January 1791 the sloop *Ballon* anchored at Trinité and delivered dispatches for Damas. Both of Martinique's factions now knew that a major expedition was coming from France, and the struggle over communications became critical. In his letter of 23 January to the minister, Damas complained that these dispatches provided no instructions to guide his conduct until the arrival of the king's commissioners: "In this absolute silence, what can I do but attach myself strongly to the principles of the new constitution?"[25] Aware that the rebels had inundated France with calumnious writings, he declared the principles to which he had adhered during these difficult circumstances. The first was that he considered the current colonial assembly to be legally constituted, according to the National Assembly's decrees of 8 and 28 March 1790, and therefore the true representative of the colony. Thus Damas characterized his actions as defending not only law and order but also popular sovereignty.[26] Second, he claimed that he had done everything in his power to prevent the outbreak of hostilities, and when his efforts proved in vain, that he employed all his means to reduce the harm inseparable from civil war. In contrast, the rebel troops' conduct could not be excused in any way.[27] Similarly the colonial assembly protested that it had been forced to take up arms to protect lives and property.[28]

According to Crassous, patriots welcomed the news that representatives of the nation were being sent to Martinique. He composed his history of the struggle to show that love for the constitution alone had animated the party of Saint-Pierre. This text challenged the claim in

Damas's memoir that it was inaccurate for patriots to call Martinique's planters "aristocrats": "Who does not know that the revolution applies the word aristocrat to all those who, abusing the name of the king from near or far, exercise against their subordinates the tyranny by which they were themselves enslaved by their superiors; to all those who, aping the great ones, believe that their nobility or their riches puts them above the people, crushing them from their fictive grandeur; one could not mistake these traits among most men of whom M. Damas declares himself the defender."[29] This portrait is a striking illustration of the extent to which colonial patriots had adopted the political culture of the metropolitan revolution. The label of "aristocrat," Crassous insisted, fit Martinique's planters perfectly: debtors who feared the law would force them to pay their creditors, men who affected contempt for other Europeans who had arrived recently in the colony's towns, a group holding a monopoly over judicial and political posts in the colony. If Crassous portrayed a social and economic division, he also suggested that the conflict between the patriots and the planters was a political and ideological one: "Examine their language, see that if in France the revolution is treated by its enemies as brigandage against property and legitimate authority, if aristocrats call the people brigands, here the awakening of the people is treated as an invasion of planters' property, as a revolt against legitimate authority, and citizens are called brigands."[30] By painting the colonial assembly and its supporters as counter-revolutionaries, Crassous and the patriots attempted to strengthen their claims to local legitimacy and to true loyalty towards metropolitan authority. Damas and the colonial assembly did the same. Both factions sent self-justifying texts to France, seeking to convince the National Assembly to send representatives to support their cause.[31]

These representatives reached Martinique on 12 March 1791, and the armada bringing them demonstrated the metropolitan state's determination to assert its authority. From his flagship, *Eole* 74, Commodore François-Emmanuel de Girardin commanded the fleet of nineteen vessels, including transports, frigates, and three other ships of the line. Girardin anchored in Fort-Royal Bay but forbade any communication with the shore.[32] The king's commissioners feared that rebel troops might resist the expedition or try to subvert its forces.[33] Béhague issued the first of a series of proclamations on 13 March. He charged two of his officers to carry copies to the rebel soldiers in Fort-Bourbon and to those in Fort-Royal, with orders to return with their responses by the following day. In demanding their surrender, the new governor general appealed to the rebel troops' loyalty to France and asked them to recognize that "perfidious counsellors" had misled them. Therefore the soldiers had to prove their loyalty by identifying the traitors and surrendering – or face the consequences.[34]

In response to Béhague's proclamation, two officers of the Martinique Regiment came aboard the *Eole* as deputies of the fourteen parishes united at Fort-Royal. They claimed that citizens were overjoyed at the fleet's arrival and that soldiers were ready to offer Béhague the forts they had guarded for the nation.[35] The new governor general dismissed this response to his proclamation, telling them that he had given his order to surrender Fort-Bourbon and Fort-Royal – not to the fourteen parishes, but to those who commanded the forts. Béhague then sent Lieutenant Colonel Fressinaux and Quartermaster General Constant to deliver a direct order to the soldiers occupying Fort-Bourbon to evacuate it immediately.[36] These two officers accompanied the deputies back to Fort-Bourbon, where they read the order to the assembled troops. The soldiers insisted, however, that they would leave only when the grenadiers destined to relieve them arrived. Fressinaux replied that if Béhague's order was not obeyed immediately, the governor general would be released from his promise of a pardon for the mutineers. After a brief display of defiance, the soldiers evacuated Fort-Bourbon as ordered.[37] Upon entering the fort himself, Béhague ordered the flag lowered; a quarter-hour later troops of the new garrison raised it and fired a gun salute. "It was thus that the Gibraltar of America was returned to the power of the nation," Béhague reported, "without spilling a drop of blood."[38]

III The King's Commissioners and the Dilemma of Factional Strife (March–October 1791)

Despite the surrender of Fort-Bourbon, and the testimonies of loyalty to the nation from both factions,[39] the situation in Martinique remained volatile. As well as calling for the immediate cessation of hostilities throughout the island,[40] Béhague proclaimed the king's order for the re-establishment of military discipline that was concerned chiefly with controlling the troops' communications. It forbade soldiers from going beyond the limits to which they were confined and declared that straying into the towns or countryside would be punished under military law. The new governor general warned soldiers that it was strictly forbidden to have any contact with other regiments. All

2 Chevalier D'Epernay and Nee, "Île Vue du Fort-Royal de la Martinique."
PAH3020/National Maritime Museum, Greenwich, London.

sedition would be punished, and they were not permitted to call for
the intervention of the administrative corps under any pretext.[41] The
initial defiance at Fort-Bourbon appeared to justify this new effort to
control communications, as did Béhague's conviction that Saint-Pierre
had openly reproached the soldiers for submitting too easily.[42] There
was other evidence to support fears of subversion. "Sordid attempts
were made to stir up the battalions from France," the king's commissioners reported, "letters, printed pamphlets capable of misleading
the soldiers were spread clandestinely; uneasiness seized spirits and
these dangerous moves determined us to join the general in issuing
several joint proclamations."[43] In a letter addressed to a soldier in the
Forez Regiment, newly arrived with the expedition, a corporal in the

Martinique Regiment expressed astonishment that commanders had forbidden him and his fellows from speaking with the new arrivals: "It is us, my dear comrade, who have conserved the forts for *la patrie*; we, here and at Saint-Pierre, are the only good citizens; anyone not with us is suspect and accustomed to lying."[44] An address from the Martinique Regiment to Fort-Bourbon's new garrison demonstrated similar consternation with the ban on its communication with the metropolitan troops, and encouraged these soldiers to defy the ban.[45] According to Girardin, radicals at Saint-Pierre attempted to win over naval crews, as well as the troops, using "money, drink, and incendiary papers."[46] The furtive distribution of such papers, often by cabaret owners, determined Béhague to garrison Fort-Bourbon only with loyal troops and to maintain the posts surrounding Fort-Royal to prevent rebel soldiers from slipping out during the night.[47]

On 20 March the governor general and the king's commissioners made the first of a series of joint proclamations, aimed more at civilians than at the soldiers, further demonstrating their resolve to control communications: "No association, corporation or individual can under any pretext enter into correspondence with the regiments which compose the army with the object of attaching them to a party ... nor can the regiments open such correspondence without being equally guilty as traitors and criminals." They warned that they would punish all instigators or authors of sedition against military subordination.[48] On 22 March they forbade travel between Saint-Pierre and Fort-Royal in an effort to keep the opposing parties apart.[49] The king's commissioners also ordered Martinique's printers not to publish writings encouraging fermentation or rekindling discord, warning them they would be held personally responsible. Like other revolutionaries after them, they justified this limitation of the right to free expression by referring to the extraordinary circumstances, some of which were unique to colonial society.[50] The commissioners stated that it was necessary to stop the spread of writings "dictated by passion and efforts to mislead weak and uneducated men," which could provoke dangerous disorder, "in a country populated by easily seduced Negroes and where the towns are, to a great part, inhabited by vulgar men without constant domicile, who know no other restraint than force, chased from all the countries of Europe by misery and often by crime."[51] The new representatives of the metropolitan state, like the former governors general, sought to limit the communications not only of troops but also of slaves and *petits Blancs*.

Béhague and the king's commissioners also deported those they regarded as threats to their authority. Learning that Saint-Pierre was collecting donations to thank rebel soldiers for their services, the new governor general ordered the troops of the Martinique Regiment to be embarked immediately on ships to await transport to France. When this was accomplished, loyal troops from the Bassigny and Turenne Regiments took up posts at Fort-Saint-Louis and Fort-Bourbon.[52] Béhague and the commissioners also ordered all inhabitants of neighbouring islands to return to their homes.[53] Yet neither troops nor patriot volunteers accepted their expulsion easily. On 26 March Béhague informed men of the Martinique Regiment that he had appointed a council to provide the minister and the National Assembly's military committee with information so that they could judge the soldiers' statements. The troops' supporters were not convinced they would get a fair hearing, however, and for the next few days cries of alarm rang out through Fort-Royal.[54] Meanwhile Linger, the king's commissioner sent to Saint-Pierre to enforce the departure of troops and volunteers from other colonies, faced serious opposition. He had no choice but to deliver a certificate to the volunteers, attesting to their submission to the law, although he insisted to his colleagues that this did not imply approval of their past conduct.[55] The volunteers sailed from Saint-Pierre on 24 March, while the bulk of the Martinique Regiment left Fort-Royal on 2 April. According to the king's commissioners, a total of 979 troops, deserters, and volunteers were deported from Martinique.[56]

For the king's commissioners the removal of rebel troops, and the measures to prevent the subversion of those brought to replace them, were necessary preconditions to their mission: to restore peace between Martinique's opposing parties and to investigate the causes of the civil war. Overwhelmed by complaints, denunciations, and requests, they did not believe they could undertake a detailed investigation immediately.[57] Yet to begin the process, on 22 March they invited colonists to submit written statements to the sénéchal at Saint-Pierre or to that at Fort-Royal.[58] A week later they issued a proclamation for the formation of a reconciliation committee.[59] This ordered the citizens composing the "party of Saint-Pierre" to divide themselves into four classes: commissioners of the fourteen united parishes, wholesale merchants and commissioners of commerce, owners of houses and warehouses, and those who exercised a public profession and had lived in the colony for at least two years. These classes were to assemble separately to elect six electors each, who together would form a single assembly. This assembly then would elect twelve of its members as commissioners to a reconciliation committee to address all appropriate means to restore unity and concord. This process imitated the indirect elections by active citizens under the liberal – but not democratic – constitution of 1791. Beyond the exclusion of Saint-Pierre's rootless *petits Blancs* from representation on this committee, the proclamation addressed only one of Martinique's factions. The colonial assembly, before dissolving on 17 March to conform to the Law of 8 December, had chosen twelve of its own members to furnish information on the civil war. The commissioners designated this group as the second reconciliation committee, while at the same time refusing to accept nominations for the other committee from either the suspended municipalities of Saint-Pierre and Fort-Royal or from the fourteen united parishes whose legality they did not recognize.[60] Thus the formation of the reconciliation committees, despite the commissioners' determination to act with impartiality, seemed to validate one faction's claim to legitimacy while denying that of the other.

The commissioners' efforts to reconcile Martinique's factions had barely begun when they received news of the ongoing revolutionary turmoil in Saint-Domingue. Troops of the Normandy and Artois Regiments, having just arrived in that colony from France, had aligned themselves with the mutinous Port-au-Prince Regiment, whose soldiers murdered their commanding officer, Colonel Thomas-Antoine de Mauduit du Plessis, on 4 March. Colonel Mauduit had led the forces against the Saint-Marc Assembly in 1790. His murder was part of an uprising by the *Pompons Rouges*, or patriots, at Port-au-Prince that forced Saint-Domingue's governor general, Philibert-François Rouxel de Blanchelande, to flee to Cap Français in the north.[61] Blanchelande appealed to the Windward Islands to send reliable troops to Saint-Domingue to restore his authority. Béhague and the king's commissioners agreed to dispatch two battalions to Saint-Domingue aboard three warships.[62] Security concerns in Martinique complicated the decision to send these forces. No battalions would depart until the last troops of the Martinique and Guadeloupe Regiments had embarked to leave the colony. Béhague proposed that only two of five battalions that they had already decided should return to France were trustworthy enough to send to Blanchelande; the others had been corrupted in France or subverted since their arrival.[63] The news from Saint-Domingue only heightened fears that *petits Blancs* sought to undermine the troops' subordination in Martinique, thus weakening the possibility of reconciling the colony's factions.[64]

Having deported rebel troops and patriot volunteers, Béhague and the king's commissioners took steps to disarm Martinique's slaves and return them to their masters. They sought not only to restore order but also to win Saint-Pierre's confidence. Defiance of the amnesty for slaves who submitted, however, worsened relations with the town. On 7 April the king's commissioners and the governor general issued a proclamation forbidding all speech or actions that threatened peace and order. It forbade all gatherings by planters at Saint-Pierre, by the town's residents in the countryside, and it particularly forbade *gens de couleur* from entering the town under any pretext. All these measures to limit communications were intended to bring the security that would foster reconciliation.[65] After contact with the leaders of armed bands, Béhague and the commissioners recognized that the slaves' submission was dependent on the proclaimed promise of amnesty.[66] The slaves had to return within eight days or be considered traitors, but their masters also had to conform to the amnesty and treat returning slaves with gentleness.[67]

Initially this strategy seemed successful. Slaves surrendered muskets and trooped back to their plantations without incident. Yet those who returned to Saint-Pierre were beaten in the town's streets. Despite another proclamation, reaffirming that these slaves had been guaranteed a general pardon,[68] whites in Saint-Pierre committed further acts of violence against blacks. The slaves' confidence in the promised amnesty evaporated; many fled to the hills, thwarting the plan to disarm them. "In the current circumstances the cruelty of the master towards his slave must be seen not as a simple abuse of power," wrote the king's commissioners, "but as a true public crime."[69] They considered such masters to be traitors – not just because they defied a proclamation by the nation's representatives, but also because their actions could plunge the colony back into civil war.

White hostility at Saint-Pierre was also directed at the *gens de couleur*. *Petits Blancs* insulted and even attacked free men of colour wearing the tricolour cockade.[70] On 13 April the governor general and the king's commissioners proclaimed that it was forbidden to insult any free man who wore the cockade.[71] That same day two free men of colour at Pointe-à-Bout responded in kind to insults from white men. Béhague ordered that the two coloured men be imprisoned for fifteen days, yet what he regarded as a show of impartiality did not end the harassment of *gens de couleur* in Saint-Pierre.[72] If the *petits Blancs'* racism undermined efforts to restore civil peace, Saint-Pierre's merchants resented the fact that the commissioners had accepted the colonial assembly naming its own members to a reconciliation committee.[73] Nevertheless, Lacoste, Magnytôt, Linger, and Montdenoix attempted to regenerate the town's commerce. Merchants and French ship captains had complained bitterly at the presence of foreign vessels at Martinique and the planters' refusal to send products to Saint-Pierre.[74] The commissioners' attempts to revive the restrictions on foreign ships elicited a flood of protests from planters, however, and they failed to persuade planters to end their boycott of the port and pay their debts.[75] Thus efforts to revive Saint-Pierre's economy foundered on the continuing animosity between the colony's factions.[76]

The king's commissioners had no illusions regarding the difficulty of ending this animosity. In keeping with their instructions, however, they believed that strict and impartial enforcement of the law was the key. This outlook characterized those in France who supported the constitution of 1791. Despite concerns about the planters' behaviour, the commissioners began to meet with the colonial assembly's delegates to the reconciliation committee. Even more encouraging, the "Party of Saint-Pierre" also named representatives in the manner prescribed.[77] Even as the commissioners reported these hopeful signs to the minister, an episode at Saint-Pierre challenged their strategy of legalism as a path to peace and reconciliation. Captain de Narbonne-Lara, an army officer arriving at Saint-Pierre on 23 May aboard the merchant ship *Jenny*, complained to the governor general and the king's commissioners of abuse he had endured at the hands of the ship's captain. The commissioners sent Narbonne-Lara before the admiralty tribunal to make a formal complaint and asked Béhague to have the *Jenny* conducted to Fort-Royal to await the court's decision. The governor general assigned the captain of the frigate *Calypso*, Louis Mallevault de Vaumorant, to this task. One of Mallevault's lieutenants went ashore at Saint-Pierre to arrest the *Jenny's* captain, but he refused to surrender. A crowd of onlookers forced the naval officer to retreat.[78] In complaints submitted to the commissioners, the merchant captain and his supporters presented their defiance as an appeal for justice under the law.[79]

This affair posed a dilemma for the king's commissioners between supporting executive authority or ensuring the rule of law, and it exposed differences between their outlook and that of Béhague. The episode also provided more evidence of enmity between merchant captains, as well as colonial patriots more generally, and the French Navy. Captain Mallevault sent a guard of thirty armed men aboard the *Jenny*, but the commissioners asked that this guard be withdrawn and suggested that Mallevault's orders for the merchant captain's arrest might have been irregular.[80] In response, Béhague defended Mallevault's conduct and insisted that the defiance of the naval officer required prompt and severe justice.[81] Commodore Girardin also worried that failure to punish the merchant captain would encourage colonists undermining his crews' discipline.[82] Yet the king's commissioners were determined to uphold the letter of the law: they agreed that arresting the *Jenny*'s captain would end the affair but insisted that they lacked the required authority to order his imprisonment. They also argued that the *sénéchal* needed to investigate the possible violence towards Mallevault's lieutenant.[83] The commissioners' belief that impartial and strict adherence to the law was necessary to reconcile Martinique's warring parties – and to assert the nation's will – was at odds with the governor general's determination to uphold executive power.[84] Nonetheless, the schism between these representatives of the metropolitan state occurred as a result of events in Guadeloupe.

Governor Clugny had expressed relief at the arrival of the fleet and the king's commissioners in March. Although Guadeloupe had not experienced open civil war, in September 1790 rebel troops had arrested Clugny at Basse-Terre and seized control of Fort-Louis at Pointe-à-Pitre. By the time that Fort-Bourbon surrendered to the new governor general, Clugny could report that the situation in Grande-Terre was peaceful. This was not the case in Basse-Terre, however, and he hoped the king's commissioners would "enlighten those who have been misled and reduce the wicked to silence."[85] Clugny and members of Guadeloupe's colonial assembly travelled to Fort-Royal to meet with the commissioners shortly after their arrival. The members of the assembly declared their submission to the decrees of the National Assembly and their confidence in its delegates, but they also appealed to the commissioners to suspend neither Guadeloupe's assembly nor its municipalities. Clugny supported their arguments, suggesting that even the provisional return to the Old Regime would cause the greatest disorder in the colony. The king's commissioners conceded. Clugny then asked that none of the battalions from France be sent to Guadeloupe, where he claimed that their indiscipline would wreak havoc. The governor and the deputies also requested copies of the commissioners' proclamations recalling soldiers to their duty, so that they could publish them in their colony.[86]

These concerns about insubordinate soldiers fit with larger obsessions regarding patriots' supposed efforts to incite rebellion among *petits Blancs* or even slaves through subversive communications. Since September 1790 Guadeloupe's colonial assembly had regarded the municipality of Basse-Terre, led by Mayor Thyrus de Pautrizel, as playing the same dangerous role in the colony that Saint-Pierre played in Martinique. In April the national guard at Basse-Terre honoured the returned volunteers as heroes, and these festivities led to a rumour that patriots intended to expel the regular troops and occupy Fort-Saint-Charles.[87] In May the municipality of Sainte-Anne discovered a plot among the slaves to burn the town, the local plantations, and even Pointe-à-Pitre. As with previous plots, the ringleaders intended to stir up the gangs by telling them that the governor was concealing a decree of the National Assembly giving blacks their freedom. Having deployed troops and arrested eighteen slaves identified as plotters, Clugny blamed the conspiracy on the colony's white radicals. He also warned Béhague to take precautions, "persuaded that branches of the insurrection extend to Martinique."[88] He did not explain, however, the alleged link between patriot machinations and slave revolt.

At the end of June Clugny appealed to Béhague to authorize the deportation of mutinous artillery troops, and the governor general dispatched the *Calypso* to Basse-Terre to prevent any resistance to the gunners' removal. Clugny informed the king's commissioners that this operation had been completed without trouble, but members of Basse-Terre's municipality later told them that the frigate's intervention had caused great alarm in the town. Captain Mallevault had publicly declared that the town's residents were "brigands," loaded the *Calypso*'s cannon, and sent armed sailors ashore. On 17 July Clugny returned from Pointe-à-Pitre to Basse-Terre to occupy the official residence he had abandoned after being held prisoner in September. His escorts included armed sailors from the frigates *Calypso* and *Didon* and possibly also armed men of colour crying "*Vive le Roi et M. de Clugny!*" Backed by this force, he suppressed the town's national guard and expelled the artillery troops. Guadeloupe's colonial assembly had suspended its sessions on 16 July, and Clugny argued that, therefore, he should also suspend Basse-Terre's municipality.[89] The commissioners refused to authorize this. Shortly afterwards the colonial assembly renewed its sessions, having received reports of the king's flight to Varennes and return to Paris. This news cast doubt on the legitimacy and viability of the liberal revolution that the commissioners represented. In August there were a number of violent confrontations between officers and non-commissioned officers of the Guadeloupe Regiment, on one side, and townsfolk, on the other. At least one civilian was killed. It was news of this violence that prompted the king's commissioners to leave Martinique on 23 August to investigate the situation in Guadeloupe themselves.[90]

The king's commissioners found themselves in conflict with Guadeloupe's governor and colonial assembly long before their arrival in that colony. This conflict involved not only the commissioners' commitment to the rule of law but also one of the central dilemmas of the French revolutionary script: Where was national authority located? On 19 April members of the assembly had asked the commissioners to prevent Masse, an administrator who had been serving in Tobago, from replacing Chabert de Prailles as interim *ordonnateur* at Guadeloupe. Members suggested that this change in personnel would threaten the "sane" coalition that had supported the governor and assembly in maintaining tranquillity.[91] The commissioners had already sent orders to Masse, whose seniority designated him for the post at Guadeloupe; thus, they told the colonial assembly: "We can permit ourselves neither the arbitrary disposition of appointments nor the arbitrary contravention of ordinances."[92] They had received no specific complaint against him and, therefore, would not deprive him of his rights under law. In May Clugny informed the commissioners that if they sent Masse to Guadeloupe, he would resign as governor.[93] The commissioners responded that they were determined to uphold the law and would not block Masse's appointment without legal cause.[94]

It was not until the middle of July that the colonial assembly explained its opposition to Masse. The deputies had assumed it would be sufficient to inform the king's commissioners of Guadeloupe's unfavourable opinion of Masse for him to resign voluntarily – and for the commissioners to confirm this. They placed their assumption in the context of recent events:

> What motives must we believe more appropriate to determine you on this subject than the example of the King who never, above all since the Revolution, suffered any part of his powers to remain in hands suspect and odious to his people, and to speak only of those cases analogous to

that of M. Masse, we will refer only to what happened to [Messieurs] Marbois and Foullon. Why was one recalled? Why did the King not permit the other to return to his *intendance*, even after his return to France was annulled by the National Assembly? Only because their conduct and sentiments had rendered them incompatible with order and public tranquillity.[95]

Patriots had driven *Intendant* François de Barbé-Marbois from Saint-Domingue in October 1789, while Damas had deported Foullon d'Écotier from Martinique in July 1790. These references represented an effort to place the assembly's demand in the context of revolutionary popular sovereignty to which the commissioners should yield. The deputies alleged that Masse had abandoned Tobago before the expedition's arrival because he feared that coloured troops from Martinique were approaching Tobago to arrest him. Supposedly he told Tobago's governor that "he was going to bury himself under the ruins of Saint-Pierre," thus showing that he "espoused the cause of the brigands."[96] Believing that Masse was an ally of their local enemies, Guadeloupe's assembly and governor made no concession to reconciliation, let alone to the impartiality of the law.[97]

The colonial assembly's refusal to accept Masse's appointment was a direct challenge to the authority of the king's commissioners. Their response to this challenge demonstrated not only the clash of competing claims to legitimacy but also the ambiguity of appeals to popular sovereignty in this struggle. Along with refuting the assembly's claim to embody the colony's will, the commissioners repudiated its accusation that their position regarding Masse was unjust. Even more revealing was the commissioners' response to the colonial assembly's charge that they had not followed the king's example of removing unpopular ministers:

Your citations are ill-informed: we were there and we have not seen since the revolution any minister removed at the demand of the people. Those who have quit the ministry gave their resignations, and if some ceded to popular clamours, the example is without application. The inhabitants of Guadeloupe would certainly not be happy to find themselves mistaken for the populace of the *faubourgs* and *halles* of Paris. No *intendant* has been recalled: Marbois left Saint-Domingue without any ministerial excitation; Foullon, whose dismissal was declared null, kept his title and his pay. But what we have seen is that the National Assembly itself has always abstained from approaching the King for the dismissal of his ministers.[98]

There is irony in the commissioners' accusation that the colonial assembly, the voice of Guadeloupe's planter aristocracy, had adopted the rhetoric of the Parisian *sans-culottes*. At the same time, this exchange reveals a fundamental truth about the struggle in the colonies. The king's commissioners represented the liberal revolution in metropolitan France, which sought to confine national sovereignty to the decrees of the National Assembly sanctioned by the king. "The Nation, the Law, the King" symbolized a determination to balance parliamentary authority and executive power, and it denied the legitimacy of claims to national will made beyond the National Assembly. Strong opposing currents in the revolutionary script had undermined this liberal project from its inception, and by mid-1791 Louis XVI's attempted flight had dealt it a fatal blow in France. But no faction in the colonies had ever been committed to the liberal revolution. Guadeloupe's colonial assembly, like both its allies and patriot enemies throughout the Windward Islands, claimed local authority using the language and logic of revolutionary popular sovereignty. Despite addresses of submission to the authority of the king's commissioners in March, there was no real consensus that these men, in conjunction with the governor general, spoke for the nation.

Lacoste, Magnytôt, Linger, and Montdenoix reached Basse-Terre on 25 August. Their arrival elicited opposite reactions from Guadeloupe's factions: the municipality and its supporters welcomed the commissioners enthusiastically, while its enemies regarded them with distrust and hostility. Lacoste and Magnytôt would later claim that this reflected the prejudice sown by Béhague, who reported to Guadeloupe's assembly their suggestion that new troops might replace Basse-Terre's garrison.[99] The colony's factional division also confronted the commissioners in news of the federations of "good citizens," which had occurred at Sainte-Anne on 3 August and at Basse-Terre on 17 August. Having sworn oaths to fight anarchy at these rallies, the *fédérés* then identified other colonists as "troublemakers."[100] The day that the king's commissioners arrived in Guadeloupe, the assembly decreed that a general federation of all the colony's parishes be held on 15 September. In response, the commissioners observed that not only did such federations promote conflict but they also assumed illegal and even tyrannical powers in opposition to national authority.[101] If the federations defined "bad citizens" in terms of acts related to the troubles occasioned by the revolution, the commissioners reminded the colonial assembly that the National Assembly had reserved to itself the right to judge all that happened in the Windward Islands before the Law of 8 December 1790: "Would the Federation claim to be above the tribunal of the nation?"[102]

The commissioners feared that the assembly hoped to provoke residents of Basse-Terre into resistance that could then be repressed.[103] Such resistance to the general federation occurred, however, at Pointe-à-Pitre. On 15 September grenadiers of the Forez Regiment swore the oath with other groups participating in the federation; but when they realized it was different from the oath they had sworn in France, they refused to sign the written version. The soldiers then raised the tricolour flag over the barracks, which their officers and Point-à-Pitre's municipality viewed as a sign of revolt. Governor Clugny led deputies of the colonial assembly, accompanied by officers of the army and navy, who marched on the barracks and disarmed the rebels. Claiming that the interrogation of prisoners revealed the existence of a larger plot, the assembly ordered that a court martial be convened to try the grenadiers and that the courts of justice begin proceedings against civilian "instigators and their accomplices."[104]

With new disorders throughout Guadeloupe, the king's commissioners travelled to Pointe-à-Pitre to meet directly with the colonial assembly. Specific disagreements emerged regarding brawls at Sainte-Anne, the commissioners' right to direct judicial officers to investigate, and the assembly's powers over municipalities and administrative bodies.[105] The last issue had immediate relevance because on 21 September the commissioners learned of a *coup d'état*: the colonial assembly had dismissed Basse-Terre's municipality on 13 September, declared its municipal officers ineligible for any public function for five years, and prescribed the formation of a new municipality.[106] The shocked commissioners insisted that the assembly did not have the authority to take such action that was not merely contrary to the letter of the law but also to the spirit of the constitution.[107] Their defence of an elected municipality was entirely in keeping with the liberal revolution they represented. In defiance, members of the colonial assembly declared that the decree of 8 March and the instructions of 28 March invested them with provisional legislative authority for anything concerning the colony's internal regime. Even more revealing, however, was their assertion that the people's will (as interpreted by the assembly) was superior to election results.[108] Despite its hostility to the patriots and their enthusiasm for the French Revolution, the colonial assembly invoked revolutionary popular sovereignty to justify breaking Basse-Terre's municipality.

IV The Nation's Representatives Divided (October–December 1791)

The conferences between the king's commissioners and members of Guadeloupe's colonial assembly failed to resolve their differences.[109] When the meetings were over, the commissioners returned to Basse-Terre and prepared a proclamation intended to counter accusations against them and to reassert their authority in the colony. It denounced the particular federations as unlawful, the *arrêté* dismissing Basse-Terre's municipality as illegal and unconstitutional, and called on the colony's inhabitants to oppose the spirit of division.[110] When Clugny and members of the assembly learned of this proclamation, they came to Basse-Terre to prevent its publication. Linger and Montdenoix agreed to submit it to the governor for his observations. With the issue still unresolved, the commissioners received news of troubles in Sainte-Lucie. The commissioners decided that Linger and Montdenoix would sail from Basse-Terre on 1 October, leaving Lacoste and Magnytôt to publish the proclamation and complete the mission in Guadeloupe.[111]

Clugny warned Lacoste and Magnytôt that the proclamation's publication would embolden Guadeloupe's "brigands" in their destructive projects, thus igniting the same kind of civil war that had torn Martinique apart. The king's commissioners then received threats that 1,500 *fédérés* would descend upon Basse-Terre and destroy the town unless they withdrew the proclamation. Finally, Clugny informed them that he was resigning his post as governor rather than sanctioning the publication of the proclamation. The commissioners appealed to René-Marie d'Arrot, Guadeloupe's *commandant-en-second*, but he also announced that he would resign before he would agree to their request. The colonial assembly forbade any municipality in the colony from publishing anything without its express permission. The real blow, however, came with the arrival of dispatches from the governor general. Béhague ordered Clugny to resume his duties but said nothing about sanctioning the proclamation, thus undermining the authority of Lacoste and Magnytôt completely. This was a resounding victory for the colonial assembly and a bitter defeat for the two commissioners.[112] On 20 October Lacoste and Magnytôt informed the assembly that Béhague's order had rendered their mission useless and that they were leaving Guadeloupe to return to Martinique and from there to France. Yet they remained defiant: "It only remains for us to give an account to the King and the National Assembly, and we will do so with celerity and exactitude."[113]

In Martinique the schism between the depositories of national authority was completed. Lacoste and Magnytôt arrived at Saint-Pierre on 21 October, the same day that Linger and Montdenoix returned from Sainte-Lucie. Meeting two days later, the four commissioners disagreed on the result of their mission to Guadeloupe and on what their next step should be. To reach a decision, they held a series of deliberations at Fort-Royal with the governor general. On 29 October Lacoste formally requested that Béhague deport Clugny and d'Arrot to France, where they would account for their disobedience to the Law of 8 December. If this request was refused, he stated that he and Magnytôt would consider the authority of all the king's commissioners to be nullified. Béhague was shocked – as much by the criticism of his order as by the demand to deport the governor of Guadeloupe and his lieutenant – but he appealed for unity. Montdenoix then offered a somewhat conciliatory opinion. Because of their refusal to publish the commissioners' proclamation, he agreed that Clugny and d'Arrot must answer to the king and National Assembly. The commissioners should send a report and await the National Assembly's verdict on the two officers, but in the meantime there was no reason their mission should end. Magnytôt was adamant, however, that Béhague must deport Clugny and d'Arrot. In response, Montdenoix and Linger reiterated their disagreement. The governor general then gave his own final opinion. While his instructions of 24 January gave him the power, he believed that expelling Clugny and d'Arrot would threaten public order. Therefore, Béhague, Montdenoix, and Linger overruled Lacoste and Magnytôt. Magnytôt announced that he and Lacoste were preparing a declaration – not only denouncing Guadeloupe's colonial assembly, as well as Clugny and d'Arrot, but also informing the king and National Assembly that Béhague had contravened the Law of 8 December and had attributed to himself superiority over the king's commissioners. Thus he and Lacoste believed that it was no longer possible to fulfil their duties and so would return to France.[114] They did not actually sail until 24 November due to a dispute over the commissioners' archives.[115] Montdenoix and Linger refused to provide access to the documents, claiming that these were their responsibility since they must continue the mission. Lacoste and Magnytôt had to sail without the crucial evidence the archives contained.[116]

In a flurry of bitter recriminations, the king's commissioners and the governor general blamed each other for the collapse of unity. Lacoste and Magnytôt explained the division as the result of intrigues on the part of the governors and also of their colleagues' weakness.[117] Montdenoix and Linger, on the other hand, attributed the break to the "arrogance and passion which carried Lacoste and Magnytôt beyond all measure."[118] They told the minister that the commissioners could have reached an understanding with Guadeloupe's assembly, but the proclamation of 29 September composed by Lacoste at Basse-Terre made this impossible. Montdenoix and Linger claimed that they had opposed the proclamation but had signed it under pressure to preserve unity among the commissioners.[119] Béhague's report also blamed the schism entirely on the arrogant, unreasonable, and treacherous behaviour of Lacoste and Magnytôt. He claimed that the two commissioners, by trying to publish their denunciations, hoped to incite an uprising of other colonies against Guadeloupe and against himself.[120] In a separate dispatch, Linger accused them of having constantly ignored the advice of their colleagues, who had twenty-four years of experience in the Windward Islands.[121] This suggests that, beyond the personal acrimony, the split reflected a fundamental difference in outlook between the two former colonial administrators, along with Béhague, and the two metropolitan bureaucrats. Neither differences in professional background nor clashes of personality, however, provide a satisfactory explanation for the division between the king's commissioners. Montdenoix and Linger's supposed opposition to the proclamation of 29 September was expressed only after the deliberations with the governor general; there is no evidence that they had disagreed previously with the commissioners' unified stance on national authority and the rule of law. Why did these two king's commissioners abandon liberal principles and give unqualified support to the holders of executive power? The answer lies in two crises that emphasized the dangers of patriot-incited insubordination and rebellion.

The first crisis was the mutiny aboard the *Embuscade*. Armed with thirty-two 12-pounder cannon, and manned by a crew of nearly two hundred, the frigate was a powerful weapon and, like all ships of the French Navy, a potent symbol of metropolitan authority. Thus its defection could threaten control of the colonies by those who claimed to represent the nation. There had been signs of trouble before the mutiny. Béhague reported that on 30 May sailors from *Embuscade* and *Ferme* had brawled with other sailors at Fort-Royal.[122] Both Commodore Girardin and the *Ferme*'s captain, the chevalier de Rivière, suspected that "ill-intentioned men" ashore sought to subvert naval crews and destroy their discipline.[123] In September Captain Orléans received orders to pick up Montdenoix and Linger at Basse-Terre and take them to Sainte-Lucie. Shortly after getting under way from Fort-Royal, however, *Embuscade*'s crew insisted instead on sailing for France.[124] The declaration that the crew signed at the time of the mutiny, and that they delivered to authorities when *Embuscade* arrived at the Île-d'Aix off France's west coast, demonstrated that revolutionary propaganda had influenced the sailors.[125] In France the vicomte d'Orléans insisted that too much time in contact with the shore had allowed patriots at Fort-Royal to seduce and corrupt a crew that previously had been loyal and disciplined.[126]

The *Embuscade*'s mutiny shocked Montdenoix and Linger. What might happen if other crews followed this example? In their reports, they urged the minister to punish the mutineers in order to prevent a similar debacle.[127] To maintain order and subordination in the rest of the naval station, Montdenoix and Linger issued a proclamation, reading it aloud before the assembled ships' companies of *Ferme* and *Eole* on 4 October. This proclamation portrayed the mutiny on the *Embuscade* as a criminal challenge to national authority and warned that the nation would punish similar disobedience. The commissioners believed most sailors and soldiers remained loyal; they directed these warnings particularly at those who sought to incite revolt. Treason would not be forgiven, however, and the proclamation concluded that the men must obey the commissioners as the representatives of the Nation, the Law, and the King.[128] This proclamation demonstrates the continuing struggle over communications, with the commissioners seeking to neutralize patriot subversion with a counter-message. It also suggests that the mutiny drove Montdenoix and Linger towards Béhague's view that executive authority must be upheld at all costs.

News of a second, even more frightening crisis reached Martinique a month after *Embuscade*'s crew defied their commander. The slave gangs of Saint-Domingue's northern plain had massacred whites and burned plantations in a massive revolt, beginning in August, and Governor General Blanchelande appealed to Béhague for ships, troops, and munitions.[129] This was the worst disaster any white colonist or administrator could imagine. It had come to Saint-Domingue only months after patriots and rebel troops had driven Blanchelande from Port-au-Prince, a sequence of events that seemed to validate Clugny's suspicions of Basse-Terre's patriots. Could radicals' defiance of executive authority and their efforts to undermine military subordination lead to slave revolt in the Windward Islands? The news from Saint-Domingue, arriving on the eve of the deliberations at Fort-Royal,[130] escalated fears of patriot communications and convinced Montdenoix and Linger to break with their colleagues.

The liberal revolution's failure in the Windward Islands was further demonstrated in the colonial reaction to two laws delivered to the governor general and the remaining king's commissioners on 24 November. The first was the National Assembly's decree of 24 September, which overturned its earlier decree of 15 May 1791 granting political rights to some free men of colour. In May the majority of deputies in Paris had approved a text that confirmed slavery but decreed that *gens de couleur* born of a free mother and a free father be admitted to parish or colonial assemblies if they met other criteria. This resolution was a victory for French abolitionists, who had championed the cause of free men of colour, but representatives of the colonies opposed it bitterly.[131] Yet in September, days before the National Constituent Assembly adjourned to make way for the new Legislative Assembly created by the constitution of 1791, the deputies reversed their position. The new decree stated that colonial assemblies would make all laws concerning "the status of non-free persons and the political status of men of colour and free Negroes."[132] According to Montdenoix and Linger, communication of the new law was timely, given recent news from Saint-Domingue: whites at Croix-des-Bouquets, seeking protection from the slave revolt, had entered a "concordat" with free men of colour by which they recognized their rights according to the decree of 15 May. Martinique's *gens de couleur* learned of this concordat and assembled to oppose the limitation of their rights. To stop these dangerous "pretensions," Montdenoix and Linger issued a proclamation to announce the decree of 24 September. The governor general also appealed to the men of colour, and they returned to submission.[133] This support from Béhague and the two commissioners for the colonial status quo, and their previous silence regarding the decree of 15 May, casts doubt on their enthusiasm for the liberal revolutionary script.

Planters seized the opportunity provided by the decree of 24 September to regulate racial status themselves and to affirm the legitimacy of political bodies they controlled. On 20 December Guadeloupe's colonial assembly voted to name six commissioners who, with others from Martinique, Sainte-Lucie, and Tobago, would form a general congress at Fort-Royal to prepare a constitution for the colonies of the Windward Islands. This constitution would fix the political existence of *gens de couleur libres*. The assembly ordered one thousand copies of this *arrêté* to be printed and posted in all parishes, so that the free men of colour would know the colony's benevolent dispositions towards them and appreciate the benefits of submission to the *grands Blancs*.[134] Planters wanted to control the status of *gens de couleur* and to keep them as allies against *petit-Blanc* patriots, whom they intended to exclude from political power. In a subsequent *arrêté* that formalized the project to create a general congress, Guadeloupe's assembly declared itself a "constituent assembly," which would give way to another legislature only after it had presented the articles of a new constitution to the king and National Assembly.[135] Thus planters would continue to control the colonial assembly while their representatives prepared a constitution intended to perpetuate that control. On 22 December Guadeloupe's assembly sent an address of thanks and devotion to the king that included the statement, "The representatives of this important colony are the true organs of all colonists."[136] The reassertion of this claim, previously refuted by the king's commissioners, was further evidence of the liberal revolution's failure in the Windward Islands.

The second law delivered to Martinique on 24 November was the National Assembly's amnesty for all offences related to the revolution. In announcing the law, Montdenoix and Linger declared that all investigations into the origins and authors of the colony's troubles would cease.[137] Yet on 2 December thirty-eight soldiers of the Forez Regiment, imprisoned after the insurrection of 15 September, were embarked for transport to France. Six civilians were also embarked for deportation. Four were residents of Pointe-à-Pitre, implicated as instigators of the troop insurrection, while the other two were men from Martinique accused of complicity in the murders of coloured militia at Saint-Pierre in June 1790. Montdenoix and Linger objected to the deportation of these civilians, which was contrary to the National Assembly's amnesty. Béhague responded that these were necessary security measures. The six men were dangerous and suspect individuals, he told the commissioners, who might cause the greatest disorders. In particular they might spread "exaggerated pretensions" among the *gens de couleur*, who were in a state of considerable excitement due to news of the Concordat of

Croix-des-Bouquets, and thus bring about the same calamities that afflicted Saint-Domingue. Montdenoix and Linger acquiesced.[138] Factional vengeance had trumped the rule of law, and the belief that unquestioned authority and complete control of communications were necessary had prevailed over the introduction of a new liberal order.

At the end of 1791 metropolitan control over the Windward Islands seemed restored, yet contention over the location of legitimate authority remained stronger than ever. Both sides in Martinique's civil war had appealed to the nation; yet the deportation of rebel troops and the formation of committees to investigate the past seemed to favour the planters. The strategy of the king's commissioners to achieve reconciliation through the strict and impartial rule of law had failed to win over Martinique's patriots. Worse, Guadeloupe's colonial assembly had defied the commissioners over the appointment of *ordonnateur* Masse, over the formation of antipatriot federations, and over the breaking of Basse-Terre's municipality; in effect, the assembly challenged the commissioners' claim to represent the nation's will. Montdenoix and Linger backed Clugny and Béhague, rather than their colleagues Lacoste and Magnytôt, because they feared that patriot communications would destroy military discipline and incite rebellion – not merely among soldiers or *petits Blancs*, but also among the slaves. Thus they abandoned liberal principles in favour of strengthened executive authority. The colonial assemblies' formation of the general congress in December demonstrated the planters' determination to resist metropolitan-imposed reform. Yet if they took advantage of ambiguity within the revolutionary script to assert their authority, rejecting the liberal revolution made it increasingly difficult for colonial assemblies to square their opposition to local patriots with claims of loyalty to the nation. When the Legislative Assembly sent a new expedition in 1792 to enforce its will on the colonies, Martinique and Guadeloupe took the drastic step of repudiating metropolitan authority and embracing royalist counter-revolution.

5 Counter-Revolution: The Revolt of Martinique and Guadeloupe, 1792–1793

In December 1792 Captain Jean-Baptiste-Raymond Lacrosse, commanding the frigate *Félicité*, arrived in the Windward Islands to bring official news of the French Republic's declaration to the colonies. He discovered that the planters of Martinique and Guadeloupe were in rebellion against metropolitan authority under the banner of the old monarchy. This revolt had begun in September when Martinique's colonial assembly and Governor General Béhague refused to allow a convoy from France to land its troops. The convoy also carried new governors and three civil commissioners sent to execute the Law of 4 April granting equality to free men of colour. Officers of the naval station supported Martinique's authorities: their warships chased the convoy from the Windward Islands. The white *fleur-de-lis* of the Bourbon monarchy replaced the tricolour of the Revolution in Guadeloupe and Martinique, and the colonial assemblies in both colonies arrested those who challenged their actions. News of this counter-revolution had not reached France when Lacrosse sailed, and his lone frigate was outnumbered by the rebel men-of-war. Yet with the support of patriots in British Dominica and Sainte-Lucie, Lacrosse conducted a vigorous political campaign against the royalists. His communications undermined the authority of Béhague and the colonial assemblies, persuaded the majority of colonists to withdraw their support or to oppose the rebels, and in January 1793 brought about the triumph of the Republic in the Windward Islands.

Communications from France provoked revolt in Martinique and Guadeloupe and brought about its collapse. If the rebellion reflected the planters' secessionist sentiments, it also expressed their growing antipathy to metropolitan revolutionaries who seemed bent on destroying racial hierarchy and, ultimately, abolishing slavery itself. With the Law of 4 April 1792, the Legislative Assembly ended the local autonomy over racial status, prescribed full political rights for free men of colour, and ordered new elections in which they would participate. Yet resistance to racial equality was not the only cause for rebellion. The Law of 4 April also called for the dispatch of new troops to ensure its execution, and the colonial assemblies feared that the intervention of radical soldiers from France would put them at the mercy of their patriot enemies. Béhague, Governor d'Arrot of Guadeloupe, and the commanders of the naval station took leading roles in the rebellion. If personal loyalty or class interest shaped their royalism, these officers supported the revolt in a desperate bid to shore up the legitimacy of executive power in the colonies. Rumours from Paris provided naval officers and colonial assemblies with a counter-revolutionary script, while subsequent news of the Republic's declaration and the victory of French armies in Europe crippled the revolt. Captain Lacrosse arrived not only as the bearer of this news but also as the Republic's representative, successfully asserting its claim to authority and discrediting the rebels' claims to legitimacy. Thus just as the rebellion arose from the bitter factional struggle among white colonists, Lacrosse's triumph demonstrated how the French revolutionary script, and the related dilemma regarding legitimate authority, helped to shape this struggle.

I The Law of 4 April (January–July 1792)

The origin of the colonies' revolt against metropolitan authority can be detected in the split between the four king's commissioners in November 1791, which demonstrated colonial defiance of the new revolutionary order and its repercussions in Paris. Béhague, Linger, and Montdenoix knew that Lacoste and Magnytôt would denounce them upon their return to France, but such denunciations had greater impact given the more radical character of the Legislative Assembly and a change in royal ministers in the spring of 1792. Lacoste and Magnytôt landed at La Rochelle on 17 January 1792 and reported their quarrel with Béhague and Clugny, the schism with their colleagues, and the seizure of the commission's records.[1] On 3 February the Legislative Assembly received a deputation of soldiers from the Aunis Regiment, who had been deported from Sainte-Lucie, claiming that they were victims of despotism. They denounced Governor General Béhague for his treatment of troops of the Martinique Regiment, "sent to France in irons for embracing the Revolution," and for ordering their own deportation because they had supported Saint-Lucie's patriots.[2] On 22 February the assembly ordered the minister of marine, Antoine-François Bertrand de Molleville, to report within eight days on the civil commissioners' mission to the Windward Islands.[3] This order demonstrated distrust of the minister and followed a roll-call vote on 1 February in which a narrow majority of the assembly rejected a motion of non-confidence. On 10 March Bertrand de Molleville submitted his resignation, and on 15 March Louis XVI accepted the nomination of Lacoste to replace him as minister of marine.[4] Lacoste thus became part of the so-called "Patriot Ministry," including Charles Dumouriez as minister of foreign affairs and Jean-Marie Roland as minister of the interior. Jacques-Pierre Brissot and other radical deputies had demanded this ministry as part of their campaign for war against the Austrian emperor.[5] For Béhague and the colonial assemblies in Martinique and Guadeloupe, Lacoste's appointment foreshadowed the metropolitan government's hostility.

The rising influence of the "Brissotins" in the Legislative Assembly had a more direct effect on colonial policy. Brissot and many of his allies were outspoken opponents of slavery and advocates of free-coloured equality. Given the continuing slave insurrection in Saint-Domingue, these deputies argued that granting political rights to *gens de couleur* was the only way to conserve the colony for France. Armand-Guy Kersaint articulated this position to the assembly on 28 March.[6] Rather than simply a tactical measure to obtain the loyalty of this intermediate class, Kersaint hoped that granting equal rights to free men of colour would be the first step towards ending colonial slavery. The decree adopted by the assembly on 28 March made no mention of such hopes, insisting instead that the slave revolt in Saint-Domingue had been the result of a conspiracy against the nation, which had profited from divisions among colonists. To end this disunity, the assembly decreed: "The National Assembly recognizes and declares that men of colour and free Negroes must enjoy, as well as the white colonists, equality in political rights."[7]

The decree of 28 March ordered specific measures to achieve free-coloured equality and initiated the dispatch of new expeditions to the colonies.[8] Following the decree's publication, colonial assemblies and municipalities were to be re-elected but with full participation by those men of colour and free blacks who fulfilled the conditions prescribed by article 4 of the instructions of 28 March 1790 concerning age, property ownership, and residency; they were also to be eligible for all elected posts. This new decree asked the king to name civil commissioners, three for Saint-Domingue and three for the Windward Islands, to execute its provisions. It empowered them to pronounce the suspension and dissolution of existing colonial assemblies and to take any steps necessary to accelerate the convocation of parish assemblies. Moreover, the decree sought to ensure the commissioners troops loyal to the nation: it charged the executive power to send to the colonies an armed force composed largely of national guards. Once the new colonial assemblies were elected, they would express in the name of each colony views on the measures appropriate to its prosperity and happiness, conforming to the principles tying the colonies to metropolitan France. This decree was a direct repudiation of the general congress formed by the existing colonial assemblies in the Windward Islands.[9]

With Louis XVI's sanction, the decree became the Law of 4 April. The king's instructions of 17 June to Leroi de Fontigny, Lamarre, and Girault, the civil commissioners delegated to execute the law in the Windward Islands, demonstrated Lacoste's determination that the colonies would obey metropolitan authority as well as his continuing commitment to the liberal revolution. The commissioners needed to silence passions and rally spirits around the law. As organs of the law, however, "not only are the civil commissioners charged to make known to all the National Will; but, depositories of the most extensive powers, they must make it triumph over any resistance they might encounter."[10] Given the colonies' manifestation of dispositions favourable to free men of colour, the king presumed that according them equality in political rights should not lead to trouble; but colonists must comply with the law.

With preparations under way for a new expedition and the dispatch of the new civil commissioners to execute the Law of 4 April, the Legislative Assembly's colonial committee presented two reports that demonstrated growing suspicion of the governors and planters in the Windward Islands. This ran parallel to general suspicion of royal executive power and the rising tide of radicalism in France, which would overthrow the monarchy and the constitution of 1791 in August. The committee's reports also reflected the influence of patriot communications on metropolitan legislators. The report on Martinique, begun on 2 May by Goyn and concluded on 22 June by Queslin, praised the "party of Saint-Pierre" and criticized the colonial assembly, Vioménil, Damas, and Béhague.[11] Queslin's report on Guadeloupe, presented on 2 July, was even harsher in its assessment of Béhague and of Clugny. It charged the two governors with being part of a conspiracy, which included military officers, the colonial assemblies, and sovereign councils, to thwart "the establishment of the regenerative system" in the French colonies.[12] Following his report, Queslin presented two decree proposals to the assembly. The first condemned the federations organized at Sainte-Anne and at Basse-Terre in August 1791; overturned the colonial assembly's *arrêté* of September 1791 breaking Basse-Terre's municipality; and forbade any colonial assembly, administrative corps, or governor from deporting any citizen.[13] The second ordered the recall of Governor General Béhague, Governor Clugny, and *commandant-en-second* d'Arrot to account for their conduct to the Legislative Assembly.[14] The assembly's adoption of these decrees on 2 July represented Lacoste's revenge for the governors' defiance of the commission's authority in 1791. These two decrees clarified that new governors would now accompany the new commissioners and suggested that Béhague would be tried for treason upon his return.[15]

II Coloured Equality, Factional Strife, and Fear of Metropolitan Intervention (May–August 1792)

Martinique's colonial assembly reacted to news of the Law of 4 April, which reached the colony on 24 May, by insisting on its loyalty to metropolitan authority and its acceptance of equality for *gens de couleur*, but it also demonstrated its fear of receiving radical troops from France.[16] While assuring Béhague that the colonial assembly would conform to the sentiments of the nation and king, the assembly's *comité intermédiare* stated: "The favourable dispositions of the colonists of Martinique for the *gens de couleur libres* are too well known for you not to feel that the forces you announce are unnecessary and would find themselves much better directed if they were joined to those which the disastrous position of the colony of Saint-Domingue demand."[17] On 3 June the full colonial assembly made its formal response to the Law of 4 April, declaring that men of colour and free blacks would enjoy the same political rights as the white colonists of Martinique. It also agreed to give way to a new assembly. This change would not happen immediately, but in the meantime the assembly assured the *gens de couleur* that their rights had not been forgotten.

If this suggested stalling on forming parish assemblies and holding elections, the context in which the colonial assembly granted equality to free men of colour was even more revealing. The assembly stated that it existed by virtue of the decree of 8 March 1790 on the one hand, "and according to the free wishes of its constituents on the other hand."[18] That decree and the instructions of 28 March 1790 had designated it as a constituent assembly for the colony's internal legislation, and the assembly claimed that all subsequent decrees had confirmed its character. Thus, in accepting the Law of 4 April, the colonial assembly asserted its claim to local legislative autonomy. Just as bourgeois radicals and popular militants challenged the new liberal order in France by insisting that the nation's will was not confined to the National Assembly, planters in the colonies also used the ambiguity of popular sovereignty to resist the liberal revolution.

Béhague disagreed with the colonial assembly's intention to delay implementing the provisions of the Law of 4 April, suggesting that elections be held within fifteen days.[19] He reminded the deputies that the eligibility of free men of colour to vote in primary assemblies was to be based on article 4 of the instructions of 28 March 1790, meaning that only a fraction could participate. Only the colony's full compliance with the law could prevent internal dissension and the dispatch of new troops.[20] Moreover, Béhague disputed the colonial assembly's claim that the decree of 8 March 1790 had given it the right to establish the colony's internal regime. The subsequent decree of 24 September 1791 had allowed the colonial assembly only to legislate on free-coloured status provisionally, he insisted, and the Law of 4 April invited the new assembly only to propose the colony's opinion on the constitution, legislation, and administration.[21] Despite the *de facto* alliance between the governor general and the colonial assembly, they had distinctly different outlooks. Béhague was a metropolitan aristocrat, not a colonial planter; more important, though, he was the king's representative. He recognized that the colonial assembly's pretensions to popular sovereignty were as much of a challenge to executive power as were the claims of Saint-Pierre's radicals.

Clugny's response to news of the Law of 4 April, like Béhague's, was that Guadeloupe should demonstrate immediate compliance to try to head off the dispatch of new troops.[22] This did not mean that he welcomed the new law. In convoking Guadeloupe's colonial assembly for 4 June, Clugny summoned its deputies to save the colony from the danger posed by metropolitan legislation.[23] Nevertheless, the governor stressed that the colony must obey the law and demonstrate its loyalty to metropolitan authority to prevent it from sending military force.[24] The colonial assembly duly ordered that the Law of 4 April be executed in Guadeloupe. Clugny's subsequent instructions to municipal officers made clear that not all *gens de couleur* would participate in the elections. Beyond the qualifications required by the instructions of 28 March 1790, men of colour would need to prove their free status by producing their legal *titres d'affranchissements* before municipal officers could include them in the list of active citizens in each parish.[25] Many deputies in Paris had intended the new law to eliminate racial hierarchy, as well as to save the colonies from slave revolt, but Guadeloupe's *grands Blancs* hoped that the colony might comply while maintaining the status quo. The colonial assembly and governor convoked the primary assemblies, admitting those few *gens de couleur* who could meet all criteria, which then proceeded to elect a new colonial assembly.[26]

Reaction to the Legislative Assembly's decree of 28 March 1792 from the Windward Islands' representatives in Paris sheds further light on the colonies' attitudes. Romain Lacaze, Arthur Dillon, Dubuc-Duferret, Bellevue-Blanchetière, and eight others signed a protest asking the king to use his veto to prevent the decree from becoming law. These *grands Blancs* claimed that all had been peaceful in Saint-Domingue until the decree of 15 May 1791 first awarded political rights to freedmen in the colonies. How could the assembly place the other colonies in similar danger in order to grant the *gens de couleur* "a purely conventional right," they asked, while recognizing the necessity of hiding "the natural right of all men to liberty" from the slaves? They argued that the new decree would not only undermine slavery but also incite slave revolt.[27] Yet equally important to the colonies' resistance to the decree was fear of the troops sent to enforce it. Troops require subordination and military spirit, which the authors of the protest stated were difficult to maintain in the colonies, and soldiers deployed in colonial towns would be seduced by the "bad subjects" who inhabited them. Martinique's *comité intermédiare* expressed this same fear that new troops from France would join hands with local patriots and put planters at their mercy. In a letter to Dubuc-Duferret in July 1792, its members claimed that the colony's free men of colour had stood firm with the colonists in opposing new troubles occasioned by the arrival of the Law of 4 April. They justified the colonial assembly's decision not to convoke the primary assemblies but to await the arrival of the civil commissioners, because Martinique remained deeply divided. Above all, however, the members of the *comité intermédiare* wanted their agent in Paris to persuade the minister to prevent the departure of the announced troops.[28]

The colonial assembly's fear of new troops from France not only reflected anxiety over the continuing factional conflict but also over the messages of the French Revolution. In February 1792 worrying rumours circulated in Martinique regarding colonists wearing white cockades to provoke patriots, violent plots by groups of *gens de couleur*, machinations by "enemies of order," and even plans to take Béhague prisoner.[29] In May the arrival of two merchant ships from France – the *Pavillon National* at Fort-Royal and the *Paix* at Saint-Pierre – triggered disorder. The *Paix*'s officers reportedly insulted the commander of the corvette *Maréchal de Castries*. When Captain Villevielle of the *Didon* arrested a merchant officer, whom he accused of singing the *Ça Ira* with marked enthusiasm, an angry mob demanded the prisoner's release. An officer of the town's garrison deployed his troops, but some of the soldiers complained: "They want us to cut throats for a song that all the universe sings, that they sang before the King."[30] Even as these events unfolded at Saint-Pierre, troops at Fort-Royal appeared to be on the verge of open rebellion. Villevielle claimed that the *Paix* and the *Pavillon National* also instigated this unrest in which revolutionary symbols and practices were prominent. On 3 June soldiers of the Turenne regiment in garrison at Fort-Bourbon broke ranks and demanded that Colonel Fressinaux provide them with a national flag, as well as powder and ball. When he refused, they descended to the harbour, seeking a tricolour flag from one of the merchant ships. Upon returning to Fort-Bourbon, the rebels tried to close the drawbridge and sang a version of *Ça ira*, threatening to hang the colonel. Fressinaux told the soldiers that he would resign his command unless they recognized legitimate authority. On 5 June a deputation offered the colonel the garrison's repentance, but further signs of sedition convinced Béhague to replace Fort-Bourbon's garrison and deport the rebel soldiers.[31] For Martinique's planters and military officers, this episode echoed the mutiny of September 1790 and left no doubt on how the colony's troops would react to the arrival of even more politicized metropolitan soldiers.

Anxiety regarding the radicalization of white troops was linked to fears of coloured equality and slave revolt. On 17 August Commandant Mollerat informed Béhague that he had imprisoned a free man of colour, Couton, who became insolent when his requested permission to travel to Sainte-Lucie referred to him as "*nommé*," the traditional title for non-whites, rather than as "*sieur*." A deputation of eight other men of colour then demanded that Mollerat release Couton and punish the clerk for his provocation to the "New French Citizens."[32] The governor general dismissed their protest over the title "*nommé*," since this was also applied to white soldiers (although not their officers), and insisted that such titles would be maintained until a new law changed them. This legalism demonstrated determination to uphold racial hierarchy.[33] The coloured protestors were not cowed. They told Mollerat that the clerk had offended their whole class, that it was not prideful to demand something that the new decree would soon accord to all men of colour when it was promulgated, and that they deserved the title "*sieur*" because they served the colony not as paid soldiers but as *gardes Bourgeois*.[34] Béhague demanded obedience from the free men of colour, insisting nothing would change in their status until the new law's execution, but suggested that these protestors had been influenced by white agitators.[35] The tension between the governor general's professed affection for free men of colour and his resistance to accepting their equality had been a constant theme in the statements of *grands Blancs* since 1789. If an alliance between planters and *gens de couleurs* against *petit-Blanc* patriots still existed in 1792, anticipation of the Law of 4 April exposed how tenuous were the common interests on which this was based. Béhague's main concern, however, was that the free-coloured pretensions would encourage similar pretensions, and therefore defiance, among white troops and naval seamen.[36] Given the terrifying example of Saint-Domingue, where military mutiny preceded a massive slave uprising, the governor general and the colonial assemblies were desperate to isolate the Windward Islands from radical troops and revolutionary messages.[37]

III Counter-Revolution (September–November 1792)

On the morning of 16 September a convoy of ten ships escorted by the French frigate *Sémillante* appeared off Martinique's southwest coast. These ships carried not only troops but also the three civil commissioners delegated to execute the Law of 4 April, as well as General Donatien-Marie-Joseph de Vimeur Rochambeau, son of the American War hero, named to replace Béhague as governor general of the Windward Islands. The new governors for Sainte-Lucie and Guadeloupe, Generals Ricard and Georges-Henri-Victor Collot, accompanied Rochambeau. As the ships passed Diamant, Eustache de Bruix, the convoy commander and *Sémillante*'s captain, launched a boat and sent one of his officers ashore to investigate the situation in the colony.[38] Lieutenant Gaillard spoke with a dozen inhabitants who told him that the convoy was expected but that the colony would refuse to receive either its national guards or the new governors.[39] Despite this ominous report, Bruix led the ships into Fort-Royal Bay. He recognized the 74-gun *Ferme* and the frigate *Calypso* at anchor; the two men-of-war appeared ready to sail at a moment's notice. The entire convoy was inside the bay when the sloop *Ballon* approached the *Sémillante* carrying three deputies with a letter from the colonial assembly. They invited the civil commissioners to come ashore so that they could see with their own eyes evidence of Martinique's submission to the law. The letter asked that they take no action until they had done so; it also insisted that the convoy not communicate with the shore.[40]

Two days before the convoy appeared, Béhague's proclamation of 14 September revealed the determination of Martinique's authorities to isolate the colony from revolutionary communications. The proclamation announced that the governor general's orders to arm the batteries guarding Fort Royal Bay, justified by news of France's declaration of war on Austria,[41] were being used as a pretext by ill-intentioned men who sought to provoke insurrection among troops, naval crews, men of colour, and even slaves. Hordes of vagabonds gathered at Grenada and Dominica, poised to descend on Martinique with fire and iron, awaiting only the explosion that internal sedition was preparing. Therefore, the proclamation insisted, apprehensions were justified in a colony loyal to the nation, law, and king, with no intention of rejecting the National Assembly's decrees. The governor general's duty – to protect colonists' property and to preserve Martinique for France – was clear. To carry out this duty, Béhague demanded complete and unquestioning obedience to his authority.[42] The message to the civil commissioners aboard *Sémillante* also implied that colonial authority was equivalent to national authority.

Following the delivery of this message, there were further signs that those who controlled Martinique planned to defy metropolitan authority. Rochambeau announced that he would deliver the National Assembly's decree and the king's orders personally to Béhague and the colonial assembly the following day. He wrote to Béhague, informing him of the decree replacing him as governor general, entrusting the letter to his aide-de-camp, Daucourt, who went ashore as night fell on 16 September. When Daucourt tried to see Béhague in Fort-Royal, he was arrested and informed that Béhague was also under arrest and could speak to no one. Some colonists told Daucourt that the convoy's arrival had spread fear in Martinique. Although he was released on the morning of 17 September, none of his captors would accept the package for Béhague; instead, they sent him back to the *Sémillante*.[43] Before he arrived, Bruix had summoned the captains of the convoy's ships aboard the frigate for a conference. The master of the *Père de Famille* reported that a pilot had come aboard during the night and told him of rumours in the colony that the convoy was full of brigands who had taken the ships by force in French ports and had come to burn Martinique and put its inhabitants to the sword. Even more ominous for Bruix was the silence from the naval station's commander: the chevalier de Rivière had not communicated with him, thus treating him as an enemy rather than a fellow French officer. Even as the boat carrying Rochambeau's aide-de-camp drew near, Bruix observed the *Calypso* raising her topsails.[44]

Convinced that *Calypso*'s intentions were hostile, Bruix signalled the convoy to get under way. His apprehension that an armed confrontation might be imminent only increased with the appearance of the corvette *Maréchal de Castries* entering the bay from the south.[45] Even as the two warships bore down on the *Sémillante*, the civil commissioners prepared a letter to Martinique's colonial assembly expressing shock at the hostile reception given to the convoy and warning its members that their defiance constituted treason.[46] The commissioners had no opportunity to deliver this document, but the clash of competing claims to legitimate authority was demonstrated starkly in the ensuing exchange between the opposing frigates. The *Calypso* overtook the *Sémillante* and closed to within range of a pistol shot with all its cannon run out. Bruix had also cleared for action but did not run out his guns so that no suggestion could be made of aggression on his part. Someone in the *Calypso*, possibly Mallevault himself, hailed Bruix across the water and ordered him to leave. The *Calypso* ignored Bruix's request to deliver a letter from the king's commissioners and acknowledged the authority only of the colonial assembly, Béhague, and Rivière.[47] The naval station's warships, *Calypso*, *Maréchal de Castries*, and *Ferme*, chased the convoy away from Martinique, thus initiating civil war within the French Navy as well as the colony's rebellion against metropolitan government.

Bruix signalled the convoy's ships to steer west and ordered the commander of the *flûte Bienvenue*, Lieutenant La Carrière, to lead them to Saint-Domingue.[48] The civil commissioners countermanded Bruix's orders and required him to lead the convoy to Guadeloupe where they would try to carry out their mission.[49] During the night of 17–18 september, however, the frigate became separated from *Bienvenue* and the other ships. The commissioners denied General Collot's request to be put ashore at Guadeloupe and asked Bruix to gather the scattered convoy. Assuming the missing ships had steered west, Bruix sought them off Puerto Rico where he hoped he could also take on water.[50] With only a few days of food remaining, Bruix abandoned his search on 23 September and sailed for Cap Français, Saint-Domingue, where the *Sémillante* anchored on 28 September.[51] By 1 October all but three ships of the convoy had also arrived at Le Cap;[52] it would be more than three weeks until Bruix and the civil commissioners learned their fate. Separated from the convoy, the *Bienvenue*, the *Balthazar*, and the *St Nicolas* had anchored at St Kitts.[53] Here they were discovered by the *Calypso*, the *Maréchal de Castries*, and the *Ballon*, all flying the *fleur-de-lis* of the old monarchy rather than the national flag. Although La Carrière claimed protection from the colony's governor, Mallevault seized the three transports.[54] British outrage at this attack reflected the drastic nature of Mallevault's actions and of the rebellion itself.[55]

At Cap Français the civil commissioners received news not only of *Bienvenue*'s capture but also the extent of the counter-revolution in the Windward Islands. Jacques-Jérémie Paige, a merchant from Saint-Pierre, arrived at Le Cap in mid-October. He reported to Leger-Félicité Sonthonax, Étienne Polverel, and Jean-Antoine Ailhaud, the civil commissioners delegated to execute the Law of 4 April in Saint-Domingue. Paige informed them that the *Calypso* and the *Maréchal de Castries* had anchored at Basse-Terre, where their crews helped to arrest the town's patriots. On 30 September the white flag of the old monarchy was raised on the two warships and over the forts at Basse-Terre and at Pointe-à-Pitre. Meanwhile, the population at Saint-Pierre feared that sailors and men of colour were preparing to arrest patriots there following the arrival of the *Ferme*. Citizens took up arms during the night of 3–4 October, prompting Commandant Mollerat to try to reassure them that the rumours were unfounded. When Paige had learned of events at Guadeloupe, however, he left Saint-Pierre on a vessel bound for Dominica, sailing from there to Saint-Domingue.[56]

Shortly after reading Paige's declarations, Leroi de Fontigny, Lamarre, and Girault received an even more detailed report that emphasized the rebels' attacks on revolutionary symbols as well their oppression of patriots. Henry, a deputy from Sainte-Lucie, had witnessed the royalist *coup d'état* at Guadeloupe. On 25 September a counter-revolutionary federation took place at Basse-Terre. When Mallevault struck the tricolour and raised the *fleur-de-lis* on *Calypso*, the fort followed his example. Meanwhile, Guadeloupe's colonial assembly decreed a general round-up of patriots. It also proclaimed René-Marie d'Arrot as governor of

Guadeloupe to formally replace Clugny, who had died in July. D'Arrot then issued orders for the colony to fly the white flag and to display only the white cockade and for municipalities to arrest citizens designated in a proscription list drawn up by the colonial assembly. Henry observed planters and men of colour insult, intimidate, and assault patriots. He claimed that these actions occurred in an atmosphere of festivity: "In almost every part of town, the planters held celebrations to mark their counter-revolution and in their orgies shot and burned the National Flag."[57]

Henry also reported opposition to the rebellion. Guadeloupe's assembly had named deputies to go to Martinique to seal the colonies' alliance. Saint-Lucie rejected the counter-revolutionary coalition, however, and refused to receive Governor Gimat when he came from Fort-Royal to "plant the standard of rebellion." Tobago and Marie-Galante also resisted joining the revolt, and hundreds of patriots had fled from Guadeloupe and Saint-Pierre to Dominica, St Vincent, and Grenada. Even as this exodus was occurring, the counter-revolutionaries vainly attempted to control news of their rebellion by forbidding coastal trading vessels from reporting on Guadeloupe's political affairs. "It would have been better," Henry stated, "to order the captains to lay down their tongues before departure."[58] Merchant ships anchored at Pointe-à-Pitre and Basse-Terre resisted flying the white flag, but their masters, like Guadeloupe's resident merchants, tried to conceal their opposition to the revolt in order to protect their commercial interests. Meanwhile the planters in Guadeloupe and Martinique portrayed themselves as the generous supporters of free men of colour. Henry suggested, however, that *gens de couleur* realized that the *grands Blancs* would take away the advantages they had gained under the constitution. Mulattos and free blacks were among those who had fled to Dominica and, he claimed, the freedmen of Sainte-Lucie and Marie-Galante supported the patriots.[59]

Following their own flight from the Windward Islands, Henry's report confirmed for the civil commissioners that Martinique and Guadeloupe were now in open revolt against metropolitan authority. The colony of Sainte-Lucie, given its continued loyalty and its strategically important windward position, seemed vital to any plan for defeating the rebellion. Leroi de Fontigny, Lamarre, and Girault appealed to Sonthonax, Polverel, and Ailhaud to send naval forces from Saint-Domingue to St Kitts immediately. These ships would pick up the convoy's troops stranded there and carry them to Sainte-Lucie, where they would strengthen its garrison and make that colony into a patriot bastion until new forces arrived from France.[60] Along with patriot accounts of events, the civil commissioners obtained a copy of an address from Martinique's colonial assembly to the king, providing categorical proof of the rebellion's expressly royalist and counter-revolutionary nature.[61]

This address, dated 8 October 1792, sought to justify Martinique's refusal to admit the convoy, or to receive either the civil commissioners or Rochambeau, and it began with a declaration of loyalty to the king. The assembly stated that just when the decree of 24 September 1791 seemed, at last, to have fixed the bases of the colonial regime, that of 28 March 1792 overturned this accomplishment. Nevertheless, Martinique's deputies sanctioned the new decree and accepted its dispositions regarding free men of colour. The assembly had hoped that the representations of colonists and of commerce alike would prevent the French government from sending troops and placing the colony in grave danger. Yet the colony's enemies were determined. It was painful to disobey those who claimed to be the king's servants, but the colony was forced to save itself: "These acts of conservation will be painted, Sire, as an act of rebellion; but we are convinced that Your Majesty will not consider it thus; we have not resisted your will, we have followed it."[62] Thus the assembly portrayed its refusal to receive the troops, king's commissioners, or new governor general as an act of loyalty.

Beyond its statements of self-justification reflecting objections to the sending of troops, the colonial assembly's address also demonstrates that communications from Europe encouraged rebellion in the Windward Islands and provided a counter-revolutionary script to justify repelling the convoy after the fact. News of the events of 10 August in Paris, where the assault on the Tuileries Palace overthrew the monarchy, had reached Martinique on 23 September.[63] The colonial assembly was aware not only of Louis XVI's suspension but also of the preparations to elect a new National Convention. In this context, the address of 8 October sought to represent the assembly's defiance of metropolitan authority as principled royalism. Subsequent news from France led Martinique's assembly to believe that the Austrian and Prussian armies were on the verge of restoring the king to his full powers. Thus the colony's actions could be justified as part of a larger counter-revolutionary crusade.[64]

As in 1789, news of the second revolution in France reached the Windward Islands initially in unverified and incomplete fragments or rumours. Henry's report to the civil commissioners, who had received no dispatches regarding the collapse of the constitution in Paris, stated that the catalyst for the royalist uprising in Guadeloupe was English newspapers, which had arrived at Montserrat by packet boat from London in August. A free-coloured trader, whose schooner visited the British island, informed D'Arrot and Guadeloupe's assembly that the English papers announced that a counter-revolution had occurred in France, that the Austrian and Prussian armies were at the gates of Paris, and that the National Assembly had been destroyed: "It was on the basis of such suspect and bizarre news that they have delivered themselves to all the vexations that they have committed."[65] Such news did not come only from the English press. An open letter attributed to Romain Lacaze had been printed and circulated at Basse-Terre. Dated from Paris, 4 to 12 September, the letter presented a tableau of catastrophe. It referred to the Prussian invasion, decrees by the assembly ordering house-to-house searches for suspects, and the September Massacres in the prisons of Paris. The letter included extracts from the revolutionary newspapers *La gazette nationale de France* and *La chronique de Paris* as evidence not only of the success of foreign armies but also of the imminent possibility of a counter-revolution. In this context, Lacaze counselled his fellow colonists to take advantage of their separation from the troubled mother country. Moreover, he warned them that, although Lacoste was no longer minister of marine, Magnytôt remained in the marine bureau and had drafted secret instructions for the new civil commissioners.[66] Lacaze did not clarify what these sinister instructions were, but many planters would have assumed that they included the abolition of slavery.

It was not only *grands Blancs* who received communications from France. In a letter from Paris, dated 15 August, La Villegégu gave a detailed account of the 10 August insurrection to a fellow Saint-Pierre merchant, Vasselin, from the perspective of a committed radical. He referred to the supposed conspiracy of the "Austrian Committee," the provincial *fédérés*' fraternization with the Parisian national guard, Paris's ultimatum to the Assembly, and the attack on the Tuileries as one who had been privy to the insurgents' plans. This revolution also had tremendous significance for the colonies. La Villegégu claimed that the events of 10 August would ensure that the "monster Béhague" and his "satellites in the colonial assembly" would be held accountable for their crimes, and he urged his colleague and all of Saint-Pierre's citizens to show them no mercy.[67] For the patriots, as for their enemies, the rumours from France raised the stakes in the colonial struggle.

Immediately after repelling the convoy both Béhague and the colonial assemblies had sought to avoid the appearance of an irreparable break with metropolitan France. In a letter to the minister of marine of 20 September, Béhague did not conceal what had occurred but defended his actions as necessary to save Martinique. Claiming that his men recognized within the convoy mutineers and arsonists who had been deported from the colony, and whom the brigands of Saint-Pierre were preparing to join, Béhague stated that Rochambeau, Bruix, and the civil commissioners "unmasked themselves" with their inexorable insistence on landing the troops. Martinique was in danger, and so the ships of the naval station repelled the convoy. He also claimed that pilots returning from the convoy's ships reported hearing their passengers say that they would seek reinforcements and then return to hang colonists and burn their plantations. He suggested that this threat implied an alliance with Saint-Domingue's insurgents.[68] On 23 September, following the arrival of the first official dispatches referring to the events of 10 August, Béhague and *ordonnateur* Petit de Viévigne wrote to Gaspard Monge to acknowledge his appointment as the new minister of marine.[69] Two days later Béhague wrote again to Monge, informing him that the naval station's warships had returned and reporting that Rochambeau's convoy had left the Windward Islands. He assured him that, "The colony, loyal to the Nation, the Law, and the King, appears to all of us more than ever perfectly calm in these principles."[70]

Similarly, the colonial assemblies of Martinique and Guadeloupe sought initially to assure metropolitan commerce that nothing had occurred to interrupt trade. In a letter of 19 September to merchants in France's seaports, Martinique's *comité intermédiaire* stated that the convoy's arrival three days earlier had threatened the tranquillity necessary for commerce. Although Martinique had accepted the decree of 28 March 1792, the new civil commissioners demanded that troops be put ashore, which, the letter alleged, alarmed citizens of all colours who feared violence and the colony's total subversion. The *comité intermédiaire* insisted that Martinique's colonists had always submitted to metropolitan laws and were always attentive to the interests of metropolitan commerce. Saint-Domingue had been overwhelmed, but the colonists of Martinique would preserve their island and its resources for France.[71] Guadeloupe's colonial assembly produced a similar letter to metropolitan commerce, claiming that the colony's actions had averted the kind of catastrophe suffered by Saint-Domingue. In these dangerous circumstances Guadeloupe supported the "firm and wise steps taken by Martinique." The assembly insisted, however, that this had not altered the colony's loyalty to France.[72]

These protestations of loyalty following the explicit defiance of the agents of metropolitan government seem disingenuous efforts to mask rebellion. Paige told the civil commissioners that the letter from Martinique's assembly to metropolitan commerce contradicted Béhague's proclamation of 14 September: repelling the convoy was not a sudden decision, as the assembly alleged, because work to arm the batteries had begun the month before.[73] Henry's report stated that Guadeloupe's letter revealed the fear of dire reprisals against the rebellious colony felt by the "more sound part of the planters," who hoped that metropolitan commerce, mindful of its own interests, might temper national vengeance.[74] Both letters suggested uncertainty, even fear, about the drastic step the colonies had taken and what would happen next. News from France regarding the fall of the monarchy, and possible counter-revolution, was unexpected and unconfirmed. In addition, as Henry pointed out, divisions existed among the rebels.

The comte de Béhague's statement of loyalty to Monge was certainly insincere and intended to gain time. Shortly after the naval station chased Rochambeau's convoy from Martinique, Béhague sent his nephew, the baron de Constant, to Europe on a secret mission. He ordered Constant to obtain information on the situation in France and to seek direction from the king himself. If this proved impossible, he was to go to London and make contact with representatives of Louis XVI's brothers, the leading *émigrés* and titular heads of the counter-revolution, to obtain instructions. Béhague told his nephew that if the princes wanted him to remain in the Windward Islands, they needed to send him not only warships and troops but also new powers. He also ordered Constant to approach the British government and seek guarantees of protection for colonial products.[75] Thus Béhague was fully prepared to commit himself and the colonies to the royal cause. Yet he was also a career servant of the French state and the representative of executive power in the Windward Islands. He had quarrelled with Martinique's planters in June over their refusal to convoke the colony's primary assemblies and their pretensions to legislative authority. His equivocal letters to the minister in September 1792 reflect acute anxiety over the decision to defy metropolitan government. The colonial assembly had arrested Béhague during the night of 16–17 September and, therefore, he did not personally give the orders to repel the convoy.[76]

In October, having been released by the assembly, Béhague advised caution and opposed calls to raise the *fleur-de-lis* in Martinique despite its appearance in Guadeloupe. Constant had not returned and the rumours of a counter-revolution in France remained unconfirmed. Declaring for the old monarchy while Sainte-Lucie held itself aloof from the other colonies would be reckless. Nonetheless the colonial assembly, which Béhague claimed was now dominated entirely by Louis-François Dubuc, ordered the white flag to be flown, decreed that the primary assemblies (with the participation of free men of colour) would meet on 15 October to elect a new assembly, and composed its declaration of loyalty to the king on 8 October.[77] The assembly named Dubuc as Martinique's representative to Louis XVI; he left for London on 15 November with Guadeloupe's representative, the baron de Clairfontaine.[78] Dubuc was committed less to the cause of the Bourbon monarchy than to the preservation of slavery and the protection of the planters' interests, and to achieve these goals he would negotiate secretly with the British government over its possible occupation of Martinique.

Officers of the Windward Islands' naval station played crucial roles in the rebellion, but important distinctions and divisions existed between them as well. Captain Mallevault had initiated counter-revolution at Guadeloupe by raising the *fleur-de-lis* on his own initiative and then had captured the *Bienvenue*. In his own account of these events, he asserted the legitimacy of royal over national authority. When *Calypso*, *Maréchal-de-Castries*, and *Ballon* arrived at St Kitts, he claimed that the British recognized the authority of the white flag, "the true flag of France," and, in his letter to the island's governor, Mallevault insisted that *Bienvenue* and the other ships from the convoy must lower the national flag and submit to his orders because the king of France had at last taken back the rights seized from him so unjustly.[79] Yet Mallevault was a Creole, born and raised in Martinique, and his close identification with its planters shaped his royalism. He was highly critical of the revolution for undermining racial hierarchy; he believed that only the vigilance of the chevalier de Rivière had saved the colony from Saint-Domingue's fate. In a memoir written from La Force prison in Paris, where he was incarcerated after travelling to France in 1802, Mallevault sought to justify his conduct in 1792–3. In the context of the dilemma regarding the location of legitimate authority, he made clear that Martinique had first claim on his loyalty.[80]

Most of Rivière's officers had been born in France, however, and hostility to colonial autonomy was part of their self-image as servants of the state. Captain Villevielle of the Didon and the chevalier de Valous, one of his lieutenants, were intransigent royalists who never concealed their antipathy for the revolution. If these aristocratic officers blamed the patriots for disorder in the colonies, they also criticized the planters. In his memoirs, Valous observed that the colonists' prosperity bred indolence and cowardice. Like the *Didon*'s captain, he expressed sympathy for men of colour and praised their loyalty.[81] More important, Villevielle and Valous were harsh critics of Béhague, whom they described as scheming, despotic, and frustratingly lenient towards mutineers and subversives. Valous claimed that the governor general had changed in 1792 as a result of the revolution's progress and became more harmful than useful.[82] Villevielle denounced Béhague for proclaiming an oath of loyalty to the nation and king to be taken by military officers and colonists on 15 July, a policy Villevielle termed "gangrenous and Jacobin."[83]

Not all naval officers serving in the Windward Islands supported the revolt. Lieutenant Pierre Duval, commanding the corvette *Perdrix*, refused orders from D'Arrot at Pointe-à-Pitre on 1 October to fly the white flag. *Perdrix* left Guadeloupe and sailed for France instead, reaching La Rochelle on 5 November. In the report he delivered to the National Convention on 8 November, which was the deputies' first news of the colonial rebellion, Duval stated: "I left my *patrie* when liberty was beginning to be born there; I upheld it as much as I could, with my crew, amidst the aristocracy which surrounded us. I saw deployed at Guadeloupe the standard of revolt."[84] A division between Duval and other naval officers was apparent at the end of July during efforts to salvage the *Didon*, which had struck a rock and sank while entering Pointe-à-Pitre's roadstead. After *Didon*'s midshipmen attacked insubordinate carpenters from the *Perdrix*, Duval defended his crew's conduct.[85] Valous saw this as evidence of contemptible weakness.[86] Therefore Duval's loyalty to metropolitan authority may have reflected a more liberal attitude towards discipline and authority aboard ship. *Sous-lieutenant* Robert de Rougemont, commander of the sloop *Ballon*, also returned to France. Despite his shock at the colonies' preparations for war with France, Rougemont claimed that lack of supplies in *Ballon* and the surveillance of other officers prevented him from leaving in September. Forced to hoist the *fleur-de-lis* and to join in operations against the *Bienvenue*, he did not manage to escape until 3 December. The delay proved fatal. The Revolutionary Tribunal at Brest condemned him to death on 9 February 1794 as an accomplice to Rivière's treason.[87]

As head of the naval station, the chevalier de Rivière was the rebellion's key military commander. If Martinique's colonial assembly decided to repel Rochambeau's convoy, it was Rivière, not Béhague, who gave the orders to the station's men-of-war to chase it from the Windward Islands, and it was he who subsequently authorized those warships to raise the white flag of the Bourbons. There is no doubt that Rivière was a royalist, but his support for the colonies' revolt was driven less by loyalty to the king than by an overriding concern to uphold executive authority. In September 1790 Rivière was at Brest, when he received orders to sail for the Caribbean, but the *Ferme*'s crew refused to weigh anchor until they were given two months' advance pay. He and his officers might have settled the dispute had the *Léopard* 74 not arrived from Saint-Domingue, touching off a mutiny that spread throughout the French fleet. The *Léopard*'s crew had taken over this ship of the line and rescued the rebel Saint Marc Assembly, even as troops loyal to Saint-Domingue's governor general had marched against it. The mutineers and their passengers claimed that the navy was poised to crush patriots in the colonies; Brest's municipality prohibited ships from sailing and ordered their commanders to submit their correspondence for examination.[88] This defiance of the minister of marine's orders delayed the *Ferme*'s departure and, more significant, it demonstrated the impotence of executive power in the face of local manifestations of popular sovereignty.

His instructions to obey orders from the governor general at Martinique fit with Rivière's conviction that executive authority, from which the navy derived its own authority, must be defended as law.[89] Throughout his tenure as commander of the naval station, he supported the colonial assembly and governor general against the colony's patriots and enforced military discipline; moreover, he sought to identify executive authority with legality.[90] Rivière continued regular correspondence with the minister of marine even after his ships had repelled the convoy. In his letter of 20 October he acknowledged the arrival of the *Espiegle*, which had delivered official news of the events of 10 August, and expressed his need for naval stores and for sailors to replace those who were sick, had deserted, or been deported to France. He also referred to Duval's departure but treated the matter as one of simple disobedience to his orders.[91] In a subsequent letter of 19 November, Rivière reported the capture of the *Bienvenue*, making no attempt to conceal that his ships had flown the white flag. He also included a routine request for new supplies of rations.[92] These dispatches in the midst of rebellion reflect both Rivière's personal insistence on the maintenance of executive authority and the larger importance of claims of legitimacy to the entire colonial struggle. Rivière even wrote to Lacrosse to inform him that, in the sea around the Windward Islands, the station commander was the only legal authority.[93]

IV Captain Lacrosse and the Revolt's Collapse
(October 1792–January 1793)

It was Captain Lacrosse, another naval officer, who defeated the revolt of Martinique and Guadeloupe. Jean-Baptiste-Raymond Lacrosse was a noble and a professional from the old navy's *Grand Corps*, like Rivière, but Monge chose him for a special mission because of his "known principles" and loyalty to the revolution.[94] The minister's formal instructions of 3 October ordered Lacrosse to depart from Brest in command of the frigate *Félicité* and proceed to the Windward Islands, where he would deliver official dispatches announcing the National Convention's proclamation of the French Republic on 22 September. The instructions also required Lacrosse to distribute various extracts from newspapers and copies of the convention's decrees in the colonies.[95] After carrying out these orders in the Windward Islands, he was then to bring news of the Republic to Saint-Domingue. Lacrosse accepted this mission reluctantly. Beyond concern for his health, he had grave reservations regarding the political sentiments of the other officers serving in the Caribbean.[96] Writing before his departure, and thus before Duval returned to France in November with news of the rebellion, Lacrosse assured Monge that "despite the counter-revolution which parades openly at Martinique," his conduct would be firm and frank: "I am proud to be the first who will speak to the royalists, in the name of the French people, the republican language."[97] Thus Lacrosse was to be the bearer of a revised revolutionary script. He had no illusions that colonial authorities would welcome this, however, and he recognized that his mission was dangerous.[98] Beyond his commitment to the revolution, Lacrosse understood the political importance of the Law of 4 April and recognized that he must convince the *gens de couleur* that only the Republic would guarantee their rights. "If the men of colour know the truth," he told Monge, "our object will be fulfilled."[99]

The *Félicité* sailed from Brest on 24 October. Lacrosse's apprehensions about the opposition he would face were confirmed when he reached the Windward Islands. The frigate made landfall at Martinique on 30 November and dawn on 1 December found her off Saint-Pierre. Lacrosse sent Devers, his principal civil aide, and one of his officers, Ensign Lepeltier, ashore to determine the situation in the colony;

specifically, he wanted to know if it had received the convoy, if it had installed Rochambeau as governor general, and whether the residents of Saint-Pierre and Fort-Royal supported the revolution of 10 August.[100] As their boat entered Saint-Pierre's roadstead, Devers was shocked to see that anchored merchant ships flew the white flag of the old monarchy. Initially, Lepeltier believed that the white portion simply obscured the red and blue of the national flag. They landed in a small cove some distance from the town and spoke to fishermen, who told them that Martinique and Guadeloupe had thrown off the metropolitan yoke. Furthermore, the fishermen claimed, Mallevault had burned his tricolour flag and pennant under the gallows, royalists at Guadeloupe had led a donkey through the streets dragging a national flag and cockade from its tail, counter-revolutionaries at Saint-Pierre had assassinated a Capuchin *curé* in his presbytery, and the *Maréchal de Castries*'s commander had ordered two of his mates shot for attempted mutiny. "In a word," Devers reported, "from General Béhague to the last officer, this was only a hoard of brigands and barbarians."[101] Devers and Lepeltier also learned that Sainte-Lucie had refused to join the revolt, its colonial assembly having declared the island independent of the authorities in Martinique, and that the citizens of Marie-Galante had taken up arms, driven out the commandant, and sworn loyalty to the nation. Lacrosse held a council of war with his officers, informing them that he intended to send a letter to Béhague before leaving Martinique to make contact with patriot refugees elsewhere. In this message, Lacrosse informed Béhague of his mission, expressed shock at seeing white flags flying from ships and forts, and learning that the colony had not received General Rochambeau's convoy. He attached news of the Republic's success to the letter and stated that he assumed Béhague had been misled regarding the events of 10 August.[102] One of the *Félicité*'s boats carried Lepeltier to the *Ballon*, anchored near Saint-Pierre's sea front. The sloop's commander signed for the packages addressed to Béhague, confirmed the extent of the revolt, and warned Lepeltier not to go ashore. In Rougemont's own account, he claimed that he also warned Lacrosse not to enter Fort-Royal Bay, where warships of the naval station would certainly attack his frigate.[103]

Lacrosse then sailed for the British island of Dominica, where he believed many patriots had taken refuge from the counter-revolution. On the morning of 2 December the *Félicité* arrived at the port of Roseau, and Lacrosse asked permission to anchor in the harbour. Immediately boats and canoes, filled with refugees from French colonies, surrounded the frigate. These patriots embraced her captain when he went ashore and confirmed the news of the rebellion at Martinique. Lacrosse paid a formal visit to Governor Bruce, who granted him permission to remain in Roseau for three days to carry out repairs. Bruce observed that the British government had given no orders to recognize the French Republic and asked the captain to allow only a few of his men to come ashore. Lacrosse then met with French refugees and informed them of his orders, reassured them of the Republic's successes, and inspired them to be ready to rise against the agents of the old executive power.[104] They told him that Marie-Galante and Sainte-Lucie remained loyal but that these islands would certainly succumb to the rebels if they received no assistance; Lacrosse decided that he would go to Saint-Lucie to hold it for the Republic and use it as his base to defeat the rebellion. On 3 December Bruce announced that the *Félicité* must leave immediately. Lacrosse protested, swearing that none of his crew had gone ashore, but the governor was adamant.[105] Therefore on 4 December Lacrosse prepared to make sail, with fifty patriot volunteers added to his crew. Letters from patriots in Martinique had warned him that both the *Calypso* and the *Ferme* had sailed with the intention of catching him at anchor. Lacrosse changed course during the night to evade his pursuers and, passing to leeward of Martinique, reached Sainte-Lucie on 5 December.[106]

Even before leaving Dominica, Lacrosse had initiated a propaganda campaign against the royalist rebellion. Devers remained in the British colony with orders to supervise the printing and distribution of a broadsheet entitled *The Last Means of Reconciliation between the Mother Country and the Rebel Colonies*. In this circular Lacrosse described his mission as bringing the Windward Islands means to cement the ties of fraternity among all Frenchmen. He came to open the eyes of those who had been deceived and to make his colonial brothers cherish "a revolution which the perfidy of the executive power had necessitated on 10 August." Yet upon arriving in Martinique, he saw the standard of revolt flying. Therefore he came to Dominica to speak, for the last time, the words of peace from a *patrie* that would pardon error, if colonists repented immediately, but that would punish rebellion.[107] Lacrosse warned that the powerful squadron en route to the colonies would crush those who did not submit to the nation's will. In fact, no such force was coming. Lacrosse told the minister that if he had even one ship of the line, the rebels would not dare to oppose him, but he recognized that it was unlikely France could send one.[108] In the broadsheet, however, he promised to come to the rescue of brothers oppressed by rogues and he exhorted patriots to resist the counter-revolution. With its multiple references to the law, *The Last Means of Reconciliation* identified the Republic as the true source of legitimate authority, thus seeking to undermine the rebels' claims to legitimacy in the king's name. Lacrosse also appealed to the colonists' interests. If the planters withdrew their support for the revolt, their property would be "under the safeguard of the nation." Moreover, he assured them that the Republic had no intention of abolishing slavery. Lacrosse linked this promise to preserve slavery with the guarantee that the Republic would ensure free-coloured equality but insisted that both were at risk if planters and *gens de couleur* backed the rebels. Lacrosse's propaganda played on the same fears that his enemies had invoked: rather than protecting the colonies from the upheaval Saint-Domingue experienced, he suggested that the rebellion against metropolitan authority would itself incite slave revolt.[109]

The appeal to colonial self-interest was accompanied by the communication of powerful news and symbolism. Along with *The Last Means of Reconciliation*, Devers printed copies of a pamphlet that included descriptions of the French army's defeat of the foreign invaders; the National Convention's decrees, from the declaration of the Republic to the order for the king to stand trial; a description of the king's imprisonment; and the complete lyrics to *La Marseillaise*.[110] This material confirmed the fall of the monarchy and it discredited rumours of Prussian and Austrian victories or of a counter-revolution in France; therefore, it represented a serious blow to the colonial assemblies. Devers used a network of patriot traders and shippers to distribute the pamphlet and Lacrosse's broadsheet not only to the rebel colonies but also to any neutral islands where patriots had taken refuge. "I believe this has already had an effect," he wrote to the minister on 9 December, "because I've learned that, despite Béhague's orders, several parishes in Martinique have again worn the national cockade and the tricolour flag is newly flown on the forts."[111]

Sainte-Lucie-la-Fidèle became Lacrosse's headquarters and the centre of his struggle against royalism in the Windward Islands. He reported that the *Félicité*'s arrival had created a sensation among the colony's patriots.[112] Lacrosse preached unity and fraternity, particularly between whites and free men of colour, and persuaded white patriots to admit *gens de couleur* to their popular society. He lost no opportunity to instruct and enlighten the "new citizens," praising a coloured patriot, Genty, for his assistance in these efforts. His role as bearer of the new republican script also included overseeing the planting of a liberty tree and encouraging the singing of *La Marseillaise*.[113] Lacrosse denounced Governor Gimat, who had joined the royalists in Martinique, but commended Sainte-Lucie's assembly, which renamed the colony *La Fidèle* and the port of Castries *Félicitéville*. He sent Captain Kermené of the Thirty-First Regiment to take command of the patriots resisting the aristocrats in Marie-Galante and he ordered a schooner to cruise to windward of Martinique, where it could warn merchant vessels coming from France of the rebellion. From Sainte-Lucie Lacrosse also attempted to coordinate the actions of other representatives of metropolitan authority in the West Indies.[114]

In particular, Lacrosse wrote to General Rochambeau at Saint-Domingue to request naval reinforcements and to report his success in undermining the rebellion. The main purpose of his letter, however, was to assert his authority as the Republic's representative in the Windward Islands.[115] Lacrosse also communicated this message to the British naval commander at St Kitts. He reminded him of the good will that existed between England and France, denouncing those royalist French officers who had led Martinique and Guadeloupe into rebellion against the mother country. Sainte-Lucie remained loyal and thus had become the capital of the French colonies: "It has recognized me as the only legitimate commander of the naval forces of the French Republic in the Windward Islands. It is in this capacity that I have the honour of writing to inform you."[116] Asserting this claim to legitimate authority was central to his campaign. With only the *Félicité*, Lacrosse could not face the combined forces of the rebel naval station in battle. As he put it to the minister, "Persuasion and instruction: such are the arms that I employ."[117]

Martinique's colonial assembly recognized the threat from Lacrosse's communications and his presence in the Windward Islands, and countered with its own propaganda. On 13 December it sought to justify its defiance of metropolitan authority in deliberations printed and distributed as a proclamation by Béhague. Since the revolution's outbreak, colonists had struggled against anarchy. The colonial assembly had submitted to decrees sanctioned by the king and, according to this proclamation, welcomed those benefiting free men of colour. Although it had received commissioners and troops sent to restore order in March 1791, it repelled those that arrived in September because they would have destroyed the colony. This brought new dangers, however, and in their letter of 8 October to the king, the colonists manifested their true loyalty. Considering the *Félicité*'s arrival in the Windward Islands, and considering the overthrow of the government and the instability in France, the safety of the colony demanded extraordinary measures: "The colonists of Martinique, expressing their unanimous view by the organ of their representatives, and persisting in the declaration of sentiments contained in their letter to the King, declare that, authorized by the Princes, brothers of the King, they will keep the white flag and will receive neither laws nor new forces from the metropole until peace; that in awaiting it, they will govern themselves according to the regime and the laws currently existing in the colony, and place themselves under the protection of the coalition powers."[118] Competing claims to legitimate authority were at the heart of the revolutionary struggle. It is significant that this proclamation justified the colonial assembly's authority and its actions on the grounds that it was the colonists' representative body: both sides invoked popular sovereignty to legitimize their position. Beyond committing Martinique to the royalist cause, the proclamation also reflected the planters' long-standing resistance to metropolitan reforms and it suggested Dubuc's hopes for British occupation. It also warned men of colour, whose status was "fixed immutably" by the assembly's *arrêtés*, that their fate would follow events: *gens de couleur* must be loyal or risk losing the equality the colony had bestowed. Finally, the assembly announced that it would open all of the colony's ports to foreign trade.

Lacrosse responded to this manifesto by Martinique's assembly with a second broadsheet, *Observations on Béhague's Proclamation, Addressed by Citizen Lacrosse to All His Fellow Citizens*, dated 25 December and printed in Saint-Lucie. In it he denounced members of the assembly as counter-revolutionaries but also as enemies of the colony's true interests. His mission, he stated, was to enlighten citizens misled by false news and to combat errors like those propagated in Béhague's proclamation of 13 December. The broadsheet portrayed the rebellion's leaders not only as oppressors of patriots but also as hypocrites who intended to plunder the colonies for their own benefit. Even more strongly than the first broadsheet, this one appealed to free men of colour. Lacrosse urged the new citizens to withdraw their support from the rebels, who would bring back racial segregation, and to rally to the Republic, which would guarantee their equality:

> The law that you do not recognize is entirely in your favour. The republican government is yours, it is that of the people; already its reign has begun in loyal Sainte-Lucie; come and see, rejoin your brothers who have

become ours, make only one family, sitting at the same table, sharing our pleasures together as we do our work and dangers in war. Do you prefer the old regime where a line of humiliating demarcation separated you from whites? You will put yourself again in this same dependence, in serving men who want to recognize only the law of a despot to impose it in their turn.[119]

This message proved highly effective because it invoked the long-standing resentment of racial hierarchy as well as the *grands Blancs'* reluctance to accept equality for *gens de couleur*. Like all of Lacrosse's propaganda, this broadsheet also attacked the rebellion's legitimacy. It challenged the colonial assembly's claim that his mission was perfidious by including Monge's instructions of 3 October, contrasting these with the rebels' actions. Lacrosse made all of his threats and promises in the name of the Republic, which he identified with the law, and he signed himself as "the legitimate commander of the Republic's naval forces in the Windward Islands."

If Lacrosse's own broadsheets were the most powerful salvos in the propaganda campaign against the rebellion, the work of Devers and of Sainte-Lucie's patriots supplemented and reinforced them. From Dominica, Devers reported on 14 December that the papers he had circulated had caused a schism among the rebels. Both patriots and counter-revolutionaries were fleeing Martinique, where violence was about to explode. Devers also claimed that this material had caused great agitation in Guadeloupe. Citizens of colour had donned the tricolour, taken up arms, and attempted to seize the fort at Basse-Terre. Although this project had been betrayed, the *gens de couleur* retained their weapons and increased their determination as their ranks swelled. "I dare almost to assure," Devers wrote to the minister, "that before eight days the revolution will be operated in the island of Guadeloupe."[120] He encouraged this outcome with a new circular of his own, *Response to the arrêté of the So-Called Intermediary Committee of Guadeloupe's Colonial Assembly, Dated 10 December 1792, Addressed to All French Patriots*, printed at Roseau. The enemies of the French nation, this broadsheet proclaimed, sought to stop the march of liberty. Guadeloupe's *comité intermédiare* called Captain Lacrosse's news of the Republic's success false and outlawed his *Last Means of Reconciliation*. Did this committee and the colony's compliant governor truly believe that they could thus stop progress and prevent the return of colonists' brothers? Devers asked rhetorically. All of France would rise against the guilty, although a prompt return to obedience might diminish the mother country's vengeance against her rebel children.[121]

A printed extract from the proceedings of Sainte-Lucie's colonial assembly, dated 22 December, delivered a similar message. In response to the claims by Guadeloupe's *comité intermédiare*, Sainte-Lucie's deputies proclaimed the truth of Lacrosse's news and the beneficence of his mission to return the colonists to obedience to the nation. They also affirmed the legitimacy of his authority both as agent of the Republic and as an officer of the French Navy, including the text of his commission as ship captain in their proceedings. The deputies urged all citizens in the colonies to answer the fraternal invitation made in *Last Means of Reconciliation*. They denounced, to the National Convention and to all true Frenchmen, "the *comité intermédiare* of Guadeloupe's colonial assembly and the traitor René-Marie d'Arrot, so-called governor of Guadeloupe and its dependencies, as rebels to the nation and traitors to *la patrie*."[122]

The factional conflict in the Windward Islands had become part of the larger political and ideological struggle between revolution and counter-revolution, and both sides received emissaries from the embattled forces in Europe. Lacrosse reported that the rebels in Martinique and Guadeloupe were in contact with the Princes and that Sainte-Lucie's assembly had intercepted correspondence providing evidence of a conspiracy to give the colonies independence from France.[123] Similarly, Devers informed the minister that an *émigré* from Coblenz had arrived in Martinique, had been announced as the Princes' envoy, and had promised foreign troops and ships for the rebels.[124] This envoy was Cougnac-Myon, a surgeon born in La Rochelle who had lived in Saint-Domingue. In 1790 he had returned to France in the *Léopard*, one of the eighty-five deputies of the Saint-Marc Assembly, but switched from being a violent patriot to a royalist intriguer. In September 1792 the comte de Provence had named him commissioner to the colonies and ordered him to promise the planters free trade and the cancellation of their debts in return for holding the islands for the king.[125] He arrived in Martinique on 1 December and delivered the Princes' instructions to Béhague. Cougnac-Myon soon perceived that Lacrosse's presence and news of the Republic's success had shaken the planters and military officers, but he claimed that the rebellion's failure was due principally to Béhague's weakness and disloyalty to the royal cause. As an example, he cited the governor general's failure to inflict harsh punishment on mulattos who had raised the tricolour over Fort-Bourbon. Defending his reputation years later, Béhague insisted that until Cougnac-Myon's arrival he had commanded the loyalty of Martinique's free men of colour, on which the revolt depended. He claimed that a cabal affiliated with Dubuc had threatened him since October and then denounced him in January 1793 to seek clemency from the republicans.[126] Beyond Béhague's greater caution than the fervent royalists, or his opposition to Dubuc's secessionist schemes,[127] the rebel leaders' recriminations reflected the revolt's collapse.

Patriots in Guadeloupe rose up against the rebel administration on 18 December. Devers reported that Governor d'Arrot's orders to disarm free men of colour had been discovered and, as a result, the colony's *gens de couleur* had broken with the *grands Blancs* and donned the tricolour. Crews of merchantmen at Pointe-à-Pitre also displayed national flags and cockades defiantly.[128] According to one of the town's residents, Cadiot *fils*, news from France caused men of colour to take up arms and sailors in the harbour to declare their support for patriots. Planters and military officers holding the fort were determined to maintain the white flag, and Pointe-à-Pitre teetered on the brink of civil war. After tense negotiations, those holding the fort agreed to terms on 19 December. Pointe-à-Pitre's primary assembly then declared that *arrêtés* opening Guadeloupe's ports to foreign trade were henceforth annulled and that the colony would remain loyal to France under whatever government it had adopted.[129] On 21 December the commandant turned over control of the fort to the municipality, which struck the *fleur-de-lis* and hoisted the tricolour to cries of "*Vive la Nation!*" in the town and gun salutes in the harbour, replacing the garrison with a guard of patriots. Cadiot *fils* described these events as a revolution and predicted, "The national cockade will soon be adopted everywhere."[130] D'Arrot marched on 26 December at the head of regular troops and militia to suppress the patriot uprising, dispatching the *Calypso* and the armed schooner *Elisabeth* to Pointe-à-Pitre to support his assault. When a significant number of planters did not rally to his aid, however, the patriots counter-attacked and the governor retreated to Basse-Terre. Abandoned by the planters, and then by the navy, d'Arrot fled to St Kitts.[131]

Lacrosse's propaganda campaign had undermined and discredited the revolt. Following the patriot uprising at Pointe-à-Pitre, *petit-Blanc* refugees and coloured deserters from Rivière's ships made their way to Sainte-Lucie in increasing numbers. Learning of the uprising, Lacrosse sent his congratulations to the merchant seamen and encouraged their continuing support for the town's defiance.[132] He met with representatives of Pointe-à-Pitre's triumphant patriots and promised to come to Guadeloupe. On 5 January 1793 the *Félicité*, adorned with a huge wooden Liberty Bonnet atop her mainmast, dropped anchor at Pointe-à-Pitre. Her captain went ashore where, as another powerful expression of the new script he brought, he gave a fraternal kiss to a citizen of colour. The town's inhabitants welcomed Lacrosse enthusiastically as representative of the Republic.[133]

The revolt also collapsed in Martinique. Lacrosse's broadsheets had persuaded the colony's *gens de couleur* that the Republic would protect their interests and was the legitimate expression of the nation's will. In an address of 9 January Martinique's citizens of colour proclaimed that they were ready to swear obedience and loyalty to the Republic. They professed continued devotion to the colonial assembly but demanded that its members reject the counter-revolution that would bring metropolitan vengeance and threatened their equality: "We will always be ready to fight and, if necessary, to die with you for the defence of the laws, for the security of persons and property; but we do not want to sacrifice ourselves for a cause which is equally foreign to us, which is also contrary to our common interests; what would we gain from a counter-revolution, if it could take place, and why should we want this? You would see the return of the privileged orders, and we the humiliating demarcation which separated us from white citizens."[134] The defection of the *gens de couleur* was crucial. During the night of 10–11 January, Béhague left Fort-Royal for exile in the British colony of St Vincent. He insisted that the colonial assembly had forced him to leave so that it could recognize the Republic. On 13 January the assembly issued a proclamation blaming Béhague for the revolt and calling on *émigrés* to return to the colony.[135] Four days later the chevalier de Rivière sailed for Trinidad to put his men-of-war at the service of the king of Spain.[136]

Meanwhile the colonial assembly sent a deputation to Sainte-Lucie to present Lacrosse with a letter from its president, begging him to come to Martinique. The departure of Béhague and the naval station had removed the obstacles to his arrival and the colony needed his help: "Lead this misled family back to the mother-country it has always loved."[137] The deputation also brought an extract from the assembly's proceedings of 13 January, which claimed that Martinique had submitted to the National Assembly's decrees even though they were contrary to its habits and prejudices. Colonists had feared that liberty had gone too far, however, and that their property was at risk. Surrounded by dangers, they were susceptible to the lies of the counter-revolutionaries, whose support for arbitrary power had given colonists the hope of conserving their property: "Now, assured by Citizen Lacrosse, convinced that the metropolitan government represents the unity of wills and forces to protect them, the colonists of Martinique retake the cockade and flag of the Nation, and revoke the *arrêté* of 13 December."[138] Thus the colonial assembly submitted to metropolitan authority and sought clemency for its rebellion. Even in their submission, however, the planters' loyalty to the revolution remained qualified.

Captain Lacrosse's success in defeating the revolt of Martinique and Guadeloupe demonstrated the importance of communications to the colonial conflict – both in terms of information and of political culture – and it demonstrated the centrality of competing claims to legitimate authority. The news he brought from Europe exposed the rumours of counter-revolution as false, while his propaganda campaign discredited the rebels' claims to legitimacy: Lacrosse's broadsheets also undermined the rebels' support by persuading planters that continued defiance of metropolitan authority placed their property, including their slaves, at risk. Perhaps even more important, he convinced free men of colour, who had backed the rebellion, that only the Republic would guarantee them equality. The triumph of the Republic in the Windward Islands was, to a large degree, Lacrosse's victory as bearer of a more radical revolutionary script. Yet the colonial assemblies' submission and the coming of new governors did not end factional animosities. The planters' fears remained, and it was far from clear that *petit-Blanc* militants would defer to the authority of new agents of republican executive authority. Free men of colour were now equal, but the Republic maintained slavery. All of these tensions, moreover, would soon be played out under the shadow of international war.

6 The Slave-Holding Republic in the Windward Islands, 1793–1794

Captain Lacrosse's defeat of the royalist revolt allowed for the formation of republican regimes in Guadeloupe and Martinique in 1793. These appeared to consolidate victory for white patriots over their planter enemies, equality for free men of colour, and metropolitan control over the colonies. Lacrosse convoked Guadeloupe's primary assemblies to elect a new colonial assembly and created political clubs modelled on the popular societies of revolutionary France. At the beginning of February General Rochambeau arrived to assume his post as governor general. In Martinique Rochambeau suspended the colonial assembly and established surveillance committees in every town and parish. General Collot, who with Rochambeau had been driven from the Windward Islands in September 1792, also arrived in Guadeloupe in February 1793. Patriots accepted him as governor reluctantly, but Collot sought to unify the colony and to strengthen its defences. The French Republic had declared war on Great Britain, and internal strife compounded the danger from external enemies. In May 1793 Martinique's planters rose in rebellion and assisted a British attempt to capture the island. Rochambeau's troops beat back the invasion, but the governor general knew that he could not resist another attack without reinforcements from France. None appeared and a new attack began in February 1794. Rochambeau sustained a lengthy siege before surrendering Martinique to British commanders in March. Meanwhile, Guadeloupe experienced slave revolt. In April 1793 slaves at Trois-Rivières massacred white planters, claiming they were royalists plotting to arm slaves against the patriots. This episode escalated hostility between the colony's radicals and the moderates allied with Collot, who perceived himself to be attacked at every turn by a malicious faction, right up to the British conquest of Guadeloupe in April 1794.

The republican regimes in the Windward Islands were based on news and a revised revolutionary script from France. Their trials and subsequent collapse reflected further communications from Europe, as well as the intrinsic ambiguities of the Republic in the colonies. The representatives of metropolitan authority insisted that equality for free men of colour was a cornerstone of the new republican order, which also included the maintenance of slavery. Planters' feared that coloured equality would lead inevitably to slavery's abolition. *Petit-Blanc* patriots purported to uphold the rights of men of colour, but many resented the weakening of racial hierarchy. Rochambeau and Collot counted on the "new citizens" to defend the slave system and their authority. Yet the governors, royalist planters, white patriots, and even free men of colour encouraged black aspirations to liberty, at different times and in different ways, as a tactic in their struggles against political enemies. While the slave insurgents of Trois-Rivières presented their revolt in terms of loyalty to the Republic, the consensus that slavery was essential to the colonies remained. The conflicts among free colonists reflected not only anxiety about racial equality and slavery but also the continuing revolutionary dilemma regarding legitimate authority. News of the Republic strengthened the position of agents of the metropolitan state initially but it did not end contestation of colonial governors' authority. War did not cut all communications with Europe. Royalists encouraged planters to resist, colonists learned of the metropolitan struggles to control the Republic during 1793, and radicals asserted claims to popular sovereignty to challenge moderate rivals and attack executive authority. As in France, the coming of war raised the political and ideological stakes in the Windward Islands.

I Establishing Republican Regimes in Guadeloupe and Martinique (January–April 1793)

As soon as the *Félicité* anchored at Pointe-à-Pitre on 8 January 1793, Captain Lacrosse took steps to consolidate republican control. He ordered the town to declare that it no longer recognized the intermediate committee of the "monstrous" colonial assembly and insisted that the rural primary assemblies pronounce Guadeloupe's schism with rebel Martinique.[1] Lacrosse received an address of loyalty from Pointe-à-Pitre's citizens of colour, declaring they were bound to the French nation by "the bonds of the sweetest equality."[2] Although this reassurance was followed by confirmation that Fort Saint-Charles was secure and that a patriot municipality had returned to office in Basse-Terre,[3] it was not clear to Lacrosse whether his propaganda and Guadeloupe's example would produce the same result in Martinique.

Yet on 9 January Martinique's colonial assembly had revoked its royalist and separatist *arrêté* of 13 December 1792.[4] The assembly sent three of its members to deliver its formal submission to Captain Lacrosse at Sainte-Lucie. Since he was no longer there, Sainte-Lucie's patriot authorities arrested the deputation but sent its documents to Lacrosse at Pointe-à-Pitre.[5] These included a letter addressed to him by the president of Martinique's assembly, declaring that the colony awaited his arrival to swear its loyalty to metropolitan law.[6] They also included a proclamation to colonists who had fled the colony, inviting them to return and to unite under Lacrosse's leadership. It also suggested, however, that the assembly intended to maintain its local authority despite submitting to the Republic.[7] On 12 January Martinique's assembly formed a provisional executive council, which it claimed had been elected by the majority of inhabitants remaining in the colony. This council informed the minister of marine in Paris that the assembly had revoked its *arrêté* of 13 December and awaited the arrival of Captain Lacrosse and the National Convention's decrees. As well as portraying itself as the continuity of legal authority in Martinique, it blamed the revolt entirely on Béhague and the military officers.[8] It remained to be seen whether this denial of culpability would persuade the Republic's representatives to treat Martinique's planters with leniency.

While preparing to go to Martinique,[9] Lacrosse sought to republicanize political culture in Guadeloupe. Patriots now controlled the island, but he believed that he needed to educate colonists: "During this time, I did not cease to demonstrate to the inhabitants that their interests must tie them to the Revolution; they seemed of good will to me, returned from their errors; but I did not know yet the depth of the Créole character."[10] He formed a popular society, "The Friends of Equality," a club modelled on those in France, at Pointe-à-Pitre, while Devers established "The Society of Friends of the Republic" at Basse-Terre. Lacrosse intended these clubs to unite citizens and to propagate the "republican spirit." The colonists' political education also included elections and the formation of new representative bodies. Lacrosse had already convoked Guadeloupe's primary assemblies, according to the regulations of the Law of 4 April enfranchising free men of colour, to name deputies who would replace the colonial assembly. These deputies, including ten new citizens, gathered at Point-à-Pitre, constituting themselves on 24 January as the General and Extraordinary Commission of Guadeloupe.[11] The commission's first act was to nominate Lacrosse as the colony's provisional governor, a duty he accepted in the Republic's name.[12] Lacrosse then ordered the election of new municipalities, and a significant number of coloured citizens were elected to these new bodies.[13] He also encouraged measures to demonstrate that the Republic represented the interests of national commerce. The commission annulled the colonial assembly's *arrêté* opening all of Guadeloupe's ports to foreign ships, and it reimposed duties on rum and syrup exported by foreigners.[14] As the commission voted these measures, and as municipal elections took place, Lacrosse received a dispatch from Basse-Terre informing him that General Rochambeau had arrived in Guadeloupe.[15]

Donatien-Marie-Joseph de Vimeur Rochambeau, along with Generals Collot and Ricard and the civil commissioners, had been in Saint-domingue since September 1792. At Le Cap he received dispatches from Paris instructing him to take command of forces loyal to the Republic and defeat the revolt in the Windward Islands. Therefore Rochambeau and Ricard sailed from Saint-Domingue, reaching Basse-Terre on 29 January 1793.[16] Their unexpected appearance provoked suspicion. Lacrosse and the town's patriots placed enormous importance on determining the legitimacy of the general's authority, given that the Republic had been proclaimed in France only four months previously and the defeat of counter-revolution in the colonies remained uncertain. Along with his own orders, Rochambeau carried a letter from the minister of marine that required *Félicité*'s captain to support him.[17] These documents convinced Lacrosse, and he ordered the municipality to recognize Rochambeau as commander-in-chief of the Republic's military forces in the Windward Islands, in essence as governor general. The two officers planted a liberty tree together before sailing to Pointe-à-Pitre. There Rochambeau submitted a copy of his orders to the commission, along with a letter asserting the legitimacy of his authority in Guadeloupe.[18] He also named Lacrosse as the colony's provisional military commander, thus nullifying the commission's appointment of the naval officer as governor and underlining that it was Rochambeau who now spoke for the Republic in the colonies.[19]

With his authority recognized in Guadeloupe, Rochambeau turned to the greater task of restoring metropolitan control over Martinique. He sailed in *Félicité* to Saint-Pierre, where residents welcomed the

Republic's officers enthusiastically.[20] The frigate then carried Rochambeau to Fort-Royal, where he announced that he was changing the name of Martinique's capital to Fort-de-la-République.[21] Members of the colony's executive council received Rochambeau and Lacrosse with great displays of respect, but the new governor general refused to recognize the council or accept its invitation to present himself to the entire colonial assembly. Instead, on 4 February, he proclaimed the assembly's suspension and quashed the executive council, denouncing the latter as illegitimate and counter-revolutionary: only republican authority was legitimate. In this initial proclamation Rochambeau defined his government as both enforcing the law and implementing the French Revolution in Martinique.[22] As well as the imminent arrival of republican civil commissioners, he also invoked the forces that the Republic had put at his disposition to crush the revolt; given that he had not arrived at the head of any new metropolitan troops, it was crucial to remind colonists that such forces could appear at any moment. Severity in the proclamation, he reported to the minister, was the only means available to intimidate the rebels.[23]

Like Lacrosse in Guadeloupe, Rochambeau saw a connection between imposing revolutionary culture and thwarting opposition to metropolitan authority. As well as forming popular societies in Saint-Pierre and Fort-de-la-République,[24] he created new political bodies. In his proclamation of 8 February Rochambeau ordered the establishment of surveillance committees in Fort-de-la-République, in Saint-Pierre, and in every parish of the colony to exercise the functions of municipalities. He did not convoke Martinique's primary assemblies to elect these committees; instead, commissioner conciliators named by the governor general nominated the committees' members. Membership was open to all free men.[25] Rochambeau was determined that patriots control the surveillance committees, which would then support his government and fill the gap created by the destruction or neglect of revolutionary institutions. It would be dangerous, he told the minister, to convoke primary assemblies when "gangrenous men" dominated both Martinique's towns and countryside.[26] His reference to the traitors' overriding concern for their fortunes showed that he regarded the planters as counter-revolutionary and that he sought support from urban patriots and free men of colour.

Leborgne, an administrative officer who had accompanied Rochambeau from Le Cap, explained and defended the governor general's strategy to Paris. In Saint-Domingue the "ignorant fanatics," as he termed the *petits Blancs* there, were bitterly opposed to the Law of 4 April. He feared that Saint-Domingue would be lost to France if these "*Léopardins*" were not stopped, because they hoped for English occupation to overturn coloured equality. In the Windward Islands, however, it was the planters who cherished these hopes. According to Leborgne, Martinique's patriots had united with free men of colour in loyalty to metropolitan authority. Rochambeau named many coloured citizens to the surveillance committees, thus demonstrating that it was the Republic that ensured their rights, and he won the confidence of white patriots through the popular societies.[27] Not all of Martinique's colonists shared this confidence. The planter Aquart, writing to his son in New England, observed that Rochambeau was neither impressed that the colony had submitted to him peacefully nor interested in moving its inhabitants beyond party hatred; rather he had simply reversed the situation. If the colonial assembly's *arrêté* of 13 December had caused residents of Saint-Pierre to emigrate, now the colony's notables sought to flee from persecution at the hands of the patriots.[28] The establishment of unelected surveillance committees gave Martinique's new republican regime the appearance of a dictatorship.

During his initial weeks in Martinique Rochambeau also addressed the state of the colony's commerce and finances, and he informed foreign powers that the Republic now controlled the French Windward Islands.[29] The governor general had to borrow money from Saint-Pierre to pay troops, but this was no solution to the calamitous state of the colony's finances.[30] News from Europe made the need for tax revenue all the more urgent; indeed, it changed the situation facing the French colonies utterly. The Republic had declared war on Great Britain and Holland on 1 February. Announcing the outbreak of war in his proclamation of 14 March, Rochambeau declared that the *patrie* needed the colonists' courage and their unity.[31] Yet even as Rochambeau appealed to Martinique's inhabitants to forget their internal divisions, there were many who hoped that war would bring a British invasion to overthrow the republican regime.[32]

While Lacrosse was in Martinique supporting Rochambeau's installation as governor general, General Collot arrived in Guadeloupe and ended the patriot consensus on republican authority in that colony. Georges-Henri-Victor Collot did not leave Saint-Domingue with Rochambeau and Ricard but sailed separately in the schooner *Ardeur* that reached Basse-Terre on 4 February. When Mayor Pautrizel asked if he was invested with new powers, Collot acknowledged that he had no documents to demonstrate that the Republic had confirmed his appointment as governor – he had come to the Windward Islands on General Rochambeau's orders alone. Informed that the colony had entrusted its government provisionally to Captain Lacrosse, Collot replied that he would wait at Basse-Terre "as a simple citizen" until he received new orders from the legally constituted authorities.[33] Yet when Lacrosse returned to Guadeloupe, Collot announced that he had come to take up a post "delegated to me by the national will" and he asked the provisional governor to convoke the commission to rule definitively on his status.[34] This request initiated a new phase of political strife in Guadeloupe, pitting Collot against Lacrosse, planters wanting order against *petits Blancs* fearing despotism, and the conception of national authority invested in executive power against the ideology of revolutionary popular sovereignty embodied in direct democracy.

Lacrosse announced that he would turn over the government to Collot if the commission recognized the validity of the general's powers, but that if it did not he would continue to carry out the duties of governor, "according to the wishes of the entire colony."[35] It was clear that patriots did not trust the general.[36] In the report he presented eight months later to the National Convention in October 1793, Lacrosse stated explicitly that Guadeloupe's counter-revolutionaries wanted Collot as governor.[37] If Lacrosse explained the ensuing conflict in the colony as a struggle between patriots loyal to him and counter-revolutionaries who supported Collot, the general presented a different interpretation. In his account of his administration of Guadeloupe, published in 1795 in Philadelphia, Collot claimed that Rochambeau's arrival and then his own appearance had foiled a plot by intriguers to gain control of the colony. Lacrosse had contested the governors' authority, which thwarted his "ambitious pretension," and encouraged a radical faction whose hostility toward Collot brought Guadeloupe to the brink of disaster.[38]

Rochambeau responded by taking a firm stand on the legitimacy and superiority of executive authority in the colonies as emanating from that of metropolitan government. He told Lacrosse that he regarded the commission's nomination of him as governor to be illegal. Rochambeau had appointed Lacrosse as Guadeloupe's military commandant because General Collot was absent and because "I had the right as the legitimate delegate of the French Republic to replace him with someone possessing the necessary talents." In contrast, "Guadeloupe's extraordinary commission had named a governor irregularly, and had on this point evaded national sovereignty and the metropole's rights over the colonies."[39] Awaiting the result of the commission's determination, he told Lacrosse, "I hope they will conform to constitutional principles."[40] Ambiguity on the location and nature of authority, however, was intrinsic to the French revolutionary script.

Rochambeau's intervention caused Lacrosse to retreat; to assure the governor general that neither he nor the colony were guilty of usurpation; and to report that as soon as Collot submitted his powers and Rochambeau's orders, he had turned over Guadeloupe's government to him.[41] Lacrosse told members of the commission that failing to obey Rochambeau's orders would break his oath of loyalty to the Republic. He urged the commission to accept his resignation and recognize the governor general's authority rather than risk dividing republicans.[42] Rochambeau's support emboldened Collot to tell the commission's members that they did not have the right to judge whether to recognize him as governor. Collot insisted that the national will had sent him to Guadeloupe in the capacity of governor. This had been confirmed by the National Convention's decree of 21 September 1792, stating that all laws not abrogated were to be executed provisionally and all powers not revoked or suspended were to be maintained provisionally. Therefore, according to Collot, if the commission refused to recognize his powers, its members would be no better than the royalist rebels.[43] He could hardly have asserted his claim to legitimate authority more provocatively.

The commission's reluctance to recognize Collot as governor reflected pressure from those patriots who distrusted agents of executive authority and believed that popular will was superior to metropolitan orders.[44] This situation created a dilemma for Lacrosse between bowing to local claims of popular sovereignty and obeying orders from his superior.[45] The governor general was unsympathetic, however, and unrelenting in his insistence on the superiority of his authority over that of colonial representatives.[46] It was the news that France was at war, rather than Rochambeau's assertion of executive authority's legitimacy, that ended the stalemate. Citing these new circumstances, as well as the Convention's decree of 21 September 1792 now known officially, the commission formally recognized Collot as governor on 20 March.[47] Many patriots did not like the decision.[48] Caussade, one of Pointe-à-Pitre's municipal officers, wrote to his brother-in-law in Bordeaux that "the aristocrats have manifested joy at the change [in governors], which has pained the patriots so much more on the eve of war."[49]

Taking up his duties, Collot called for colonists to support him in preparing Guadeloupe's defences. In a speech before the commission on 23 March, Collot expressed confidence that discord would cease. Referring to "unprincipled men" who had deceived the people, however, Collot implicitly criticized the radicals who had sought to block his recognition as governor.[50] In a proclamation issued the same day, he declared that he had accepted the government of Guadeloupe to restore the tranquillity that "cruel divisions had banished." His mission was that of the French Revolution – to bring liberty and equality to the colony. The proclamation condemned the injustice of the colony's old social inequities; it promised careers open to talents; and it guaranteed that properties, "whatever their nature or type," would be respected. Collot thus reassured masters that slavery would not be abolished. The proclamation placed such reassurance in the context of the larger revolutionary struggle, including not only the Republic's war against international enemies but also political threats to representative democracy.[51] Collot was aware of the turmoil in metropolitan France, where popular militants challenged the National Convention, now bitterly divided between the radical Montagnards and the more moderate Girondins. If he sought to unite colonists against foreign enemies, he also perceived the radical patriots as a threat to Guadeloupe's republican regime.[52]

Collot believed that he must unite citizens to save the colony,[53] and this required communications to win hearts and minds. He undertook an inspection of Grande-Terre's parishes and portrayed his tour as evidence of reconciliation: residents of the countryside demonstrated their desire to forget conflicts with town dwellers, while club members showed similarly generous dispositions. Collot emphasized the loyalty shown by citizens of colour, appointing one of them as an aide-de-camp.[54] Residents in the parish of Morne-à-l'Eau beseeched the governor to extend clemency to *Sieur* Clugny, son of the late former governor and one of the revolt's leaders, who had been a fugitive since the rising of Pointe-à-Pitre. Hoping to convince planters of the new citizens' desire for reconciliation, and thus end their fear of racial equality, Collot visited Clugny's wife to inform her that he had granted her husband a pardon.[55] Collot presented Madame Clugny's tears of gratitude, and the virtuous conduct of the coloured citizens of Morne-à-l'Eau, as the presage of success in his efforts to unify the colony: significantly, his account to the commission was published in the colony's press.[56] Yet he also adopted punitive measures against *émigrés*. On 1 April the commissioners who had accompanied Collot on the inspection tour announced at Pointe-à-Pitre that all citizens who had attempted to leave the colony at a time of danger betrayed the *patrie,* and all who remained in enemy territories, now that hostilities had begun, would be treated as enemies themselves.[57] The governor himself identified the danger to Guadeloupe's republican regime from royalist intriguers such as Romain Lacaze, whose pamphlets circulated in the countryside.[58]

Collot's top priority was to defend Guadeloupe and he believed that it was essential to establish four new battalions of paid national guards. The governor told members of the commission on 5 April that a regular armed force would help to re-establish the order necessary to collect taxes.[59] He proposed granting property concessions to needy citizens in return for their enlistment and announced a voluntary subscription collected by the municipalities to help fund the battalions.[60] Two days later he was furious to discover that the commission had approved neither his measures against internal agitators nor the establishment of paid battalions.[61] In a pamphlet dated 8 April, Collot defended his proposal in terms of republican principles. Soldiers would defend liberty and protect property, he argued, only if they were committed to the public good and anticipated its rewards. Eager to merit public esteem, such troops would understand the governor's insistence that the country's safety depended on their submission to discipline and obedience to the law. This emphasis on discipline reflected not only Collot's outlook as a professional officer and agent of the metropolitan state but also a conception of republicanism identifying national sovereignty with law rather than with direct expressions of popular will. Collot concluded his pamphlet with a quotation from Minister of the Interior Jean-Marie Roland warning of the danger posed by demagogues challenging public authority in their quest for popular support.[62] Roland's speech did not refer to the colonies but to the situation in metropolitan France, where he and other moderates were locked in political conflict with the Montagnards in the National Convention and the sans-culottes of Paris. Linking the defence of his authority to the Girondins' struggle, Collot saw the situation in Guadeloupe as part of the larger drama of the French Revolution.

Collot's proclamation of 18 April further demonstrated his conviction that threats to his authority undermined the colony's defences. He announced that the law of 2 September 1792, identifying as traitors all who refused to defend the patrie personally or to turn over their arms for this purpose, also declared that those who refused to execute the orders of executive power deserved the death penalty. This included citizens who, "under the appearance of patriotism," propagated hatred or vengeance to discourage the timid or the desperate or "who by injurious and incendiary speech seek to turn the weak from obedience to the law and the constituted authorities."[63] Two days later a bloody revolt provided stark evidence that internal conflict threatened Guadeloupe's republican regime.

II War and Rebellion in Martinique (April 1793–January 1794)

The National Convention's declaration of war against Great Britain revived counter-revolutionary hopes in the Windward Islands and communications with the planters' representatives in Europe, Dubuc, and De Curt, who opened negotiations with the British government. Such schemes ran counter to the aspirations of Béhague and Rivière, however, who sought to regain the colonies for the Bourbon monarchy. Many British statesmen believed that seizing the French West Indies would destroy France as a maritime rival. William Pitt's government signed a treaty on 19 February with the representatives of Martinique and Guadeloupe that specified that Britain would occupy the colonies in the name of the French king until the restoration of peace.[64] Even before he learned of Dubuc's machinations in London, Béhague had denounced Martinique's colonial assembly for hypocrisy and cowardice. The assembly had claimed in its proclamation of 13 January that he had forced the colony to fly the white flag of the monarchy. Writing from St Vincent, Béhague accused the assembly's members of being unprincipled opportunists.[65] There is truth in this charge, but, more important, it provides further evidence of the differences in outlook between planters and metropolitan officers.

Despite tension between the governor general and naval officers in 1792, Béhague and Rivière had maintained respectful relations following the revolt's collapse.[66] Rivière and his officers had sailed to Port-of-Spain, Trinidad, in January 1793 with the intention of putting their ships and themselves at the service of the king of Spain. Governor Chacon had been sympathetic but had no authority to accept the rebels into the Spanish navy. Therefore the royalist squadron's situation at Port-of-Spain was tenuous.[67] Learning of the outbreak of war in March, Béhague urged Rivière to sail immediately; Rivière informed him, however, that *Ferme* was in no condition to put to sea.[68] Yet on 26 April, the day that a British fleet arrived at Barbados, Rivière received a deputation from Martinique that beseeched him to come immediately and assist loyal colonists to throw off Rochambeau's tyranny. Despite the poor state of his ships, Rivière prepared to sail.[69]

The rebellion against Martinique's republican regime began before the arrival of either *émigrés* or British forces. During the first two weeks of April, many of the colony's planters left their estates to form an armed camp at Morne-le-Maître, not far from Fort-de-la-République. Rochambeau responded by marching regular troops against the camp, but his two columns became separated and had to retreat.[70] On 17 April the governor general issued a proclamation ordering citizens who had assembled in arms without his permission to disperse within two days and return to their residences – those who did not would be guilty of treason.[71] Six days later the colonial assembly's intermediate committee, reconstituted at Lamentin to provide the rebellion with political leadership, responded to the proclamation. While republicans dismissed it as insincere, the committee's letter to Rochambeau provides insight into the rebels' motivations. The committee claimed that after 13 January the entire colony had been united under the national flag. Martinique's planters had gladly submitted to Rochambeau for the sake of peace. Yet soon after he took up the reins of government, threatening proclamations had appeared. It was not Rochambeau's assertion of authority to which planters objected but rather that *petit-Blanc* radicals had influenced his use of authority. If this demonstrated a sense of class conflict between planters and propertyless patriots, the letter also emphasized the planters' fear that radicals, ensconced in Martinique's popular societies, had recklessly incited the slaves to revolt in order to wreak vengeance on their enemies:

> But what held them in continual worry were these clubs composed in part of men from Heaven or rather from Hell; men who do not respect property, the instrument on which they count to assassinate us, and whose impudence is so indecent that it means little to them to give voice to those who so painfully cultivate this colony but who they still want to keep in irons. It is in nighttime assemblies that the best citizens of the colony were denounced, it was there that the most incendiary projects were developed to the noise of clamorous approbation of all spectators; it is there that they speak only of liberty and equality in a country which can exist only with slaves.[72]

The planters' complaints against irresponsible and hypocritical patriots thus illustrate the inherent tensions and contradictions within the slave-holding Republic. The committee made two demands of Rochambeau: first, he must exchange the planter Dérivau, jailed by republicans, for two prisoners held by rebels; second, he must suppress the "infernal clubs." If these demands were met, all colonists would return to their homes. If they were not, the committee warned that Rochambeau would face a fight to the death.

Soon after the rebellion's outbreak, royalist *émigrés* made their way to Martinique. In the final days of April a British frigate brought Gimat, the former governor of Sainte-Lucie, to the colony to inform the rebels of Dubuc's treaty and of a British fleet's imminent arrival. The intermediate committee recognized Gimat as Martinique's governor and prepared to cooperate with British forces.[73] On 7 May *Ferme* appeared off Martinique. Rivière issued a proclamation urging inhabitants "to recognize their error, to leave the abyss into which they had plunged voluntarily, and to range themselves under the standard of their king, the only one they could recognize as their master."[74] Royalist *émigrés*, however, were divided in their objectives and loyalties. Béhague reacted bitterly to news that Rivière had responded to the intermediate committee's summons, since the naval officer had refused his request, and that colonists had recognized Gimat as governor. He also learned that the British government expected him to cooperate with Dubuc's agents.[75] One of these, Le Merle, was already in Barbados when Béhague reached the island on 6 May, and two others, Dubuc *fils* and Clairfontaine, arrived in June. Béhague advised Major General Bruce, commander of the British troops preparing for the attack on Martinique, to have the colony's sovereign council publish the Declaration of the French Regent. He also recommended moderation in dealing with the defeated republicans.[76] Yet Béhague became convinced that Dubuc's emissaries were blocking his efforts to influence British operations.

Martinique's republicans were more united than their enemies but they were outnumbered and under siege. Rochambeau proclaimed the formation of a new corps of light troops, the Martinique *chasseurs*, on 2 May. This would be a standing force, paid analogously to regulars and with officers named by the governor general. The *chasseurs* would be recruited not only from the colony's free men of colour but also from its slaves.[77] Rochambeau's proclamation did not include a clear promise of freedom to these slave-soldiers, but *émigrés* accused him of having done just that.[78] On 10 May nine British men-of-war arrived at Martinique. Rivière asked that troops be landed immediately, but Major General Bruce and his soldiers were still in Barbados.[79] The following day a force of coloured soldiers led by the free-coloured officer Bellegarde struck at rebels encamped on the Levassor plantation and succeeded in driving them from Lamentin. The republicans set fire to three plantations as the royalists fled. Lacrosse defended the violence in his account of the action: "It was necessary to make war on persons and property; we were fighting for our lives."[80] Rochambeau promoted Bellegarde to command of the *chasseurs* and began preparations for a methodical campaign against the rebels. On 15 May he dispatched a force of almost four hundred men to attack the rebels at Trois Islets, a position crucial to the control of Fort-Royal Bay. The republicans captured the village and Bellegarde's *chasseurs* drove the planters from several adjacent plantations.[81] According to Rochambeau it was retreating royalists, and not only republicans, who set fire to buildings and cane fields. On 28 May the governor general launched attacks against rebel positions north-east of Fort-de-la-République. His goal was to regain access to the port of Trinité on the Atlantic coast. Rochambeau marched out of Fort-de-la-Convention, the renamed Fort-Bourbon, at the head of three hundred regulars deployed in three columns. Under his command these disciplined soldiers forced the planters to evacuate Gros Morne.[82] Although Rochambeau had regained control of a broad swathe of the colony, on 11 June the British fleet reappeared, bringing General Bruce and over one thousand red-coats.

Following the siege, royalist *émigrés* bitterly criticized British commanders for not landing troops sooner. Dubuc *fils* and Clairfontaine, writing to a mysterious agent "X" in London, claimed that if an invasion had been carried out at the end of April, "the English would today be masters of Martinique," but instead they had "remained spectators" while "the factious" burned plantations and attacked the colonists who had risen up in expectation of assistance.[83] On 17 June the British fleet landed soldiers and armed planters south of Carbet, from where they intended to march overland to assault Saint-Pierre. Rochambeau, who had gone to Saint-Pierre to prepare its defences, ordered a night attack, taking the enemy by surprise. In the confusion, planters and British troops fired on each other. The mêlée convinced British commanders to abandon the operation, and they ordered their forces to return to the ships. The fleet embarked planters fleeing the colony before leaving Martinique on 24 June.[84] Rivière also took perhaps eight hundred colonists and their slaves aboard *Ferme* before he returned to Trinidad.[85] Dubuc *fils* and Clairfontaine blamed the disaster on Bruce's hesitation and treachery,[86] but the *émigrés* had misled the British government regarding the strength of royalist forces in the colony. Rochambeau's counteroffensives had thwarted the invasion but they also ensured that

Britain's next attempt to capture Martinique would not involve cooperation with dubious French allies.[87]

The siege reinforced the alliance between the governor general and Martinique's patriots, but it also exposed the republican script's ambiguity towards slavery. Rochambeau attributed his triumph over rebels and the British to the bravery of Saint-Pierre's inhabitants and praised the free men of colour led by Bellegarde.[88] In its address of 2 July to the National Convention, Saint-Pierre's surveillance committee characterized the recent siege as yet another episode in the patriots' revolutionary struggle since 1789. Echoing the governor general's request, the committee asked the convention to send Martinique troops and funds.[89] Rochambeau's reports on the siege also emphasized its impact on the slaves. Both sides had armed slaves during the struggle, he told the minister, and subsequently the colony's gangs pillaged the countryside. Worse, these slaves now demanded liberty and received encouragement from some whites and free men of colour. Rochambeau had received no indication that the National Convention intended to abolish slavery, however, and he felt bound to preserve slavery as well as to defend the colony: "The Convention can rest assured that I will hold my post to the last extremity, and that I will fight all rebels to the law of whatever colour they may be."[90]

On 2 July Rochambeau proclaimed that all patriots, including those of colour, must unite in returning Martinique's slaves to their gangs. The proclamation ordered the surveillance committees to disarm all slaves, except for those enrolled in the *chasseurs*. Rochambeau promised to reward loyalty by freeing slaves identified as having distinguished themselves in the recent fighting. He insisted that all slaves return peacefully to their masters and surrender their weapons, however, and warned that those who did not within three days of its publication would be arrested and shot without trial.[91] Rochambeau informed the minister that this proclamation responded to ideas of general emancipation spread in the colony by secret agitators and that disarming the slaves was a painful and difficult task. The problem also contributed to the danger posed by foreign powers. If loyal colonists believed metropolitan government had abandoned them, Rochambeau warned, they would be susceptible to English promises to protect their property and commerce.[92] Although he blamed abolitionist propaganda for encouraging slave defiance, Rochambeau and his government differed from those that preceded them. The governor general defended the rights of free men of colour and identified coloured individuals for praise and promotion. "New Citizens," Rochambeau declared, "are the children of the constitution."[93] The republican regime upheld racial equality even as it sought to maintain slavery.

If the royalist uprising demonstrated that planters had not accepted the Republic sincerely in February, it also reflected the provisional nature of the republican regime in Martinique. The rebels could claim with some justification that the old colonial assembly was more representative than the radical-dominated clubs or the appointed surveillance committees.[94] Therefore, to strengthen the regime and its legitimacy, and to inculcate republican principles and practices in the inhabitants, Rochambeau convoked the colony's primary assemblies in September to elect a new representative assembly. It held its first session on 22 September in Saint-Pierre. This was the appropriate location, according to Rochambeau, because of the services the town's inhabitants had rendered to the French Revolution and because it was in Saint-Pierre that "the people *en masse* can enlighten its delegates and defend them against common enemies."[95] The governor general invoked the legitimacy of popular sovereignty to strengthen his demands that the metropolitan government send military and financial support for the colony. Between September 1793 and January 1794 the representative assembly supervised the election and operation of new municipalities, issued new regulations regarding the administration of sequestered properties, and in December declared Martinique to be a department of France.[96]

Four themes dominated the assembly's deliberations and indicated the republican regime's priorities: controlling slaves and the legal institution of slavery, reforming manumission, defending the revolution and punishing political enemies, and strengthening the colony's defences. On 25 September the assembly formalized the Corps of *Chasseurs* as a corps of auxiliary troops of the line to be paid by the Republic. This designation distinguished these soldiers from those in the national guard because most *chasseurs* were not citizens – they were slaves.[97] The corps was crucial to the colony's defence, but it was not intended to undermine slavery. On 20 October the assembly ordered the creation of a commission to estimate the value of the individual slaves within the corps, so that their owners could be provided with a receipt for future reimbursement.[98] While this *arrêté* reaffirmed that slaves were property, it also implied that these troops would not return to their masters following their military service. In his letter to the minister of 25 October, Rochambeau confirmed that he had augmented his military forces with 1,334 men of colour or "Negroes whom I have freed" to form the Corps of *Chasseurs*. They had fought both rebels and English in defence of French territory, "and for the liberty which I promised, conducting themselves as men worthy of it."[99]

The republican regime's ambiguity towards slavery was also evident in the new assembly's reforms to the process of manumission. On 9 October it declared that when a master renounced ownership of a slave, he would no longer be required to pay an arbitrary sum to register the enfranchisement, as under the Old Regime. The slave would be free, provided the master could prove his ownership in the declaration in which he renounced his rights over the slave. Furthermore, slaves could request freedom on the basis of service in the old militia or the national guard, provided they possessed a certificate from the captain under whom they had served.[100] On the other hand, the assembly stated in another *arrêté* that slaves freed in a foreign colony needed to have their acts of manumission registered by a municipality in Martinique and stamped by the government. The act would not be registered if it had been acquired against the will of a master living in the French colonies, however, and an act acquired fraudulently would be declared null and void and the slave returned under the old master's power.[101] The assembly also made clear that the republican regime would tolerate neither slave revolt nor those who incited it.[102]

If its validation of slavery suggested continuity with the old colonial regime, the representative assembly was still a republican legislature committed to the triumph of the French Revolution. Both the steps it took and the language it used demonstrated the powerful influence of metropolitan revolutionary culture on colonial patriots.[103] One of its first acts was to nationalize all church property in the colony.[104] In subsequent sessions, the deputies ordered the expropriation of the Saint-Jean-Baptiste hospital in Saint-Pierre.[105] A higher priority than de-Christianization for Martinique's republican regime, however, was its determination to deter and to punish rebels, *émigrés*, and aristocrats.[106] To that end, the assembly established a revolutionary tribunal between 28 September and 18 October. The deputies justified the creation of this extraordinary court in part because, cut off from metropolitan France by the war, it was their duty to protect society and to punish crime. They also claimed that the large number of rebels locked up in Martinique's prisons, forts, and ships represented a serious potential danger, particularly in the event of another enemy attack, and needed to be cowed by an "example of terrible justice." This echoed the words of Georges Danton in the National Convention on

10 March, when he called for the formation of the revolutionary tribunal in Paris: "Let us be terrible, to spare the people the need to be terrible themselves."[107] While the deputies ordered Martinique's tribunal to investigate all counter-revolutionaries, their *arrêté* stated that it would not pursue those who had previously supported the colonial assembly but subsequently fought for the Republic against the coalesced rebels and English. Colonists who had committed murder, pillage, or arson between the publication of the amnesty of 30 November 1791 and Rochambeau's proclamation of 4 February 1793 would be tried by the colony's ordinary criminal courts. Thus the revolutionary tribunal was intended to suppress opposition to the republican regime specifically. The assembly charged the governor general to provide space for the tribunal to conduct trials and to order the construction of a guillotine.[108]

The republican regime's determination to discover and punish internal enemies was connected to a fourth priority, the need to prepare Martinique's defences for another British assault.[109] This required the mobilization of colonists. The representative assembly declared on 3 October that all male citizens between sixteen and fifty-five years of age were required to do military service in the island's citadels and camps. Companies of "veterans" over fifty-five years old would be formed for police duties.[110] Two days later the assembly ordered that a replacement tax be levied against the properties of landowners whose absence prevented them from fulfilling their military service.[111] Martinique had not received the National Convention's decree of 23 August announcing the *Levée en masse*, but these measures show that colonial patriots were familiar with the rhetoric accompanying the Levy of 300,000 decreed on 24 February.[112] Similarly, on 6 December, Martinique's assembly declared the National Assembly's decree of 25 July 1792 be applied to the colony. Any commander surrendering his fort before its defences had been breached – and before it had endured at least one assault – would be punished with death. Any inhabitants requesting the surrender of their stronghold would be treated as traitors to the *patrie*.[113] In keeping with the revolutionary script, members of the assembly believed threats of punishment were necessary to deter treachery and military defeatism.

In August the unexpected departure of *Félicité*, the only major warship on station in the Windward Islands, made Martinique even more vulnerable to attack. The episode further suggests the corrosive effect of revolutionary communications on military discipline. Lacrosse remained a revered figure among patriots for his defeat of the royalist revolt at the beginning of 1793. Fort-de-la-République's popular society,

"The Friends of the French Republic and of the Convention," sent him a testimonial on 12 August, declaring that, even if he were recalled to France, Martinique's republicans would continue to remember and draw inspiration from "Lacrosse and the brave sailors of all ranks who helped him to chase the ferocious and bloodthirsty men from the colony."[114] If the club thought *Félicité*'s captain might be leaving the colonies, the governor general had no intention of releasing the only frigate at his disposal. On 21 August Rochambeau ordered Lacrosse to carry out a patrol to the windward of Barbados but then to return to Fort-de-la-République.[115] Yet *Félicité* vanished after leaving Martinique. Merchant seamen told Rochambeau that before getting underway the frigate's officers had said openly that they were leaving for France.[116] On 3 October *Félicité* had arrived at Brest, where Lacrosse reported the rebel uprising and British assault on Martinique to republican authorities.[117] He claimed he had come to demand reinforcements for the colonies, but neither the urgency of this request nor his personal desire to return to France had caused Lacrosse to abandon the Windward Islands.

Félicité's crew, like that of *Embuscade* in 1791, had mutinied. On the morning of 27 August, the sailors had demanded that the captain sail for France. Lacrosse refused, telling them that he must carry out Rochambeau's orders just as they must obey his. The sailors remained defiant and changed tack to put the ship on course for France. Lacrosse and his officers submitted to the crew's will but signed an account of events registering their protest.[118] Death and sickness had taken their toll on the crew, forcing Lacrosse to recruit thirty-six merchant seamen prior to the patrol, and this may have contributed to the crew's desire to leave the colonies. The sailors' justification for their actions, however, suggests that political struggle ashore provoked the mutiny. The crew claimed that Lacrosse had promised that *Félicité* would escort a convoy to Europe but that Martinique's clubs and surveillance committees persuaded Rochambeau to change these orders. The sailors then resolved not to return to the colony because they believed it was headed for civil war that would also engulf the navy. While describing the *petits Blancs* as Martinique's "true patriots," the sailors did not believe the republican regime had united white and coloured patriots. They feared the two groups would soon be at each other's throats, and they knew that the slaves now demanded liberty. *Félicité*'s crew claimed it was willing to fight rebels or the English, but they insisted that a single frigate could not save the colony when the English returned in force. The sailors had no confidence in the governor general, expressing the fear that they might become "the blind instrument of intriguers, of the factious or of rebels" as had the crews of *Ferme, Calypso,* and *Didon.* Given the crisis in which the colony found itself, every course of action appeared equally dangerous, and so they had resolved to return to France.[119] The revolutionary struggle and the dynamic of popular sovereignty had rendered all authority tenuous.

For Rochambeau, *Félicité's* disappearance contributed to a growing anxiety that metropolitan government had abandoned the Windward Islands. In his letter of 16 October, reporting the frigate's failure to return from patrol, he accused the executive council in Paris of having broken sacred promises that the colonies were part of the French empire.[120] Rochambeau suspected Lacrosse of deserting his post by returning to Europe, and this only worsened the situation in which Martinique found itself.[121] On 27 December Rochambeau reported the capture of the brig *Lutin,* reducing even farther the number of vessels at his disposal, while he had learned that the British in the eastern Caribbean anticipated the arrival of a fleet from Europe.[122] In response to the arrival of official dispatches, the governor general declared Martinique's loyalty to the Republic on 22 January 1794, but he reiterated that France must send reinforcements.[123] Less than three weeks later Martinique was again under siege.

III Slave Revolt and Factional Strife in Guadeloupe (April 1793–January 1794)

In the same month that Martinique's planters rose in rebellion, events in Guadeloupe demonstrated the ambiguities of that colony's republican regime and its inability to control communications. On the night of 20–21 April 1793, a band of slaves from several gangs in the vicinity of Trois-Rivières murdered twenty-three men, women, and children from the families of six wealthy planters. The insurgents, numbering perhaps two hundred, then advanced on the town of Basse-Terre. News of their revolt preceded them. When national guard companies confronted the column, the slaves identified themselves as "citizens and friends," who had thwarted a conspiracy to deliver the colony to the English. Four of their leaders told national guard officers that the slaves had acted entirely on their own accord and that they had killed royalists who had armed them to assassinate patriots. According to the account published on 24 April in the *Journal républicain de la Guadeloupe,* the national guard then escorted the slaves, who offered no resistance and cried repeatedly *"Vive la République,"* to Basse-Terre, where they were confined in the courtyard of the arsenal but not disarmed immediately. The patriot newspaper also accepted the slaves' claims and justification for their insurrection.[124]

Guadeloupe's general and extraordinary commission was less willing to take the slaves' claims at face value and saw the revolt itself as a threat to the colony. On 25 April it issued an *arrêté* ordering harsh punishments for slaves who committed crimes and for anyone who fomented their insurrection. The commission insisted that free men of colour were attached to the cause of the French Revolution and that they recognized it was in their interests to oppose slave revolt. The deputies stated that the slaves, too, should be loyal to the Republic, which assured them humane treatment and made enfranchisement not an arbitrary disposition but the reward for loyal service. Beyond this validation of slavery, the commission called on all colonists to unite against the common threat.[125] While this might refer to a threat from royalist conspirators, it also implied a danger posed by radical opposition to Governor Collot. Reactions to the slave revolt at Trois-Rivières were linked inextricably to the conflict between Guadeloupe's moderate and radical republicans.

The commission's Committee of General Security interrogated the rebels escorted to Basse-Terre and investigated the revolt. Despite the commission's initial reaction, the slaves' own account set the agenda for the committee's inquiry.[126] The committee's report, presented on 8 May, referred to the machinations of the "royalist party" since September 1792 as the background to the events of April. The report claimed that these counter-revolutionaries had plotted to destroy the colony by inciting the slaves to revolt, in part with the promise of liberty and in part with rumours that new citizens had demanded that slaves be branded on the face. Along with evidence of such subversion in February and March, the committee possessed correspondence intercepted from *émigrés* to royalists in Guadeloupe, which revealed a plot to assist an assault on the colony. Therefore the committee argued that the royalists had armed slaves to attack patriots, and thus to facilitate a British conquest, but that the slaves had turned on them instead. The report also identified several citizens who had been arrested – suspected of conspiracy or of fomenting insurrection among the gangs – but made no reference to the whites killed at Trois-Rivières.[127] The commission, having accepted the committee's report, ordered that a special tribunal be formed to judge the slaves detained at Basse-Terre and Baillif and to investigate citizens implicated in those proceedings. The deputies also ordered that arrests be limited to those accused of planning to deliver the colony to the enemy or of inciting the slaves to revolt.[128] It would prove impossible to contain the radicals' desire for vengeance, however, against their moderate republican rivals as well as against royalists.

Collot saw the slave revolt's danger in the context of factional conflict. He reported the killings at Trois-Rivières to the minister in his dispatch of 10 May, expressing fear that the slaves' expectation of liberty could set a dangerous precedent.[129] In his 1795 memoir he described his shock when he returned to Basse-Terre on 22 April to discover that the national guard had not disarmed the insurgents. The governor disarmed the slaves himself, demanding that the committee imprison them in the fort or aboard ship until their trial. The committee refused, insisting that this would prejudge the investigation's outcome. Collot claimed that his demand to imprison these insurgents, and his refusal to sanction arming them as a company to hunt down counter-revolutionaries, had provoked the committee members' implacable hostility.[130] The governor did respond to the danger of a possible royalist plot.[131] Stating that royalists had removed weapons from state magazines during the 1792 revolt, and that conspirators had subsequently hidden these throughout the colony, Collot proclaimed that all municipalities must search the slave gangs for arms and ensure that no citizen possessed weapons beyond the needs of his own defence.[132] Collot informed the minister that investigation of the revolt had revealed the existence of a conspiracy to deliver the colony, and he praised the Committee of General Security for breaking the plot by the arrest of suspect inhabitants.[133] Yet the governor's opposition to a lengthy proscription list led radical patriots to challenge his authority directly.

On the morning of 15 May the Committee of General Security denounced Collot as an aristocrat, as a supporter of royalist planters who was in correspondence with them, and as an opponent of free-coloured equality. Many of Basse-Terre's new citizens who heard these accusations cried "To Arms!" and called for the governor's head. Collot convoked an extraordinary session of the commission and sought to defend himself. Surrounded by a hostile crowd, he characterized those who had spread calumnies against him as false patriots who accused him of tyranny because he preached submission to the law. Agitators had portrayed his proposal for paid battalions as an attack on citizens' rights, especially those of new citizens, when it was part of his efforts to strengthen Guadeloupe's defences. Collot also responded to the charge that he had not attended sessions of the popular societies, stating that he had more urgent tasks than mere deliberation and, moreover, that it was dangerous for a public functionary to court popular influence rather than simply being accessible to citizens' requests.[134] This attitude towards the clubs points to a fundamental division between the governor and the radical patriots, who soon began to call themselves "*sans-culottes.*"[135] Collot believed that his authority rested on the National Convention's decrees and the orders of metropolitan government, not on the approval of local manifestations of popular will. A majority of the commission's members, men who could be described as moderate republicans, wanted to unite citizens against the threats of slave revolt and counter-revolution; therefore, they sought to avoid a clash between these opposing definitions of popular sovereignty. After Collot's speech the deputies announced that the Committee of General Security merited the greatest praise, but they also declared that the governor enjoyed the colony's confidence. Collot then asked Thyrus Pautrizel, a member of the Committee of General Security, to become his aide-de-camp and, to the cheers of the crowd observing the session, the patriot accepted the post.[136]

Collot initially interpreted the session's outcome as a triumph over his enemies. Yet radical distrust of the governor continued.[137] News from France, arriving in an American ship coming from Bordeaux, made Collot's position even more tenuous. Beyond confirming that the frigate carrying the expected civil commissioners had returned to port, these reports described the French army's defeat in the Austrian Netherlands, the treason of General Dumouriez, and the political turmoil that shook the Republic.[138] The fact that Dumouriez, who was a friend of the Girondins, had tried to rally his troops to march against Paris and the National Convention only heightened radical suspicions. In his dispatch of 5 July Collot reported that a spirit of disorganization and insubordination gripped the colony: "I can attribute this only to the affection that [the colonists] bear Citizen Lacrosse and to the aversion that they have shown to my commission signed by Louis XVI, a prejudice that nothing can destroy," and he asked to be recalled.[139]

On 7 July a crowd armed with axes and iron bars forced its way into the jail at Pointe-à-Pitre and murdered seven men imprisoned as counter-revolutionary suspects. That morning a free-coloured guard had been wounded in a scuffle with one of the prisoners, and his cries caused the crowd to converge on the jail. The town's mayor and military commandant were powerless spectators to the killings. "Pointe-à-Pitre was the theatre of a tragic scene which has brought consternation to all sensitive souls," Collot announced to the colony's municipalities and parish commandants, "The voice of the municipal officers was smothered, and the law was scorned in the most outrageous manner."[140] The prison massacre reflected an atmosphere of intense suspicion in Guadeloupe, as well as free-coloured fears that counter-revolutionaries would restore racial inequality. In his memoir, Collot suggested that the episode's origin lay in demands by Pointe-à-Pitre's popular society that prisoners detained in the town as a result of the warrants issued by the Committee of General Security should be transferred to Basse-Terre. To the governor's assertion that its prisons were already full, club members responded, "Best then to cut off their heads!" Collot claimed that Pointe-à-Pitre had become the headquarters of the colony's worst agitators, that the club had taken the name of the "Jacobins of the Antilles," and that this faction modelled itself on the "Terrorists" in France.[141]

Collot published his self-justifying memoir in 1795, at the time of the Thermidorian Reaction, when associating his enemies with Robespierre and the Terror could be expected to discredit them. Nonetheless, Collot's accusations fit with other evidence that the communication of an increasingly radical revolutionary script from France had a powerful influence in the colonies.

Just as the governor feared subversive communications, so his enemies tried to block news that might bolster his authority, which they saw as antithetical to popular will. This obstruction was evident in both the reaction to the arrival of the new metropolitan constitution and in a subsequent challenge to the governor's right to sanction decrees. In October Collot received the new Constitutional Act, accepted by the National Convention on 24 June 1793, in a package from Rochambeau. He immediately submitted it to a printer in Basse-Terre so that copies might be distributed throughout the colony. This action provoked protests from the town's popular society and from members of the Committee of General Security.[142] On 29 October the commission ordered nine of its members to question the governor regarding the Constitutional Act. Collot told them he could doubt neither its authenticity nor that it had been accepted by the French people, given the newspaper reports in the United States and in British colonies. He gave them the original he had received from Rochambeau and stated that, since it had been printed in Martinique, he believed that the people in Guadeloupe should also have the opportunity to express their view. Thus the governor in this instance could portray himself as the defender of popular sovereignty. The following day the commission declared the colony's provisional acceptance of the Constitutional Act and ordered all municipalities to convoke both the primary assemblies and the popular societies.[143] All but two parishes accepted the new constitution. Of the popular societies only Pointe-à-Pitre's opposed the Constitutional Act, claiming to doubt its authenticity but in fact fearing that it undermined slavery.[144]

Following these votes, the tension between Guadeloupe's moderate and radical republicans produced a public schism. Radicals within the commission shifted their deliberations from Basse-Terre to Pointe-à-Pitre. On 21 December they declared the colony in crisis, ordering that the commission's *arrêté* of 20 March be nullified and the governor's veto be abolished.[145] Warned that the faction allied with the Committee of General Security was preparing some kind of coup, Collot travelled to Pointe-à-Pitre on the evening of 20 December. He found the town full of armed men and in a state of agitation. Crowds threatened him as he made his way through the streets to the *Morne du Gouvernment*; they yelled, "No more veto! No more royal commission!" the latter referring to Collot's original appointment. The following day Collot presented himself before the deputies, refusing to surrender his powers as governor. Amid angry shouting one orator accused Collot of complicity in all the crimes of previous governors and counter-revolutionaries. In reply Collot coolly requested that four commissioners be named to investigate these charges. He claimed this tactic turned the tables on his accusers and resulted in the majority of deputies avowing that such accusations were without foundation.[146] Nonetheless, the deputies at Pointe-à-Pitre declared themselves to be the "Revolutionary Representative Corps of Guadeloupe" and established a provisional executive council formed by the joint Committees of Security and Administration.

Moderate republicans in Basse-Terre did not accept the radicals' arrogation of executive authority. On 26 December the joint committees at Pointe-à-Pitre forwarded their *arrêté* of 21 December to Gerlain, the colony's national attorney.[147] If the radicals assumed that this official would validate their actions, they were to be disappointed. In a brief submitted to the district tribunal at Basse-Terre, Gerlain criticized both the deputies' invocation of direct democracy and their defiance of national legislation that confirmed the governor's right to approve the commission's orders. In reconstituting themselves and in erecting an executive, Gerlain contended that the deputies at Pointe-à-Pitre had defied the Constitutional Act that they had previously approved.[148] The national attorney's critique reflected the insistence of moderate republicans on the rule of law and obedience to metropolitan authority; he recommended that the district tribunal denounce the *arrêté* to the National Convention. The tribunal assembled on 2 January 1794, and the judges pronounced their refusal to register the *arrêté* of 21 December.[149]

Despite judicial disapproval, the joint committees at Pointe-à-Pitre continued to hold sessions as a provisional executive council. According to Collot, their supporters threatened and intimidated all those who would not acknowledge their authority. Deputies of the general and extraordinary commission who had remained in Basse-Terre called for the dissolution of the usurping assembly. This move provoked an insurrection on 10 January in which sailors at Basse-Terre sought to rouse the town's artillerymen into killing prisoners held in Fort Saint-Charles. The governor and municipal officers prevented the massacre, restoring calm only with great difficulty. If this incident gave radicals even more reason to accuse Collot of protecting aristocrats, their hostility towards him cannot be reduced to a clear or simple conflict between enthusiastic republicans and a conservative governor, or between advocates of racial equality and a supporter of the old colonial order. Prior to 10 January the joint committees had voted and ordered the printing of an act of accusation against Collot, representing him not only as an "enemy of equality" but also as a "Philanthropist," a "Negrophile," and as someone "wanting to be a French republican and not a colonial republican."[150] Despite their response to the Trois-Rivières insurgents, Guadeloupe's radical patriots feared slavery's abolition, and they charged the governor with holding abolitionist sentiments. Despite radical accusations, Collot and his moderate supporters were committed to equal rights for free men of colour, whose support they believed was crucial to upholding slavery and the colony's republican regime.[151] The factions were not divided essentially over slavery or racial equality; rather, the fundamental conflict concerned the legitimacy of executive authority and the location of the nation's will. This division – complicated and embittered by fear of slave revolt and counter-revolutionary intrigue, and by white prejudice and coloured suspicions – rendered the colony incapable of firm resistance when British forces arrived in April.

IV The British Conquest of Martinique and Guadeloupe (February–April 1794)

Following its failure to gain control of the French Windward Islands through cooperation with colonial royalists in June 1793, the British government began preparations for a major expedition to capture the colonies. The ministry offered Lieutenant General Sir Charles Grey command of the troops, while the Admiralty appointed Vice Admiral Sir John Jervis as naval commander. Originally this effort was to be part of an ambitious strategy to conquer Saint-Domingue as well as the smaller colonies, but the objective of the expedition that sailed from England in November, including twelve men-of-war and carrying seven thousand troops, was limited to the French Windward Islands. When they reached Barbados on 6 January 1794, however, a dispatch from London encouraged Grey and Jervis to go directly to Saint-Domingue in order to exploit the situation there. Planters from Saint-Domingue had appealed to British authorities in Jamaica, particularly following the general emancipation of slaves by commissioners Sonthonax and Polverel in August, and in September British forces had seized the Môle Saint-Nicolas. Nevertheless, Grey decided to begin his campaign with the capture of Martinique.[152]

The British armada appeared off Martinique on 4 February and began a siege lasting forty-eight days. In the journal he kept to record events of this siege, Rochambeau noted that the British had chosen their moment well – there were fewer than five hundred regular French troops in the Windward Islands.[153] Grey and Jervis put troops ashore in multiple locations in order to divide Martinique's defenders. Communications intended to neutralize opposition exposed the ambiguities of the republican regime. British officers distributed copies of a declaration inviting colonists to surrender Martinique to His Britannic Majesty's government and, in return, promising them personal security and protection of their property under their old laws; thus, British occupation would maintain slavery.[154] With the limited forces at his disposal, Rochambeau tried to block the enemy from moving inland. But national guard companies failed to take up assigned positions or surrendered, and Bellegarde, the coloured officer Rochambeau had entrusted with command of the *chasseurs*, retreated from Trinité without a fight. By 16 February British troops had captured Républiqueville's outer defences and taken the town of Saint-Pierre, while Jervis's fleet had anchored in Fort-Royal Bay and placed the forts under blockade.[155]

Even as the enemy began preparations for a methodical siege of Républiqueville (formerly Fort-Royal) and the citadel of Fort-de-la-Convention (formerly Fort-Bourbon), Rochambeau faced internal dissension. On 15 February he foiled a plot by three coloured officers to assassinate him and take over the forts. Rochambeau linked the incident to the larger divisions plaguing the republican regime.[156] He did not approve Bellegarde's attack against enemy forces unloading supplies at Cohé Lamentin on 18 February. British troops repelled the *chasseurs*, who fled to Républiqueville and abandoned the post they had occupied on heights overlooking Fort-de-la-Convention.[157] On 19 February Rochambeau received a message from General Grey to surrender the forts to avoid unnecessary bloodshed.[158] The governor general informed Républiqueville's municipality and Committee of Public Safety of Grey's message, but the troops in Fort-de-la-Convention declared that they preferred defending themselves to the shame of capitulation.[159] Grey gave his enemy another twenty-four hours to consider his proposition for an honourable surrender. French troops were resolved to fight, however, and Rochambeau informed Grey of their determination. The British commander's response signalled the violence of the coming siege: "I see with pain the stubbornness of your garrison. I have done everything required of me to spare you the ferocious extremities to which you remain exposed. I will have nothing for which to reproach myself."[160]

On 22 February British forces opened their first irregular parallel, a major step in the pattern of eighteenth-century siege craft in which the attacking troops dug trenches to advance troops and artillery towards the besieged town and fortress. While the enemy prepared to bombard and assault the strongholds, republican unity and defiance were crumbling. Rumours circulated that the coloured troops awaited the beginning of a general bombardment to plunge into the countryside and raise the slave gangs in revolt; this would serve as a diversion to allow Bellegarde to arrange a truce with the British.[161] On 26 February Rochambeau received a more tangible indication of republican defeatism: officers of Fort-de-la-Convention's garrison submitted a petition requesting that he surrender, since there was no hope of saving the colony.[162] The following day a British officer delivered another message from Grey to Républiqueville's municipality calling on the town to surrender.[163] The governor general did not respond formally to the petition or to Grey's new offer of terms, but on 28 February Bellegarde and his lieutenant abandoned the republican cause. The two officers rallied the *chasseurs* for an attack on the enemy posts, persuading them that this was only way to salvage their reputation. When the black troops reached the Dillon Plantation, however, their commanders disarmed and delivered them to British forces as prisoners.

This was a bitter betrayal for Rochambeau, who had formed the *chasseurs* and hand-picked their commander.[164] While he claimed that the

Dodd, del.

Page, sculp

View of the storming and taking the Fort and Town of Fort Royal,
in the Island of Martinico, by General Sir Charles Grey, &
and Vice Admiral Sir John Jervis, March 24.1794.

Published as the Act directs, May 20.1794.

3 Robert Dodd and J. Pass, "View of the Storming and Taking of the Fort
and Town of Fort Royal in the Island of Martinico, by General Sir Charles
Grey, and Vice Admiral Sir John Jervis, March 24th 1794," 1794. PU5468/
National Maritime Museum, Greenwich, London.

enemy had purchased Bellegarde's treason, it is likely that the coloured
officer remained loyal until shortly before his defection and that his
decision had been influenced by Rochambeau's harsh criticism of his
failed attack on 18 February.[165] Free-coloured loyalty to the Republic,
like previous loyalty to royal authority, was always conditional upon
changing assessments of which faction would uphold the equality and
interests of the *gens de couleur*. Despite desertion and discouragement,
Rochambeau believed that his troops continued to have confidence in
him – that even the "intriguers" recognized that he alone had the authority to negotiate a surrender.[166] Yet he had no illusions regarding his
situation: he commanded fewer than eight hundred troops within the

besieged town and fort, while he needed forty-five hundred men to defend them. In his final dispatch to the Republic's executive council, Rochambeau laid the blame for impending defeat squarely on metropolitan government.[167]

The siege's final stage began on 7 March with a general bombardment. No part of Fort-de-la-Convention was sheltered from the fire of British batteries, which dismounted several French guns and killed or wounded between forty and fifty men. Much worse, the bombardment cut the channels conducting water into the fort and destroyed the building gutters, which fed rainwater into the cistern. It was now only a matter of time before the fort's defenders would be without water to drink and dysentery began to ravage the beleaguered garrison.[168] The following day shells from gunboats in the harbour set fire to Républiqueville's powder magazine, causing it to explode. Nevertheless, republicans continued to defy the attackers. Grey and Jervis sent a third ultimatum to Rochambeau and to the constituted authorities of Républiqueville on 12 March.[169] Although enemy fire had put over two hundred of his men out of action, and dysentery afflicted another hundred, Rochambeau again refused to surrender.[170] Therefore the bombardment continued – its terrible intensity demonstrated when a cannon ball decapitated the French artillery commander and covered Rochambeau with his blood.[171] On 20 March British troops assaulted and captured Fort-de-la-République (formerly Fort-Louis). Républiqueville's municipality and Committee of Public Safety again appealed for Rochambeau to capitulate, and this time the regular troops in Fort-de-la-Convention supported them.[172] The governor general asked the British commander to offer his troops honourable terms. He proposed that each side send three commissioners to the Dillon plantation to draft the articles of a formal capitulation.[173] The British commissioners accepted Rochambeau's insistence on guarantees of the regular troops' honour and the white colonists' security, but they refused his proposals to recognize the rights of free-coloured national guards or the liberty of slave soldiers.[174] The six commissioners signed the terms of surrender on 22 March. As British troops took possession of the citadel's exterior works, Fort-de-la-Convention's garrison marched out in arms, with flags deployed, and embarked in ships to take them to France.[175] Their commander departed separately, sailing to New England where, in his first dispatch to Paris, he blamed the loss of Martinique on the metropolitan government since it had abandoned him without reinforcements. Martinique had succumbed to military conquest, but Rochambeau recognized that the divisions between colonists, the tensions over free-coloured rights, and the growing agitation among the colony's slaves had rendered the republican regime particularly vulnerable.[176]

Colonial divisions and factional conflict, which played out according to the metropolitan revolutionary script, also contributed to Guadeloupe's fall one month later. When Collot learned that Martinique was under attack, he declared Guadeloupe to be in a state of siege. He reminded colonists that, according to the decree of 26 August 1792, anyone calling for surrender before he deemed it necessary would be considered a traitor.[177] Yet the governor's enemies blocked communication of this proclamation and news of the British attack.[178] Collot claimed that the faction at Pointe-à-Pitre had undermined his efforts to prepare for the coming invasion by persecuting moderate republicans and by disarming Forts Fleur d'Épée and Islet à Cochon. Radicals had earlier opposed the governor's attempt to raise a battalion of black *chasseurs*, accusing him of wanting to arm slaves but not free men of colour. Collot denied this, but the accusation thwarted the recruitment of *chasseurs*.[179] When a vessel from Saint-Pierre arrived at Pointe-à-Pitre, bringing patriot news of the British attack, several members of the Committee of General Security tried to flee Guadeloupe. Officials loyal to the governor arrested four of them aboard an American ship on 22 March, and Collot accused these men and their comrades of betraying the colony.[180] If these arrests discredited the Committee of General Security, news of an impending attack failed to unify colonists behind the governor's authority. Upon learning that Rochambeau had surrendered, Collot ordered the evacuation of Basse-Terre and tried to imprison the 200 slave insurgents from Trois-Rivières in Fort Saint-Charles. The slaves attacked the detachment sent to accomplish this, however, and the troops were only able to force them into the town's jail. Three days later the circulation of a rumour that free men of colour were plotting to kill all white colonists panicked the governor's supporters, and on 9 April a British fleet appeared in the Saints Channel.[181] To defend Guadeloupe Collot had only 611 troops, of which 220 were poorly armed and untrained black *chasseurs*.[182] General Grey, who had taken Sainte-Lucie in five days, had over 4,000 disciplined British regulars at his disposal.[183]

The demoralization of Guadeloupe's defenders wrecked Collot's plans to resist the British invasion. Grey landed two battalions at Gosier on 11 April, and these troops stormed Fort Fleur d'Épée the following day, causing the republicans to abandon Pointe-à-Pitre. National guards from the adjacent parishes refused to march, and deserters from

Pointe-à-Pitre spread panic to the island of Basse-Terre.[184] On 13 April Grey landed with the main body of his troops at Petit-Bourg, advancing down the island's east coast. At the approach of British soldiers, national guards abandoned their batteries and spiked their guns without firing a shot.[185] With all of his advance positions abandoned, Collot ordered his remaining forces to Palmiste, where he intended to make a last stand. On 17 April Collot learned that the British were in possession of Matouba to the north, and thus they were able to turn his right flank. That night arsonists started a major fire in the town of Basse-Terre.[186] The following day Grey demanded that Collot surrender. The governor told members of the administrative chamber and of Basse-Terre's commune that he considered his second line of defence impregnable, but only if those manning its redoubts and earthworks were prepared to defend them. The mayor of Trois-Rivières replied that, in the present circumstances, the danger from the enemy was less than that from imminent slave insurrection in the colony's interior; therefore, he believed, the governor must surrender. In contrast, a member of the administrative chamber urged the constituted authorities to rally to the colony's last citadel.[187] Before others could express their views, however, Collot learned that most of Fort Saint-Charles's garrison had fled during the night and that the two remaining companies wanted to surrender.[188] The limited will to resist now evaporated. Only two civilians refused to sign a capitulation.[189]

Guadeloupe's remaining defences collapsed quickly. During the night arsonists again set fire to the town of Basse-Terre. The new conflagration, according to Collot, provoked despair and mutual accusations: "Moderates accused the Terrorists, Terrorists in turn accused me."[190] On the morning of 19 April the governor received the constituted authorities' formal request for capitulation and assembled his council of war in Fort Saint-Charles.[191] Yet Grey did not offer an armistice to arrange terms, and on 20 April he demanded that French forces in Basse-Terre and Fort Saint-Charles surrender immediately and unconditionally.[192] The garrison marched out of Fort Saint-Charles on 22 April, boarding ships for transport to France. Although he requested two weeks to wrap up his administration, French émigrés persuaded Grey to force Collot's departure two days later.[193]

Collot did not return directly to France but, like Rochambeau, sailed first to New England. Awaiting exchange and appropriate transport, both governors quarrelled with Joseph Fauchet, the new French minister plenipotentiary to the United States.[194] They defended their actions in surrendering the colonies, asserting that metropolitan government had abandoned them and that colonists had betrayed them. Bitter internal conflicts had contributed to the British conquest of Martinique and Guadeloupe. These conflicts reflected the ambiguity of the republican regimes in the Windward Islands, which affirmed coloured equality but defended slavery. Martinique's planters believed these positions were incompatible and rose against Rochambeau's government in April 1793. If the governor general armed slaves to defeat the rebellion and to repel the first British invasion, he was determined to return slaves to their gangs after the siege. In Guadeloupe the slaves who killed their masters at Trois-Rivières claimed that they had thwarted a counter-revolutionary plot. White radicals praised the insurgents and accepted this claim because it fit with their hostility towards planters and Governor Collot, yet these patriots feared slavery's abolition.

The French revolutionary script not only inspired the aspirations of slave insurgents and the fears of royalist planters but it also shaped the factional strife among whites. Conflicting interpretations of popular sovereignty and the location of the nation's will divided colonists. If moderate republicans accepted Collot's authority as emanating from that of the metropolitan government, radicals could never accept a commission originating with Louis XVI. Emboldened by news and rhetoric from France, Guadeloupe's *sans-culottes* challenged the legitimacy of executive authority itself. In Martinique the new representative assembly echoed revolutionary political culture by instituting de-Christianization and by creating a revolutionary tribunal to punish counter-revolutionaries. If patriots supported Rochambeau, the mutiny of *Félicité* demonstrated that the revolutionary struggle undermined the defence of the Windward Islands. Writing from Philadelphia in 1795, Collot referred to those who had opposed his authority and thwarted his efforts to defend Guadeloupe as "Terrorists."[195] This characterization of the patriots and of the situation in the colony was premature. In June 1794 a French expedition that authentically embodied the Jacobin Terror recaptured Guadeloupe, and its leaders came armed with the most radical of revolutionary communications: the National Convention's decree abolishing slavery.

7 Reign of Terror: Victor Hugues's Regime in Guadeloupe, 1794–1798

Six weeks after General Collot surrendered to British forces, a handful of ships carrying just over one thousand soldiers from France reached Guadeloupe. This small expedition would reconquer the colony for the Republic and transform it into a bastion of radical revolution in the eastern Caribbean. Victor Hugues, one of two civil commissioners sent to the Windward Islands, led French troops in capturing Pointe-á-Pitre and repelling a subsequent British siege. He also proclaimed the National Convention's decree of 16 *Pluviôse* Year II (4 February 1794) abolishing slavery in the French empire. Mobilizing the liberated slaves to supplement his white troops, Hugues drove the British from Guadeloupe by the end of 1794. Despite British naval superiority, from 1795 to 1798 French warships and privateers harassed British shipping and delivered a steady flow of prizes to Guadeloupe. Hugues also used the subversive power of the decree of 16 *Pluviôse* to incite rebellion in British colonies. The resulting insurgencies, which he backed with munitions and troops, forced the British to abandon Sainte-Lucie (St Lucia) and threatened their control of Grenada and St Vincent.

Hugues carried the decree of revolutionary emancipation to Guadeloupe, but he also brought the guillotine of revolutionary Terror. His treatment of French colonists who supported the British occupation of Guadeloupe was brutal, and he dealt ruthlessly with all internal opposition. News of the Thermidorian Reaction in France, however, threatened Hugues's authority in Guadeloupe after 1795 by providing a conservative counter-script that could be used to discredit him. White colonists' denunciations of Hugues as a corrupt tyrant undermined his reputation with metropolitan government until his recall to France in 1798. Recent scholarship has focused on the contradiction between the emancipation of Guadeloupe's slaves and the denial of their equality. Hugues forced the black cultivators to return to work on the plantations, refusing to implement the new constitution of 1795 in Guadeloupe because it would grant them political rights. Laurent Dubois has argued that Hugues's regime foreshadowed the republican racism of France's nineteenth-century colonial empire.[1] Yet Hugues relied on the support and loyalty of the black *sans-culottes* to maintain power, and opposition to abolition lay behind much of the contemporary criticism he faced. Beyond the colonial context, including the tension between the goals of ending slavery and maintaining plantation agriculture, the ideological dynamic of the French Revolution helps to explain the regime's ambiguity. Proclaiming the decree of 16 *Pluviôse* was part of Hugues's imposition of an even more radical version of the revolutionary script than his republican predecessors. In its calls for universal liberation, its ruthless use of violence, and its justification for absolute authority, his dictatorship reflected the Revolutionary Government in France that sent him. Victor Hugues's regime in Guadeloupe represented the extension of the Jacobin Terror to the Windward Islands.

I The Abolition of Slavery (June 1793–April 1794)

The National Convention's decision in February 1794 to abolish slavery was the outcome, as Jeremy Popkin has demonstrated, of a series of contingencies on both sides of the Atlantic.[2] In June 1793 Léger-Félicité Sonthonax and Étienne Polverel, entirely on their own initiative, offered freedom to slaves in Saint-Domingue who would fight for the Republic because of an unexpected crisis in the city of Cap Français. The Legislative Assembly had sent these civil commissioners to Saint-Domingue in 1792 to enforce the Law of 4 April and to end the slave revolt. White patriots reacted to the commissioners' arrival with deep suspicion.[3] General François-Thomas Galbaud, who arrived in May 1793 as Saint-Domingue's new military governor, provided a focus for resistance. After Sonthonax and Polverel confined Galbaud aboard a warship in the harbour of Cap Français, sailors and patriot prisoners persuaded the general to lead them against the commissioners and the free men of colour. On 20 June some six hundred to two thousand sailors stormed ashore to attack Cap Français. Sonthonax and Polverel believed that they had no choice but to recruit slaves as additional defenders. Their offer of freedom to "black warriors" to fight the Republic's enemies marked the beginning of slavery's abolition by

French Revolutionary authority.[4] Pressure to maintain French control of Saint-Domingue pushed Sonthonax to announce general emancipation for all slaves in the North Province on 29 August. This decree broke the link between freedom and military service, stating explicitly that slavery was incompatible with revolutionary principles.[5] Even before Polverel made the same announcement in the West and South Provinces, Sonthonax dispatched deputies to carry copies of his general emancipation decree to Paris: Jean-Baptiste Belley, who was black, Louis Dufay, who was white, and the mulatto Jean-Baptiste Mills.[6] It remained to be seen, however, whether the National Convention would give its approval to a local decision made by civil commissioners tainted by association with "counter-revolutionary" politicians.

In January 1794 Sonthonax's delegation arrived in metropolitan France just as the Revolution entered its most radical phase. Support for the abolition of slavery, however, had declined because it was associated with Brissot and other Girondin deputies. On 2 June 1793 the sections of Paris had purged these enemies of Robespierre and the Montagnards from the National Convention. A blatant violation of national representation, the purge inspired widespread protest and even outright rebellion by moderate republicans in the provinces.[7] The Girondins' association with what the Montagnards called the "Federalist Revolt" helped send some of them to the guillotine in October 1793. The indictment of Brissot and his colleagues before the Revolutionary Tribunal also included accusations by white colonists from Saint-Domingue. Pierre-François Page and Augustin-Jean Brulley – representatives of the colonial assembly at Cap Français, sent to Paris in 1792 to insist that Saint-Domingue could not exist without slavery – had already persuaded the Montagnards that Sonthonax and Polverel, whom Brissot had recommended as civil commissioners, were linked to the Girondins' alleged crimes. Consequently, the convention voted the commissioners' recall and arrest on 16 July 1793.[8] When news of the 20 June events at Cap Français reached Paris, Page and Brulley claimed it as further proof of the commissioners' counter-revolutionary conspiracy. Even when they learned at the end of December that Saint-Domingue's planters had concluded a treaty with the British government, the Montagnards accepted Page and Brulley's defence of the colonists.[9] Developments in the colonies, however, were overshadowed by the emergence of the Terror. The Federalist Revolt as well as the counter-revolution in the Vendée and the ongoing war with the European coalition had convinced many deputies that ruthless measures were needed to save the Republic. The National Convention was also under pressure from the *sans-culottes* of Paris, who demanded greater economic controls and harsh measures against hoarders and traitors. The formal declaration of Terror as the "order of the day," following a popular uprising in Paris on 5 September, however, was not simply a response to lower-class agitation or to the circumstances facing the Republic – it also reflected Jacobin ideology. On 10 October the convention decreed that the government would remain "revolutionary" until peace, thus suspending the new constitution indefinitely and concentrating executive power in the Committees of Public Safety and General Security. As Louis-Antoine Saint-Just's speech introducing the decree made clear, the new Revolutionary Government embodied the people's will; dissent or opposition would not be tolerated.[10]

Just as the sailors' attack on Cap Français led the civil commissioners to proclaim general liberty in Saint-Domingue, so the unexpected arrival of Sonthonax's delegation in Paris proved decisive in bringing about the National Convention's abolition of slavery. Even as the planters' representatives demanded their arrest, the new Saint-Domingue deputies convinced the Committee of Public Safety that Sonthonax and Polverel were not counter-revolutionaries. On 3 February 1794, or 15 *Pluviôse* Year II according to the new republican calendar, they addressed the National Convention and were admitted as legitimate representatives of Saint-Domingue's North Province. The following day Dufay, the delegation's white member, delivered a lengthy speech to the convention. He blamed the events of 20 June at Cap Français on General Galbaud, claiming that the blacks had offered their assistance spontaneously; he insisted that Sonthonax and Polverel had given them freedom in order to maintain national sovereignty in the colony. He also argued that this emancipation would not harm commercial interests because it had simply transformed the slaves into loyal paid labourers. The National Convention subsequently declared, "the abolition of Negro slavery in all the colonies; in consequence it decrees that all men, without distinction of colour, residing in the colonies, are French citizens and will enjoy all the rights assured by the constitution."[11] The Paris Commune celebrated the decree of 16 *Pluviôse*,[12] but the convention might not have voted for abolition without the intervention of Sonthonax's delegation.

The Revolutionary Government's measures to enforce the emancipation decree, including the appointment of civil commissioners to carry it to the Windward Islands, were also shaped by contingency, the circumstances of war, and the political struggles of the Terror. Although members of the Committee of Public Safety did not rescind its order for the arrest and recall of Sonthonax and Polverel, they issued an arrest warrant for Page and Brulley in Paris. On 12 April they ordered the minister of marine to send a copy of the decree of 16 *Pluviôse* to Saint-Domingue, where it was to be promulgated without delay. The same *arrêté* called for the minister to submit another copy of the emancipation decree, "destined for the Windward Islands to the civil commissioners who must go there, with the order that it must also be published upon arrival."[13] The Committee of Public Safety had already decided to send commissioners to the Windward Islands before 16 *Pluviôse*. Those sent earlier by the Legislative Assembly to execute the Law of 4 April 1792 had been repelled by the royalist squadron and then recalled to France as politically suspect. The committee's instructions for new civil commissioners, drafted on 22 January 1794, indicated the Revolutionary Government's suspicion of existing republican authorities in Martinique and Guadeloupe.[14] Thus enforcement of the decree of 16 *Pluviôse* was simply added to the civil commissioners' primary mission of enforcing the Revolutionary Government's will in the Windward Islands.

Similarly, the choice of civil commissioners was determined less by commitment to slavery's abolition than by revolutionary politics. When the Committee of Public Safety drafted the 22 January instructions, it had selected Pierre Chrétien, Bertrine, and Sijas for the mission to the Windward Islands. Yet for reasons unknown, the committee later replaced Bertrine with Victor Hugues. Son of a Marseilles baker, Hugues had moved to Saint-Domingue as a young man. He became modestly successful as a mariner and small merchant involved in intercolonial trade. An enthusiastic patriot during the early phase of the revolution in the colony, he became a member of the colonial assembly of the West Province at Port-au-Prince; thus he was hostile to Saint-Domingue's "aristocrats" but also opposed free-coloured equality. Following the slave revolt's outbreak in 1791, he lost his brother and most of his property in the ensuing violence. He returned to metropolitan France in 1792 via London; there he wrote to the minister of marine to denounce a conspiracy against Saint-Domingue by *émigrés*, the British and Spanish governments, and former Governor General Blanchelande, and to offer his services to the Republic.[15] He was not given the naval commission he sought, however, and instead became involved in revolutionary politics in Lorient and an ally of proslavery lobbyists. In January 1794, acting in concert with Page and Brulley, he tried unsuccessfully to prevent Sonthonax's delegation from reaching Paris.[16] Belley, Mills, and Dufay later denounced Hugues to members of the Committee of Public Safety, linking him to the "*Léopardins*" of the Saint-Marc Assembly.[17] While the reason for the Committee of Public Safety's selection of Hugues is unclear, it appears that his reputation as a vigorous enforcer of revolutionary justice was crucial.

In October 1793 representatives on mission Joseph-François Laignelot and Marie-Joseph Lequino had appointed Hugues as public prosecutor to the revolutionary tribunal at Rochefort, which tried naval officers and sailors who arrived in November aboard the ship of the line *Apollon* from Toulon.[18] That city's administrative corps, in rebellion against the National Convention and facing an imminent siege, had opened the port to a British fleet under the command of Admiral Hood on 27 August.[19] Hood deported five thousand to six thousand naval prisoners from Toulon in four disarmed French battleships. When these men reached Brest, Lorient, and Rochefort, they were imprisoned as traitors. Ten naval officers were executed at Rochefort following Hugues's ferocious indictment of 19 November 1793.[20] Hugues subsequently became the prosecutor for the revolutionary tribunal at Brest. He quarrelled with André Jeanbon Saint-André, member of the Committee of Public Safety on mission to rebuild the navy, whom he reproached for moderation.[21] Nonetheless, the Revolutionary Government appointed Hugues along with Chrétien as civil commissioners to the Windward Islands. They wrote to the Committee of Public Safety in April 1794 to request that Sijas, one of the three original commissioners, accompany them. This request for a third commissioner may have reflected tension between the two: Chrétien had known Hugues in Saint-Domingue and did not regard him as an appropriate colleague for the mission entrusted to them. Their ships sailed before Sijas had received orders to join the expedition, however, and before the Committee of Public Safety had received a deposition denouncing Hugues for supporting slavery.[22]

The Revolutionary Government assembled the military expedition at Rochefort, with which Hugues and Chrétien sailed, to strengthen the Republic's defences in the Windward Islands. News that Martinique had fallen to British forces reached France shortly before the expedition's departure; thus its objective was to reinforce Guadeloupe's garrison and to recapture Martinique. It included Generals Aubert, Cartier, and Rouyer, who were to replace the military commanders of Martinique, Guadeloupe, and Sainte-Lucie. Yet the expedition's strength was far below the number of reinforcements requested by Rochambeau. The entire force numbered only 1,150 men. The main contingent of troops

was a battalion formed in the Basses-Pyrénées from various companies of volunteers. Lieutenant-Colonel Jean Boudet commanded these
800 men who took the name "*Bataillon des Sans-Culottes*." The expedition
also included a company of regular infantry soldiers and two artillery
companies under Captain Mathieu Pelardy. All of these troops, along
with their equipment and munitions for Guadeloupe, were loaded into
six transport vessels. Three warships commanded by Captain Corentin-
Urbain de Leissègues, the frigates *Pique* and *Thétis* and the brig *Cerf-
Volant*, escorted the convoy, which sailed from the Île-d'Aix outside
Rochefort's harbour on 23 April 1794.[23] While far from a powerful armada, this little expedition transformed the situation in the Windward
Islands both politically and militarily.

II The Reconquest of Guadeloupe (June–December 1794)

After a crossing of forty-four days the convoy made landfall off the
southern coast of Grande-Terre. Captain Leissègues sent one of his lieutenants ashore; the officer returned with the news that Guadeloupe, like
Martinique, was in British hands. The convoy's commander then convened a council of war at which the civil commissioners decided that
the expedition's troops should be landed in an attempt to retake the colony. French soldiers went ashore near the village of Gosier on the evening of 3 June.[24] Having established a beachhead, Hugues and Chrétien
prepared to assault Fort Fleur-d'Épée. This stronghold mounted fifteen
heavy guns, commanding the entrance to Pointe-à-Pitre's harbour. The
British forces in Grande-Terre, however, were poorly prepared to repel
an attack. Many British troops were sick in hospital and the colony's
governor, Major General Thomas Dundas, died of yellow fever the
very day the French expedition appeared.[25] In the early hours of 6 June
Boudet's battalion, led by Chrétien and supported by French sailors,
stormed Fort Fleur-d'Épée, capturing it after a second assault.[26] The surviving British soldiers abandoned not only the fort but also the town
of Pointe-à-Pitre, retreating across the harbour to Basse-Terre even as
Leissègues's ships entered the port. Taking control of the town, Hugues
reported that the French troops liberated many patriot prisoners from
Pointe-à-Pitre's jail, which the "aristocrats" had tried to set on fire before their departure.[27] In less than three days, the French expedition had
regained half the colony.

Even more dramatic changes soon followed. Two days after the capture of Fort Fleur-d'Épée, Hugues and Chrétien issued the first in a

series of proclamations. It announced that the Republic had conquered Grande-Terre and called on all citizens to rally to national representation. Because the Republic needed to distinguish between its friends and its enemies, however, all those who had not appeared within fifteen days, and were then discovered as fugitives, would be considered rebels: there would be no mercy for those who resisted the nation's will.[28] Far more important was the announcement of general liberty. In a lengthy printed broadsheet, also dated 19 *Prairial* or 8 June, the commissioners first reproduced the National Convention's decree of 16 *Pluviôse* abolishing slavery, and then they proclaimed that the execution of this law had been entrusted to them: "Citizens of all colours, your happiness depends on this law and its execution; the delegates of the nation will guarantee you a way of life which will be the safeguard of all friends of the French Republic against those who already have been and want again to be their oppressors."[29] The revolutionary significance of this proclamation should not be underestimated. Unlike Sonthonax's decrees in Saint-Domingue, this announcement in Guadeloupe that slavery had been abolished was backed by metropolitan legislation and the authority of the French state. Yet if the abolition of slavery destroyed the existing system of colonial labour, it was not intended to overthrow all property relations. While Chrétien and Hugues proclaimed that the law would result in "benevolent equality," they also pledged to guarantee the property held by some and the product of the labour of all others. The proclamation made clear that freedom came with responsibilities: "It is necessary that white citizens offer, cordially, fraternally, and at a fair salary, work to their black and coloured brothers; and it is also necessary that the latter learn and never forget that those who have no property are obliged to provide, by work, their subsistence and that of their family, and furthermore to contribute by these means to the support of their country." It would prove easier to proclaim the obligation to work and the promise of wages, however, than to implement such a system in the colony.

Guadeloupe's former slaves were not only obliged to work, they were also expected to defend the Republic that had freed them. In a proclamation of 9 June the commissioners invited citizens of all colours in the vicinity of Pointe-à-Pitre to enlist in the colony's armed force as national volunteers.[30] If they were to regain control of the colony, it was crucial for the republicans to mobilize large numbers of black troops. This succeeded because former field slaves preferred military service to working the plantations. Yet in the immediate aftermath of the proclamation of general liberty, most former slaves in Grande-Terre simply deserted their work gangs. Chrétien and Hugues sought to restore order by proclaiming death for any citizen who pillaged the plantations' food supplies.[31] Hugues issued an even stronger proclamation on 18 June, denouncing black citizens who had left the plantations and lived through brigandage.[32] The proclamation insisted that not all citizens could be employed in the defence of the colony; the rest had to cultivate the earth and plant food crops as soon as possible. It asked those not under arms to return to the plantations or to remain at work there, declaring that those who did not would be considered traitors and delivered to the rigour of the law. In his report of 17 June to the Committee of Public Safety, Hugues noted the disorder following the publication of the decree of 16 *Pluviôse*. He suggested that severe measures were needed to impose discipline on the former slaves: "There is much confusion, they think sooner of defending themselves than of guarding the colony, and the black citizens whom I command do not yet know the price of liberty and serve only to steal or destroy."[33]

Beyond the challenges arising from the sudden abolition of slavery, the republicans found themselves under siege and awaiting a British attack. Upon learning of the expedition's arrival at Guadeloupe, Admiral Jervis had sailed immediately from Martinique with ships of the line hoping to destroy the French convoy at sea. Leissègues had anchored his ships under the guns of Forts Louis and Fleur-d'Épée, however, so Jervis could only place Pointe-à-Pitre under blockade while the British garrison in Basse-Terre prepared to assault the town. As of 14 June, when Chrétien died as a result of fever and exhaustion, French leadership rested solely with Hugues. The commissioner formed a provisional council of war composed of Captain Leissègues, General Cartier, Lieutenant-Colonel Boudet, Captain Frémont, and Pierre Villegégu, the head of civilian administration who had accompanied the expedition.[34] Even as he awaited the enemy's assault, Hugues took steps to strengthen his control and to communicate the new order in Grande-Terre. With Villegégu's assistance he organized a new popular society and established new municipalities at Saint-François, Sainte-Anne, Moule, and Pointe-à-Pitre. Complaining that colonists who claimed to support the Republic lacked revolutionary fervour, he ensured that those who opposed it would face revolutionary justice. On 17 June Hugues reported to the Committee of Public Safety that he had formed a military commission to try "aristocrats captured under arms," meaning colonists who had fought with the British, and that several had already been guillotined.[35]

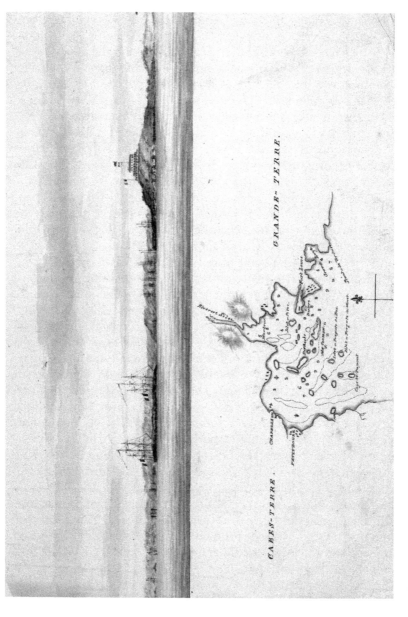

4 "View and Plan of French-Occupied Guadeloupe." PAH5035/National Maritime Museum, Greenwich, London.

Admiral Jervis and General Grey landed troops to the east of Pointe-à-Pitre on 19 June. Five days later their batteries opened fire on Fort Fleur-d'Épée and the town in concert with British guns across the harbour and the Rivière Salée. Cut off from the town's water supply by the bombardment, many of the besieged in Pointe-à-Pitre perished from dysentery. Grey's soldiers advanced, seizing the high ground that dominated both the town and the fort, and beat back a republican counterattack to regain the position. The siege's climax came on 2 July, when British troops assaulted Fleur-d'Épée from the east and the town from the west. Pointe-à-Pitre's defenders took refuge in the fortified Morne du Gouvernement; from there they directed lethal musket fire and grape shot at the attackers. Gunfire from French ships in the harbour caused the explosion of a powder magazine in Pointe-à-Pitre, decimating and demoralizing the British troops, who retreated back to Basse-Terre. Grey called off his attack on Fort Fleur-d'Épée; three days later he disembarked his army from Grande-Terre.[36]

The British retreat from Grande-Terre solidified both Hugues's leadership and the importance of abolition to his regime. None of the French generals survived the siege, two of whom Hugues had denounced as cowards, but he was effusive in his praise for the "brave Boudet" and his men. He also commended the conduct of the expedition's sailors and naval officers, recommending that Leissègues be promoted to the rank of rear admiral.[37] More important than his commendations of loyal subordinates in official dispatches, however, were Hugues's communications celebrating the end of the siege as the Republic's victory in Guadeloupe. In a printed *Address to the Republicans of the Armies of Land and Sea*, he compared French troops to those of ancient Rome, who had defeated an army of superior numbers because of their virtue and courage. Republican heroes now included black men, however, and if the English had previously conquered French possessions, "this was not difficult because then there were masters and slaves."[38] Thus the address represented emancipation as being crucial to victory. Hugues delivered a similar message with his order of 16 July that Pointe-à-Pitre henceforth be called Port-de-la-Liberté, as the place where the delegates of the National Convention first announced the freedom decreed on 16 *Pluviôse* and as commemoration of the Republic's victory over enemies and traitors.[39] Behind the public pronouncements, Hugues's private report on these events suggests that the siege had altered his attitude towards the former slaves:

I declare by my soul and conscience to the Committee of Public Safety that having passed twenty years in the colonies and having always owned Negroes, I had always doubted that they could be given freedom, but I must in truth declare that they showed themselves worthy of it by the conduct they have held. Beyond the theft and the laziness, vices innate to enslaved men due to the debasement in which they are kept, they have not carried themselves to any extremes against their former masters. They have pillaged much, but have limited themselves to that only. Many have taken up arms and these have shown themselves worthy to fight for liberty.[40]

He stated that black soldiers would always need European leadership, but he also ordered the amalgamation of former slaves into the same units with the *sans-culottes* from France where they would receive the same pay.[41] Hugues had come to understand, as he had not before leaving Rochefort in April, that his success as a revolutionary leader in the colonies depended upon backing emancipation in Guadeloupe and promoting it elsewhere.

Hugues's immediate objective was to conquer the entire colony. After Grey withdrew from Grande-Terre on 5 July, British forces in Guadeloupe limited themselves to fortifying their camp at Berville and bombarding Port-de-la-Liberté. They had suffered over five hundred casualties in the recent operations, causing Grey to appeal to England for reinforcements. Similarly, most of the French troops who had arrived with the expedition had been killed, died of wounds, or succumbed to disease.[42] Yet the decree of general liberty enabled Hugues to overcome these losses.[43] Along with white and coloured patriots, the republicans mobilized more than two thousand black soldiers. The new army achieved its first success at the end of July when it regained the island of Désirade, north-west of Grande-Terre.[44] To outfit this army, Hugues sent cargoes of sugar and coffee to the Swedish colony of Saint-Barthélemy, and he used funds from their sale to purchase arms. He also issued letters of marque to small privateers, encouraging them to capture needed supplies and harass enemy shipping.[45]

The communication of Terror was central to Victor Hugues's political and military strategy. His proclamation of 17 July declared that treachery had caused the loss of French possessions throughout the Windward Islands. If the English had corrupted French colonists, it would be republican courage and virtue that would assure the French conquest of all the Antilles. Republican virtue was now inseparable from the abolition of slavery: "The decree of 16 *Pluviôse* while assuring us our colonies, will also assure the destruction of those of the enemy: men degraded by slavery, recognizing the price of liberty, will fight for us. They will carry liberty into the English colonies. Already terror proceeds them and assures their success. The arms of the Republic, triumphant in Europe, will be so in America."[46] Yet it was as important to purge the "monsters" from within the Republic's territory – and the vices associated with them – as it was to terrorize the foreign enemy. To end brigandage, public spirit had to be introduced and the reign of law assured to bring about the rebirth of tranquillity. In keeping with the new version of the revolutionary script from France, Hugues formalized a system of revolutionary justice to punish the wicked. He ordered the renewal of the military commission to try "national crimes" and the establishment of tribunals in every municipality.

Having raised a new army, Hugues went on the offensive. During the night of 26–27 September, thirteen hundred French troops embarked in canoes to outflank the British lines. One column commanded by Pelardy, whom Hugues had promoted to the rank of general of division, captured the magazine near Petit-Bourg. The other column, under Brigadier General Boudet, forced the British to abandon their post directly across the harbour from Port-de-la-Liberté. This allowed Hugues to throw a bridge of boats across the span of water, giving the rest of the republican army free communication between Grande-Terre and Basse-Terre. Uniting his forces, Hugues attacked the Berville camp on 1 October. Its defenders repelled three French assaults with both sides suffering heavy casualties. Hugues demanded that the British commander, Brigadier General Colin Graham, surrender with his army or no quarter would be given. Graham asked for the same terms to be applied to the French royalists as to the British troops, but Hugues refused. On 7 October Graham signed the surrender and marched out of the camp at the head of his men, a capitulation Hugues compared to that of General Burgoyne at Saratoga during the War of American Independence.[47]

Cooper Willyams, the chaplain aboard Admiral Jervis's flagship, claimed that Graham succeeded in smuggling twenty-five French officers to the safety of *HMS Boyne*, but Willyams also witnessed the fate of the other royalists who remained:

> their unfortunate brethren, to the number of three hundred, who had defended their posts to the last, with the most determined resolution, were doomed to suffer death by the hands of their republican countrymen in cold blood, in a manner hitherto, I believe, unheard of, at least unrecorded

in the annals of the most savage and abandoned people. Humanity must shudder at the idea; the republicans erected a guillotine, with which they struck off the heads of fifty of them. Thinking, however, this made of proceeding too tedious, they invented a more summary plan; they tied the remainder of these unhappy men fast together, and placed them on the brink of the trenches which they had so gallantly defended; they then drew up some of their undisciplined recruits in front, who firing an irregular volley at their miserable victims, killed some, wounded others, and some, in all probability, were untouched; the weight however of the former dragged the rest into the ditch, where the living, the wounded, and the dead, shared the same grave, the soil being instantly thrown upon them.[48]

Willyams was incorrect that no precedents existed for such action. Republican forces in France had carried out similar mass executions of prisoners in 1793 following the defeat of the counter-revolutionaries in the Vendée and the rebel cities of Lyon and Toulon. Such repression characterized the Terror.[49] Hugues was well aware of such episodes; indeed he knew officials who had ordered them in western France, and he served as an agent of the Revolutionary Government that considered them as necessary and just. His own account of the executions following Graham's surrender is matter of fact: "From the 7th to the 16th [of Vendémiaire Year III; 28 September to 7 October 1794] close to 1200 Frenchmen were taken arms in hand; all those who were free before 1789 have suffered the punishment due their crimes."[50] Hugues spared the slaves who had fought with the royalists because they had no say in their fate and had been kept in ignorance of the decree of 16 *Pluviôse*; instead, he condemned them to labour at public works projects.

As these executions were taking place, the remaining British troops in Guadeloupe under Major General Robert Prescott evacuated all other posts and took refuge in Fort Saint-Charles, which commanded the town of Basse-Terre. Because British warships remained close to shore, the republicans had to haul the artillery and munitions overland for the coming siege. The French army began to bombard the fort on 21 October and soon cut off its water supply. Even as the siege dragged on, Hugues issued an order on 21 November, inspired by the revolution in France, that determined how the colony's plantations would be run. All land belonging to *émigrés* would be designated "National Property," while that of absent owners, whose emigration could not be verified, would be designated as "Sequestered Property." There was precedent for such expropriation. In late February and early March 1794 the Committee of Public Safety had proposed the disposal of lands confiscated from enemies of the revolution, and the National Convention had approved what became known as the Laws of Ventôse.[51] If these laws called for such lands to be redistributed to "indigent patriots," Hugues declared sequestered properties in Guadeloupe indivisible: they would not be broken up and there would be only one principal renter.[52] Like the insistence that black citizens continue to work, this order suggested that Hugues's regime did not intend to alter the basic structure of the colony's plantation economy. This decision was premised on French control of Guadeloupe. After a siege of fifty-eight days, General Prescott evacuated Fort Saint-Charles on 10 December. He abandoned the fort's guns and powder to the republicans, who shortly before his evacuation had regained the island of Marie-Galante.[53] Even as Prescott's men embarked on ships of the Royal Navy in Basse-Terre's roadstead, Hugues devised a symbolic act to terrorize both the retreating enemy and those colonists in Guadeloupe who sympathized with them: he ordered the remains of General Thomas Dundas, the British governor who had died in June, to be dug up and scattered to the winds.[54] The Terror had come to the Windward Islands.

III Spreading Revolution in the Windward Islands (1795–1796)

Victor Hugues's strategy to regain the Republic's possessions and to defeat its enemies was to communicate subversion and revolt throughout the Windward Islands using printed propaganda and revolutionary agents. In the immediate aftermath of the British evacuation, however, he first took steps to consolidate his control of Guadeloupe. Hugues appointed new municipalities, with increased powers of surveillance, from lists of trusted revolutionaries.[55] He ordered that all effects from the homes and plantations of *émigrés* be seized.[56] *Émigré* property was not to be looted but to be held and administered by revolutionary authority. In February 1795 Hugues ordered specific measures to control commerce in colonial commodities and to prevent speculation in basic supplies. All trading with neutral ships was forbidden. A provisional commercial agency was established to set the prices for commodities. It also set the prices and quantities of merchandise, sold on behalf of the Republic's account, which citizens could purchase.[57] To encourage former slaves to remain on the plantations, and as a gesture of de-Christianization, in March the commissioners decreed that cultivators should not rest on Sundays but could use the *nonidi*, the ninth day of the republican week, for their private business and the *decadi* for rest.[58] Hugues also beefed up Guadeloupe's defences and sent commissions into the countryside to root out royalists and to educate the population.[59] The arrival of reinforcements from France in January 1795 strengthened Hugues's hold on Guadeloupe and also demonstrated the serious obstacle posed by the British naval blockade. Hugues sent the *Pique* to warn the approaching convoy, which brought two more civil commissioners, Goyrand and Lebas, as well as two thousand French troops, that at least six enemy men-of-war were cruising to windward of Guadeloupe.[60] *HMS Blanche* intercepted and captured the *Pique* after a hard-fought engagement. Most of the convoy entered Port-de-la-Liberté safely, although the British took one transport carrying over five hundred soldiers.[61]

Despite the blockade, in 1795 Hugues succeeded in fomenting and then assisting insurrections in Sainte-Lucie, Grenada, and St Vincent. Although British forces had taken Sainte-Lucie in April 1794, they soon encountered resistance from republican insurgents in the island's interior, who referred to themselves as *"l'armée française au bois."* The insurgency became general throughout the colony after news of the decree of 16 *Pluviôse* allowed republicans to rouse Sainte-Lucie's slaves into rebellion. The British commander, Brigadier General Stewart, offered an amnesty to rebels who would surrender, but only eight did so. In February 1795 Hugues sent an agent to Sainte-Lucie with a commission in the army of the Republic for the insurgents' leader and an order for all French inhabitants to join the revolt.[62] The republicans soon gained control of most of the island, bottling up Stewart's men in the town of Castries and the fort of Morne Fortuné. Lieutenant General Sir John Vaughan, who had replaced Grey as British commander-in-chief in the Windward Islands, dispatched a newly raised corps of black soldiers from Martinique to Sainte-Lucie to put down the rebellion. This tactic had only limited success, however, and in April Hugues sent his colleague Goyrand to take command of the republicans.[63] Goyrand's forces routed British troops on 22 April, forcing Stewart again to take refuge in Morne Fortuné. Hugues's flotilla of small vessels transported fifteen hundred additional troops, siege artillery, and munitions from Guadeloupe to Sainte-Lucie; on 17 June the republicans began to bombard the fort. Stewart evacuated his garrison that night into British ships in the harbour, abandoning the colony to the French.[64]

Hugues also incited rebellion in Grenada and St Vincent. France had settled both islands originally but lost them to Great Britain in 1763 after the Seven Years' War. The British government doubted the loyalty of its

5 John Thomas Baines, "Action between HMS Blanche and the Picque, 5 January 1795," 1830. BHC0478/National Maritime Museum, Greenwich, London.

French-speaking subjects, since they had supported the French occupation of the two colonies during the War of American Independence. The islands were returned to British control in 1786. French planters' resentment of British administration in Grenada increased with the appointment of Ninian Home as governor in 1793 and his enforcement of 1763 instructions to confiscate property belonging to the Roman Catholic Church. If such actions undermined solidarity between French- and English-speaking whites in Grenada, the British administration also introduced further discriminatory regulations against free people of colour, most of whom were of French origin. Therefore French colonists welcomed Hugues's emissaries in February 1795, and the coloured planter Julien Fédon accepted his commission as leader of the revolt in Grenada, which began on 2 March. The republican forces, including slaves inspired by the French promise of emancipation, attacked the British inhabitants of Gouyave and Grenville and captured Governor Home. The acting governor proclaimed martial law, held his forces in the capital of St George's, and appealed to Martinique for reinforcements. Fédon demanded the surrender of the colony's forts, warning that he would kill all his hostages if the governor attacked his headquarters. The rebel leader also declared that he would kill any colonists who opposed him and burn their property. Vaughan ordered part of Sainte-Lucie's garrison to Grenada, but on 7 April these troops failed to dislodge Fédon from his interior stronghold and retreated to St George's.[65]

The British difficulties in Grenada were compounded by a simultaneous uprising in St Vincent. In this colony Hugues's communications appealed not only to disaffected French colonists and to slaves but also to the indigenous Caribs. While the French had divided St Vincent with the Caribs, after 1763 British colonists tried to push the Black Caribs, those who had interbred with runaway slaves, off their land in order to extend plantations. Carib resistance resulted in a negotiated peace in 1773, but the Caribs never accepted British rule and supported French forces during the American War.[66] On 4 March 1795 republican agents landed in St Vincent with a message for the Carib Chief Chatoyer, addressed by Hugues not only as an ally but also as a French general, to rise up against the English. Learning of the rebellion in Grenada, Governor James Seton requested that Chatoyer and the other Carib chiefs attend a meeting of the colony's council. Chatoyer refused and on 8 March the Black Caribs, armed by French republicans, attacked militia troops in St Vincent, forced their retreat into Kingston, and defiantly flew the tricolour flag on Dorsetshire Hill overlooking the island's capital. On 12 March Chatoyer issued a proclamation to the island's French colonists demanding that they support his rebellion. If they did not, "we swear to them that fire and sword will be used against them, that we will burn their goods and that we will slit the throats of their wives and children to wipe out their race."[67] Two days later British forces stormed the hill, dispersed its defenders, and killed Chatoyer and perhaps twenty other Carib warriors.[68]

Hugues denounced Chatoyer's death as an atrocity, claiming that he had been hanged rather than killed in battle, but he also reported to the Committee of Public Safety that the Caribs had massacred all British planters who fell into their power.[69] His own address inciting the Caribs to revolt had encouraged such action.[70] Brutality and ruth-lessness characterized both the insurrections and the efforts to defeat them. Reporting on the atrocities that accompanied the fighting in Grenada, Hugues blamed the British.[71] Reflecting the language and ideology of radical revolutionaries in metropolitan France, Hugues both condemned the actions of the Republic's enemies and called for violent reprisals. In a published *arrêté* of 31 March, he described the bounties placed on republicans and Caribs by the councils and governors of Grenada, St Vincent, and Dominica as "an attack on the rights of humanity, nations and peoples." He charged the Caribs and their republican allies to retaliate against the British in these islands. He also ordered Fédon's lieutenants and the Republic's delegate in Grenada to inform enemy commanders of his *arrêté*. Once this had been done, he enjoined all French officers "in islands conquered or to be conquered" to "observe the laws of war": if the British killed any republican prisoners, despite Hugues's formal warning, French officers were to exact revenge "until they efface the name and memory [of the enemy] from the country where the crime was committed."[72] This declaration was propaganda and was intended both to motivate the insurgents and to intimidate the enemy. As Lebas observed, "Hugues has spread terror among the English."[73]

The conquest of Sainte-Lucie in June 1795 marked the republicans' greatest achievement in the Windward Islands and the high point of Hugues's campaign of subversion.[74] The commissioners' primary objective, however, was to regain Martinique. To prepare for that conquest, Hugues ordered an attack on Dominica. In June five hundred French troops under General Pelardy landed in the colony, but their arrival neither inspired a slave revolt nor received support from the island's French planters. British soldiers soon forced the republicans to surrender. Hugues blamed the raid's failure on the "weakness and incapacity" of its leader; his dismissal of Pelardy marked the beginning of the alienation of many of Hugues's former supporters. The commissioners informed the Committee of Public Safety in July that, if the British relinquished command of the sea during the coming hurricane season, they would make every effort to assault Martinique.[75] While the republican successes had been achieved in large part using arms captured from the enemy, they demanded greater support from the metropolitan government.[76] On 21 November Hugues and Lebas stated that their next dispatch would report either that republicans were in Martinique or that they were defending Guadeloupe against a British invasion.[77]

Hugues's strategy of spreading revolution, requiring both the communication of *agents provocateurs* and amphibious military operations to support insurgents, was closely linked to the actions of privateers based at Guadeloupe. As republicans waged guerrilla war against the British on land, French privateers waged *guerre de course*, or war on trade, throughout the eastern Caribbean. "Our efforts are not circumscribed by the limits of the islands that we occupy, the sea can attest to our temerity," Hugues and Lebas boasted to the Committee of Public Safety. "The small fleet of our corsairs, after transporting troops, sometimes to one island, sometimes to another, worry the enemy and ruin his commerce," they added.[78] On 8 June they reported that since late October 1794 French privateers had captured fifty vessels and sunk or burned at least eighty others.[79] Along with issuing letters of marque to privateers, Hugues also committed warships of the French Navy to the campaign against enemy commerce.[80] These operations were highly successful despite, according to Hugues, "the repugnance of certain sailors to sortie and face the enemy."[81] This criticism reflected a growing conflict between the commissioner and naval crews. In his dispatch of 15 November Rear Admiral Leissègues reported a mutiny among his sailors, who were furious that Hugues refused to distribute prize money the crews expected from the vessels their frigates had taken.[82] Hugues punished this insubordination with exile. He dispatched the frigate *Concorde* to Sainte-Lucie, where it remained trapped during the rainy season as fever decimated its crew. He confined the *Thétis* and the *Hercule* to a distant anchorage on northern Grande-Terre – far from the taverns of Port-de-la-Liberté or Basse-Terre – to carry out necessary repairs.[83] This act encouraged desertion, which exacerbated Leissègues's difficulties in manning his ships. British men-of-war captured French ships, and their sailors could not be replaced because no prisoner exchanges occurred. Moreover, the civil commissioner repeatedly countermanded the orders the admiral received from Paris.[84] Hugues viewed the navy as subordinate to revolutionary authority that, like the Jacobin regime that sent him, he embodied.

Privateers were more important to the war against British commerce than ships of the French Navy. By October 1795 more than forty privateers were based at Guadeloupe, not counting the sloops, longboats, and canoes republicans used to attack enemy vessels. Initially most privateers were fitted out directly by the republican administration, but in July 1796 Hugues and Lebas issued regulations for individual merchants to arm corsairs. After paying a fee for a commission, the private outfitter could profit from the sale of his corsair's prizes and their cargos, although the profit was shared with the captain and crew. The records of the colony's tribunal of commerce demonstrate the success of these operations during Hugues's tenure: between 14 October 1794 and 28 October 1798, privateers and French warships brought in 880 vessels to be assessed and sold as prizes.[85] If commerce raiding allowed Guadeloupe to be provisioned and supplied with munitions despite the British blockade, by 1795 it also brought an influx of money and economic activity to the colony's ports. It was not only the outfitters of privateers who benefited but also all those who supplied the privateers' needs. This economic boom was not enjoyed exclusively by whites. Privateers' crews included mulatto and black sailors, and privateering contributed to the social rise of a coloured merchant elite in Guadeloupe, most of whom had been free before the decree of 16 *Pluviôse*.[86] Hugues made significant personal investments in privateers, accumulating considerable wealth as a result. His enemies accused him of making a fortune from the war on trade by forcing other merchants to give him a share of their enterprises and by stacking the tribunal of commerce with his creatures to ensure maximum profits from the sale of prizes in which he had an interest.[87]

Privateers flying French colours were based not only at Caribbean islands under the Republic's authority but also in neutral colonies and in ports of the southern United States.[88] Hugues sought to control these operations beyond Guadeloupe. On 9 September 1795 the commissioners issued an *arrêté* stating that Guadeloupe's privateers had been denounced in the United States for attacks on neutral shipping. They blamed this on corsairs lacking legitimate letters of marque or on those who had received commissions from suspect republican officials, "which they use to plunder even patriots who fled English persecution." Given the complaints of neutral powers, Hugues and Lebas ordered the owners of all vessels requisitioned for the Republic's service, if resident in the United States, to liquidate their titles before the French consul general and submit documentation to prove that they were not *émigrés*.[89] Yet in 1796, believing that New England merchants were supplying British garrisons in the Windward Islands, Hugues ordered his privateers and warships to stop and search neutral ships sailing under British protection.[90] Hugues denounced the American government for signing the Jay Treaty of November 1794, which had established favourable commercial relations with Great Britain, and began to target American vessels specifically.[91] By 1797 French privateers were seizing American and other neutral vessels as prizes, actions that led to the so-called Quasi War between France and the United States.[92]

Even as Hugues spread revolution in the Windward Islands, political developments in France threatened his position as revolutionary leader in the colonies. On 27 July 1794 deputies in the National Convention denounced Robespierre and his closest associates, accusing them of dictatorship. They were guillotined the following day. The conspirators behind the *coup d'état* of 9 *Thermidor* had not intended to moderate the revolution, but the pressure from the majority within the convention and from the nation at large to end the Terror proved overwhelming. The convention released those imprisoned as suspects and reorganized the government to prevent the concentration of power in the committees. In November and December the deputies closed the Jacobin Club, put some of the most infamous terrorists on trial, and abolished the maximum on the prices of basic commodities. The end of economic controls led to the popular uprisings in Paris of *Germinal* and *Prairial* in the spring of 1795. Their failure marked the final defeat of the *sans-culottes* and allowed the National Convention to prepare a new constitution for the Republic.[93] It was not clear, however, what the Terror's repudiation in metropolitan France would mean for the abolition of slavery or for Hugues's regime in Guadeloupe.

Rumours and news of Thermidor in the British press reached the Windward Islands long before any official account from France. Beginning in July 1795 the correspondence of Hugues and Lebas revealed growing concern to demonstrate their non-partisan loyalty to the Republic and their affirmation that the abolition of slavery had been a success. In a letter to Étienne Lavaux, Saint-Domingue's new governor general, they contrasted the tranquillity in Guadeloupe under their leadership with the turmoil in his colony, where most former slaves had abandoned the plantations.[94] They also contrasted their military exploits with Lavaux's failure to drive the British from Saint-Domingue. This letter was intended to bolster Hugues's reputation in metropolitan France and, also to this end, on 8 July he and Lebas wrote to the president of the National Convention. For eight months their only news from Europe had come from "perfidious English newspapers," but they informed him that "the success of the Republic's arms in this hemisphere merits the regard of the National Convention."[95] Along with their conquest of Guadeloupe and Sainte-Lucie and the attacks on

St Vincent, Grenada, and Dominica, they referred to the immense quantity of prizes captured at sea. Much more important, however, they insisted that they were loyal only to the National Convention. Hugues was aware of the events of Thermidor and recognized that he was now vulnerable to denunciation, dismissal, and arrest as a terrorist.

The commissioners' efforts to portray themselves as loyal and nonpartisan republicans, and to defend emancipation in Guadeloupe, were also demonstrated in their proclamation of 10 September, addressed to French colonists who had taken refuge in the United States. Hugues and Lebas sought to distance themselves from other civil commissioners, particularly Sonthonax, whom most colonial refugees hated and held responsible for the anarchy they associated with the abolition of slavery. Hugues denied accusations that he had instituted a reign of terror, an impression he had previously embraced. If this demonstrated his awareness of the new Thermidorian context in metropolitan France, so did the proclamation's insistence that he had not introduced radical social levelling in Guadeloupe. The real fear for French colonists who had fled to the United States was that abolition had destroyed the plantation economy and produced racial equality. The proclamation assured them that agriculture had been restored in Guadeloupe, property was respected, the armed forces were disciplined, and, perhaps most important, that the freedom of former slaves was qualified. Hugues recognized that Thermidor encouraged colonial *émigrés* and their supporters in France to hope that the decree of 16 *Pluviôse* might be repealed and that those who implemented it might be denounced and replaced. Therefore, he and Lebas portrayed themselves as republicans distinct from the royalists who had devastated the colonies, from the philanthropists who excited the slaves' vengeance against their masters in Saint-Domingue, and from the dictators, the latter a reference to the now discredited Robespierrists in France.[96]

The fate of Hugues and his regime remained uncertain at the end of 1795. Through reports in the British press and intelligence from his own agents, he was aware that the British government was preparing a major expedition to the West Indies.[97] The commissioners also learned of political developments in France, where the National Convention had completed the Constitution of the Year III and defeated the monarchist uprising of 13 *Vendémiaire* (5 October 1795) in Paris, which allowed it to dissolve peacefully and usher in the new constitutional regime of the Directory.[98] This development had been welcome news to Guadeloupe's republicans, who had been discouraged by royalist propaganda spread

by *émigrés* arriving in the *Andromique*. This propaganda caused particular concern to the colony's former slaves, suggesting that black citizens
regarded their fate as being tied to that of the Republic.[99] The commissioners received a letter from the Committee of Public Safety, written
only weeks before the National Convention disbanded, which praised
their victories over the British. It also referred to the Republic's recent
deliverance from the yoke of cruel tyrants and stated that the convention awaited a profession of the same principles from its delegates.[100] In
their dispatch of 28 December, Hugues and Lebas again affirmed their
steadfast loyalty to the Republic despite the vicissitudes of the revolution and the difficulties of their colonial mission. They knew, however,
that the convention had received "calumnies from malevolent men,"
including the "imbecile Pelardy."[101] It remained to be seen whether the
Directory would confirm Hugues and his colleagues in their positions
or act on the accusations against them.

IV Revolutionary Dictatorship (1795–1797)

The denunciations of Victor Hugues submitted to the French government provide evidence of the range of opposition he faced, and
they also shed light on the nature of the revolutionary dictatorship in
Guadeloupe. Perhaps the most damaging to his reputation in the long
run was the denunciation made by Mathieu Pelardy, the artillery officer
that Hugues had promoted to the rank of general. Hugues dismissed
Pelardy from his command and deported him to France following the
failed attack on Dominica in June 1795. Yet tension between the two
men had emerged before that crisis.[102] While Pelardy knew that Hugues
had criticized his actions, he was shocked when Bordeaux's commune
arrested him upon his arrival on 21 August. Writing to the Committee
of Public Safety, he requested permission to travel to Paris, declaring
that he possessed sufficient evidence not only to prove his own innocence "but also to open your eyes to the immorality, the abuse of power
and the vexations of a man who dishonours national representation."[103]
Hugues's quarrel with Pelardy was part of a larger pattern of conflict
with military officers who questioned his authority, his strategy, or his
accomplishments.

While still imprisoned at Bordeaux in September 1795, Pelardy sent a
report to the Commission of Marine and Colonies condemning Hugues
for continuing the Terror at Guadeloupe. It was Pelardy's record as an
officer – he had been praised and promoted by Hugues – that made his

accusations potentially damaging. He claimed that it was his criticism of the civil commissioner, rather than any failings in his own conduct, that had led to his dismissal and return to France. To support his allegation of injustice, and as evidence of Hugues's violent and erratic behaviour, he also referred to the case of two naval officers whom Hugues had sent before a court martial on trumped-up charges of professional misconduct. According to Pelardy, Hugues was enraged when the judges declared them innocent. Beyond his treatment of military officers, Pelardy accused Hugues of terrorism and corruption. He reminded the commission of Hugues's connection to Rochefort's revolutionary tribunal and claimed that the former public prosecutor continued the same pattern in Guadeloupe.[104]

Almost six months after he submitted his condemnation of Hugues to state officials, Pelardy received support from Janvier Littée, who had the distinction of being the first man of colour elected to a French national assembly; patriot refugees in Dominica had elected him on 28 October 1792 to represent Martinique in the National Convention.[105] In June 1796 he wrote to the Directory asking its members to give an audience to General Pelardy, whose testimony and original documents, Littée declared, would convince them that "the conduct of Victor Hugues is reprehensible."[106] His backing of Pelardy is evidence that Hugues did not command the loyalty of former free men of colour. This designation no longer existed after the proclamation of general liberty in Guadeloupe. The old juridical castes associated with slavery were abolished and the colony's population was divided for census purposes or notarial records into the three categories of *noirs*, *blancs*, and *rouges* (persons of mixed race). Frédéric Régent has examined the social and economic rise of the *rouges* in Guadeloupe after 1794 but concluded that it was primarily those who had been free before 1794 who benefited. Moreover, despite the end of legal discrimination, he argued that racial prejudice continued under the new regime.[107] Hugues did not trust members of the old free-coloured elite; rather, he believed that they had a subversive effect on Guadeloupe's cultivators and was hostile to their desire for greater influence.[108]

Even before Pelardy arrived in France, a representative of Guadeloupe's white colonists had denounced Hugues to a deputy of the National Convention from Bordeaux. Hapel de La Channie was a chemist who, before 1789, had been a member of the Royal Society of Arts and Sciences of Cap-Français and a correspondent from Guadeloupe to the Royal Society of Medicine in Paris.[109] The memoir he submitted to

Antoine François de Fourcroy shortly after arriving at Bordeaux in June 1795 referred to Hugues as a "cruel despot" and an "execrable monster" whose crimes were unknown to the Committee of Public Safety, even though all of Bordeaux groaned with the knowledge. La Channie claimed that the civil commissioners in Guadeloupe had reduced its inhabitants to poverty. Not only had they seized their money and goods but, because Hugues alone could trade with foreigners, they also forced colonists to pay whatever prices he set in order to purchase supplies from the state magazines. It is not surprising that white colonists resented the economic controls characterizing Hugues's regime. Similarly La Channie's sinister depiction of Guadeloupe's black army as the basis for Hugues's power reflected former slave owners' opposition to abolition. Yet in a more general sense, white colonists perceived Hugues as a corrupt tyrant. La Channie referred to his absolute control of communications with metropolitan France, claiming that he forbade all private correspondence, and accused him of forcing the colony's women to become his concubines. The chemist also attributed to Hugues the most unconscionable hypocrisy in first promising protection to all colonists who returned to Guadeloupe – provided that they supported the Republic – but then delivering them to persecution and even the guillotine for supposed counter-revolutionary crimes committed before they had left the colony.[110]

Hugues insisted that most of those seeking to return to Guadeloupe were troublemakers. He sent his own delegation to France in the summer of 1795, and its members informed the Committee of Public Safety that "Tranquillity reigns, but old hatreds are ready to reignite as soon as the old leaders set foot in the colonies."[111] In their own report of 18 November 1795, Hugues and Lebas stated that complaints against them came from inhabitants engaged in illegal commerce with enemy colonies. They went even further to assert strongly that most planters were traitors whose opposition to the abolition of slavery caused them first to support the British and now to attack the civil commissioners.[112] In a subsequent dispatch, Hugues and Lebas accused Pierre-Auguste Adet, France's minister to the United States, of facilitating the entry of émigrés who published records of the slaves they had owned in preparation for what they hoped would be the re-establishment of slavery. With the same hope, those émigrés who returned to France made false reports of calamities in Guadeloupe. According to the commissioners, rumours of this agitation caused great anxiety among the colony's blacks, who feared the return of their old masters. Although these émigrés

6 Photograph of guillotine blade, which was used in Guadeloupe by French republicans and brought to Great Britain as a war trophy by Captain Matthew Scott of HMS Rose. TOA0079/National Maritime Museum, Greenwich, London.

called themselves "deportees," Hugues and Lebas were adamant that "we have deported nobody."[113]

There is justice in Hugues's argument that much of the hostility towards him reflected white resistance to emancipation. Yet it was also true that his regime was a dictatorship and, in the context of the Thermidorian Reaction in France, he knew that he was particularly vulnerable to such a charge. Therefore, he made significant efforts to both justify and deny the arbitrary and authoritarian aspects of his administration. Much of the report his delegation submitted to the Committee of Public Safety in August 1795 represented a defence of the provisional organization Hugues had established in Guadeloupe. Beyond the decree of 16 *Pluviôse*, the report claimed that the National Convention's laws were unknown in the colony; therefore, constituted authorities had to base their conduct on the civil commissioner's *arrêtés*. Since this caused them to exercise seemingly arbitrary rule over citizens, the report requested that metropolitan legislators pass new laws for the colonies. Similarly, Hugues's delegates asked that the Convention provide laws to replace Guadeloupe's system of revolutionary justice, which they claimed had been absolutely necessary to deal with traitors. They recognized that metropolitan government would replace the commissioners but urged leaving at least one of them in place to ensure continuity – and not to establish a colonial assembly.[114] Such arguments were tailored to appeal to the Thermidorian deputies who themselves had been associated with emergency measures. Thus Hugues and Lebas portrayed themselves as agents of the Republic, who had taken equally difficult but necessary actions without partisan motivations. They called their administration in Guadeloupe a model for other colonies. Some colonists accused them of "aristocracy" because they had not been the instruments of vengeance, while they claimed others accused them of "terrorism" because they punished those who had taken up arms with the enemy: "In a country torn by factions, our efforts were against the English: we showed no party greater advantage."[115]

Despite the efforts of pro-slavery activists, the Thermidorian Convention maintained the emancipation decree of 16 *Pluviôse*.[116] In this context, neither the accusations against Hugues nor his efforts to defend his administration had as much impact on the political leadership in France as his record of military success. In August 1795 deputy Joseph-Jacques Defermond delivered a report on the situation in the Windward Islands to the National Convention. He lauded the republicans in Guadeloupe for regaining French possessions and for attacking the enemy's colonies and commerce. In light of these achievements, Defermond argued, deputies should ignore malicious criticism of Hugues and his colleagues.[117] Members of the new Executive Directory, who took up their functions on 2 November 1795, accepted this argument and retained Hugues, Lebas, and Goyrand as the Directory's agents in the Windward Islands. Writing to inform them of this decision on 2 January 1796, Laurent-Jean-François Truguet, the new minister of marine and colonies, declared that they must now serve the Constitution of the Year III. He instructed them to organize the institutions of civil government, but he also urged them not to lose sight of the crucial importance of agriculture. The minister alluded to the accusations of tyranny when he stated that "public functionaries should make nobody fear the weight of their authority, but should excite confidence and public esteem."[118] In his dispatch of 6 March, confirming that Hugues, Lebas, and Goyrand had been named definitively as agents of the Directory, he again recommended that they distinguish between weak and misled men, who could be returned to duty with indulgence, and malevolent ones, who should be restrained by the force of law. This reflected the Directory's larger strategy to end political conflict in France.[119] Much more significant in its implications for their regime in Guadeloupe, however, was the minister's insistence that the agents ensure equality under the new constitution.[120] Hugues's refusal to comply sheds light on a completely different aspect of his dictatorship.

Hugues declared that the control of black citizens and the maintenance of plantation agriculture were incompatible with the constitution. In their report of 9 August Hugues and Lebas informed the minister that they had neither promulgated the constitution in Guadeloupe nor did they intend to, because it would lead inevitably to the colony's destruction.[121] They contended that the new constitution would make it impossible to restrain the blacks' fury against the island's white population. Moreover most of Guadeloupe's whites, aside from two or three hundred men of principle, were sworn enemies of the blacks and of the republican government. Hugues and Lebas claimed that it would become impossible to contain these hatreds under a constitutional order. The problem lay in the definition of citizenship. Citizens had the right to participate in primary assemblies to choose electors, who would then determine their representatives. Article 8 of the constitution of 1795 defined a citizen as a man subject to direct taxation; yet nobody in the colony paid such taxes. Who then would form the primary assemblies? Hugues and Lebas insisted that it would be disaster to allow the blacks to participate in primary assemblies or to form primary assemblies and exclude them from participation.

More important than the dangers of holding primary assemblies, however, was the incompatibility between constitutional principles and the continuation of colonial agriculture. Hugues and Lebas warned the minister that if the government intended to distribute national property to the Africans, the Republic would lose great capital but gain no advantage. Without constraint black cultivators would cease to work the plantations, raising only the few crops they needed to live comfortably. This tendency resulted not from their natural idleness but from the painful nature of the work. The crux of the problem, according to the agents, was the impossibility of reconciling the constitution with the government's instructions to maintain agriculture; forcing cultivators to work for others clearly violated the spirit of the constitution. They insisted that implementing the constitution would not only end agricultural production but also risked upsetting the delicate equilibrium in Guadeloupe. The colony's most enlightened black citizens had distinguished themselves in military service, and the agents praised their performance and discipline. While constraint was essential to keep the plantations in operation, Hugues and Lebas declared that they were taking all measures necessary to improve the cultivators' fate. In their dispatch of 8 August 1796 Hugues and Lebas told the minister that neither individual interest nor recognition of what they owed the Republic stimulated the cultivators: "They naturally hate work and only inspiring fear in them can defeat this apathy."[122] Slave owners had used identical logic, but the decree of 16 *Pluviôse* was supposed to have transformed slaves into free workers who would be paid for their labour. The promise of wages, however, went unfulfilled. Villegégu reported in May 1795 that cultivators on national properties now believed they were entitled to a salary, but this was impossible to pay, and the administration could furnish them only with food.[123]

If the besieged colony's limited resources made it impossible to pay cultivators, thus allowing Hugues to argue that he must rely on coercion to keep plantations operating, his reluctance to implement the constitution also reflected his belief that black citizens lacked the necessary capacity to exercise political rights. The Directory had been deceived, he told the minister in December 1796, regarding the possibility that former slaves might participate in primary assemblies as independent and responsible citizens: "We are no friends of slavery ... but the government must make blacks happy, they are incapable of making themselves happy; their wills will never be other than vile instruments in the hands of others."[124] His opposition to implementing the constitution and permitting such participation was even more adamant in his letter of 16 December to Fourniols, deputy for Martinique to the Legislative Corps, in which he stated: "I have not believed it my duty to assemble black people to name deputies, I never will: honour and my conscience forbid it."[125]

Hugues's refusal to implement the constitution of 1795 reflected his ambivalent attitude towards black liberation. Laurent Dubois argued that Hugues's exclusion of former slaves from full citizenship was part of the larger phenomenon of republican racism, which emerged during the French Revolution's experiment with emancipation and later characterized French imperialism in the nineteenth and twentieth centuries. Dubois also suggested that Hugues's initial demand that slaves work in return for wages was probably influenced by the system Sonthonax tried to establish in Saint-Domingue. Above all, however, Dubois linked Hugues's exclusion of blacks from political rights to the ideas of abolitionists such as the marquis de Condorcet, who had called for the gradual emancipation of slaves. Specifically, Condorcet suggested that freed black workers could not enjoy the full rights of citizenship immediately, having been too degraded by their enslavement, but must be gradually reformed for integration into society.[126] Given Hugues's language in defending his refusal to implement the constitution in Guadeloupe, there is validity to this connection. Yet there was also an enormous difference between the attitudes of Condorcet, the liberal intellectual who condemned slavery as antithetical to reason and justice, and those of Hugues who tried to prevent Sonthonax's delegation from reaching the National Convention. Condorcet's gradualism was not based in racism; if he argued that former slaves needed to be reformed before they could exercise their rights, he also argued that members of the lower classes in France must undergo political and moral education before they could govern themselves.[127] Dubois acknowledged that Hugues's outlook on black citizens was complex. As a former slave owner, Hugues had assumed blacks could not be given freedom, but as a Jacobin he believed that republicanism could transform the former slaves. His determination to maintain an economic order requiring the forced labour of black cultivators was crucial.[128] Hugues's limitation of black liberty, however, was also entirely in keeping with a revolutionary dictatorship modelled on the Terror in France. Just as the Montagnards suspended the constitution of 1793, restricting local freedom and direct democracy in the name of popular sovereignty, Hugues's authority alone represented the nation's will in Guadeloupe.

V Fall of the New Robespierre (1796–1798)

In 1796 the tide of the war in the Windward Islands turned in favour of Great Britain. Determined to regain the initiative in the Caribbean, the British government mounted a major expedition in late 1795 under the command of Major General Ralph Abercromby and Rear Admiral Hugh Christian. Violent storms delayed its departure, but Abercromby reached Barbados in March 1796.[129] His objective was to regain control of Sainte-Lucie, St Vincent, and Grenada before attacking Guadeloupe. The assault on Sainte-Lucie began on 26 April when British regulars landed on either side of Castries harbour, forcing Goyrand to take refuge in Morne Fortuné. Goyrand refused to surrender,[130] and British forces began a regular siege early in May. The French were outnumbered and soon began to run out of water and ammunition. When the British succeeded in establishing their third parallel on 24 May, Goyrand called for a ceasefire; he surrendered the following day.[131] Although Goyrand and his men marched out of the fort and aboard ships to be transported to Europe, other republican soldiers escaped into the woods, joining the island's slaves in continued guerrilla resistance to British occupation. When Abercromby embarked his forces to continue the campaign against St Vincent and Grenada, he had to leave three thousand troops under the command of Brigadier General John Moore to deal with the insurgency.[132]

Although the time spent besieging Morne Fortuné ended the possibility that Abercromby would attack Guadeloupe in 1796, the loss of Sainte-Lucie was a major blow to the republican cause. Hugues and Lebas reported that many French colonists had gone to Sainte-Lucie to join the enemy.[133] News from St Vincent deepened their sense of alarm. Abercromby landed troops there on 9 June and immediately assaulted the republican stronghold on Vigie Ridge. After a day of artillery bombardment and fierce fighting, Marinier, one of the original leaders of the revolt in Sainte-Lucie, surrendered along with 460 black and white republicans on 11 June.[134] The Caribs, cut off from French support, proposed a truce four days later. As in Sainte-Lucie, however, bitter conflict continued following the formal surrender.[135] The same day that Marinier surrendered in St Vincent, 3,000 British troops landed in Grenada south of the republican-held town of Gouyave. Their attack caused 180 republicans to surrender, but Fédon escaped to the Belvidere camp on the slopes of Mount Quoca with 1,000 insurgents. They held this position only until 19 June. While low-intensity resistance would continue, the capture of the Belvidere camp ended Grenada's rebellion and the 1796 campaign. If Abercromby had failed to assault Guadeloupe, he had reversed the French gains made in the Windward Islands in 1795. The British expedition effectively ended Hugues's export of revolution, placing him firmly on the defensive.[136]

News of diplomatic and military developments in Europe also affected the situation in the Windward Islands in 1796–7. After invading Holland, France had signed the Treaty of the Hague with the new Batavian Republic in May 1795 and then concluded a peace settlement with Spain in July 1796. At the end of August 1796 the metropolitan government informed the Directory's agents in Guadeloupe that Spain had declared war on Great Britain.[137] Hugues and Lebas warned Spanish officials at Trinidad of the danger they now faced, but Hugues was more concerned that the Dutch colony of Curaçao not fall into British hands.[138] In September 1796 Hugues sent the frigate *Pensée* to Curaçao, where it supported the island's republicans in expelling the stadtholder, the royal governor who intended to seek British protection. Ironically, Hugues's assurance that he would not impose the abolition of slavery on Curaçao was crucial to the Dutch republicans' alliance with France.[139]

In 1797 the military situation facing the French Republic in the Windward Islands deteriorated further. British forces captured Trinidad on 17 February.[140] Hugues and Lebas reported that, despite their warnings, the Spanish commanders had made no preparations to resist an invasion. Moreover, the Directory's agents claimed that none of Spain's colonial governments accepted the alliance with France because of their fears regarding the abolition of slavery.[141] In their dispatch of 10 March Hugues and Lebas insisted even more forcefully that the decree of 16 *Pluviôse* and the example of Saint-Domingue had turned the Spanish colonies towards England. Black republicans from Saint-Domingue had provoked fears of slave insurrection among both neutrals and French allies.[142] From promoting emancipation as an ideological weapon against the Republic's enemies, Hugues had moved to complaining that France's sponsorship of abolition was alienating its allies in the struggle against Great Britain. The strategy of subversion had failed.

The decline in Hugues's military prestige was accompanied by new communications of opposition to his regime. These denunciations reiterated old charges of tyranny, immorality, and financial corruption but did so in the new context of military defeat. In the first of a series of letters to the minister of marine and colonies, the Guadeloupe merchant Thouluyre Mahé accused Hugues of despotism in February 1796.[143] He claimed that Hugues was a "stranger to virtue," who used public funds to pay for his own pleasures and for a retinue of private agents. Moreover, he accused Hugues of fomenting a "spirit of license" among the blacks, which was directed against the whites whose number in the colony, he claimed, had dropped alarmingly. In a second letter of 23 May, Mahé told the minister that the appointment of Hugues as the Directory's agent was "for all of us here a more cruel sentence than death."[144] He asserted that representative Lion not only protected Hugues from criticism but also gave him the names of those who addressed complaints to metropolitan authorities: these colonists soon found themselves dismissed from public employment, imprisoned, or deported. He asked the minister for permission to travel to France in order to make the case against the Directory's agent in person. Mahé's next letter of 25 November 1796 was written from prison in Port-de-la-Liberté. He had been imprisoned and threatened with the sequester of his property on the charge that he had not delivered all commodities in his possession to government magazines when the English left the colony.[145] In a subsequent letter from prison, dated 12 December, he maintained that this was not the real reason for his imprisonment: "My crime is to have revealed to those who represented Guadeloupe in the Convention, and who represent it again in the Legislative Corps, the outrageous vexations, the criminal and arbitrary acts, and the tyranny of citizens Victor Hugues and Lebas."[146]

It is unclear whether Mahé travelled to France, but in 1797 he submitted a detailed memoir on the situation in Guadeloupe to the minister, insisting that the Directory must replace Hugues. This memoir contained an analysis of the colony's population to support the contention that Hugues had "emptied the island of whites."[147] It denounced the colony's administration as lawless and financially corrupt, claimed that Hugues had chosen his delegates in the communes from the ranks of the propertyless, and stated that "weeds cover most of the old plantations and their buildings have fallen into ruins." Beyond these standard grievances of the colony's white planters and merchants, Mahé also blamed Hugues for the "disasters" at St Vincent and Grenada. He contrasted Hugues's vices with the virtues of General Pelardy and called on the metropolitan government to appoint a new agent for Guadeloupe.

The demand for Hugues's recall was also made in an anonymous memoir submitted to the minister of marine and colonies in 1797 that echoed the Thermidorian language of earlier denunciations: "The most perfect student of Robespierre, this is Victor Hugues."[148] Like Mahé, the author of this memoir contrasted General Pelardy as a true republican, who deserved the credit for Guadeloupe's conquest, with the corrupt Hugues, who had claimed it undeservedly: "Pelardy had the glory, the new Robespierre wanted it and wanted to collect its fruits." The memoir criticized Hugues's abysmal conduct of the war, which included his abandonment of Goyrand at Sainte-Lucie and of the republican forces at St Vincent. Beyond these familiar charges, however, the memoir denounced Hugues for failing to implement the new constitution, claiming colonists only became aware of it when General Girod returned to Guadeloupe from a British prison with a copy he had received from a British officer. It alleged that Guadeloupe's deputy Lion had pressed

Hugues to hold primary assemblies as the constitution required, but that Hugues refused. Moreover, the memoir suggested that in a larger sense he had alienated the colony's black population, thus creating the danger of black revolt. These accusations, regarding the constitution and the former slaves, reflected the fundamental ambiguity of Hugues's regime.

Revolutionary communications, as much as Hugues's failure to open primary assemblies, provoked a black uprising in Guadeloupe late in 1797. On 11 December cultivators in Marie-Galante abandoned the fields and gathered at the market town of Grand-Bourg. Incited by a former free man of colour, who exhorted them to "Cut all white throats!" the cultivators pillaged the town and attacked property owners. Hugues dispatched troops from Guadeloupe to restore order. The revolt's ring-leaders fled when the troops arrived and the majority of the insurgents submitted, returning to their plantations and surrendering their weapons. In his report on these events Hugues suggested that the uprising had been inspired by rumours from France, regarding calls for the full assimilation of black citizens, and by news from Saint-Domingue where Sonthonax had returned as head of a new civil commission in May 1796 and mulattos had massacred whites at Les Cayes in August 1796.[149] Even as troops restored order at Marie-Galante, Hugues claimed that former free men of colour hatched a conspiracy in Guadeloupe. Several "ci-devant Libres," he told the minister, had sought to incite rebellion by encouraging the colony's cultivators to overthrow white oppression as blacks had done in Saint-Domingue. The language Hugues imputed to the conspirators reflected the deepest fears of colonial whites regarding the reversal of racial and economic hierarchies. Hugues and Lebas ordered the arrest of several coloured men who had tried to subvert black and coloured army officers; shortly after these arrests a second insurrection broke out near the market town of Lamentin in Basse-Terre. Led by four "ci-devant Libres," cultivators rampaged through a number of estates and killed four white planters before converging on Lamentin. After General Boudet's attempt to negotiate failed, his troops scattered the insurgents. Hugues proclaimed an amnesty for all rebels who surrendered and returned to their plantations. This announcement had the desired effect, and cultivators turned over the insurrection's leaders to republican authorities. Although he claimed that tranquillity had been restored, Hugues placed the colony under a state of siege.[150]

Hugues's report on the cultivators' insurrections began with a tirade against the situation in Saint-Domingue, against former free men of colour in general and against Julien Raimond in particular.[151] Just as the *ci-devant Libres* sought to gain control of Saint-Domingue, he claimed that they had identical ambitions in Guadeloupe. At the same time, the Directory's agents faced constant opposition from the colony's white planters. Hugues was aware that pamphlets and petitions in metropolitan France denounced him as a terrorist. He blamed these on the planters who were not only enemies of the decree of 16 Pluviôse but also "infamous royalists" and "partners of the English." According to Hugues, Guadeloupe's black cultivators had risen at the instigation of former free men of colour and because of the imprudent speech and provocative actions of their former masters. He did not acknowledge that this discontent might reflect either his regime's failure to pay plantation workers or his refusal to promulgate the new constitution giving black citizens equal rights. The colony's black troops showed no sympathy for the insurgent cultivators, however, and Hugues's report suggested that his regime continued to enjoy their full support in 1798.[152]

If Hugues continued to command the loyalty of his black soldiers, plantation workers had come to regard his regime as oppressive. Yet their insurrection only strengthened his determination not to extend equal rights to Guadeloupe's black citizens. He was adamant that the new Law of 12 Nivôse Year VI (1 January 1798) concerning the colonies' constitutional organization represented impending disaster. Writing to the minister on 11 June, three days after the gravely ill Lebas departed for France, Hugues expressed bitterness that the Directory had ordered him to remain at his post for another eighteen months and to execute a law which heralded Guadeloupe's destruction.[153] While denying accusations that he opposed liberty for Africans in the colonies, he contended that they remained too ignorant and savage to become full citizens' and that without compulsion they would cease to work. If this echoed the arguments of gradual abolitionists, his insistence that only strong government authority could "inoculate them with liberty" – and prevent freedom from leading to licence and anarchy – was in keeping with his former role as commissioner of the Jacobin Terror.

The Directory had already decided to recall Victor Hugues. This decision reflected the denunciations of his conduct submitted to the minister of marine and colonies. It was also inspired by criticism from Guadeloupe's representatives, Lion and Dupuch, that he had neither implemented the constitution nor paid the colony's cultivators, as well as by fear that his regime was dragging France into war with the United States. On 5 June 1798 the directors appointed General Étienne

Desfourneaux, who had served in Saint-Domingue in 1793 and 1796–8, to replace Hugues. He was to enforce the Law of 12 Nivôse as well as the earlier Law of 4 Brumaire Year VI (25 October 1797), which transformed Guadeloupe and its dependencies into a department of France.[154] Desfourneaux's arrival in the Windward Islands demonstrated that reversing Hugues's policies would not be easy. The Directory's new agent left Lorient on 28 September in the *Insurgente* that, along with the frigate *Volontaire*, escorted a small convoy carrying troops commanded by Hugues's enemy, General Pelardy.[155] On 20 November the two French frigates captured *USS Retaliation*, bringing it to Guadeloupe as a prize. Despite Desfourneaux's pledge in a letter to President John Adams that Guadeloupe's privateers would respect American neutrality, and his permission for *Retaliation* and her crew to leave and to take with them 250 other Americans languishing in the island's prisons, the incident contributed to the outbreak of the Quasi War between France and the United States.[156]

Desfourneaux's immediate concern, however, was whether the colony would accept him as the new representative of metropolitan authority. When the convoy reached Guadeloupe, an officer informed Desfourneaux that Hugues's partisans would not permit him or the expedition's troops to land. Desfourneaux invited Hugues aboard the *Insurgente*, where the general accused him of seeking to prevent the convoy's arrival and hold on to power. Hugues denied the charges, but Desfourneaux insisted that he show his approval publicly for the transfer of authority. On 22 November the Directory's new agent announced his powers in the town of Basse-Terre; his initial fears of resistance to his authority appeared unfounded. After taking up residence with Hugues at government headquarters, however, Desfourneaux began to receive reports that troublemakers were preparing an uprising against him by claiming that he intended to overturn the Republic in Guadeloupe and to re-establish slavery.[157] His suspicions soon fell on the man he had replaced. The new head of civil administration intercepted a document suggesting the existence of a plot to murder Desfourneaux and return Hugues to power. The general persuaded Hugues that he must install himself in the *Volontaire* because his presence in town was compromising Basse-Terre's security. When Hugues came aboard the frigate on 4 December, Desfourneaux placed him under arrest. He also demanded that Hugues write letters to disassociate himself from disorder in the colony. Soon after Hugues delivered these, he was transferred to another ship and sailed for Europe on 2 January 1799.[158]

The same day that Desfourneaux announced his powers at Basse-Terre, the colonist Pons-Martin wrote to the minister of marine and colonies to express his relief that the Directory had delivered Guadeloupe from its tyrant: "The voices of citizens of every colour, who could hardly breath under oppression, have broken out in transports of joy at the appearance of their liberator, Citizen Desfourneaux." Yet given that Hugues had used bribery and intimidation to silence his critics and to generate undeserved praise, Pons-Martin worried that he might escape national justice; his punishment was necessary to set the record straight.[159] If many of the colony's residents agreed that Hugues was a corrupt tyrant who deserved to be punished, the turmoil and anxiety that accompanied Desfourneaux's arrival demonstrated that others saw Hugues as the republican warrior who had abolished slavery. Just as the communication of criticism and denunciations had undermined Hugues's reputation in the eyes of metropolitan government, the transmission of news and opinion regarding the waning support for emancipation in France had provoked opposition to his replacement in Guadeloupe.

Victor Hugues's regime represented the climax of revolutionary radicalism in the Windward Islands. Bearing the decree of 16 *Pluviôse*, Hugues freed Guadeloupe's slaves and armed them to drive the British from the colony. He then carried the war to the enemy by inciting rebellion in Sainte-Lucie, St Vincent, and Grenada and by unleashing privateers against British shipping. Many former slaves found new status as soldiers in the Republic's army, but Hugues forced black cultivators to continue to work the fields. He refused to implement the new republican constitution because he did not think blacks had the capacity to exercise political rights and he did not believe Guadeloupe's agriculture could be maintained without coercion. The contradictions in Hugues's regime resulted from the ambiguity of revolutionary principles in a colonial setting, but they also reflected the new version of the revolutionary script that he brought from France.

Hugues was ruthless in his treatment of anyone who opposed or questioned his authority, including French military officers. He was suspicious of the coloured elite and hostile towards white planters. While Hugues used subversive propaganda effectively against his British adversaries, he could not control communications, which undermined his authority in Guadeloupe. Accounts of developments in Saint-Domingue sharpened the grievances of black and coloured citizens. Moreover, news of the Thermidorian Reaction in France enabled his white enemies to denounce him as a tyrant, and the metropolitan government became more receptive to such accusations as the tide of the war in the Caribbean turned against the Republic. If such denunciations revealed white hostility to black emancipation, their characterization of his regime as a tyranny was valid. In keeping with the Revolutionary Government's justification for absolute authority in France, Hugues's will in Guadeloupe became equivalent to that of the nation: neither the dissent of black cultivators nor the opposition of white planters would be tolerated. In establishing a revolutionary dictatorship, as well as in abolishing slavery and encouraging black insurgency, Hugues brought the Jacobin Terror to the Windward Islands. During this same period, however, French planters in Martinique took advantage of British occupation to play out a counter-revolutionary script.

8 Return of the Old Regime: Martinique under British Occupation, 1794–1802

If Guadeloupe under Victor Hugues became a bastion of the French Republic and the epicentre of slave insurgency in the Windward Islands, counter-revolution triumphed in Martinique. Rochambeau's surrender in March 1794 marked the beginning of eight years of occupation, which ended only when Great Britain returned the colony to France as part of the Peace of Amiens in 1802. Martinique's planters welcomed the British conquest. They had bitterly opposed Rochambeau's republican regime, which favoured their patriot enemies, and they believed it had undermined slavery. General Grey's proposal to administer the colony according to pre-1789 French law was eagerly taken up by the members of Martinique's sovereign council. The high court not only affirmed British authority but also used its restored judicial powers to purge republicans and to secure the appointment of Martinique's principal royalist intriguer within the colony's new administration. Yet French collaboration was based less on royalist principles than on opposition to revolutionary abolition. The planters' support for British rule only became stronger when Hugues's agents tried to incite revolt in Martinique as a prelude to republican invasion. With the assistance of French colonists, British forces foiled all such attempts and used Martinique as a base from which to defeat insurrections in other colonies of the eastern Caribbean.

Determination to control communications helps to explain the planter elite's support for British occupation – and Martinique's sovereign council was a crucial structure to this collaboration. The court gave legal sanction to the orders of British governors and insisted that the colony be ruled by law, by which it meant the Old Regime ordinances and regulations that preserved colonial hierarchy. This decision was in keeping with the previous struggles of Martinique's elite against as-sertions of popular sovereignty by merchant and *petit-Blanc* patriots. The court's emphasis on Old Regime law was intended to silence revo-lutionary claims that legitimate authority lay with the nation or the people and was intended to purge all remnants of the revolutionary script from the colony. Even though British governors upheld slavery and limited racial equality, the court's rulings and deliberations reveal a pervasive dread of disorder, conspiracy, and subversive news and messages. In part this reflected Hugues's campaign of spreading revo-lution, as well as the example of slave rebellion in Saint-Domingue, but it also reflected long-standing anxieties in the Windward Islands about poor whites, free people of colour, and black slaves. The fear of revo-lutionary example and enthusiasm made all of these more acute. Thus the sovereign council and Martinique's planter aristocracy collaborated with the British occupation to maintain slavery; to block communica-tions threatening the colonial order; and, in a more general sense, to thwart the French Revolution.

I The Triumph of Counter-Revolution (March–May 1794)

Even before their troops landed in February 1794, British commanders used propaganda to minimize resistance from Martinique's population and to quell revolution in the colony. General Grey and Vice Admiral Jervis issued a declaration on 1 January 1794 that framed the British cause in terms of opposition to the National Convention in France. This despotic assembly, according to the declaration, intended the destruc-tion of the French as well as the British colonies in the West Indies. All persons who submitted peacefully were promised a full amnesty for acts committed under previous authority. With the re-establishment of peace, Martinique would enjoy the rights and privileges of British commerce. More important, all who would put themselves under His Majesty's protection were guaranteed personal security "and the full and immediate enjoyment of all their legitimate properties, conform-ing to their old laws and customs, and under the most advantageous conditions."[1] In other words, the declaration assured planters that British conquest would maintain slavery. The harsh security measures presented in a supplement to the declaration also made this point. If Rochambeau had promised liberty to slaves who took up arms in de-fence of Martinique, "it was impossible for His Majesty's Generals to distinguish between these brigands and people of colour born free or legally enfranchised." While promising amnesty for slaves who surrendered to British forces, or who returned peacefully to their plantations, Grey and Jervis warned that any people of colour taken in arms – "or who fought but escaped British bayonets" – would be treated as slaves and "transported to the coast of Africa and abandoned to their fate."

As he laid siege to Rochambeau's forces in Fort-de-la-Convention (Fort-Bourbon), Grey also sought to restore order in the rest of Martinique. His proclamation of 8 February declared that those guilty of setting fire to cane fields would be punished with summary execution.[2] While such arson was associated with military resistance to the invasion, it also suggested the breakdown of discipline on the plantations. British forces were determined to restore labour discipline and control slaves and free people of colour. Shortly after Saint-Pierre's capture, Colonel William Meyers issued a proclamation regarding the operation of cabarets. Beyond ordering the owners of the town's inns, cafes, and cabarets to obtain new licenses – and forbidding them from receiving soldiers or free persons of colour after six o'clock in the evening – Meyers warned that those who received or served slaves would be fined 500 *livres*.[3] In a subsequent proclamation Meyers announced that the owners and renters of houses in Saint-Pierre would be held responsible for the conduct of all persons residing in them. He ordered them to submit exact statements of all family members and other persons staying with them, distinguishing whites, mulattos, free blacks, and slaves.[4] If the regulation of cabarets was deemed essential to the maintenance of order, the limitation of vagrancy, and the monitoring of suspicious persons in Saint-Pierre, British officers believed that this regulation required the control of communications and the policing of race.

Quarrels and mutual accusations among French republicans followed Martinique's conquest. Grey's account to the British government of Fort-Bourbon's surrender included praise for the French commander: "The skilful defence of General Rochambeau and his garrison brings them the greatest honour; there exists not one square of earth which was not torn up by our bombs and shot."[5] Rochambeau, who had been transported to Newport, Rhode Island, did not express similar admiration for Martinique's conquerors. In a dispatch of 18 April to the minister of marine in Paris, Rochambeau denounced Grey and Jervis for seizing merchants' warehouses and deporting republicans. His primary concern, however, was to establish that he had not been responsible for the loss of the colony. Given the threats posed by the expected British invasion as well as by rebellious slaves, he blamed the minister for abandoning him and failing to send necessary reinforcements. He accused white colonists of deserting the republican cause and claimed that the English had partisans throughout the Windward Islands because of the inhabitants' hatred for the Law of 4 April 1792. Rochambeau also condemned the free men of colour for their cowardice and their leader Bellegarde, his former trusted subordinate, for perfidiously selling his battalion to the enemy.[6]

Rochambeau's claim that the loss of Martinique resulted from racial tension and coloured treachery was echoed in another republican account. Berclery, who described himself as an inhabitant deported by the English, submitted a "Historical summary of the events of the Revolution at Martinique" to the Committee of Public Safety in December 1795. The text, reflecting the bitter divisions among colonists resident in metropolitan France, represented the perspective of many *petit-Blanc* patriots. Berclery's history not only denounced the *grands Blancs* and the royal governors but it also insisted that on multiple occasions free men of colour had backed these aristocrats against the colony's white patriots, despite the latter's support for equality. The text conceded that the *gens de couleur* had been debased by the inequality they had suffered but claimed that this allowed wicked men to turn them against republican authority. The success of this royalist subversion was demonstrated in Bellegarde's machinations and treachery, which undermined Rochambeau's defence and forced his capitulation to the British. Thus, according to Berclery, free men of colour contributed to the victory of the *émigrés*.[7] Continuing republican suspicion and hostility towards the *gens de couleur* helps to explain why there was no significant resistance to the British occupation after the military surrender on 25 March.

As their declaration of 1 January indicated, Grey and Jervis intended to administer Martinique according to pre-1789 French law, which they hoped would promote stability and win the inhabitants' loyalty. Grey issued a proclamation on 30 March, recalling the magistrates and officers of all courts established under Louis XVI to their duties and ordering them to submit their names to Lieutenant General Robert Prescott. These courts were to resume their functions in order to provide the colony with justice and civil government until the British crown determined an alternative system.[8] Following the departure of Grey and Jervis to begin operations against Guadeloupe, Prescott ordered officers of Martinique's sovereign council and *sénéchaussées* to return to their duties and also charged them to swear an oath of loyalty to George III. The same oath was to be sworn subsequently by notaries and all the colony's residents over sixteen years of age.[9] The swearing of oaths were powerful political communications in the eyes of both royalists and republicans.

On 23 April Prescott addressed the sovereign council assembled at Fort-Royal, calling upon its members to "put aside all animosities of the past and hold the true character of judges. Decide all pressing affairs with the impartiality and attention to the laws of your country which can be expected of your dignity and high estate."[10] In response the high court announced its intention to register the proclamations and orders of the British governor according to pre-revolutionary French law, to reactivate the colony's lower courts, and to render its own judgments in the name of His Britannic Majesty. The *procureur général du Roi*, or king's attorney, went even farther in stating that the council must name commissioners to draft an address of homage and loyalty to the British monarch.[11] Two days later the court delivered its formal response to General Prescott. The magistrates declared that, having been restored to their functions by the British governor, they were "infinitely convinced that submission to the laws can assure the happiness of the whole country, making disappear from this unhappy colony the anarchy which has desolated it for so long."[12] Yet rather than a commitment to the impartial rule of law, which Prescott hoped would end Martinique's internal divisions, this declaration reflected the sovereign council's determination to use judicial authority to silence any challenge to the planter oligarchy.

British governors restored pre-revolutionary law as well as aspects of Martinique's old civil administration. In March and April General Grey appointed a series of officials including a provost marshal, a secretary register, a treasurer, an attorney general, a coroner, and a postmaster. All of those chosen for these positions were either British officers or members of Martinique's small English community, however, demonstrating Grey's distrust of French colonists.[13] Such an attitude was at odds with the re-establishment of the pre-revolutionary judicial system and with the strategy of gaining the population's support and loyalty. Thus Grey decided to appoint a French colonist to a key post. In a letter to the sovereign council, he stated that in order to assure the colony's prosperity and tranquillity, "the wisest thing is to overturn as little as possible the form of government established previously in this island."[14] Specifically, Grey proposed entrusting the responsibilities held previously by the *intendant* to a new position of administrator general; he asked the court to submit the names of three of its members as possible candidates. Unanimously, the sovereign council nominated only one candidate: Louis-François Dubuc.[15] The appointment of Dubuc suggests that the restoration of Old Regime law was linked to the larger triumph of counter-revolution. Dubuc had been in London in 1793, where he negotiated a treaty with the British government to intervene in the Windward Islands in the name of the Bourbon monarchy. In according him a provisional commission as administrator general, Grey acknowledged this previous relationship with British authority.[16] The administrator general was to preside over the sovereign council, oversee justice and civil administration, ensure the internal police of the island, and would "enjoy the privileges, honours and prerogatives attributed to the *intendant.*" A supplement to the commission stipulated that Dubuc receive a yearly salary of £2,500 sterling to be paid from the colony's funds.[17]

The sovereign council's enthusiasm for British occupation was further demonstrated in its address of 23 May to George III. Along with expressions of submission and loyalty, the councillors reminded their new sovereign that the colonists of Martinique had previously sent deputies to request British intervention. Although the British crown had welcomed these deputies, the address referred to "unforeseen circumstances" (the republican success in repelling the June 1793 attack), which dashed their hopes and forced the colonists to flee while their plantations were pillaged or burned. Thus the sovereign council spoke on behalf of Martinique's royalist *émigrés* and thanked George III for the conquest that had allowed them to return to the colony.[18] Beyond the declarations of allegiance to the British monarch, the implications of the *émigrés'* triumph was revealed on 24 April, when a member of the sovereign council called for the removal of all judicial officers who had "betrayed the colony and their duties" and who had "conducted themselves badly … during the troubles."[19] On 20 May the court ordered parish commissioners throughout the colony to prepare lists of "dangerous subjects." From these a general list was compiled and then presented to General Grey and Admiral Jervis, who were asked to order the arrest and deportation of those it named. In establishing a formal list, the sovereign council declared: "It is necessary to set a term to the arrests in order to calm spirits and to accelerate the return of order and peace."[20] If setting legal limits appeared to be in keeping with British calls for impartiality, the arrests constituted a purge of political enemies and of those who had supported the revolution.

Counter-revolution in the colonial context should be defined less in terms of royalism and more in terms of the defence of slavery and opposition to racial equality. British occupation and the restoration of Old Regime law enabled Martinique's planters to reinforce the slave system and to curtail free-coloured rights. In the same session that the sovereign council pledged initially to support the British governor, the *procureur général* announced that the colony was infested with runaway slaves. Not only must these slaves be rounded up, he insisted, but the court must also enforce old regulations to police slaves rigorously.[21] When he renewed Colonel Meyers's ordinance of 22 February for the police of inns, cafes, and cabarets, General Prescott also revived an ordinance of 16 August 1763 forbidding the admission of slaves: owners who served blacks within their establishments, rather than in their ground-floor shops or in the street, would be liable to fines or imprisonment.[22] Members of Roman Catholic religious orders doing pastoral work among the colony's slaves also came under scrutiny. Father Trepsac, head of the Dominican mission in Martinique, wrote to General Grey to denounce one of his priests. Trepsac had forced Sieur Courtiers to retire as *curé* of Vauclin, "where he was very dangerous," but he claimed that the priest, a former member of the Club of Saint-Pierre, had continued to preach trouble, disorder, and disobedience. Supporting Trepsac's call for Courtiers's deportation, on 24 May the sovereign council requested that Grey use his authority, conforming to the ordinance of 24 November 1781, to expel and return to France any missionary threatening order and public tranquillity.[23]

The planters' determination to restore the colonial order as it had existed before the revolution was further demonstrated in an address from the civil commissioner of Lamentin, Le Merle, presented to the sovereign council on 24 May. Just as it had always been understood that colonial production required slave labour, Le Merle suggested that masters had always been able to free individual slaves. Since this right of manumission could be abused – exercised as a result of crime or caprice rather than to reward merit – the colony's leading families had insisted that freedom be taxed and regulated; to enfranchise a slave required a fixed payment and permission from the governor. Yet lax governors had failed to enforce the law, causing the number of freedmen to soar. Le Merle also blamed the "so-called colonial assembly" under Rochambeau, composed mostly of non-slave-owners, which broke the barriers that the law had placed between slavery and liberty: "Thus liberty has become the reward for insurrection, for pillage, for arson, and for murder."[24] Therefore Le Merle asked the sovereign council, on behalf of all civil commissioners, to nullify false acts of enfranchisement and to return those freed illegally to their masters as slaves. Following the reading of the memoir, the *procureur général* declared null and void all liberties accorded since 12 January 1793. The court decreed that the British commander-in-chief would be asked to deport all slaves "abusively enfranchised" who did not return immediately to their master's service.[25] Enfranchisements communicated powerful and not easily controlled messages; thus, limiting manumission and the number of free people of colour remained an obsession of Martinique's planters throughout the period of British occupation.

II Conflict and Collaboration (May 1794–November 1796)

While planters welcomed the conquest of Martinique, conflict between the French inhabitants and the British authorities emerged over the latter's initial treatment of the colony and its wealth as prizes of war.[26] Grey and Jervis justified such actions by their interpretation of the British government's authorization to distribute prize money between the army and the navy. They claimed that under prize law the expedition was entitled to all arms and military stores belonging to the French government, to any French warships seized, and to all property found in towns taken by storm. Beyond these traditional claims, however, the two commanders asserted that all goods and property in the conquered islands were legitimate prizes. Jervis also used the British Order in Council of 6 November 1793, empowering him to detain all ships carrying French colonial produce or supplying French colonies, to justify a sweeping campaign against American shipping in the eastern Caribbean. On his own authority, Grey established an Admiralty court at Saint-Pierre to adjudicate the sale of the captured ships and cargoes. The seizure of its merchant vessels by Jervis's frigates provoked outrage in the United States. Similarly, inhabitants of Martinique perceived the British policy of plunder as a betrayal of the promises made in the declaration of 1 January.[27]

For the planters this policy was linked to the imposition of taxation on the colony to pay the costs of British administration. In April the sovereign council approached the governor to suggest that the existing *corvée*, which required masters to supply slave labour for the repair of fortifications and other public works at Fort-Royal and Saint-Pierre, was difficult and dangerous. The court favoured an alternative "less onerous to the colony," suggesting support for some form of financial taxation.[28] Yet on 19 May the king's attorney described Prescott's proclamation of a tax on all property owners as simply an arrangement more convenient than "general confiscation," with no justification other than the "absolute right of conquest." Addressing the sovereign council, he denounced this taxation as a betrayal of royal intentions and of the promises made to Martinique's inhabitants in general and to the *émigrés* in particular. The *procureur général* also argued that the levy of such taxation was simply not practical given the colony's devastation.[29]

The sovereign council elaborated on this theme of economic distress in its subsequent address to Grey and Jervis, requesting that they authorize free trade for the colony to prevent a dangerous subsistence crisis. Unless planters could freely sell or exchange their commodities, they could not purchase food for their slaves.[30] Despite this respectful address, members of the planter elite did not trust Grey and Jervis. They contacted Louis De Curt, the Guadeloupe *émigré* who had remained in London, and asked him to make their request directly to the British government.[31] Martinique lacked basic necessities and colonists had legitimate grievances against Grey and Jervis's policy of plunder. Yet these requests were also a manifestation of the planters' longstanding resistance to any form of taxation or any regulation of trade, which they often justified by invoking the threats of subsistence crisis and slave unrest.

Another source of tension between colonists and British rule was the Régie, or the administration of sequestered property. On 25 May the sovereign council registered Grey's ordinance for the administration of properties confiscated from persons killed or taken prisoner during the siege, those deported from the colony as threats to its security, and those currently residing in France. The ordinance's preamble suggested that because "dangerous persons" had been deported, it was necessary to rule on the administration of their property to prevent its dilapidation, just as it was necessary to assure the conservation of the goods of Martinique's colonists residing in France.[32] Those managing these sequestered properties were required to submit inventories of all slaves, animals, and movable goods to the parish commissioners, who in turn had to forward these to a registrar general. This official then determined whether to appoint managers to specific properties or to rent properties at public auction to the highest bidders. These managers or renters had complete discretion over residences on the estates; therefore, the families of absent or deceased owners could be turned out of their homes. The registrar general was also to appoint a receiver general to receive all payments generated by revenue from properties within the Régie. The final articles of Grey's ordinance ordered that all movable goods and other effects deemed not essential to the operation of the estates be auctioned off in the presence of the registrar and a parish commissioner. The profits from such auctions went mostly to British officers or officials, as part of the larger pattern of plundering, and the administration of the Régie was open to widespread corruption.[33]

The British military government continued to press Martinique's colonists to accept taxation, while planters persevered with their demands to end the regulation of trade. As a concession to such demands, Grey and Jervis ordered that coasting vessels transporting provisions or produce suffer no interruption in their navigation; upon producing a passport issued by Dubuc, they were to be subject to no duty.[34] But the commanders also issued instructions to the administrator general for the levy of taxation according to pre-revolutionary regulations.[35] On 6 August the court registered a new ordinance from Prescott and Dubuc. It stated that the necessity to provide for the colony's expenses made the prompt levy of a corresponding sum essential. While suppressing most colonial duties, this ordinance introduced a head tax of twenty-five *livres* on slaves employed in towns or in industries other than sugar production. It also levied a head tax of eighteen *livres* on slaves attached to sugar plantations. Stating that the needs of the colony's services were urgent, the ordinance ordered all contributors to pay half of what they owed immediately. Those who defaulted on their contribution would have their slaves seized and sold.[36] In the same session of 6 August, the *procureur général* presented the sovereign council with a remonstrance that referred to the terrible state of the colony.[37] The only means of preventing famine, it claimed, was the free admission of foreign ships carrying food supplies to all the colony's ports.

General Grey refused to open Martinique's ports before he left for England in November 1794, to be replaced as governor by Sir John Vaughan.[38] On 5 January 1795 a member of the sovereign council, Charles Cerand Souvigne Bonnaire, reiterated that the colony's situation was critical due to the growing shortage of food supplies. Shipowners who could provide the required provisions needed to be reassured that they would not be subject to duties, often applied arbitrarily by officials engaged in speculation. Attempts to corner the market in various provisions was all too common in Martinique, according to Souvigne Bonnaire, because it was an *entrepôt* for all of the Windward Islands. The growing shortage of "the three sisters of daily nourishment" – cod, flour, and manioc – was leading to a crisis that could "favour the activities of malevolent persons for the seduction of those so easily misled."[39] Therefore, the councillor argued, British commercial laws must be modified by the circumstances and the need that is the highest law: "*salus populi suprema lex esto.*" With no acknowledgment of the irony of counter-revolutionaries invoking the law of public safety to prevent slave revolt, the sovereign council declared that a formal request be sent to Governor Vaughan to open all of the colony's ports to foreign ships carrying essential provisions, free from all duties, for eight months.[40] Two days later the *procureur général* and his assistants addressed the court concerning the critical importance of cod as food for the slave gangs, stating that the colony could not wait for British commerce to provide sufficient quantities of this necessity. The delegation insisted that selfish merchants were blocking the introduction of foreign cod.[41] Despite the new context of British occupation, the old conflict between planters and merchants continued. On 26 January Vaughan conceded, ordering Martinique's ports opened to foreign ships.[42]

Despite these tensions over economic policy, the republican conquest of Guadeloupe in 1794 strengthened French collaboration with British authority in Martinique. Even before the arrival of Hugues's expedition, Martinique's planters had been aware of the danger posed by communication of the National Convention's decree of 16 *Pluviôse*. On 18 May Grey informed the sovereign council that several persons from France, who had arrived at Saint-Pierre aboard a Danish vessel from St Thomas, had caused such disorder that both ship and passengers were being conducted to Fort-Royal for interrogation. Having examined the documents carried by these passengers, and their petitions to remain in Martinique, members of the court concluded that all of the British governor's efforts to restore calm and tranquillity in the colony would be in vain unless he ordered the troublemakers' expulsion and took measures to prevent the entry of others whose principles or sentiments compromised public security: "This salutary goal can be obtained only by proscribing absolutely all direct or indirect communication with France."[43] Grey complied with the sovereign council's request to quarantine the colony from dangerous news or ideas; he issued a proclamation on 23 May that forbade entry to anyone arriving from France via St Thomas.[44]

Fear of such contamination was soon eclipsed by an even greater threat. The 7 June issue of *The Martinico Gazette and General Advertiser*, a bilingual newspaper aimed primarily at Martinique's small English community, reported that a number of French warships had appeared off Guadeloupe. The article sought to minimize the danger, contrasting the "swaggering exaggerations of Republican leaders" with Grey's modest account of his success. It also reported on the solemn mass held in Saint-Pierre the day before in commemoration of the deaths of Louis XVI and Marie Antoinette. The article's final paragraph, printed in French rather than in English, announced General Prescott's proclamation of 4 June: no person could be arrested without legal cause, with the exception of debtors and murderers, and neither civil commissioners nor anyone else could arrest a resident of the colony without a written warrant signed by Prescott or Grey.[45] This announcement suggests that the British governor was attempting to maintain some semblance of the rule of law in the context of rising panic among planters. An extract from a letter written by an unknown author, dated 17 June from Fort-Royal, provides evidence of the planters' reaction to news of the French expedition's arrival at Guadeloupe. The captain of a trading schooner reported that Pointe-à-Pitre was under attack, that Fort Fleur d'Épée had been stormed, and that women from Sainte-Anne had fled the attackers with only the clothes on their backs: "These monsters wanted to take no prisoners; they massacred everyone."[46] More appalling to the Fort-Royal correspondent than accounts of violence was the confirmation that the French republicans had announced the abolition of slavery: "The *Carmagnoles* passed to Gosier and there these rogues published the famous decree of liberty for the Negroes." In response, the sovereign council enthusiastically registered Grey's ordinance of 15 July, ordering that no person currently a slave, whatever his or her colour, be freed in the conquered islands of Martinique, Sainte-Lucie, Guadeloupe, and their dependencies for any reason or under any pretext until His Majesty's pleasure was known.[47]

Yet the republicans gained control of Guadeloupe. Grandprey, a French officer serving there under British command, provided a detailed account of the struggle in the colony from a royalist perspective: "The events since the conquest [of Guadeloupe by British forces] have taken a turn much opposed to our hopes."[48] He observed that the decree of general liberty allowed the republicans to recruit black troops, but he claimed that they had to deceive the blacks in order to make them fight. As a white colonist, Grandprey could not accept that freed slaves could become dependable or effective soldiers. He became General Graham's aide-de-camp and was among those besieged at the Berville camp in October. Grandprey expressed deep suspicion of the terms of surrender offered by the republicans, which refused to allow French royalists to leave with British forces. He was one of twenty-five French officers transported to Jervis's flagship in a covered boat, thus saving them from the massacre following the capitulation. Grandprey's account ended with the inhabitants of the town of Basse-Terre seeking to escape Guadeloupe with the British fleet, and General Prescott shutting himself in Fort Saint-Charles to await reinforcements. If these reinforcements did not arrive, Grandprey predicted that the republicans would attack elsewhere and wreak havoc throughout the Windward Islands.

Even before Prescott had evacuated Fort Saint-Charles on 10 December, Martinique's sovereign council approved new security measures. These included Grey's formation of a free-coloured militia.[49] On 22 November, the same day that it registered the powers of Sir John Vaughan as the new commander of British forces in the Windward Islands, the sovereign council deliberated on a petition from various inhabitants of Saint-Pierre to Vaughan, in which they asked to be excused from service in the militia and from the required oath. Members of the court ruled unanimously that the commander-in-chief should refuse this petition.[50] Thus the republican conquest of Guadeloupe only reinforced old animosities in Martinique and increased planters' suspicions of Saint-Pierre's residents.

Control of Guadeloupe had allowed Hugues to spread revolution throughout the Windward Islands. A journal of events in February and March 1795 written by Frédéric Guillot, an inhabitant of Martinique, demonstrates the rising fear of republican subversion. Guillot believed that 1,500 prisoners of war confined aboard transports in Fort-Royal's roadstead should not be sent to Europe, – since they would violate their oaths to remain there – instead returning "to swell the number of *sans-culottes* at Pointe-à-Pitre to whom they belong."[51] More worrying to him, however, was the discovery of a cabal among the prisoners, resulting from the mixing together of soldiers, sailors, and officers, "under the immoral and impolitic pretext of republican equality." The soul of this conspiracy was the captain of the frigate *Pique*, who was in contact with Hugues, "who has correspondence and friends everywhere." When a guard discovered packages of letters in a laundry hamper being sent ashore, the republican naval officer was confined to a cell. Guillot claimed that the prisoners had planned to seize control of Fort Bourbon and that they had conspired to poison British soldiers using rum sold by women of colour; fear of revolutionary plotting fit easily with white suspicion of the seductive *mulâtresses*.

Fears of subversion and radical communications escalated with news that the republicans had incited rebellion elsewhere in the Windward

Islands. According to Guillot, news reached Martinique on 5 March that republican corsairs had landed troops in Grenada. The following day inhabitants learned that planters in Sainte-Lucie, faced with a growing insurgency, had fled their estates to take refuge in Castries or Morne Fortuné. A schooner carrying families from that colony arrived at Saint-Pierre on 9 March; the governor allowed only the women and children to disembark, however, and returned the men to Sainte-Lucie to prevent revolutionary contagion. The same day, Martinique received confirmation that more republicans had landed in Grenada at Gouyave. In alliance with the island's "patriot party," to whom they supplied arms and munitions, they had captured Grenada's governor. Guillot predicted that, unless the awaited convoy arrived with reinforcements from Great Britain, the island of St Vincent would soon see insurrection as well: "It has long been known that the Caribs are all patriots." His deeper fear was that a republican invasion might spark a similar revolt in Martinique: "All have come to believe that the patriot party of this island awaits Victor Hugues to rise up and show themselves when armed and protected by him."[52] Guillot included in his journal the complete text of Hugues's printed declaration of 28 February to British commanders. In this broadsheet Hugues announced that in retaliation for the "assassination of any Republican, whatever his colour," he would guillotine two British officers. Hugues did not only threaten his British enemies. He also declared that the Republic had decreed that all Frenchmen who served the British – or who had delivered France's colonies to them – would be punished as traitors: "The law which has pronounced the penalty of death against them will conserve always its full vigour."[53]

On 12 March Guillot learned that an attempted republican landing at Grenada had been repelled. The colony's governor remained a prisoner, however, and even more worrying was the confirmation that intercepted letters from Grenada's French inhabitants proved that they had summoned the republicans and promised them the support of the island's blacks. The following day two vessels from England arrived at Fort-Royal; according to Guillot, their report that the expected convoy of reinforcements had not yet left Plymouth caused panic in Martinique.[54] In the context of further news of rebellion in Grenada and St Vincent, authorities arrested a vagabond for distributing placards. Signed by Hugues, Le Bas, and Jourau, they invited Martinique's blacks, mulattos, and white patriots to rise up en masse to destroy the English and the royalists.

Such propaganda heightened not only fears of subversion but also hostility towards *petits Blancs* and people of colour. Two republican privateers tried to put boats ashore near Trinité on 15 March but stood off when the militia assembled. The British navy had placed Guadeloupe under blockade in an effort to prevent the sortie of amphibious expeditions. Yet republican privateers continued to appear off Martinique; royalists assumed they intended to land spies and instigators. The widow Rounier, a rich shopkeeper from Lyon, was jailed for seditious speech to blacks and *gens de couleur*, as well as for seeking to reform the opinions of *émigrés* from Guadeloupe. "Women in general have made much trouble at Saint-Pierre," Guillot claimed, "and the *mulâtresses* have perverted many young people."[55] Most of the young men had fled the town to avoid militia duty. While acknowledging that some colonists believed this was due to British conduct in the colony, Guillot suggested that these young men anticipated a republican invasion and feared retribution if they took up arms for the British. On 21 March more news arrived from Grenada containing details about the conspiracy among the colony's French inhabitants that lay behind the rebellion. These white Frenchmen included rich sugar planters, as well as coffee planters and *petits Blancs*, and they had admitted blacks and men of colour to their coalition. Here was the royalist planter's worst nightmare: white men of property, with the encouragement and support of metropolitan radicals, had deliberately incited slave revolt in the name of liberty and equality.

Hugues's proclamation of 27 May 1795, "to the citizens of Martinique," spoke directly to such white men of property. Printed in both French and English, it warned colonists not to trust the British, who had conquered France's colonies only to plunder them and sacrifice their inhabitants. Hugues declared that even if the love of their mother country had been extinguished, planters should consult their interests. Guadeloupe's economy was prospering under the French Republic; its blacks, while now free citizens, remained a disciplined workforce. If he insisted that his regime and its commitment to abolition would not destroy the colonial economy, Hugues also reminded Martinique's colonists that the Republic had pronounced the death penalty for traitors. He warned that all who did not rally to republican forces when they appeared in Martinique – or who did not report to agents of the Republic within three days of their arrival – would be considered traitors and have their property confiscated. The proclamation concluded with encouragement for non-whites serving under British colours to

7 Nicholas Pocock and Robert Pollard, "His Majesty's Ship the Mermaid on the 10th of October 1795, at Requin, Grenada, Run Aground in Chase of the French Corvette Brutus, To Prevent the Landing of Ammunition," 1798. PAH7889/National Maritime Museum, Greenwich, London.

defect: "All and every coloured citizen armed by the English, of any nation and in whatever colony, who joins the republican army with arms and baggage shall be admitted, if agreeable to him, according to his former station, and a gratification of thirty *livres* shall be paid to him."[56] Hugues's effort to subvert coloured troops reflected Governor Vaughan's decision in April to recruit slaves in Martinique for the *Corps des Chasseurs* to supplement his inadequate number of British regulars and colonial militia. Vaughan emphasized to parish commandants that only reliable blacks should be admitted, but he also made clear that these slaves would be freed after their service in the *Chasseurs*.[57] Planters had condemned Rochambeau's arming of slaves to defend the colony, but the sovereign council endorsed Vaughan's measure without protest.[58] In May all "royalist planters and property owners" swore a new oath of loyalty to George III.[59] Republican threats and propaganda only strengthened planters' support for British authority in Martinique.

This collaboration helped to thwart republican success in the colony. Martinique's residents learned from translated English newspapers that General Stewart had abandoned Sainte-Lucie and that insurgents had besieged British forces in the capitals of Grenada and St Vincent.[60] In December, however, an effort to instigate rebellion in Martinique failed. On 6 December a French ship flying British colours entered Vauclin Bay on the colony's south-east coast, putting sixty-five men ashore. These republicans immediately took possession of a hill overlooking the town of Vauclin and called on slaves in the vicinity to rise up against their masters and the British occupation.[61] Goyrand, Hugues's fellow commissioner who commanded republican troops in Sainte-Lucie, sent two naval officers in a sailing canoe to make contact with this advance party and to arrange for the landing of reinforcements. Arriving at Martinique during the night of 16–17 December, these agents first encountered a woman who told them to remain hidden in the woods or they would be captured and shot. She then brought the republican commander who told them his forces had been destroyed in action with British troops and French colonists. Beyond accusing the enemy of atrocities, including shooting prisoners after the battle and confiscating patriots' properties, the commander reported: "The English and the aristocrats say that they want to finish off all 'brigands' and that forces from France will never come."[62] In his dispatch to Goyrand, the canoe's captain suggested that the capture of Martinique would require a major force, given the strength of the island's defences.[63] According to the sovereign council, it was not only white planters who supported British authority against the revolutionary menace. Two months later, in February 1796, the court asked the governor to recognize the loyalty of two black freedmen, who had exposed a conspiracy to incite slave revolt in the parish of Rivière-Pilote. If the council condemned the plot's three ringleaders to death, "virtue in any of the classes must receive its reward from the tribunals just as vice receives its punishment."[64] Beyond the court's wish to encourage people of colour to report plots among slaves or republican machinations, this ruling demonstrated the planters' belief that bonds of loyalty and paternalism still existed in colonial society; their collaboration with British authority was intended to preserve such bonds.

Planters' grievances regarding economic policy remained despite their support for the British occupation. Many of these grievances were addressed, however, by the replacement of military rule with a civil administration. Sir John Vaughan died at the end of June 1795, but in December 1794 he had asked the Duke of Portland, the home secretary in London, to appoint a civilian governor for Martinique.[65] The British government named Robert Shore Milnes to the post, and he arrived at Fort-Royal on 4 July 1795. Attending the session in which the sovereign council registered his commission as governor, Milnes responded to the official statements of welcome with a speech in French, greeted with enthusiastic applause.[66] The bilingual new governor moved quickly to introduce reforms to the colony's administration. He created a privy council, which included several prominent planters, to assist him. He appointed two members of the sovereign council to investigate mismanagement of the Régie and a second committee of the council to prepare a detailed report on the structures of the colony's French administration before 1789. Milnes's biggest challenge was the state of the colony's finances – expenses significantly exceeded revenue from taxes and duties. The governor insisted, however, that the British government, rather than the French colonists, must cover military expenses. He also moved to reduce harbour duties and to minimize trade regulations.[67] One of the strongest indications that the governor had won the inhabitants' goodwill was their new willingness to cooperate with the levy of slaves for the British army. In August General Paulus Aemilius Irving, who had replaced Vaughan as British commander-in-chief, reiterated the call for raising a corps of troops from Martinique's slaves; planters, however, delivered only two hundred slaves. Irving and the government in London questioned the inhabitants' loyalty, but Milnes defended them. In November the sovereign council registered Milnes's ordinance calling for the levy of one thousand slave pioneers – or military labourers – and planters cooperated to meet this target.[68]

Because of ill health, Milnes left Martinique in April 1796 and was replaced as governor by William Keppel. Addresses of praise for the departing governor were sent from Martinique to the British government.[69] A month before Milnes's departure, General Abercromby's military expedition reached the Windward Islands. By June his forces had retaken Sainte-Lucie from the republicans and had crushed the insurrections in Grenada and St Vincent. Abercromby's arrival assured British domination in the Windward Islands and thus the safety of French royalists; while Milnes's administration ended French discontent.[70] Despite their appreciation for Milnes's reforms, members of Martinique's sovereign council and its planter aristocracy more generally continued to defend their privileges jealously. On 2 November 1795, the court registered Milnes's new regulation regarding the police of slaves. While councillors highly approved of the regulation, which included articles forbidding slaves from assembling or wearing distinct emblems, they also believed it necessary to remind the governor that the court must register all ordinances before they were published or sent to the *sénéchaussées*: "Without this, judicial order and hierarchy would find themselves reversed."[71]

In a formal statement of grievance addressed to the king one year later, the sovereign council further demonstrated its determination to protect the planters' domination of colonial society. The councillors complained that the royal Order in Council of 20 July 1796, allowing the crown to annul the sovereign council's orders, represented an attack on their prerogatives. They cited the case of Pocquet de Puilhery, a planter who had fled to Dominica in 1793. He had owed Madame de Fourniols 158,941 *livres*; part of his crop had been sold to pay the debt. When Pocquet's family returned to Martinique, they appealed to the sovereign council. Madame de Fourniols appealed to London to have its ruling overturned, however. The councillors were adamant that the court's authority was at risk if its decisions could be challenged and nullified. Preserving their judicial authority was not their only concern. The councillors acknowledged that Madame de Fourniols had legitimate recourse but claimed that she had not taken it and instead "had seen with indifference the property of her debtor pass into the hands of the Republic by the decree confiscating the goods of *émigrés*." Pocquet, a "victim of the revolution," should not be held responsible for Madame de Fourniols's "negligence."[72] Thus beyond its hostility towards those who might have benefited from the republican regime, the sovereign council's statement of grievance demonstrated its determination to defend Martinique's planters against their creditors. The economic conflict dividing "patriots" and "aristocrats" in 1789 had not disappeared under British occupation.

III Continuing Fears (November 1796–January 1801)

If the danger of a republican invasion from Guadeloupe subsided, fear persisted in Martinique during the last five years of British occupation. Planters loathed the revolutionary script: that is, the ideas and language of the metropolitan revolution, which they saw as a threat to the slave system and to their social and economic hegemony. Yet their continuing fears of revolutionary communications reflected tensions and anxieties that had existed in colonial society long before 1789. One such traditional anxiety concerned the growing numbers of free people of colour and the need to maintain control over manumission, an anxiety made more acute by the republicans' abolition of slavery. The king's attorney presented the sovereign council with a remonstrance on 10 November 1796 regarding the continuous entry into Martinique from other Windward Islands of "a prodigious quantity of *gens de couleur* of both sexes who all call themselves free and are treated as such; there are among this number, however, many slaves or at least many whose status is suspect."[73] Claiming that this influx had a dangerous influence in the colony's towns and villages, he proposed that all people of colour be required to produce legal titles of their enfranchisement or other documents proving their free status; those who could not should be imprisoned or deported to the colony from which they came. The same concern regarding the validity of enfranchisements was apparent in the court's deliberations of 3 July 1798 on petitions by women of colour who were seeking to reclaim free status that had been refuted. Marie Anne, a woman of mixed race, appealed to the sovereign council because the civil commissioner of Lamentin, Le Merle, refused to enumerate her free status on the basis of the court's order annulling all enfranchisements conferred since 13 January 1793. Rochambeau had confirmed her liberty in 1793, but Marie Anne's master had freed her in 1780, paid the required sum of 500 *livres* to the colonial government, and died shortly afterwards. She was not in the category of slaves who had forced liberty from their masters or who had obtained it despite their objections. Therefore, the *procureur général* suggested that the court could order the *sénéchaussée* at Lamentin to register her free status; instead, it sent Marie Anne to petition the governor. If this ruling indicated unwillingness to acknowledge coloured liberty if any uncertainty existed regarding status, the sovereign council's position was even clearer in its decision on a subsequent request by seven other women, three identified as *"mulâtresses"* and four as *"métisses."* These women, also residents of Lamentin, had been freed by their master as a reward for loyalty and good service. Rochambeau had confirmed their liberty in December 1793, but Le Merle refused to enumerate their free status. The supplicants suggested that the general disposition to annul all liberties since 13 January 1793 could not be authorized by a judicial *arrêté*, but it surely required a law passed by legislators. Therefore, their request that the court confirm their free status rested on the possibility that Le Merle had misread or misunderstood its order. Such an argument carried no weight with the councillors, who acknowledged few limits to their authority. Since Rochambeau had awarded liberties to slaves in the absence or without the consent of their masters, the king's attorney told the court that it could annul those liberties. The sovereign council was silent on the supplicants' request and simply ordered them returned to their master as slaves.[74]

Fear that colonial authority's control over manumission was diminishing, and that the line between slavery and freedom was blurring, became particularly evident in the 3 November 1800 session of the sovereign council. The king's attorney reminded the court of a recent letter from the governor, which reported daily attempts to elude the order forbidding new acts of enfranchisement and of the councillors' subsequent request for information from the island's lower courts. The officers of the *sénéchaussée* of Saint-Pierre had responded with evidence of enfranchisements granted as the result of the sale of slaves to themselves. Denouncing such acts as illegal, the *procureur général* decried the existence of these "amphibious beings, free in appearance but slaves in reality."[75] He then summarized Old Regime laws limiting enfranchisements. The council of state's *arrêt* of 24 October 1713 forbade masters from freeing slaves without the written permission of the governor general and the *intendant*. A royal ordinance of 15 June 1736 had required that all enfranchisements made without this written permission be nullified, that the masters be fined, and the slaves be confiscated. A subsequent government ordinance of 5 February 1768, intended to prevent slaves from purchasing their liberty, had prohibited notaries from receiving an act of enfranchisement without written authorization. The same ordinance also forbade the transportation of slaves to a foreign island in order to free them there. Finally the council of state's *arrêt* of 8 June 1776 had ordered that priests baptize no child of colour as free without written acts of liberty. These laws were precise and often renewed, the king's attorney concluded, and they made clear that government permissions must precede all manumissions and gifts of liberty. He also referred to Grey's order of 6 August 1794, issued in response to Hugues's arrival at Guadeloupe with the decree of 16 *Pluviôse*, which he claimed had fixed these legal requirements for manumission. In response, the sovereign council declared null three specific acts of enfranchisement dated 14 June 1797, 25 August 1799, and 21 June 1800.

The court's determination to control and limit the number the enfranchisements in Martinique was linked to a more general anxiety regarding disorder and threats to racial and social hierarchy. Planters were suspicious of people of colour whose activities appeared to be outside their traditional roles. On 6 September 1797 a member of the sovereign council denounced, "the existence at Saint-Pierre of a society of Negro jugglers, conjurers, fortune-tellers, and doctors who not only permit themselves to exercise their charlatanism there, but who also seek to make proselytes with the most dangerous consequences."[76] The court's suspicion was not limited to people of colour. Its examination of crime and disorder at Saint-Pierre during the session of 11 November 1798 echoed the colonial assembly's accusations against *petit-Blanc* patriots in the early phase of the revolution: "Vices of all kinds, disorders of all types, crimes, and also the most frightful attacks threaten the colony with total and impending subversion."[77] According to the *procureur général*, greed lay behind a rash of thefts, duels, and assassinations committed by individuals who carried concealed daggers and sword canes. Since a murder had been committed on the town's Grande Rue in broad daylight, for which no one had been arrested, alarm had become general. Moreover, duellists and assassins had found apologists in Saint-Pierre who defended their crimes publicly, which suggested the communication of revolutionary sympathies.

Beyond the failure to uphold the law in Saint-Pierre, the king's attorney attributed the violence to corruption and pervasive immorality: "which due to the difficulties of the times and circumstances has gradually frozen within all classes of society, including those who were honest and engaged in useful occupations but are now stupefied by indolence and libertinage, and think only of intrigue, debauchery and crime."[78] Planters and colonial authorities had used similar language before and after 1789 in reference to the unruly merchant seamen and rootless *petits Blancs* of Saint-Pierre. The *procureur général* claimed that the heart of the town's corruption was in its gambling dens, frequented by men with nothing to lose. Yet denunciations of corruption and immorality were connected to fears of subversion, possibly revolutionary subversion. The king's attorney insisted that it was urgent to "dam this contagious torrent," which would soon overflow from the town into the countryside. This goal would require the unity of all authorities, in concert with honest and virtuous citizens, so that active surveillance and exemplary punishments could enable the colony to defend itself against "the perverse enemies of its happiness and tranquillity." In response to this report, the sovereign council ordered that existing regulations against gambling, duelling, and carrying concealed weapons be reaffirmed and enforced rigorously. It forbade merchants from selling canes or sticks concealing swords, ordering them to surrender any such weapons in their possession. The court also ordered a crackdown on the "public apologists for crimes and offenses," appealing to honest citizens to support these efforts, and it requested that Governor Keppel use all his powers against "vagabonds and disturbers of the public peace."

The fear of slave conspiracy and revolt was even more pervasive and deep-seated among Martinique's planter aristocracy than fear of *petit-Blanc* disorder. The sovereign council's deliberations regarding subsistence crises, and its requests that governors relax trade regulations to increase the importation of foodstuffs, often invoked that fear. In May 1797 the *procureur général* announced that the dearth of fish and other necessities meant that inhabitants could barely feed themselves, let alone their slaves: "Meanwhile the movements which result, the dangers and evils to which this dearth could give place, are as terrible as they are alarming."[79] The presence of republican abolitionists and insurgents elsewhere in the Windward Islands made the fear of slaves more acute. On 29 December 1797 the *procureur général* alerted the sovereign council to the danger of the British authorities employing black prisoners of war from Sainte-Lucie as labourers in Martinique's forts and magazines: "This service facilitates the most dangerous communication between them and the Negroes of this colony, and allows them at the same time to propagate deadly principles they have so cruelly practised."[80] While acknowledging that such employment spared inhabitants from the levy of their own slaves for military labour, he warned that lax supervision of the prisoners not only allowed them to form liaisons with blacks in the towns but also offered them opportunities to escape – "to disperse themselves through the countryside and there to foment the most perverse arrangements." The court agreed that this possibility represented a real threat, thus perceiving the black prisoners as revolutionary subversives who might incite slave revolt.

Fear of slaves poisoning livestock, other slaves, and even white colonists long preceded 1789, but planters believed that the revolution encouraged this crime. The sovereign council deliberated on a remonstrance from the *procureur général* on 8 March 1799, which informed its members that the colony's apothecaries and drug merchants, in contempt of existing regulations, were selling drugs to anyone: whites, coloureds, and even slaves. These drugs could even be procured by individuals in prison. The fear was that the drugs could be used as poison. Even more alarming, the court also learned that the practice of medicine, surgery, and pharmacy by untrained or unlicensed persons was widespread throughout the colony; that is, non-whites were claiming to be doctors or healers. In response, the sovereign council ordered that all persons practising pharmacy must report to the king's attorney, they had to be inscribed on his list, and they were forbidden from selling any drugs reputed to be poisonous. Such drugs needed to be locked up and dispensed only by white clerks to approved physicians and surgeons. Furthermore, the court expressly forbade all blacks or people of colour from practising medicine or surgery.[81]

Despite these measures to ban coloured doctors and to control the dispensing of drugs, the fear of poisoning intensified. The sovereign council received reports in May 1799 of poisonings in various parishes, "which have multiplied themselves for some time to a frightful point."[82] In July the *procureur général* called the court's attention to "the ravages caused by poisonings in almost all parts of the colony."[83] He claimed that these were harming the economy and required a vigorous judicial response. Specifically, the *procureur général* recommended that individuals other than officers of the courts should conduct investigations quickly and unexpectedly in order to gain evidence that would lead to arrests. In response, the court ordered surgeons to investigate suspected poisonings of slaves or beasts on plantations immediately, to prepare accounts of their investigations noting the presence of any drugs in the bodies, and to submit these accounts to civil commissioners. The court's ordinance also authorized the commissioners to lay charges against "the slave authors, instigators and participants of the crime" and to arrest and interrogate them. Planters assumed that poisoning was how slaves attacked their masters secretly. Just as the measures to control drug dispensing and the practice of medicine were intended to curb clandestine resistance, the suppression of *marronage* was intended to prevent open revolt. In January 1800 the sovereign council reaffirmed its *arrêt* of 9 November 1785 regarding the pursuit of *marrons* or runaway slaves. Ordering that it be newly published and posted throughout the colony, the council altered the regulation that accounts of blacks killed during the pursuit be submitted to the clerks of the *sénéchaussées* rather than to parish commandants. This modification reflected the changed circumstances under British occupation.[84]

Jean Kina's revolt in December 1800 appeared to justify white suspicions regarding free men of colour, as well as white fears of conspiracy and subversion. This episode also demonstrated the tension between the pragmatism of the British occupation and the French planters' obsession with maintaining the Old Regime status quo. Part of the context for these events was the declining number of effective troops in the Windward Islands due to illness and mortality from tropical disease. By April 1800 there were more French prisoners of war in Martinique than British soldiers.[85] Following the Abercromby expedition in 1796, however, British commanders could not expect reinforcements from Europe, relying instead upon black units recruited from the colony's slaves. Such recruitment raised the question of how black troops would be treated. In ordering the formation of black regiments, both Grey and Vaughan had insisted that slaves would gain their freedom after six years of loyal military service. Given his understanding that these men would be drilled and disciplined no differently than white soldiers, General Kenneth Bowyer was disturbed by the sight of black troops being whipped in the manner reserved for slaves. In September 1798, shortly before he was replaced as commander-in-chief by Lieutenant General Thomas Trigge, Bowyer wrote to the secretary of state for war in London to propose that colonial legislatures pass special laws to exempt black soldiers from such degrading treatment. The British government did not support Bowyer's proposal and, even worse, Trigge reported that on 3 December 1800 the sovereign council had annulled Grey's order of 1794, which had made military service an exception to the restriction on all acts of enfranchisement.[86] While Trigge suggested that this was the specific provocation for the revolt, the records of the sovereign council contain no reference to such an annulment on that date. In his own examination of the Jean Kina revolt, David Geggus points instead to the court's decision of 3 November: by reaffirming old restrictions on enfranchisement, it threatened the status of many free people of colour and thus triggered the revolt.[87]

Jean Kina was an unlikely rebel. He had been a slave in Saint-Domingue who not only fought for the white planters against free-coloured revolt and slave insurgency but also rallied his fellow slaves against revolution. This loyalty and his reputation as a leader of black troops for the royalist cause had gained him his freedom. During the British occupation of Saint-Domingue, he rose to the rank of colonel in the British army and became a slave owner himself. When the British evacuated the colony in 1798, Kina travelled to London. In 1800 the

British government sent him to Martinique as a possible commander of a black regiment there. General Trigge feared that Martinique's white inhabitants would never accept such a command being given to a former slave from Saint-Domingue, who had gained wealth and military rank during that colony's destruction. He waited instead to see if he could assign Kina to a post in Demerara, Surinam, or Jamaica. While stranded in Martinique, Kina may have been aware that he was the object of suspicion. He was humble and submissive towards whites, and his strict religious observances demonstrated devout Catholicism. In the revolt's aftermath, the sovereign council condemned this as treacherous hypocrisy intended to deceive the colony.[88] This denunciation of Kina reflected the planters' distrust of all *gens de couleur*.

On the night of 4 December Kina and perhaps thirty men of colour, most of them members of the militia wearing uniforms and bearing arms, left the town of Fort-Royal carrying a British flag to which they attached a banner inscribed "*La Loi Britannique.*" On the way to Morne Le Maître, near Case Navire, Kina stopped at a number of plantations. Seeking to recruit followers, he proclaimed: "I do this to maintain the order of British law and to protect my brothers, because the colonists have been executioners and eaters of flesh; that they will seize all Negroes and force them to work and have decided to sell all free blacks."[89] The following morning British troops and colonial militia arrived to confront Kina's band, which may have numbered as few as forty. Colonel Maitland approached alone, promising to investigate the rebels' grievances and guaranteeing them a pardon if they surrendered. Kina agreed to surrender, but only to the British officer, and Maitland ordered the French colonists to withdraw. General Trigge quickly confirmed the pardon and, more important, he suspended the law restricting enfranchisements even for black soldiers.

The sovereign council registered the commander-in-chief's proclamation on the revolt reluctantly, but in a subsequent letter to the Duke of Portland the court complained that Trigge's pardon prevented a proper judicial investigation, allowing the rebels to disperse without punishment and leaving the colony threatened by their example and sedition. In contrast to their criticism of General Trigge, who they said had been "fooled by the false pretexts given by this rebel," the councillors praised civilian Governor Keppel, who was sympathetic to the hard line they wished to take.[90] While the court emphasized his effort to rally plantation slaves, Kina's revolt was rooted in the grievances of the colony's free men of colour, particularly those in the militia, who believed their status had been threatened. The fact that Kina had appealed to slaves, however, contradicted his previous actions. Louis de Curt, the French colonial representative in London, claimed that Kina was driven by a desire for vengeance because of the humiliation he had experienced in Martinique. Other contemporaries suggested that Kina had acted on the basis of secret instructions from Trigge, who sought an excuse to overturn the sovereign council's ruling on enfranchisements.[91] Whether or not a conspiracy existed between Kina and the British commander, and this seems doubtful given Kina's subsequent deportation to England and incarceration in Newgate Prison, the revolt of December 1800 demonstrated the limits of planters' collaboration. British authority regarded the recruitment of black troops as a military necessity; officers like Trigge, Bowyer, and Vaughan believed the promise of emancipation could provide loyal and effective black soldiers. Yet the sovereign council remained intransigent in its determination to limit manumission and, more fundamentally, to maintain strict racial hierarchy in Martinique. It is not surprising that Jean Kina appealed to the protection of British law against the hostility of French colonists.

IV Return to French Rule (February 1801–September 1802)

Neither republican invasion nor revolutionary subversion ended the British occupation of Martinique, and the colony returned to French rule as a result of developments in Europe. In November 1799 General Napoleon Bonaparte overthrew the Directory; established a new constitutional regime, the Consulate; and proclaimed that the French Revolution was over. To justify this claim, Bonaparte as first consul had to resolve the issues underlying the instability and division in France. First among these was the war with other European powers. Following French victories at Marengo and Hohenlinden, the Austrian Empire sought an armistice, signing a peace treaty at Lunéville on 9 February 1801. The Second Coalition against France collapsed. Only Great Britain remained at war with the French Republic, but in February 1801 William Pitt resigned as prime minister. Henry Addington formed a government and, given war weariness in Britain, initiated peace talks with France. Britain's initial conditions included maintaining Martinique, along with other conquests, which reflected the West Indies' importance to its original war aims. Bonaparte refused, however, and the British delegation offered new terms in July 1801, renouncing all conquests except Ceylon and Trinidad. In October Bonaparte forced Addington's government to agree to a preliminary treaty by threatening to break off negotiations, and on 25 March 1802 representatives of both countries signed the final peace treaty at Amiens. Among other concessions, Great Britain relinquished Martinique.[92]

British authorities and French colonists in Martinique learned that a preliminary treaty had suspended hostilities, and by December 1801 rumours circulated that peace and the colony's restoration to France were imminent. The sovereign council's reactions to such rumours, and to definitive news of the Peace of Amiens, demonstrated that members of the high court saw the new regime in France as being fundamentally different than the revolutionary Republic. More specifically, planters believed that Bonaparte would not abolish slavery in Martinique.[93] On 20 January 1802 the sovereign council deliberated, with the full support of Governor Keppel, on the choice of a deputy to represent the colony's interests to the French government. The court chose Louis-François Dubuc, assuming that the Consulate would accept this royalist and British collaborator as an appropriate representative. The following day councillors named both Dubuc and Louis De Curt to carry a declaration of their gratitude to George III, in particular for the wise administration of Governor Keppel.[94] On 14 June the governor wrote to the sovereign council to request that it register the peace treaty signed at Amiens. The court did so on 6 July and, during the same session, its members praised Keppel for governing Martinique by justice and love rather than by force.[95]

Keppel's subsequent reply to its formal address of thanks helps to explain the positive relationship between the sovereign council and the British governor. While neighbouring colonies had fallen prey to convulsions, the governor claimed that the colonists of Martinique remained tranquil because of excellent laws and worthy magistrates.[96] Keppel's words should be seen as more than flattery; they represented an endorsement of the sovereign council's resurrection of pre-1789 ordinances regulating slavery, policing racial status, and maintaining order. Military officers such as Grey and Prescott had distrusted Martinique's French inhabitants, but they hoped that the restoration of Old Regime law might win their loyalty and end the colony's political divisions. In contrast Milnes and Keppel, as civilian governors, had showed sympathy for the French planters and approved of the sovereign council's efforts to defend their social and economic domination of the colony. Keppel told the court that his regret at leaving was qualified by the satisfaction of knowing Martinique had been preserved from revolutionary subversion and upheaval, implying that the new regime in France would maintain slavery in Martinique.

Like the British commanders, the sovereign council made final preparations for the return to French rule. On 15 July the *procureur général* recommended that the court take advantage of the period preceding the formal transition of sovereignty to present the first consul of the French Republic with a testament of its submission. The opportunity to do so was provided by the imminent arrival of Charles Henri Bertin, the French government's new colonial prefect for Martinique and its dependencies.[97] Bertin, who would head the colony's civilian administration, negotiated with Keppel regarding the amount of tax revenue still owed to the British government.[98] In September Admiral Louis-Thomas Villaret Joyeuse, appointed by Bonaparte as captain general to take possession of the colony in the name of France, arrived in Martinique. The sovereign council received its final instructions from the British governor on 13 September. The following day authority over the island was transferred to Villaret-Joyeuse in a simple ceremony, and British troops evacuated all forts and strategic points.[99]

The British occupation of Martinique was an episode of the war that had begun in 1793, but it also represented the triumph of counterrevolution in the Windward Islands. Martinique's planters welcomed the British conquest in 1794, which put an end to the local republican regime. They acceded to General Grey's authority and swore their loyalty to George III, but this submission was based less on royalist principle than on the desire to maintain slavery and preserve the colonial status quo. Martinique's sovereign council exemplified the colony's collaboration, and its registration of British governors' orders gave them the legitimacy of Old Regime law. The court's statements and decisions also demonstrated that the planter elite expected collaboration to control communications, which threatened social and racial hierarchies. Planters backed British commanders in their efforts to defend the colony from republican invasion and the insurgency that Victor Hugues tried to incite with propaganda and *agents provocateurs*. Beyond these overt threats, however, the sovereign council's insistence that the colony would be ruled by Old Regime law was intended to purge republican ideas and sympathies and to silence revolutionary claims to authority. Furthermore, the court's deliberations provide evidence not only of the continuation of planters' anxieties regarding *gens de couleur*, *petit-Blanc* disorder, and slave conspiracy. They also reveal planters' determination to control communication among these groups and to block subversion. These colonial anxieties had existed before 1789, and they would not vanish after 1802, but they had been intensified by planters' fear of a radical metropolitan Republic and its local agents or supporters. Bonaparte had not only ended the war associated with that Republic and discredited the revolutionary script that challenged executive authority, but he also appeared to have abandoned its most radical policy of all: the abolition of slavery. Therefore, the peace that ended Great Britain's occupation of Martinique also marked the end of the French Revolution in the Windward Islands.

Conclusion

If rumours of emancipation had a profound impact on the revolution's beginning in the Windward Islands, anticipations of slavery's restoration played a crucial role in the dramatic reversal of radical revolution in Guadeloupe. Shortly after deporting Victor Hugues in January 1799, General Desfourneaux ordered the arrest of those deemed responsible for the uprising against his assumption of authority. Despite his proclamation promising that his administration would preserve liberty, the trials of those accused of conspiring against him revealed that both soldiers and cultivators feared he would return blacks to servitude. After publishing the Constitution of the Year III, Desfourneaux proclaimed a new law on cultivators in February 1799. This new regulation insisted that cultivators must be paid, but it also made clear they would not be given land. Moreover, in announcing that national plantations would be rented to private individuals in an effort to increase productivity, the law stated that the cultivators assigned to those plantations would be transferred to the new managers along with the land. Such measures hardly reassured Guadeloupe's non-white population that the new agent of metropolitan authority was committed to preserving their freedom. In response to a very different rumour, in October 1799 Desfourneaux stated that he would never accept the reappointment of Hugues and would use force to prevent Terror from returning to the colony. If such a stance was in keeping with the Directory's constitutional principles in France, it heightened fears regarding the end of liberty and equality in Guadeloupe. Desfourneaux's subordinates accused him of treason; on 19 October crowds forced his arrest and deportation.[1]

The rumours that undermined Desfourneaux reflected changing metropolitan attitudes towards the abolition of slavery. Since 1795 planters from Saint-Domingue and Guadeloupe had been telling the government in Paris that the decree of 16 *Pluviôse* had been a catastrophe for the colonies. The political context in France also changed when the Directory was overthrown in the Coup of 18 *Brumaire* Year VIII (9 November 1799), which brought Napoleon Bonaparte to power as first consul. The new regime's policy towards the colonies was not clear immediately. In a proclamation of 25 December 1799, Bonaparte guaranteed freedom for the "brave blacks" of Saint-Domingue.[2] Rather than reaffirm the integration of the colonies and metropolitan France, however, the new Constitution of the Year VIII stated that particular laws would govern each of the colonies: their inhabitants would neither enjoy the same rights as metropolitan citizens nor elect representatives to national parliament.[3] Some of Bonaparte's advisors like Admiral Truguet defended slavery's abolition as an essential republican principle, but the first consul also appointed pro-slavery figures such as Moreau de Saint-Méry from Martinique to positions in the ministry of marine. If Bonaparte's intentions regarding slavery remained equivocal, his determination to restore absolute metropolitan control over the colonies was clear. Bonaparte appointed three new officials to impose the nation's will on Guadeloupe, including Admiral Lacrosse as the colony's captain general. In 1792 Lacrosse had come to the Windward Islands as the herald of the democratic Republic and of racial equality; in 1801 he returned as the agent of Napoleonic authoritarianism.[4]

Lacrosse would take over from three commissioners named by the Directory to replace Desfourneaux but who had sailed from France after the coup of Brumaire with Bonaparte's approval. These commissioners arrived in Guadeloupe in January 1800 and continued Desfourneaux's plan of renting national properties in an attempt to boost sugar and coffee production. They subjected black cultivators to greater discipline and complained that the colony's mixed-race population was disloyal and insubordinate. Even before Lacrosse's arrival, therefore, metropolitan agents sought to roll back emancipation and racial equality.[5] Yet their authority depended on an army that was predominantly non-white. Two coloured officers who commanded great respect in the army were *Chef de brigade* Magloire Pélage, Guadeloupe's second in command, and *Chef de bataillon* Louis Delgrès. Both men had been born in Martinique where they fought with the republicans, were captured during the British conquest in 1794, and deported to France. Integrated into the *Bataillon des Antilles*, they were promoted and sent to Guadeloupe as part of the military reinforcements for Hugues's garrison. Pélage subsequently served at Sainte-Lucie under Goyrand and was wounded, captured, and spent eighteen months in a British jail before returning to France in a prisoner exchange. Similarly Delgrès fought with the rebels in St Vincent before being captured, imprisoned in England, and returned to France. Promoted again, both officers returned to the Windward Islands in 1800 with the troops accompanying Desfourneaux's replacements.[6] The careers of Pélage and Delgrès represented the advances made by non-whites since the decree of 16 *Pluviôse*, but the different roles they played in 1802 also demonstrated the terrible dilemma that Bonaparte's imposition of metropolitan control created for coloured officers: Should they support the authority to which they had sworn their loyalty, and that was associated with ending Old Regime injustice, or should they resist what many blacks and people of colour perceived as a bid to return them to servitude and subservience?

Lacrosse's expedition reached Guadeloupe on 30 May 1801. Crowds cheered the admiral as the returning hero of the Republic, but his harsh measures and attacks on racial equality soon alienated the colony's population. Shortly after arriving the new captain general began to purge black and coloured soldiers from the army: he accused them of rebelling against Desfourneaux and imprisoned them in preparation for deportation. Lacrosse also invited *émigrés* to return to the colony. While metropolitan authorities might see this in keeping with Bonaparte's amnesty for French royalists in Europe, in Guadeloupe it meant that black cultivators found themselves working under the supervision of former masters who had never concealed their opposition to the Republic or to the abolition of slavery. Workers poisoned livestock in defiance. Lacrosse responded by convening a military commission in June that condemned thirteen cultivators to death. When popular General Antoine-Charles de Béthencourt died from fever on 5 August, Lacrosse did not promote Pélage but took command of Guadeloupe's army himself. Troops protested this sign of racial discrimination, which led Lacrosse to order more arrests and to propose the deportation of all men of colour who he called "enemies of the government." The attempt by white officers to arrest Pélage on 21 October provoked an insurrection against Lacrosse's authority by both soldiers and cultivators at Port-de-la-Liberté. Ransacking his headquarters, crowds discovered a letter from

Lacrosse stating that imprisoned troops were to be sent to Madagascar. When the captain general arrived from Basse-Terre, the black soldiers accompanying him joined the insurgents who seized him and threw him in jail. Pélage, whom troops proclaimed as their commander-in-chief, sought to regain control of the colony in the name of metropolitan authority. He prevented violence between soldiers, encouraged cultivators to return to work, and formed a provisional council composed mostly of white merchants. Fearing that furious coloured troops would murder Lacrosse, Pélage transferred him from prison to a Danish vessel, which then departed Guadeloupe. A British warship captured the vessel and took Lacrosse to Dominica as a prisoner of war.[7]

The arrival of diplomatic news from Europe transformed the situation in the Caribbean. Learning of the preliminaries of peace between France and Great Britain, the British governor of Dominica treated Lacrosse not as a prisoner but as the legitimate governor of Guadeloupe and assisted him in placing the colony under blockade and calling on its inhabitants to resist the rebels. A British officer brought a newspaper to Guadeloupe in November that described the imminent peace settlement, but many black and coloured soldiers denounced the news as false: they recognized that the war's end would undermine their military value to France and allow the metropolitan government to send a major expedition to regain control of the colony. Bonaparte was already preparing such an expedition for Saint-Domingue. The government in Paris suspected Toussaint Louverture, the black general whom French commissioner Sonthonax had named the colony's commander-in-chief in May 1797 and who negotiated the British evacuation in 1798, of aspiring to become the ruler of an independent state. Toussaint issued his own constitution in July 1801 that declared the colony part of the French Empire, but it was to be governed by its own laws that abolished slavery in perpetuity and made him governor for life.[8] The first consul's instructions for General Charles-Victor-Emmanuel Leclerc, whom he had appointed to command the force to be sent to smash Toussaint's regime, indicated that he was not to re-establish slavery in Saint-Domingue. They ordered him, however, to disarm the colony's black armies and force its cultivators back to their plantations.[9] It is not entirely clear whether Bonaparte initially held a pragmatic attitude regarding the continuation of free labour in Saint-Domingue, or whether from the beginning he merely sought to conceal preparations to restore slavery as soon as practical.[10] His decision regarding colonies to be returned by Great Britain as part of the Peace of Amiens, however, suggested his disdain for the Republic's experiment with black emancipation. Bonaparte informed Lacrosse in a letter of October 1801 that slavery would continue in colonies like Martinique where it had never been abolished. Shortly after Leclerc's expedition sailed for Saint-Domingue in December 1801, news of Lacrosse's expulsion from Guadeloupe reached Paris. In response, Bonaparte ordered the preparation of a second military expedition under the command of General Antoine Richepance. As with Leclerc, Bonaparte instructed Richepance to proclaim that liberty would be preserved in Guadeloupe in order to minimize resistance. The general's mission, however, was to crush defiance of metropolitan authority ruthlessly.[11]

The ships carrying Richepance and his thirty-five hundred white troops arrived at Guadeloupe on 6 May 1802 and, to the general's surprise, received a friendly welcome at Port-de-la-Liberté. Pélage and his council declared their loyalty to Bonaparte and to Richepance, but Pélage's control of the colony was tenuous. He had faced an uprising by cultivators in December, and many of his troops distrusted his insistence on the maintenance of metropolitan authority given Lacrosse's hostility to people of colour, news of the fighting in Saint-Domingue between the forces of Leclerc and Toussaint Louverture, and the rumours of slavery's imminent restoration. Richepance validated this distrust when he demanded the evacuation of the colony's forts and his soldiers began to disarm all black troops. Pélage ordered his men to comply, but some kept their weapons and escaped to Basse-Terre where Delgrès, whom Pélage had appointed commander of Fort Saint-Charles, rallied all those prepared to resist the return of racial inequality and slavery. Delgrès issued a proclamation that appealed to the first consul for justice but declared the rebels' determination to "Live Free or Die!"[12] On 10 May ships landed most of Richepance's troops at Basse-Terre, while a smaller column marched overland to confront the rebels. After fierce fighting in the town, Delgrès's forces retreated into Fort Saint-Charles. Preparing to assault the stronghold, Pélage freed five hundred of the black troops imprisoned in the holds of ships where they awaited deportation, and he persuaded them to fight alongside Richepance's white soldiers. After enduring several days of artillery bombardment, the rebels escaped from the fort: some crept back across the mountains to try in vain to incite the population of Port-de-la-Liberté to rise up against Richepance and Pélage, the others under Delgrès entrenched themselves on the heights of Matouba to make their last stand. On 28 May, with Richepance's troops advancing on their position, Delgrès's rebels ignited multiple barrels of gunpowder and blew themselves up in a final devastating gesture of defiance. This dramatic resistance was not the end of the violence in Guadeloupe. Richepance ordered mass executions and deportations not only to stamp out the continuing insurrection but also to eliminate all black and coloured soldiers who had served in the colony's army: he viewed such men as the root of resistance to metropolitan control. In July 1802 Richepance unofficially reestablished slavery in Guadeloupe, a decision that the government in Paris authorized subsequently.[13]

Even before the restoration of slavery, communication of the events in Guadeloupe helped trigger a new phase of revolution in Saint-Domingue. After his troops gained control of the colony's key ports, Leclerc negotiated a peace settlement in May 1802 that allowed Toussaint Louverture to retire to a place of his choosing while retaining his rank and his staff. The agreement also obliged his generals to submit to metropolitan rule. In June, however, Leclerc betrayed his promise, arrested Toussaint, and deported him to France where he would die in a prison cell in the Jura Mountains. French troops' efforts to disarm Saint-Domingue's cultivators and force them back to their plantations provoked upheaval. Leclerc, like Richepance, became convinced that he had to eliminate all black and coloured soldiers in order to end opposition to metropolitan authority. Insurrection became general in the colony by September, in part because accounts of Delgrès's rebellion and the subsequent massacres in Guadeloupe had reached Saint-Domingue and convinced the population that their only options were enslavement or resistance. The black generals Henri Christophe and Jean-Jacques Dessalines broke with French authority in October and assumed the leadership of what had become a war of independence.[14]

The irony of Lacrosse's role in the destruction of radical republicanism in Guadeloupe was not unique. Other key figures from the revolution in the Windward Islands also contributed to the end of emancipation and the restoration of Old Regime patterns. When Leclerc died of fever on 1 November 1802, Rochambeau replaced him as commander-in-chief of French forces in Saint-Domingue. As governor general of Martinique in 1793 General Rochambeau had established a republican regime that enforced equality for free men of colour against opposition from royalist planters. He had surrendered the colony to British forces in March 1794 only after leading a heroic defence conducted according to established laws of war. Yet after taking over from Leclerc, Rochambeau was responsible for atrocities in Saint-Domingue, including drowning and torturing prisoners and the use of man-killing dogs imported from Cuba. In April 1803 he asked the government in Paris to send Toussaint Louverture back to the colony so that he could hang him as an example to the rebels. By then Rochambeau's forces in North Province, decimated by fever and battle, only held the town of Cap Français. The resumption of war between France and Great Britain ended any hope of reinforcements and, therefore, of renewed French control. In November Rochambeau abandoned Le Cap, the last French troops in the colony evacuated Le Mole in December, and Dessalines proclaimed the independence of Haiti in January 1804.[15] The willingness of Rochambeau and Lacrosse to attack liberty and equality for nonwhites betrayed the principles they had communicated to the colonies in 1793. They had been agents of the slave-holding Republic, however, and Victor Hugues's actions after 1798 were perhaps even more ironic. Although he returned to France in disgrace, Hugues succeeded in rehabilitating his reputation to the extent that the Directory appointed him governor of the French colony of Guyana in September 1799. In that role, the man who brought the Jacobin Terror to Guadeloupe and incited slave rebellion throughout the Windward Islands presided over the re-enslavement of Guyana's cultivators in 1803; he then swore allegiance to Emperor Napoleon in 1804.[16]

The end of the revolution in the Windward Islands, like its earlier stages, demonstrated not only the ambiguity of revolutionary principles in the colonial context but also the crucial importance of struggles to control news, ideas, language, and symbols: these were the elements of the French revolutionary script that helped to give meaning to conflict in the colonies. France did not abolish slavery definitively in its overseas empire until 1848, again under the inspiration of revolution in Paris,[17] but racial inequality and resentment of colonial rule continued to characterize French possessions in the Caribbean and elsewhere. This study of colonial revolution at the end of the eighteenth century perhaps suggests a useful perspective for examining how modern colonial insurgents (including those linked to the wars of decolonization in the twentieth century) adopted, transformed, and rejected European revolutionary scripts. While the realities of race and slavery affected everything in the Caribbean, the struggles in Martinique and Guadeloupe were also shaped and inspired by the political drama unfolding in France. Patriots, royalists, and terrorists adopted its language; fought over the meaning of its concepts and symbols; and sought to monopolize the circulation and interpretation of its news. Their conflict often took the form of competing claims to speak for the nation – echo-ing the ideological dynamic of popular sovereignty – and the colonies' residents faced similar dilemmas of loyalty experienced by men and women in France. The developments in the Windward Islands between 1789 and 1802, therefore, should be seen as part of the larger story of the French Revolution.

Notes

Abbreviations

AD Gironde   Archives départementales de la Gironde, Bordeaux
AD Guadeloupe   Archives départementales de la Guadeloupe, Basse-Terre, Guadeloupe
AD Martinique   Archives départementales de la Martinique, Fort-de-France, Martinique
AP   Archives parlementaires de 1787 à 1860, Paris, 1875–1987
Bordeaux   Archives municipales de Bordeaux, Bordeaux
Colonies   Archives des colonies, Aix-en-Provence and Paris
Marine   Archives de la marine, Vincennes
Moniteur   Réimpression de l'ancien moniteur, Paris, 1840–54

Introduction

1 Robert L. Stein, "The Revolution of 1789 and the Abolition of Slavery," *Canadian Journal of History* 17 (1982): 447–68.
2 One of the most important works marking this shift was Yves Bénot, *La révolution française et la fin des colonies* (Paris: Éditions la Découverte, 1989). See also: Anne Pérotin-Dumon, *Être patriote sous les tropiques: La Guadeloupe, la colonisation et la révolution* (Basse-Terre: Société d'histoire de la Guadeloupe, 1985); Henri Bangou, *La révolution et l'esclavage à la Guadeloupe 1789–1802* (Paris: Messidor / Éditions sociales, 1989); Léo Élisabeth, "Gens de couleur et révolution dans les Îles du Vent (1789–Janvier 1793)," *Revue française d'histoire d'outre-mer* 76, no. 282–3 (1989): 75–95 and "La république dans les Îles du Vent, décembre 1792–avril 1794," *Annales historiques de la révolution française* no. 3, 4 (1993): 373–408.
3 See for example David Patrick Geggus, *The Impact of the Haitian Revolution in the Atlantic World* (Columbia: University of South Carolina Press, 2001).

4 Frédéric Régent, *Esclavage, métissage, liberté: La révolution française en Guadeloupe 1789–1802* (Paris: Bernard Grasset, 2004), esp. 234–47, 285–354.

5 Laurent Dubois, *A Colony of Citizens: Revolution and Slave Emancipation in the French Caribbean, 1787–1804* (Chapel Hill: University of North Carolina Press, 2004), esp. 1–14, 23–9, 124–54, 167–8, 187–221.

6 See for example Suzanne Desan, Lynn Hunt, and William Max Nelson, eds., *The French Revolution in Global Perspective* (Ithaca, NY: Cornell University Press, 2013).

7 David A. Bell, "Questioning the Global Turn: The Case of the French Revolution," *French Historical Studies* 37, no. 1 (Winter 2014): 1–24.

8 Jeremy D. Popkin, *You Are All Free: The Haitian Revolution and the Abolition of Slavery* (New York: Cambridge University Press, 2010).

9 For discussions of the nature and importance of political culture in the French Revolution, see François Furet, *Interpreting the French Revolution*, trans. Elborg Forster (Cambridge: Cambridge University Press, 1981; repr. 1985); Lynn Hunt, *Politics, Culture, and Class in the French Revolution* (Berkeley: University of California Press, 1984); Colin Lucas, ed., *The Political Culture of the French Revolution* (Oxford: Pergammon Press, 1988), esp. "Introduction," xi–xvii; Keith Michael Baker, *Inventing the French Revolution: Essays on French Political Culture in the Eighteenth Century* (Cambridge: Cambridge University Press, 1990). The development of scholarly interest in political culture was linked to the revisionist challenge to the "classical" interpretation of the French Revolution, which emphasized socio-economic factors. For discussions of this historiographical debate, see William Doyle, *Origins of the French Revolution*, 2nd ed. (Oxford: Oxford University Press, 1988), 7–40 and Gary Kates, ed., *The French Revolution: Recent Debates and New Controversies* (London: Routledge, 1998).

10 Kenneth J. Banks, *Chasing Empire across the Sea: Communications and the State in the French Atlantic, 1713–1763* (Montreal and Kingston: McGill-Queen's University Press, 2002), 3–13.

11 Ibid., 43–64.

12 Ibid., 127–52.

13 Ibid., 184–216.

14 Keith Michael Baker and Dan Edelstein, eds., *Scripting Revolution: A Historical Approach to the Comparative Study of Revolutions* (Stanford: Stanford University Press, 2015), esp. 1–21.

15 Keith Michael Baker, "Revolutionizing Revolution," in *Scripting Revolution*, ed. Baker and Edelstein, 71–102. See also Keith Michael Baker, "A Script for a French Revolution: The Political Consciousness of the Abbé Mably," in *Inventing the French Revolution*, 86–106.

1 The Windward Islands

1 Robert Louis Stein, *The French Sugar Business in the Eighteenth Century* (Baton Rouge: Louisiana State University Press, 1988), ix.

2 Lucien Abenon, Jacques Cauna, and Lilianne Chauleau, *Antilles 1789: La révolution aux Caraïbes* (Paris: Éditions Nathan, 1989), 26.

3 William L. Grant, "Canada versus Guadeloupe: An Episode of the Seven Years' War," *American Historical Review* 17 (1912): 735–43. See also Lucien-René Abenon, *Petite histoire de la Guadeloupe* (Paris: Éditions l'Harmattan, 1992), 69–72 and J.H. Parry, *Trade and Dominion: The European Overseas Empires in the Eighteenth Century* (London: Weidenfield and Nicolson, 1971), 124–8.

4 Jacques Adélaïde-Merlande, *La Caraïbe et la Guyane au temps de la révolution et de l'empire* (Paris: Éditions Karthala, 1992), 12–14. See also Abenon, Cauna and Chauleau, *Antilles 1789*, 16–21.

5 Abenon, *Petite histoire de la Guadeloupe*, 10–11; and Anne Pérotin-Dumon, *La ville aux îles, la ville dans l'île: Basse-Terre et Pointe-à-Pitre, Guadeloupe, 1650–1820* (Paris: Karthala, 2000), 16–19, 381–97.

6 Lilianne Chauleau, *Dans les Îles du Vent: La Martinique XVIIe–XIXe siècle* (Paris: éditions l'Harmattan, 1993), 5–6.

7 Paul Butel, *Histoire des Antilles françaises XVIIe–XXe siècle* (Paris: Perrin, 2002), 10–11.

8 W.J. Eccles, *France in America* (Toronto: Fitzhenry and Whiteside Ltd, 1972), 31; Robin Blackburn, *The Making of New World Slavery: From the Baroque to the Modern 1492–1800* (London: Verso, 1997), 280–1; and Butel, *Histoire des Antilles françaises*, 23–7. See also "La formation des bourgs dans les Antilles françaises: Ordres du roi et actes d'assemblée de la compagnie des îles d'Amérique, 1636–1645," in Pérotin-Dumon, *La ville aux îles*, 723–4.

9 Nellis M. Crouse, *French Pioneers in the West Indies (1624–1664)* (New York, 1940; repr., Octagon Books, 1977). See also Butel, *Histoire des Antilles françaises*, 27–35 and Abenon, *Petite histoire de la Guadeloupe*, 26–30.

10 Stewart L. Mims, *Colbert's West India Policy* (New Haven, CT: Yale University Press, 1912), 121, 142–75, 180–94, 223. See also Butel, *Histoire des Antilles françaises*, 39–57; Eccles, pp. 32, 60–4; Blackburn, *Making of New World Slavery*, 282–6; Abenon, *Petite histoire de la Guadeloupe*, 35–46; Chauleau, *Dans les Îles du Vent*, 17–24.

11 Abenon, Cauna and Chauleau, *Antilles 1789*, 52–6; Abenon, *Petite histoire de la Guadeloupe*, 53–5; Chauleau, *Dans les Îles du Vent*, 38–60; Butel, *Histoire des Antilles françaises*, 57–63, 130–2.

12 Originally this colonial high court was the *Conseil souverain*, but in the eighteenth century metropolitan government and its agents called it the

Conseil supérieur to emphasize that sovereignty was the property of the crown. The colonial judges, however, continued to refer to the court as the sovereign council. See Liliane Chauleau, *Conseil souverain de la Martinique (Série B): Inventaire analytique*, vol. 1, 1712–1791 (Fort-de-France: Archives départementales de la Martinique, 1985), 5–16.

13 C.A. Banbuck, *Histoire politique, économique et sociale de la Martinique sous l'ancien régime (1635–1789)* (Paris: Marcel Rivière, 1935; repr., Fort-de-France: Société de distribution et de culture, 1972), 155–73. See also: Abenon, Cauna and Chauleau, *Antilles 1789*, 57; Abenon, *Petite histoire de la Guadeloupe*, 54–5; Chauleau, *Dans les Îles du Vent*, 64–9; Butel, *Histoire des Antilles françaises*, 130–6.

14 Gabriel Debien, "Les engagés pour les Antilles (1634–1715)," *Revue d'histoire des colonies* 38 (1951): 5–274. See also Butel, *Histoire des Antilles françaises*, 35–9; Abenon, *Petite histoire de la Guadeloupe*, 49–50; Chauleau, *Dans les Îles du Vent*, 109–13, 144–6.

15 Blackburn, *Making of New World Slavery*, 166–213.

16 David Eltis, *The Rise of African Slavery in the Americas* (Cambridge: Cambridge University Press, 2000), 195–204.

17 Robert C. Batie, "Why Sugar? Economic Cycles and the Changing of Staples on the English and French Antilles, 1624–54," *Journal of Caribbean History* 8–9 (1976): 1–41. See also Richard Sheridan, *The Development of the Plantations to 1750: An Era of West Indian Prosperity 1750–1775* (Kingston, Jamaica: Caribbean Universities Press, 1970), 16 and Stein, *Sugar Business*, 41–2.

18 Clarence J. Munford, *The Black Ordeal of Slavery and Slave Trading in the French West Indies 1625–1715*, 3 vols. (Lewiston, NY: Edwin Mellen, 1991), 505–22. See also Blackburn, *Making of New World Slavery*, 279–95.

19 Paul Butel, "France, the Antilles, and Europe in the Seventeenth and Eighteenth Centuries: Renewals of Foreign Trade," in *Caribbean Slavery in the Atlantic World*, ed. Verene Shepherd and Hilary McD. Beckles (Oxford: James Currey Publishers, 2000), 194–205. See also T.M. Doerflinger, "The Antilles Trade of the Old Regime," *Journal of Interdisciplinary History* 6 (1976): 397–415 and François Crouzet, "England and France in the Eighteenth Century: A Comparative Analysis of Two Economic Growths," in *Social Historians in Contemporary France: Essays from Annales*, ed. Marc Ferro (New York: Harper and Row, 1972), 59–86.

20 Michael Duffy, *Soldiers, Sugar and Seapower: The British Expeditions to the West Indies and the War against Revolutionary France* (Oxford: Clarendon Press, 1987), 11–12. See also Jean Tarrade, *Le commerce coloniale de la France à la fin de l'ancien régime: L'évolution du régime de "l'exclusif" de 1763 à 1789*, 2 vols. (Paris: Presses universitaires de France, 1972), 1: 22–3, 113–44. Both

Tarrade and Stein, *Sugar Business*. 85–7, 93–105 emphasize that this commerce was not without major risk and did not generate enormous profits for all involved.

21 Robert L. Stein, *The French Slave Trade in the Eighteenth Century: An Old Regime Business* (Madison: University of Wisconsin Press, 1979), 14, 40–1.

22 Ibid., 13–42.

23 Ibid., 55–6. See also Jean Meyer, *L'armement nantais dans la deuxième moitié du XVIIIème siècle* (Paris: SEVPEN, 1969).

24 Alan Forrest, *Society and Politics in Revolutionary Bordeaux* (London: Oxford University Press, 1975), 14. Silvia Marzagalli, *Bordeaux et les États-Unis 1776–1815: Politique et stratégies négociantes dans les genèse d'un réseau commercial* (Geneva: Librarie Droz, 2015), esp. 76, 87, 127 argues that Bordeaux's success in establishing connections with American commercial houses reflected the port's central role in France's colonial trade upon which its merchant elite depended.

25 Jeremy Black, *Natural and Necessary Enemies: Anglo-French Relations in the Eighteenth Century* (Athens: University of Georgia Press, 1987). See also Parry, 107–29.

26 Richard Pares, *War and Trade in the West Indies 1739–1763* (London: F. Cass, 1963).

27 Richard Middleton, *The Bells of Victory: The Pitt-Newcastle Ministry and the Conduct of the Seven Years' War 1757–1762* (Cambridge: Cambridge University Press, 1985). See also Eccles, 215–16.

28 Jonathan R. Dull, *The French Navy and American Independence: A Study of Arms and Diplomacy 1774–1787* (Princeton, NJ: Princeton University Press, 1975), esp. 211–61. See also Étienne Taillemite, *L'histoire ignorée de la marine française* (Paris: Librarie académique Perrin, 1988), 177–91.

29 Duffy, 3–25.

30 Butel, *Histoire des Antilles françaises*, 125–7.

31 Jacques Petitjean Roget, *La Gaoulé, la révolte de la Martinique en 1717*, (Fort-de-France: Société d'histoire de la Martinique and Paris: Librarie du pont-neuf, 1966). See also Butel, *Histoire des Antilles françaises*, 136–9.

32 Tarrade, *Le commerce coloniale*, 1: 88–94.

33 Ibid., 94–5.

34 Ibid., 101–11. For a discussion of illegal commerce in Guadeloupe after 1759, see Pérotin-Dumon, *La ville aux Îles*, 148–52.

35 Tarrade, *Le commerce coloniale*, 1: 96–8, 100.

36 Ibid., 98–9. Regarding Guadeloupe under British occupation, 1759–63, see Pérotin-Dumon, *La ville aux îles*, 159–63.

37 Butel, *Histoire des Antilles françaises*, 130–1.

38 Tarrade, *Le commerce coloniale*, 1: 99, 167–74.

39 Charles Frostin, *Les révoltes blanches à Saint-Domingue aux XVIIe–XVIIIe siécles (Haïti avant 1789)* (Paris: Éditions de l'École, 1975), esp. 297–352, 396–402.

40 Tarrade, *Le commerce coloniale*, 1: 190–5.

41 Ibid., 195–201, 223–86.

42 Ibid., 287–327. In part the *entrepôts* were justified by the British project to establish "free ports" in Dominica and Jamaica, and in part they were to address the need for adequate provisioning of the colonies, which was exposed by the hurricane that devastated Martinique in August 1766.

43 Tarrade, *Le commerce coloniale*, 1: 373–437. The granting of special permissions by administrators in the Windward Islands, and the blind eye turned to *interlope*, was driven by a provisioning crisis: metropolitan commerce failed to supply the colonies adequately with flour, cod, and other necessities. This crisis had become acute by the spring of 1776.

44 Tarrade, *Le commerce coloniale*, 1: 438–49.

45 Ibid., 451–92. See also "L'ordonnance royale du 13 juillet 1778 ouvre les ports de la Guadeloupe aux étrangers," in Pérotin-Dumon, *La ville aux îles*, 741.

46 Tarrade, *Le commerce coloniale*, 1: 468–72.

47 In 1786 Guadeloupe's *entrepôt* was transferred to Basse-Terre after suggestions that Pointe-à-Pitre be made the administrative capital, as well as *entrepôt*, were rejected. Castries did authorize the transfer of the *entrepôt* to Pointe-à-Pitre, however, during the months of *hivernage*; Tarrade, *Le commerce coloniale*, 1: 593–4.

48 Tarrade, *Le commerce coloniale*, 2: 531–90. Jean-Jacques de Bethmann, a Bordeaux merchant and ship owner, echoed the resentment and anxiety of many of his peers towards Castries' measures: "L'arrêt du conseil du 30 août écrase le commerce de France et l'État … le commerce de France ne reprendra jamais le même lustre … car on s'est chaussée à la Cour des idées les plus pernicieuses à sa prospérité"; quoted in Butel, *Histoire des Antilles françaises*, 112. Regarding merchant resentment towards American trade with the French Caribbean colonies, see also Marzagalli, 34, 43, 71–4, 87.

49 Tarrade, *Le commerce coloniale*, 2: 591–614.

50 See M.A. Lacour, *Histoire de la Guadeloupe* (Basse-Terre, 1855–1860; repr. Paris: Édition et diffusion de la culture Antillaise, 1976) 1: 375–6 and Henry Lémery, *La révolution française à la Martinique* (Paris: Larose, 1936), 13–14.

51 Damas and Foulquier to Minister of Marine, 25 February 1788; Colonies C⁸ᴬ 88, 1–8. See also *Procès-verbal des séances tenues par l'assemblée coloniale de la Martinique (27 décembre 1787–1er janvier 1788)*. Colonies C⁸ᴬ 88, 9–28.

See also: Abenon, Cauna and Chauleau, *Antilles 1789*, 43–4, 58–9; Chauleau, *Dans les Îles du Vent*, 70–2; Jules-François Saintoyant, *La colonisation française pendant la révolution (1789–1799)* (Paris: La renaissance du livre, 1930), 2: 183.

52 Foullon d'Écotier to Minister of Marine, 18 February 1788; Colonies C[7A] 43, 84–93. See also Clugny to Minister of Marine, 12 January 1788, Colonies C[7A] 43, 24–8, and *Procès-verbal des délibérations de l'assemblée coloniale de Guadeloupe, tenue au mois de janvier 1788* (Guadeloupe, 1788), Colonies C[7A] 43, 94–113.

53 Barnave's Report on Martinique, 29 November 1790, *AP*, vol. 21, 125. This same explanation was given in "Rapport fait à l'assemblée nationale, au nom du comité coloniale, sur les troubles de la Martinique, par P. Goyn, député du département de la Haute-Garonne," 2 May 1792, *AP*, vol. 42, 677.

54 Lémery, 4–13; Abenon, Cauna, and Chauleau, *Antilles 1789*, 32–3; Butel, *Histoire des Antilles françaises*, 107–112.

55 "Les commissionaires de Saint-Pierre vus par le directeur du domaine à la Guadeloupe, 1754," in Pérotin-Dumon, *La ville aux îles*, 735. See also Abenon, Cauna and Chauleau, *Antilles 1789*, 42–4 and Tarrade, *Le commerce coloniale*, 1: 30.

56 Butel, *Histoire des Antilles françaises*, 111. See also Abenon, *Petite Histoire de la Guadeloupe*, 52, 59.

57 Damas and Foulquier to Minister of Marine, 23 October 1788; Colonies C[8A] 88, 68–70. Regarding the protests from Saint-Pierre, see *Observations des commissaires du commerce de la Martinique sur le procès-verbal de l'assemblée coloniale de cette îsle du 14 janvier 1788* (Saint-Pierre, 31 March 1788), Colonies C[8A] 88, 281–331.

58 Abenon, Cauna and Chauleau, *Antilles 1789*, 44.

59 Ibid., 35–6.

60 Butel, *Histoire des Antilles françaises*, 146–51.

61 Quoted in Abenon, Cauna and Chauleau, *Antilles 1789*, 37–8.

62 Butel, *Histoire des Antilles françaises*, 155–7, 108–9. For a detailed discussion of the floating population in Guadeloupe's towns, see Pérotin-Dumon, *La ville aux Îles* 285–306.

63 Tarrade, *Le commerce coloniale*, 1: 30.

64 Abenon, Cauna and Chauleau, *Antilles 1789*, 40–2.

65 Julius S. Scott, "Crisscrossing Empires: Ships, Sailors, and Resistance in the Lesser Antilles in the Eighteenth Century," in *The Lesser Antilles in the Age of European Expansion*, ed. Robert L. Paquette and Stanley L. Engerman (Gainesville: University Press of Florida, 1996), 128–43. See also Anne Pérotin-Dumon, "Ambiguous Revolution in the Caribbean: The White

Jacobins, 1789–1800," *Historical Reflections / Réflexions historiques* 13, no. 2 and 3 (1986): 499–515.

66 Benot, *La révolution française et la fin des colonies*, 60.

67 The figures for Guadeloupe are taken from Abenon, *Petite histoire de la Guadeloupe*, 80; those for Martinique from Léo Élisabeth, "The French Antilles," in *Neither Free nor Slave: The Freedmen of African Descent in the Slave Societies of the New World*, ed. David W. Cohen and Jack P. Greene (Baltimore, MD: Johns Hopkins University Press, 1972), 150–1.

68 Gabriel Debien, *Les Esclaves aux Antilles françaises (XVIIe–XVIIIe siècles)* (Basse-Terre and Fort-de-France: Sociétés d'histoire de la Guadeloupe et de la Martinque, 1974), 54–8. See also Butel, *Histoire de Antilles françaises*, 165–7 and Munford, 1: 104–25. Regarding Guadeloupe's slave population, see Régent, 21–6.

69 Cited in Stein, *The French Sugar Business*, 44–5.

70 Debien, *Les esclaves*, 135–8. See also Dale Tomich, "Slavery in Martinique in the French Caribbean," in *Caribbean Slavery*, ed. Shepherd and Beckles, 415–18.

71 Debien, *Les esclaves*, 139, 147–61. See also Régent, 79–83.

72 Tomich, 422.

73 Butel, *Histoire des Antilles françaises*, 169. See also Debien, *Les esclaves*, 140–4.

74 Tomich, 418–19. See also Debien, *Les esclaves*, 96–7.

75 Debien, *Les esclaves*, 98–104. See also Régent. 83–93 and Stein, *The French Sugar Business*, 56.

76 Abenon, Cauna and Chauleau, *Antilles 1789*, 74–5. Regarding female domestics, see Arlette Gautier, *Les soeurs de solitude: La condition féminine dans l'esclavage aux Antilles du XVIIe au XIXe siècle* (Paris: Éditions Caribéennes, 1985), 203–11.

77 Pérotin-Dumon, *La ville aux Îles*, 652–62. See also Regent, 94–102.

78 "Code noir ou édit du Roy, servant de réglement pour le gouvernement et l'administration de justice et la police des Isles françaises de l'Amérique, et pour la discipline et le commerce des nègres et esclaves dans les dits pays (1685)," in *Traite des noirs au siècle des lumières (Témoignages de négriers)*, ed. I. and J.L. Vissière (Paris: Édition A.M. Métailié, 1982), 163–70. For discussions of the origins and implementation of the *code noir*, see: Régent, 26–34; Blackburn, *Making of New World Slavery*, 290–2; Stein, *French Sugar Business*, 51–3; Chauleau, *Dans les Îles du Vent*, 119–22; Abenon, *Petite histoire de la Guadeloupe*, 51–2.

79 "Code noir," (Article XXII) in *Traite des noirs*, ed. I. and J.L. Vissière, 166. With regard to the diet and undernourishment of slaves in the French colonies, see Debien, *Les esclaves*, 186–91 and Munford, 3: 615–51. Regarding

the religious instruction of slaves, which colonial authorities saw as a necessary means of control but also as potentially dangerous, see Antoine Gisler, *L'esclavage aux Antilles française (XVIIe–XIXe siècle): Contribution au problème de l'esclavage* (Fribourg: Éditions universitaires Fribourg Suisse, 1965), 169–92 and Sue Peabody, "'A Dangerous Zeal': Catholic Missions to Slaves in the French Antilles, 1635–1800," *French Historical Studies* 25 (2002): 53–90.

80 Debien, *Les esclaves*, 179–86. See also Munford, 2: 557–62.

81 Damas and Guillot de Rochpierre to the Minister of Marine, 4 March 1789 and 25 May 1789, Colonies C⁸ᴬ 89, 3–4, 13. See also "Conseil souverain – séance du 6 mai 1789: Représentations du conseil à MM. Les administrateurs sur l'état de la colonie," in *La Martinique au temps de la révolution française 1789–1794*, ed. Marie-Hélène Leotin (Fort-de-France, 1989), 15–16.

82 Tomich, 413, 427, 434.

83 Debien, *Les esclaves*, 107–33. See also Tomich, 428 and Stein, *French Sugar Business*, 57–9. Regarding the ambiguous relationship between white overseers, *économes*, and black drivers, *commandeurs*, see the excerpt from "Manuscript d'un voyage de France à Saint-Domingue, à la Havanne et aux Unis états [sic] d'Amérique," in Jeremy Popkin, ed., *Facing Racial Revolution: Eyewitness Accounts of the Haitian Insurrection* (Chicago: University of Chicago Press, 2007), 37–42. See also Régent, 34–60.

84 "Code noir," (Articles XLII, XLIII) *Traite des noirs*, ed. I. and J.L. Vissière, 170. See also Chauleau, *Dans les Îles du Vent*, 122.

85 Debien, *Les esclaves*, 471–95. See also Butel, *Histoire des Antilles françaises*, 171.

86 Benjamin Frossard, *La cause des esclaves nègres et des habitants de la Guinée … ou histoire de la traite et de l'esclavage* (Lyon, 1789), excerpted in *Traite des noirs*, ed. I. and J.L. Vissière, 97–100. See also Munford, vol. 3, 831–57.

87 Chauleau, *Dans les Îles du Vent*, 127. See also Butel, *Histoire des Antilles françaises*, 175–8 and Munford, 3: 910–13.

88 Debien, *Les esclaves*, 411–24. See also: Régent, 42–6; Abenon, Cauna and Chauleau, *Antilles 1789*, 77–9; Munford, 3: 933–71.

89 Debien, *Les esclaves*, 456–65. See also Butel, *Histoire des Antilles françaises*, 172–3.

90 Vincent di Ruggiero, "Le Marronage en Guadeloupe à la veille de la révolution française de 1789," *Bulletin de la société d'histoire de la Guadeloupe* 116–18 (1998): 5–64. See also Abenon, *Petite histoire de la Guadeloupe*, 64; Chauleau, *Dans les Îles du Vent*, 125–6; Debien, *Les esclaves*, 414.

91 Debien, *Les esclaves*, 465–6, 413–22. Whether *marronage* in the French colonies represented a systematic struggle against slavery or merely flight from oppression has been a subject of historical debate. See Jean Fouchard, *The Haitian Maroons: Liberty or Death*, trans. A. Faulkner Watts (New York: E.W.

Blyden Press, 1981). See also Carolyn Fick, "The Haitian Revolution in an Atlantic Context," and David Geggus, "The Haitian Revolution: New Approaches and Old," in *Proceedings of the Nineteenth Meeting of the French Colonial Historical Society, Providence, R.I., May 1993,* ed. James Pritchard (Cleveland, 1994), 128–55.

92 "Code noir," (Article XXXVIII) in *Traite des noirs,* ed. I. and J.L. Vissière, 169.

93 Debien, *Les esclaves,* 424–31.

94 For a detailed discussion of free-coloured participation in the *maréchaussée* and militia, see Stewart R. King, *Blue Coat or Powdered Wig: Free People of Color in Pre-revolutionary Saint Domingue* (Athens: The University of Georgia Press, 2001), 56–65. See also John D. Garrigus, *Before Haiti: Race and Citizenship in French Saint-Domingue* (New York: Palgrave MacMillan, 2006), 42–3, 114–18.

95 *Mestizo* referred originally to the offspring of a European and an Indian, but by the 1730s was applied to a person of mixed origins whose features appeared more white than black; *mulatre,* or mulatto, referred to the offspring of a European and an African, but the term became increasingly vague and in the Windward Islands was often used interchangeably with *gens de couleur;* a *quateron* was the child of a white man and a mulatto woman. This racial ambiguity was further complicated by different terms for different patterns of manumission: an *affranchi* was a freedman or freedwoman whose white father had paid the tax to free him or her; *nègres libres,* on the other hand, usually referred to slaves who had saved enough to purchase their freedom or who had been freed as the reward for good and loyal service. See Élisabeth, "French Antilles," 134. See also Butel, *Histoire des Antilles françaises,* 158, Régent, 143–58, and Garrigus, *Before Haiti,* 41–50.

96 Élisabeth, "French Antilles," 147–50.

97 The figure for Martinique in 1789 is taken from Élisabeth, "French Antilles," 150; that for Guadeloupe in 1790 from Anne Pérotin-Dumon, "Free Coloreds and Slaves in Revolutionary Guadeloupe: Politics and Political Consciousness," in *The Lesser Antilles,* ed. Paquette and Engerman, 260. Léo Élisabeth, "Gens de couleur et révolution dans les Îles du Vent (1789–janvier 1793)," *Revue française d'histoire d'outre-mer* 76, no. 282–3 (1989): 76 gives the figures of 4,851 free coloureds in Martinique and 3,044 in Guadeloupe in 1788. Lower figures for 1787 of 4,166 in Martinique and 1,877 in Guadeloupe are given in Bénot, *La révolution française et la fin des colonies,* 60.

98 King, *Blue Coat or Powdered Wig,* 45. See also Garrigus, *Before Haiti,* 168–9.

99 Élisabeth, "French Antilles," 137–45.

100 "Code noir," (Article IX), in *Traite des noirs*, ed. I. and J.L. Vissière, 163–4.
101 Butel, *Histoire des Antilles françaises*, 159–62.
102 Élisabeth, "French Antilles," 157–62. See also Régent, 158–62, 171–3.
103 Butel, *Histoire des Antilles françaises*, 163. Regarding the discriminatory legislation in Saint-Domingue, see King, *Blue Coat or Powdered Wig*, 124, 130–1, 163–6.
104 Élisabeth, "French Antilles," 162, 150. Bénot, *La révolution française et la fin des colonies*, 60–2 suggests that economic competition from free coloureds in the Windward Islands was less acute than in Saint-Domingue since few were becoming wealthy planters.
105 Pérotin-Dumon, "Free Coloreds and Slaves," 260–1 and Élisabeth, "French Antilles," 163–4. Regarding free-coloured landholding in Saint-Domingue, and the development of a free-coloured planter group, see King, *Blue Coat or Powdered Wig*, 121–41, 205–25. See also John Garrigus, "Blue and Brown: Contraband Indigo and the Rise of a Free Colored Planter Class in French Saint-Domingue," *Americas* 50, no. 2 (October 1993): 233–63.
106 Élisabeth, "French Antilles," 164–5 and Régent, 191–207. According to Émile Hayot, *Les gens de couleur libres du Fort-Royal 1679–1823* (Paris: Société française d'histoire d'outre-mer, 1971), 20, free coloureds enjoyed great economic success in the building trades, especially as joiners. Regarding free-coloured entrepreneurs in Saint-Domingue, see King, *Blue Coat or Powdered Wig*, 142–57.
107 Élisabeth, "French Antilles," 165 argues that such solidarity was hindered deliberately by colonial custom and legislation. Régent, 34–8 suggests that the attitude of Guadeloupe's *gens de couleur* towards slaves was shaped by an ambiguous mix of exploitation and solidarity. King, *Blue Coat or Powdered Wig*, 81–120 argues that the slaveholding practices of free coloureds in Saint-Domingue were significantly different from those of whites, but he sees no evidence of racial solidarity.
108 Butel, *Histoire des Antilles françaises*, 161–2. See also Pérotin-Dumon, *La ville aux Îles*, 674–6.
109 Banbuck, 303. Regarding the praise for free-coloured troops in Saint-Domingue, see King, *Blue Coat or Powdered Wig*, 68–9, 75–7 and John D. Garrigus, "'Sons of the Same Father': Gender, Race and Citizenship in French Saint-Domingue, 1760–1792," in *Visions and Revisions of Eighteenth-Century France*, ed. Christine Adams, Jack R. Censer and Lisa Jane Graham (University Park: Pennsylvania State University Press, 1997), 144–5.
110 For a discussion of the social and cultural segregation experienced by the *gens de couleur*, which was intended to reinforce their juridical inequality, see Régent, 162–71.

111 Pérotin-Dumon, "Free Coloreds and Slaves," 262.

112 Élisabeth, "Gens de Couleur et Révolution," 77.

113 Ibid., 78. Regarding literary challenges to racial inequality, see Edward Derbyshire Seeber, *Anti-slavery Opinion in France during the Second Half of the Eighteenth Century* (Baltimore, 1937; repr. New York: Greenwood Press, 1969), 126–8.

114 Garrigus, "'Sons of the Same Father,'" 150. See also Bénot, *La révolution française et la fin des colonies*, 63.

115 King, *Blue Coat or Powdered Wig*, 158, 224–5.

116 Butel, *Histoire des Antilles françaises*, 163.

117 *Motion faite par M. Vincent Ogé, à l'assemblée des colons, habitans de St-Domingue, à l'hôtel de Massiac, place des Victoires* (n.p., n.d. but probably Paris, 1789); excerpt in Lynn Hunt, ed., *The French Revolution and Human Rights: A Brief Documentary History* (Boston, MA: Bedford / St Martins, 1996), 103–4. See also "The Free Citizens of Color: Address to the National Assembly, October 22, 1789," in *Slave Revolution in the Caribbean 1789–1804: A Brief History with Documents*, ed. Laurent Dubois and John D. Garrigus (Boston, MA: Bedford / St Martin's, 2006), 67–70.

118 Valerie Quinney, "The Problem of Civil Rights for Free Men of Color in the Early French Revolution," *French Historical Studies* 7, no. 4 (Fall 1972): 550. See also Abenon, Cauna and Chauleau, *Antilles 1789*, 85. For a detailed examination of the Club Massiac, its foundation and activities, see Gabriel Debien, *Les colons de Saint-Domingue et la révolution: Essai sur le club massiac (août 1789–août 1792)*, (Paris, 1953).

119 Bénot, *La révolution française et la fin des colonies*, 65.

120 *Mémoire en faveur des gens de couleur ou sang-mêlés de St-Domingue, et des autres Iles françoises de l'Amérique, adressé à l'assemblée nationale*, par M. Grégoire, curé d'Emberménil, Député de Lorraine (Paris: Chez Bellin, 1789); excerpt in Hunt, ed., *The French Revolution and Human Rights*, 105–6. For discussion of this text, see Benot, *La révolution française et la fin des colonies*, 66–9.

121 Peter Gay, *The Enlightenment: Volume II the Science of Freedom* (New York, 1969; repr. 1996), 407–23.

122 Charles de Secondat, Baron de Montesquieu, *Pensées et fragments inédits de Montesquieu*, ed. H. Barckhausen (Bordeaux, 1901), 374; cited in Seeber, 61. For discussion of Montesquieu's arguments against slavery, see 28–33.

123 Seeber, 76–89.

124 Ibid., 61–2, 90–3.

125 Ibid., 92–107.

126   Abbé Raynal, *Philosophical and Political History of the Settlements and Trade of the Europeans in the East and West Indies*, revised, augmented and published, 10 vols. Newly translated from the French by J.O. Justamond, F.R.S., 8 vols. (London, 1783). Excerpted from vol. 5, bk. 11: 292–6, 302–4, 307–10; excerpt in Hunt, ed., *The French Revolution and Human Rights*, 52–3.

127   Ibid., 54–5. See also "Prophesies of Slave Revolution, 1771 and 1780," in Dubois and Garrigus, eds., *Slave Revolution in the Caribbean*, 54–6. For a discussion of Raynal's ambivalence toward slavery, in the context of "The Enlightenment and the exotic," see Dorinda Outram, *The Enlightenment* (Cambridge: Cambridge University Press, 1995), 72–4. See also the discussion of the limitations of European anti-slavery thought and action prior to the revolutionary period in Robin Blackburn, *The Overthrow of Colonial Slavery 1776–1848*, (London: Verso, 1988), 35–63.

128   D.J. Garat and P.J.G. Cabanis, eds., *Oeuvres complètes de Condorcet*, 21 vols. (Paris, 1802), 11:85, 88, 93, 124–5, 191–4; excerpt in Hunt, ed., *The French Revolution and Human Rights*, 56–7. For a discussion of Condorcet's opposition to slavery and its place within his larger system of thought, see David Williams, *Condorcet and Modernity* (Cambridge: Cambridge University Press, 2004), 139–58.

129   Marcel Dorigny and Bernard Gainot, *La société des amis des noirs 1788–1799* (Paris: Éditions UNESCO, 1998), esp. 59–298. See also: Jeremy D. Popkin, "Saint-Domingue, Slavery, and the Origins of the French Revolution," in *From Deficit to Deluge: The Origins of the French Revolution*, ed. Thomas E. Kaiser and Dale K. Van Kley (Stanford, CA: Stanford University Press, 2011), 220–7; Jean-Daniel Piquet, *L'émancipation des noirs dans la révolution française (1789–1795)* (Paris: Karthala, 2002), 47–50; Daniel P. Resnick, "The Société des Amis des Noirs and the Abolition of Slavery," *French Historical Studies* 7, no. 4 (Fall 1972): 559–61; David Brion Davis, *The Problem of Slavery in the Age of Revolution 1770–1823* (Ithaca, NY: Cornell University Press, 1975), 95. Regarding the abolitionist movement in Great Britain, see Adam Hochschild, *Bury the Chains: Prophets and Rebels in the Fight to Free an Empire's Slaves* (Boston, MA: Houghton Mifflin, 2005).

130   Condorcet, *Lettre écrit par la société des amis des noirs en France, aux differens baillages et districts ayant droit d'envoyer les deputés aux etats-generaux* (n.p., n.d.), cited in Davis, 97. See also Abenon, Cauna and Chauleau, *Antilles 1789*, 88.

131   Bénot, *La révolution française et la fin des colonies*, 66–9, 89–91. Popkin, "Saint-Domingue, Slavery, and the Origins of the French Revolution,"

231–6 argues that the *cahiers de doléances* demonstrate that French public opinion was influenced by abolitionist arguments, but also by contradictory impulses which emphasized the rights of slave-owing colonists.

132 Bénot, *La révolution française et la fin des colonies*, 91–2. Popkin, "Saint-Domingue, Slavery and the Origins of the French Revolution," 237 notes that while Necker referred to the injustice of slavery and the slave trade in his address to deputies of 5 May 1789, he was careful not to translate his pro-abolition sentiments into concrete proposals.

133 Resnick, 563–7. Bénot, *La révolution française et la fin des colonies*, 97–8, 111–14 notes that Mirabeau's speech to the Jacobin Club of 26 February 1790 was exceptional in contesting the profitability of the slave trade and in offering a alternative vision of the French economy.

134 Bénot, *La révolution française et la fin des colonies*, 69–71, 95–9.

135 *Adresse à l'assemblée nationale, pour l'abolition de la traite des noirs.* Par la société des amis des noirs de Paris (Paris, 1790); excerpt in Hunt, ed., *The French Revolution and Human Rights*, 107–8.

136 Popkin, "Saint-Domingue, Slavery and the Origins of the French Revolution," 227–30. See also Bénot, *La révolution française et la fin des colonies*, 64, 70–1, 100–2 and Davis, 97–9 and Perry Viles, "The Slaving Interest in the Atlantic Ports, 1763–1792," *French Historical Studies* 7. no. 4 (Fall 1972): 529–43.

137 Bénot, *La révolution française et la fin des colonies*, 106–8.

2 Rumours of Revolution

1 Georges Lefebvre, *The Great Fear of 1789: Rural Panic in Revolutionary France*, trans. Joan White (Princeton, NJ: Princeton University Press, 1973; repr., 1982), see esp. 64–74, 122–42. For a general discussion of the disorientation resulting not only from rapid change and disorder during the revolution but also from the lack of reliable information and delays in communication between Paris and the provinces, see Bette W. Oliver, *Surviving the French Revolution: A Bridge across Time* (Lanham, MD: Lexington Books, 2013).

2 Bronislaw Baczko, *Ending the Terror: The French Revolution after Robespierre*, trans. Michel Petheram (Cambridge: Cambridge University Press, 1994), 21; see also 1–32.

3 William Doyle, *The Oxford History of the French Revolution* (Oxford: Clarendon Press, 1989), 66–85. See also William Doyle, *Origins of the French Revolution*, 3rd ed. (Oxford: Oxford University Press, 1999) and François

Furet, *Revolutionary France 1770–1880*, trans. Antonia Nevill (Oxford: Blackwell Publishing, 1992; repr., 1995), 33–63.

4 Baron de Clugny and Iger to Minister of Marine, 10 March 1789, Colonies C[7A] 43, 234 and Comte de Damas and Guillot de Rochepierre to Minister of Marine, 4 March 1789, Colonies C[8A] 89, 3–4. See also "Comité de la Guadeloupe: De la délibération de l'assemblée coloniale du 27 février 1789", Colonies C[7A] 43, 333, and *À messieurs les colons de l'Isle de la Martinique*, (Paris: De l'imprimerie de Demonville, 1789), Colonies F[3] 29, 2–46.

5 Regarding the assertion of national sovereignty, associated with both the declaration of the National Assembly and the uprising of Paris, see: Doyle, *Oxford History of the French Revolution*, 101–20, esp. 104–5; Furet, *Revolutionary France*, 63–78; M.J. Sydenham, *The French Revolution* (London, 1961; repr., Westport, CT: Greenwood Press, 1985), 35–62, esp. 42–3. Regarding the popular uprising and the attack on Bastille, see George Rudé, *The Crowd in the French Revolution* (Oxford: Oxford University Press, 1959; repr., 1972), 45–60.

6 Comte de Damas and Guillot de Rochepierre to Minister of Marine, 4 March 1789, Colonies C[8A] 89, 34. See also Comte de Damas and Foullon d'Écotier to Minister of Marine, 25 May 1789, Colonies C[8A] 89, 13–15.

7 "Séance du conseil souverain du 6 mai 1789," AD Martinique B 18, 182–3.

8 "Réponse de MM. de Damas et Foullon d'Écotier à l'arrêt du conseil supérieur, 7 mai 1789", Colonies C[8A] 89, 18. See also "Ordonnance du général Damas et l'intendant Foullon d'Écotier portant permission d'importer jusqu'au 15 octobre les farines et biscuits d'origine étrangère mais cependant par le seul port d'entrepôt, 10 mai 1789," AD Martinique B 18, 192–3.

9 Foullon d'Écotier to Minister of Marine, 25 March 1789, Colonies C[8A] 90, 5–9.

10 Foullon d'Écotier to Minister of Marine, 9 May 1789, Colonies C[8A] 90, 32–4.

11 Foullon d'Écotier to Minister of Marine, 18 February 1788, Colonies C[7A] 43, 84–93.

12 "Extrait des registres du conseil souverain de l'Isle Guadeloupe, 22 décembre 1788," Colonies C[7A] 43, 154–7.

13 "Séance du conseil souverain du 9 mars 1789," AD Martinique B 18, 174. Regarding the death of Foulquier, see AD Martinique B 18, 161, 168 and Colonies C[8A] 89, f.3. Viévigne arrived from France in July to replace Foullon, who soon complained of his conduct to the minister, Colonies C[7A] 43, 235–7 and C[8A] 90, 76–7.

14 Chauleau, *Dans les Îles du Vent*, 160–1. See also Sidney Daney, *Histoire de la Martinique depuis colonisation jusqu'en 1815* (Fort-Royal, 1846; repr.,

Fort-de-France: Société d'histoire de la Martinique, 1963), 3: 7–8. The comte de Vioménil should not be confused with his brother, Antoine Charles du Houx, baron de Vioménil, who served as Rochambeau's second-in-command in America and who helped to direct the royalist defense of the Tuileries on 10 August 1792; see le Comte de Montmort, *Antoine Charles du Houx, Baron de Vioménil: Lieutenant-General of the Armies of the King, Second in Command under Rochambeau* (Baltimore, MD: The Johns Hopkins Press, 1935).

15 Pierre-François-Régis Dessales, *Historique des troubles survenus à la Martinique pendant la révolution*, ed. Henri de Frémont (Fort-de-France: Société d'histoire de la Martinique, 1982), 17–26. See also: David Geggus, "The Slaves and Free Coloreds of Martinique during the Age of the French and Haitian Revolutions: Three Moments of Resistance," in *The Lesser Antilles in the Age of European Expansion*, ed. Paquette and Engerman, 282–3; Butel, *Histoire des Antilles françaises*, 209–12, Chauleau, *Dans les Îles du Vent*, 182–4.

16 "Séance du Conseil souverain du 7 septembre 1789," AD Martinique B 18, 211.

17 "Arrêt du conseil sourverain de la Martinique, 11 septembre 1789," Colonies F^3 29, 96. Regarding the special commission's discovery of a plot and its identification of ringleaders, see also Comte de Vioménil to Minister of Marine, 28 September 1789, Colonies C^{8A} 89, 71.

18 Colonies F^3 29, 97. Colonial paranoia regarding poisoning was widespread and long-standing. See Abenon, Cauna, Chauleau, *Antilles 1789*, 79–80 and Madison Smart Bell, *Toussaint Louverture: A Biography* (New York: Random House, 2007), 66–9.

19 Comte de Vioménil to Minister of Marine, 14 September 1789, Colonies C^{8A} 89, 57–60.

20 "Ordonance prise par le gouverneur Vioménil et l'intendant Foullon d'Écotier au sujet de l'enrigistrement des titres de liberté," AD Martinique B 18, 216.

21 Comte de Vioménil to Minister of Marine, 14 September 1789, Colonies C^{8A} 89, 59.

22 Foullon d'Écotier to Minister of Marine, 24 October 1789, Colonies C^{8A} 90, 105–7.

23 "Lettres écrites à M. de Vioménil par plusieurs commandants de quartiers au sujet de la révolte des Nègres, 11–19 novembre 1789," Colonies C^{8A} 89, 62–7.

24 "Copie d'une lettre anonime addressée à M. Mollérat, dattée de Saint-Pierre le 28 août 1789," Colonies C^{8A} 89, 68.

25 "Copie de la lettre des esclaves de la Martinique, Saint-Pierre, le 29 août 1789," Colonies C⁸ᴬ 89, 69–70.

26 Ibid., 69.

27 Baron de Clugny to Minister of Marine, 29 September 1789, Colonies C⁷ᴬ 43, 264–5. *Affiches, annonces et avis divers de l'Île Guadeloupe* (Du jeudi, 24 septembre 1789), gives the names of five passengers who arrived on *la Jeune Bayonnais* but does not mention the cockade or the reaction to the ship's arrival, AD Guadeloupe 4 Mi 21.

28 Baron de Clugny and M. de Viévigne to Minister of Marine, 15 October 1789, Colonies C⁷ᴬ 43, 239. See also Pérotin-Dumon, *Être patriote sous les tropiques*, 121–2 and Lacour, 2: 11–12.

29 Baron de Clugny and M. de Viévigne to Minister of Marine, 15 October 1789, Colonies C⁷ᴬ 43, 240. See also Pérotin-Dumon, *La ville aux îles*, 199.

30 Baron de Clugny and M. de Viévigne to Minister of Marine, 15 October 1789, Colonies C⁷ᴬ 43, 240.

31 Baron de Clugny and M. de Viévigne to Minister of Marine, 29 October and 16 November 1789, Colonies C⁷ᴬ 43, 243, 245–6. See also Lacour, 2: 12–13 and Bangou, *La révolution et l'esclavage à la Guadeloupe*, 36.

32 "Arrêt du conseil souverain du 22 octobre 1789", Colonies C⁷ᴬ 43, 328–9.

33 Baron de Clugny and M. de Viévigne to Minister of Marine, 29 November 1789, Colonies C⁷ᴬ 43, 248–9.

34 Ibid, Colonies C⁷ᴬ 43, 251.

35 Comte de Vioménil to Minister of Marine, 17 October 1789, Colonies C⁸ᴬ 89, 81.

36 *Précis de ce qui s'est passé à Saint-Pierre, depuis le moment qu'on reçu la nouvelle de la réunion des trois ordres en France, jusqu'au 29 septembre dernier* (Saint-Pierre, Martinique: l'Imprimerie de Pierre Richard, 1789), Colonies F³ 29, 103.

37 Ibid. 29, 102. See also Dessalles, *Historique des troubles*, 26–31.

38 Comte de Vioménil to Minister of Marine, 17 October 1789, Colonies C⁸ᴬ 89, 81.

39 Comte de Vioménil to Commissioners of Commerce, 25 September 1789, Colonies C⁸ᴬ 89, 89.

40 Foullon d'Écotier to Minister of Marine, 25 October 1789, Colonies C⁸ᴬ 90, 111. If the *Intendant* suggested that the arrest touched off the riot against De Laumoy on 25 September, in Vioménil's account this arrest occurred eight days earlier following his initial proscription of the cockade: Comte de Vioménil to Minister of Marine, 17 October 1789, Colonies C⁸ᴬ 89, 82.

41 *Précis de ce qui s'est passé à Saint-Pierre*, Colonies F³ 29, 104.

42 Comte de Vioménil to Minister of Marine, 17 October 1789, and to Commissioners of Commerce, 26 September 1789, Colonies C^{8A} 89, 82, 90. See also *Précis de ce qui s'est passé à Saint-Pierre*, Colonies F^3 29, 104.

43 Comte de Vioménil to Minister of Marine, 17 October 1789, Colonies C^{8A} 89, 83.

44 Ibid.

45 Baron de Clugny to Minister of Marine, 29 September 1789, Colonies C^{7A} 43, 265. See also Régent, 218–19.

46 Comte de Vioménil to Minister of Marine, 17 October 1789, Colonies C^{8A} 89, 84. See also: Daney, 2: 10–11; Lémery, 29–33; Abenon, Cauna, Chauleau, *Antilles 1789*, 149–50.

47 *Journal de St Pierre – Martinique, depuis la formation de son comité, contenant les mouvemens occasionnés par la conduite de M. le Comte de Vioménil, gouverneur général* (Saint-Pierre: Imprimerie de Pierre Richard, 1789), Colonies F^3 29, 106.

48 "Délibération du peuple, assemblé à l'Église du Fort, le 30 septembre 1789", Colonies F^3 29, 122–3.

49 *Journal de St Pierre – Martinique*, Colonies F^3 29, 107.

50 Ibid., Colonies F^3 29, 107–8. See also Dessalles, *Historique des troubles*, 32–4.

51 Comte to Vioménil to Minister of Marine, 17 October 1789, Colonies C^{8A} 89, 84–5. See also Comte de Vioménil to Minister of Marine, 6 October 1789, Colonies C^{8A} 89, 74.

52 *Journal de St Pierre – Martinique*, Colonies F^3 29, 107.

53 Ibid., 108. See also Response of the Commissioners of Fort-Royal to the Deputies of the Saint-Pierre Committee, 1 October 1789, Colonies C^{8A} 89, 92.

54 Comte de Vioménil to M. Ruste, Commissioner of Commerce at Saint-Pierre, 1 October 1789, Colonies C^{8A} 89, 93.

55 Commandant Laumoy to M. Ruste, 1 October 1789, Colonies F^3 29, 123–4.

56 Response of M. Ruste to M. the Comte de Vioménil, 2 October 1789, Colonies F^3 29, 124.

57 Comte de Vioménil to M. Ruste, 2 October 1789, Colonies C^{8A} 90, 119.

58 Declaration of several inhabitants of Fort-Royal, submitted to the thirteen deputies of Saint-Pierre, Colonies F^3 29, 127–8.

59 *Journal de St Pierre – Martinique*, Colonies F^3 29, 110.

60 M. Ruste, President of the Saint-Pierre Committee, to M. de Lacoste, commandant of the parish of Fort-Royal, 3 October 1789, Colonies C^{8A} 89, 94.

61 *Journal de St Pierre – Martinique*, Colonies F^3 29, 111.

62 Ibid., 112.

63 Comte de Vioménil to Foullon d'Écotier, 2 October 1789, Colonies C⁸ᴬ 90, 121.

64 Colonies C⁸ᴬ 90, 122–3.

65 Comte de Vioménil to Foullon d'Écotier, 4 October 1789, Colonies C⁸ᴬ 90, 124.

66 M. Ruste, president, and M. Crassous de Médeuil, secretary of the Saint-Pierre Committee, to M. Foullon and M. de Laumoy, 5 October 1789, Colonies C⁸ᴬ 89, 95.

67 Ibid., 95.

68 Ibid.

69 Comte de Vioménil to Commandant de Laumoy, 5 October 1789, Colonies C⁸ᴬ 90, 125.

70 Comte de Vioménil to Minister of Marine, 17 October 1789, Colonies C⁸ᴬ 89, 85.

71 "Copie de la déclaration de MM. le chefs de corps militaires au comité de Saint-Pierre, 7 octobre 1789," "Copie de la déclaration générale faite par les chefs de corps et officiers du corps royal d'artillerie des Colonies et du régiment de la Martinique, 8 octobre 1789," "Copie de la déclaration de M. de Laubenque, major commandant de la place du Fort-Royal, 8 octobre 1789," all in Colonies C⁸ᴬ 89, 102–4.

72 Acts of which the Comte de Vioménil is accused, drawn from the reports and memoirs submitted by the Saint-Pierre Committee, Colonies C⁸ᴬ 89, 96–101. Lémery, 41 suggests that in contrast to the patriots' hypocrisy, the Comte de Vioménil was the "real revolutionary": this metropolitan aristocrat had no qualms about paying public tribute to the loyalty of free-coloured auxiliaries.

73 Comte de Vioménil to Minister of Marine, 17 October 1789, Colonies C⁸ᴬ 89, 86.

74 Saint-Pierre Committee to Comte de Vioménil, 8 October 1789, Colonies C⁸ᴬ 89, 107.

75 See the Comte de Vioménil's opening address to the assembly on 9 October 1789 in "Procès-verbal des délibérations de l'assemblée coloniale extraor-dinairement convoquée avec adjoints attendu la situation de la colonie, 9–17 octobre 1789", Colonies C⁸ᴬ 90, 129–30. See also Comte de Vioménil to President of the Colonial Assembly (same letter addressed to the President of Martinique's Sovereign Council at Fort-Royal), 11 October 1789, in which he emphasizes that Saint-Pierre's demands for a general assembly lack any legal justification, Colonies F³ 30, 6.

76 "Procès-verbal des délibérations de l'assemblée coloniale," Colonies C⁸ᴬ 90, 132–4. See also Dessalles, *Historique des troubles*, 49–52.

77 "Discours prononcé à l'assemblée coloniale le 16 octobre 1789 ... par M. Le Camus, un des députés du Fort-Royal", Colonies C⁸ᴬ 89, 123–4.

78 "Procès-verbal des délibérations de l'assemblée colonial," Colonies C⁸ᴬ 90, 146–51. See also "Copie de l'arrêté formé par MM. de l'assemblée coloniale de la Martinique, 15 octobre 1789," Colonies F³ 30, 8–9.

79 "Séance extraordinaire du mois d'octobre 1789," AD Martinique B 18, 217.

80 Officers of Martinique's Sovereign Council to Comte de Vioménil, 15 October 1789, Colonies F³ 30, 10.

81 Foullon d'Écotier to members of the Saint-Pierre Committee, 6 October 1789, Colonies C⁸ᴬ 90, 120.

82 Foullon d'Écotier to Minister of Marine, 25 October 1789, Colonies C⁸ᴬ 90, 114–15.

83 Ibid., Colonies C⁸ᴬ 90, 112.

84 Doyle, *Oxford History of the French Revolution*, 112–13. See also Furet, *Revolutionary France*, 68 and Sydenham, *French Revolution*, 55.

85 Foullon d'Écotier to Minister of Marine, 25 October 1789, Colonies C⁸ᴬ 90, 112–13.

86 Comte de Vioménil to Minister of Marine, 16 October 1789, Colonies C⁸ᴬ 89, 77–8.

87 "Extrait de la délibérations de l'assemblée coloniale, extraordinairement convoquée dans sa séance du 17 Octobre 1789," in *Ordonnance portant convocation d'une assemblée générale de la colonie ... Du 22 octobre 1789* (Saint-Pierre: Imprimerie de Pierre Richard, 1789), Colonies C⁸ᴬ 89, 48–9. See also Adélaïde-Merlande, 51–2.

88 *Ordonnance ... Du 22 octobre 1789*, Colonies C⁸ᴬ 89, 48. See also Dessalles, *Historique des troubles*, 52–3, 65–6 and Daney, 3: 14–16.

89 Comte de Vioménil to Minister of Marine, 18 October 1789, Colonies C⁸ᴬ 89, 135–6. See also Dessalles, *Historique des troubles*, 54–6.

90 Doyle, *Oxford History of the French Revolution*, 113–16. See also Lefebvre, *Great Fear*, 75–90 and Furet, *Revolutionary France*, 68–9.

91 "Procès-verbal des délibérations de l'assemblée coloniale," Colonies C⁸ᴬ 90, 139–40.

92 Ibid., 142–4.

93 *Extrait du registre des délibérations de l'assemblée du peuple de Saint-Pierre, du Mardi 20 octobre 1789*, Colonies F³ 30, 40.

94 Ibid., 40.

95 Speech given by M. le Comte de Vioménil at the opening of the General Assembly of the colony of Martinique, 16 November 1789, Colonies C⁸ᴬ 89, 158–61.

96 Comte de Vioménil to Minister of Marine, 18 November 1789, Colonies C[8A] 89, 155–6.

97 Response of the Committee to M. de Laumoy ... 11 November 1789, Colonies C[8A] 89, 161.

98 Baron de Clugny and M. de Viévigne to Minister of Marine, 29 November 1789, Colonies C[7A] 43, 251.

99 Ibid., 251.

3 Patriots versus Aristocrats

1 AP, vol. 42, 675–99. See also: Saintoyant, 2: 182–93; Lémery, 4–66; Pérotin-Dumon, *Être patriote sous les tropiques*, esp. 137–40; Adélaïde-Merlande, 51–6.

2 Moreau de Saint-Méry, le comte Dillon, le chevalier de Perpigna, le marquis Duquesne, Croquet de Belligny, *À Messieurs les colons de l'isle de la Martinique* (De L'imprimerie de Demonville, 1789), Colonies F[3] 29, 2–46. Regarding the debate in the National Assembly in June and July 1789 on the admission of deputies to represent Saint-Domingue, see Popkin, "Saint-Domingue, Slavery, and the Origins of the French Revolution," 238–48.

3 "Compte Rendu des travaux de l'assemblée générale de l'Isle de la Martinique, convonquée le 16 novembre 1789," Colonies F[3] 30, 160–2.

4 Comte de Vioménil to Minister of Marine, 22 November 1789, Colonies C[8A] 89, 162–4. See also "Compte Rendu des travaux de l'assemblée générale," Colonies F[3] 30, 165–7 and Daney, 3: 20–1.

5 "Extrait des délibérations du comité de Saint-Pierre, du 11 Novembre 1789," Colonies F[3] 30, 122. See also *Reponse d'un citoyen de la Martinique, aux questions suivantes, sur la réunion opérée entre la ville de St Pierre et M. le général, comte de Vioménil*, Colonies C[8A] 95, 135.

6 Comte de Vioménil to Minister of Marine, 7 December 1789, Colonies C[8A] 89, 165.

7 "Extrait de la délibération de l'assemblée générale de la colonie de la Martinique dans sa séance de 1er décembre 1789: Règlement pour les milices qui doivent faire les fonctions de Maréchaussé," AD Martinique B 18, 225–6. See also Comte de Vioménil to Minister of Marine, 28 October 1789, Colonies C[8A] 89, 144.

8 "Extrait de la délibération de l'assemblée générale de la colonie de la Martinique dans ses séances des 4 et 10 décembre 1789: Règlement pour les affranchisements et gens de couleur libres," AD Martinique B 18, 234–5.

9   "Compte Rendu des travaux de l'assemblée générale," Colonies F³ 30, 190.
10 "Extrait de la délibération de l'assemblée générale de la colonie de la Martinique dans sa séance du 5 décembre 1789: Règlement sur la forme des affranchisements," AD Martinique B 18, 235.
11 "Extrait de la délibération de l'assemblée générale de la colonie de la Martinique dans sa séance du 2 décembre 1789: Règlement pour l'establissement des municipalités," AD Martinique B 18, 229–31.
12 "Extrait de la délibération de l'assemblée générale de la colonie de la Martinique dans sa séance du 3 décembre 1789," AD Martinique B 18, 228.
13 "Extrait de la délibération de l'assemblée générale de la colonie de la Martinique dans sa séance du 8 décembre 1789: Règlement pour la constitution d'une nouvelle assemblée," AD Martinique B 18, 227–8.
14 "Decree on Martial Law, 21 October 1789," in *A Documentary Survey of the French Revolution*, ed. John Hall Stewart (Toronto: Macmillan, 1951), 117–19. See also Doyle, *Oxford History of the French Revolution*, 127 and Sydenham, *French Revolution*, 66.
15 "Extrait de la délibération de l'assemblée générale de la colonie de la Martinique dans sa séance du 9 décembre 1789," AD Martinique B 18, 233–4.
16 Dessales, *Historique des troubles*, 99–103. See also Daney, 3: 22–3 and Lémery, 51.
17 Comte de Vioménil to Minister of Marine, 20 December 1789, Colonies C⁸ᴬ 89, 166–9. Regarding the *Sénéchal*'s claim, in support of protests from Saint-Pierre, that the martial law decree was illegal, see: *Extrait des registres du Greffe de la sénéchaussée du Fort-Saint-Pierre, île Martinique: Imprimée par ordre du peuple* (Saint-Pierre: Imprimerie de Pierre Richard), Colonies F³ 31, 125.
18 Foullon d'Écotier to Minister of Marine, 16 January 1790, Colonies C⁸ᴬ 94, 14–16.
19 Ibid., 11–13.
20 "Mémoire remis par M. le Comte de Vioménil à l'assemblée générale de la colonie dans sa dernière séance du 10 décembre 1789," Colonies C⁸ᴬ 89, 177–9.
21 "Sanction donnée le 10 décembre 1789 par M. le Comte de Vioménil aux délibérations de l'assemblée générale de la colonie avec celle de M. Foullon d'Écotier, données le 19 décembre 1789," Colonies C⁸ᴬ 89, 209–11.
22 "Séances du 19 décembre, de relevée, et du 26 décembre 1789," AD Martinique B 18, 232, 233.
23 "Copie d'une lettre écrite à M. le Comte de Vioménil par MM. les commissaires du commerce de Saint-Pierre (Ruste, Billouin, Delhorme, Dupont), 18

décembre 1789," Colonies C^{8A} 89, 196–7. See also "Protestations de la ville de Saint-Pierre contre l'ouverture des ports du Fort-Royal, de la Trinité, du Français et du Marin aux Américains, 15 décembre 1789" and "Protestations de la ville de Saint-Pierre contre les décrets de l'assemblée générale de la colonie depuis le 30 novembre 1789," Colonies F^3 31, 141–7, 152–4.

24 Foullon d'Écotier to Minister of Marine, 16 January 1790, Colonies C^{8A} 94, 17–18. Regarding Saint-Pierre's encouragement of other parishes to boycott the general assembly, see *Les Citoyens de la ville de Saint-Pierre, à tous les colons de la Martinique. À Saint-Pierre, le 3 janvier 1790*, Colonies F^3 32, 19. See also Daney, 3: 25 and Lémery, 52–3.

25 "Copie d'une lettre écrite à M. le Comte de Vioménil par M. de Thoumazeau, 28 décembre 1789," Colonies C^{8A} 89, 182–4.

26 Foullon d'Écotier to Minister of Marine, 16 January 1790, Colonies C^{8A} 94, 18–27.

27 Comte de Vioménil to Minister of Marine, 20 December 1789, Colonies C^{8A} 89, 170–1.

28 Comte de Vioménil to Minister of Marine, 3 January 1790, Colonies C^{8A} 93, 54–6.

29 "Copie d'une lettre anonime addressée à M. le comte de Vioménil," Colonies C^{8A} 93, 57.

30 Comte de Vioménil to Minister of Marine, 15 January 1790, Colonies C^{8A} 93, 59–62.

31 Commandant Laumoy to Minister of Marine, 18 January 1790, Colonies C^{8A} 95, 14–15.

32 "Extrait des registres des délibérations de l'assemblée générale de la Guadeloupe et dépendances, tenant au Petit Bourg, le 2 décembre 1789," Colonies C^{7A} 43, 336.

33 Baron de Clugny and M. de Viévigne to Minister of Marine, 30 December 1789, Colonies C^{7A} 43, 256–7. See also Lacour, 2: 13–15.

34 Baron de Clugny and M. de Viévigne to Minister of Marine, 20 May 1790, Colonies C^{7A} 44, 16–17. See also Pérotin-Dumon, *Être patriote sous les tropiques*, 124–6.

35 Baron de Clugny and M. de Viévigne to Minister of Marine, 10 February 1790, Colonies C^{7A} 44, 4.

36 See Bangou, 38–9 and Lacour, 2: 18–19.

37 Baron de Clugny and M. de Viévigne to Minister of Marine, 20 May 1790, Colonies C^{7A} 44, 16–17. See also Pérotin-Dumon, *Être patriote sous les tropiques*, 127–31.

38 Baron de Clugny and M. de Viévigne to Minister of Marine, 1 May 1790, Colonies C^{7A} 44, 14.

39 Baron de Clugny and M. de Viévigne to Minister of Marine, 20 May 1790, Colonies C^{7A} 44, 16–17.

40 Baron de Clugny to Minister of Marine, 10 February 1790, Colonies C^{7A} 44, 21–2.

41 "Extrait du compte rendu par les administrateurs de la Martinique, de nouveaux troubles survenus dans cette colonie, 23 avril 1790," Colonies C^{8A} 93, 46–9. See also Commandant Laumoy to Minister of Marine, 20 February 1790, Colonies C^{8A} 95, 16–17.

42 Foullon d'Écotier to Minister of Marine, 15 February 1790, Colonies C^{8A} 94, 61–3. See also Comte de Vioménil and Foullon d'Écotier to Minister of Marine, 9 February and 23 April 1790, Colonies C^{8A} 93, 38–40, 49.

43 Comte de Vioménil and Foullon d'Écotier to Minister of Marine, 23 April 1790; Colonies C^{8A} 93, 49.

44 Baron de Clugny to Minister of Marine, 24 February 1790, Colonies C^{7A} 44, 23–4.

45 See "Extrait du compte rendu … 23 avril 1790," and Comte de Vioménil to Minister of Marine, 28 February 1790, Colonies C^{8A} 93, 49–50, 78–80. See also Foullon d'Écotier to Minister of Marine, 25 February 1790, Colonies C^{8A} 94, 70–2.

46 *Relation circonstanciée de ce qui s'est passé à Saint-Pierre, entre les braves patriotes et bons citoyens, et le régiment de la Martinique, en garnison dans cette ville* (De la Martinique, le 25 février 1790), 2–5, AD Gironde 8 J 422, no. 28 (also in Colonies F^3 32, 165–8). See also Foullon d'Écotier to Minister of Marine, 25 February 1790, Colonies C^{8A} 94, 70–2.

47 *Relation circonstanciée,* 8; AD Gironde 8 J 422, #28.

48 "Copie d'une lettre des officiers municipaux de Saint-Pierre à M. de Vioménil, 22 février 1790," and "Copie d'une lettre de M. de Laumoy, commandant en second, à M. de Vioménil, 22 février 1790," Colonies C^{8A} 93, 86–7, 88.

49 "Copie d'une lettre de M. de Vioménil à M. Thoumazeau, maire de Saint-Pierre, 23 février 1790," Colonies C^{8A} 93, 89–90.

50 *Gazette de la Martinique* (du samedi, 6 mars 1790, No. IX), Colonies F^3 32, 255.

51 *Relation circonstanciée,* 6–8; AD Gironde 8 J 422, no. 28. See also Comte de Vioménil to Minister of Marine, 28 February 1790, Colonies C^{8A} 93, 81.

52 "Copie d'une lettre écrite à M. le comte de Vioménil par MM. les officiers municipaux de la ville de Saint-Pierre, 23 février 1790," Colonies C^{8A} 93, 91.

53 "Copie de la réquisition faite à M. de Vioménil par les officiers du régiment de la Martinique, 23 [sic] février 1790," Colonies C^{8A} 93, 92.

54 Comte de Vioménil to Minister of Marine, 28 February 1790, Colonies C[8A] 93, 82. See also Foullon d'Écotier to Minister of Marine, 25 February 1790, Colonies C[8A] 94, 72.

55 The intendant claimed that Fort-Royal was "silent" on 25 February, despite Vioménil's report that soldiers demanded revenge: Foullon d'Écoter to Minister of Marine, 28 March 1790, Colonies C[8A] 94, 127.

56 "Copie d'une lettre écrite par M. le comte de Vioménil à M. Thoumazeau, 24 [sic] février 1790," Colonies C[8A] 93, 93–4.

57 "Copie d'une lettre écrite à M. le comte de Vioménil par M. de Thoumazeau, maire de la ville de Saint-Pierre, 25 février 1790," Colonies C[8A] 93, 95.

58 "Copie d'une lettre à M. le comte de Vioménil par MM. les officiers municipaux de la ville de Saint-Pierre, 25 février 1790," Colonies C[8A] 93, 98–9.

59 Lémery, 70–3.

60 "Instructions de la Martinique à ses députés, 10 mars 1790," in Dessalles, *Historique des troubles*, 153–4.

61 Ibid., 156–66. See also Daney, 3: 35–41

62 Foullon d'Écotier to Minister of Marine, 27 April 1790, Colonies C[8A] 94, 188.

63 "Le peuple de la Pointe-à-Pitre, île Grande-Terre Guadeloupe, au peuple de Saint-Pierre, île Martinique, 1 mars 1790," in *Gazette de la Martinique* (du samedi, 6 mars 1790, No. IX), Colonies F[3] 32, 257. For similar declarations from the volunteers of Moule and Sainte-Anne in Guadeloupe, and those of Soufrière in Saint-Lucie, see Dessalles, *Historique des troubles*, 133–4, 137–8.

64 See the Basse-Terre volunteers' *procès-verbal*, and the letter from the Baron de Clugny to Mayor Thoumazeau, 5 April 1790 in Dessalles, *Historique des troubles*, 131–3. See also Pérotin-Dumon, *Être patriote sous les tropiques*, 139–41.

65 Baron de Clugny to Minister of Marine, 15 March 1790, Colonies C[8A] 95, 28–9. See also "Procès-verbal de la Basse-Terre Guadeloupe," and "Copie d'une lettre de M. le baron de Clugny, gouverneur-général [sic] de la Guadeloupe, écrite le 6 mars 1790, à bord la frégate *la Sensible*, en rade de Saint-Pierre, à M. de Thoumazeau, maire," in *Gazette de la Martinique* (Mardi, 16 mars 1790, Supplément au No. X), Colonies F[3] 32, 252.

66 Baron de Clugny to Minister of Marine, 15 March 1790, Colonies C[8A] 95, 30–1.

67 "Extrait des registres des délibérations de la municipalité et de la commune de Saint-Pierre, 7 mars 1790," in *Gazette de la Martinique* (du Samedi, 13 mars 1790, No. X), Colonies C[8A] 96, 144–6 (also in Colonies F[3] 32, 286–7).

68 "Extrait des délibérations du régiment de la Martinique, dans la séance du 9 mars 1790," in *Gazette de la Martinique* (Samedi, 13 mars 1790, No. X), Colonies C⁸ᴬ 96, 146.

69 "Délibération de la commune de Saint-Pierre du 10 mars 1790," in *Gazette de la Martinique* (Samedi, 13 mars 1790, No. X), Colonies C⁸ᴬ 96, 146. See also "Le peuple de Saint-Pierre-Martinique à tous les citoyens français des Îles du vent, 12 mars 1790" and "Vers chanté à la comédie, le 10 de ce mois, par Mlle Dantin," in *Gazette de la Martinique* (mardi, 16 mars 1790, supplément au no. X), Colonies F³ 32, 252–3.

70 *Gazette de la Martinique* (Samedi, 13 mars 1790, No. X), Colonies C⁸ᴬ 96, 146.

71 Foullon d'Écotier to Minister of Marine, 28 March 1790, Colonies C⁸ᴬ 94, 131. See also Daney, 25.

72 "Copie d'une déclaration faite par un citoyen de Lamentin, 29 mars 1790" and "Copie d'une lettre écrite à M. Lavau du Fort-Royal" and "Copie de la déclaration faite par MM. de Seutre et Charron, députés [de Saint-Pierre] au Fort-Royal, 23 mars 1790" and "Copie de lettres particulières relatives à la révolte des nègres libres du quartier du Lamentin, 24 mars–2 avril 1790," Colonies C⁸ᴬ 96, 16–17, 147, 148, 149–50.

73 Dessalles, *Historique des troubles*, 150–1.

74 Vicomte de Damas to Minister of Marine, 1 June 1790, Colonies C⁸ᴬ 93, 120.

75 Comte de Vioménil to Minister of Marine, 6 May 1790, Colonies C⁸ᴬ 93, 104–5. See also Minister of Marine to comte de Vioménil, 1, 11 January and 13 May 1790, Colonies C⁸ᴬ 93, 18, 20, 26.

76 Baron de Clugny to Minister of Marine, 19 April 1790, Colonies C⁷ᴬ 44, 25–6. See also "Extrait du registre des délibérations du comité municipal de la Basse-Terre, 7 avril 1790," Colonies C⁷ᴬ 44, 121 and *Adresse des volontaires-confédérés de la Guadeloupe, aux colons de la Martinique*, Colonies F³ 32, 543.

77 Vicomte de Pontevès-Gien to Minister of Marine, 9 April 1790; Marine BB 4 / 3, 17. See also Vicomte de Pontevès-Gien to Minister of Marine, 5 April 1790, Colonies C⁸ᴬ 95, 87.

78 Dessalles, *Historique des troubles*, p. 178. See also Foullon d'Écotier to Minister of Marine, 16 April 1790, Colonies C⁸ᴬ 94, 175–6.

79 *Profession de foi de l'assemblée générale de la Martinique, 10 avril 1790* (Au Fort-Royal, Martinique, de l'imprimerie de l'assemblée générale de la colonie. Avec permission de M. le Général), Colonies F³ 32, 524–5.

80 Baron de Clugny to Minister of Marine, 19 April 1790, Colonies C⁷ᴬ 44, 27. See also Vicomte de Pontevès-Gien to Minister of Marine, 23 April 1790; Marine BB 4 / 3, 21–2.

81 Daney, 3: 42–3.

82 "Procès-verbal du Comité de l'assemblée générale du colonie, 5 avril 1790," AD Martinique B 18, 258–9. See also Dessalles, *Historique des troubles*, 174.

83 Baron de Clugny to Minister of Marine, 19 April 1790, Colonies C⁷ᴬ 44, 28.

84 Ibid., 25.

85 M. de Viévigne to Minister of Marine, 20 April 1790, Colonies C⁷ᴬ 44, 56.

86 Baron de Clugny to Minister of Marine, 25 April 1790, Colonies C⁷ᴬ 44, 31–2.

87 Baron de Clugny to Minister of Marine, 22 May 1790, Colonies C⁷ᴬ 44, 36–7.

88 M. de Viévigne to Minister of Marine, 4 June 1790, Colonies C⁷ᴬ 44, 57. See also Lucien-René Abenon, "Les révoltes serviles à la Guadeloupe au début de la révolution (1789–1793)," in Marcel Dorigny, ed., *Esclavage, résistances, et abolitions* (Paris: Éditions du CTHS, 1999), 211–12.

89 Foullon d'Écotier to Minister of Marine, 16 April 1790, Colonies C⁸ᴬ 94, 175–6.

90 Foullon d'Écotier to Minister of Marine, 27 April 1790, Colonies C⁸ᴬ 94, 188–92.

91 Dessalles, *Historique des troubles*, 179–80.

92 Bénot, *La révolution française et la fin des colonies*, 72–3. See also: David Patrick Geggus, "Racial Equality, Slavery and Colonial Secession during the Constituent Assembly," *American Historical Review* 94, no. 5 (Dec. 1989): 1292–6; Norman Hampson, *Prelude to Terror: The Constituent Assembly and the Failure of Consensus, 1789–1792* (Oxford: Basil Blackwell, 1988), 95–7; Quinney, 544–57.

93 "Décret concernant la formation et la compétence des assemblées coloniales, 8 mars 1790," in Saintoyant, 1: 380–1. See also National Assembly, "Decree of March 8 and Instructions of March 28, 1790," in *Slave Revolution in the Caribbean*, ed. Dubois and Garrigus, 70–2.

94 "Instruction pour les colonies destinée à accompagner le décret du 8 mars 1790, 28 mars 1790," in Saintoyant, 1: 382–7. See also *Instruction adressée par l'assemblée nationale à la colonie de la Martinique. Du 28 mars 1790*, Colonies C⁸ᴬ 93, 7–17.

95 *Itératives protestations du commerce de Saint-Pierre-Martinique, contre l'ouverture des quatre ports du Fort-Royal, de la Trinité, du François et du Marin aux Américains* (Imprimé à Saint-Pierre par Pierre Richard, 1790), Colonies C⁸ᴬ 94, 214–15. See also "Ordonnance: Le comte de Vioménil et Foullon d'Écotier, 1 mars 1790," and "Représentations du conseil à MM. les administrateurs au sujet de leur ordonnance du 1er mars qui proroge

l'admission des farines et biscuits de fabriques étrangères dans la colonie," in Session of 6 May 1790; AD Martinique B 18, 246–7, 253.

96 Baron de Clugny to Minister of Marine, 30 May 1790, Colonies C[7A] 44, 38–9.

97 *Gazette de la Martinique: Supplément au No. XXIII*, (Lundi, 7 juin 1790), Colonies C[8A] 96, 158. See also Foullon d'Écotier to Minister of Marine, 20 June 1790, Colonies C[8A] 94, 224–6.

98 Vicomte de Damas to Minister of Marine, 4 June 1790, Colonies C[8A] 93, 122–3.

99 Vicomte de Damas to Minister of Marine, 5 and 6 June 1790, Colonies C[8A] 93, 124–5.

100 "Copie de la lettre de MM. de officiers municipaux de la ville de Saint-Pierre en date du 6 juin 1790," Colonies C[8A] 93, 153.

101 *Extrait de la délibération de l'assemblée générale de la colonie, dans la séance du sept Juin 1790, après-midi* (À Saint-Pierre-Martinique, de l'imprimerie de Pierre Richard et Al. Bourne), Colonies C[8A] 93, 130–1.

102 Vicomte de Damas to Minister of Marine, 5 and 6 June 1790, Colonies C[8A] 93, 125.

103 Vicomte de Damas to Minister of Marine, 13 June 1790, Colonies C[8A] 93, 126.

104 *Lettre de M. le vicomte de Damas, gouverneur générale des Îles du Vent, à MM. les officiers municipaux de la ville de Saint-Pierre. Au Fort-Royal le 8 juin 1790* (À Saint-Pierre-Martinique, de l'imprimerie de Pierre Richard et Al. Bourne) and "Copie d'une lettre de M. de Damas aux officiers municipaux de Saint-Pierre, 8 juine 1790," Colonies C[8A] 93, 131, 132–3.

105 Vicomte de Pontevès-Gien to Minister of Marine, 13 June 1790; Marine BB 4 / 3, 41.

106 Vicomte de Damas to Minister of Marine, 13 June 1790, Colonies C[8A] 93, 127. See also "Copie de la lettre de M. de Lambert, officier du régiment de la Martinique, à M. Dumonchel, officier du même régiment, en congé à la Basse-Terre Guadeloupe, contenant le même événement. Saint-Pierre, 11 juin 1790," in *Relation de ce qui s'est passé à Saint-Pierre Martinique, lors de l'arrivée de M. de Damas avec les troupes, par un colon de la Basse-Terre Guadeloupe, témoin oculaire. Saint-Pierre Martinique, le 8 juin 1790*; Bordeaux C 15, no. 39.

107 "Copie d'une lettre écrite à M. de Damas par la municipalité et les citoyens de Saint-Pierre, (n.d.)," Colonies C[8A] 93, 138–9. See also *Adresse des citoyens de Saint-Pierre, à M. le vicomte de Damas, gouverneur général des Îles du vent, et aux corps militaires en garnison en cette île* (12 juin 1790); Marine BB 4 / 3, 53.

108 *Relation de ce qui s'est passé à Saint-Pierre*; Bordeaux C 15, #39.

109 Foullon d'Écotier to Minister of Marine, 20 June 1790, Colonies C⁸ᴬ 94, 227–9.

110 *Extrait de la délibération de l'assemblée générale de la colonie, dans la séance du 14 Juin 1790* and *Extrait de la délibération de l'assemblée générale de la colonie dans la séance du 14 Juin 1790*, in Marine BB 4 / 3, 49, 50.

111 Foullon d'Écotier to Minister of Marine, 20 June 1790, Colonies C⁸ᴬ 94, 230.

112 Baron de Clugny to Minister of Marine, 1 July 1790, Colonies C⁷ᴬ 44, 41–4.

113 Vicomte de Damas to Minister of Marine, 2 July 1790, Colonies C⁸ᴬ 93, 158–9.

114 Members of the Directory of the Colonial Assembly (Dubuc, Gallet-Charlery, Guignod, Fiquepau de Caritan, Fontaine, Lemarle) to Minister of Marine, 21 July 1790, Colonies C⁸ᴬ 96, 71–2. See also Foullon d'Écotier to Minister of Marine, 8 August 1790, Colonies C⁸ᴬ 94, 236.

115 Vicomte de Damas to Minister of Marine, 14 July 1790, Colonies C⁸ᴬ 93, 171.

116 Baron de Clugny to Minister of Marine, 27 August 1790, Colonies C⁷ᴬ 44, 45–6.

117 "Extrait de la délibération de l'assemblée coloniale de la Martinique dans sa séance du 6 août 1790" and *Décret de l'assemblée coloniale, sur l'organisation et les fonctions des municipalités du 6 août 1790* (Imprimé au Fort-Royal par Jean-François Bazille), Colonies C⁸ᴬ 96, 124, 119–23.

118 "Extrait de la délibération de l'assemblée coloniale de la Martinique dans sa séance du 7 août 1790," Colonies C⁸ᴬ 96, 127.

119 Vicomte de Damas to Minister of Marine, 12 August 1790, Colonies C⁸ᴬ 93, 181.

120 Dessalles, *Historique des troubles*, 249–50. See also Daney, 3: 63–4.

121 *Prospectus Du courrier des Petites Antilles, du 15 juillet 1790*, AD Guadeloupe 4 Mi 21.

122 *Courrier des Petites Antilles, no. 1* (24 juillet 1790), AD Guadeloupe 4 Mi 21

123 *Courrier des Petites Antilles, no. 2* (31 juillet 1790), AD Guadeloupe 4 Mi 21.

124 *Courrier des Petites Antilles, no. 3* (7 août 1790), AD Guadeloupe 4 Mi 21.

125 *Courrier des Petites Antilles, no. 4* (14 août 1790), AD Guadeloupe 4 Mi 21.

126 *Courrier des Petites Antilles, no. 5* (21 août 1790), AD Guadeloupe 4 Mi 21.

127 *Courrier des Petites Antilles, no. 6* (28 août 1790), AD Guadeloupe 4 Mi 21.

128 See R.B. Rose, *The Making of the Sans-Culottes: Democratic Ideas and Institutions in Paris, 1789–92* (Manchester: Manchester University Press, 1983), esp. 58–116 and Jack Richard Censer, *Prelude to Power: The Parisian Radical Press, 1789–1791* (Baltimore, MD: Johns Hopkins University Press,

1976), esp. 1–12, 37–72. See also: David Andress, *The Terror: The Civil War in the French Revolution*, (London: Little, Brown, 2005), 44–8; Doyle, *Oxford History of the French Revolution*, 120–4, 142; Furet, *Revolutionary France*, 85–94; Sydenham, *French Revolution*, 58–67.

129 *Courrier des petites Antilles, no. 7* (4 septembre 1790), AD Guadeloupe 4 Mi 21.

130 Damas, "Journal des troubles de la Martinique à commencer du 1er September 1790," Colonies C⁸ᴬ 93, 191–4. See also *Mémoire de M. de Damas, gouverneur de la Martinique, sur les troubles de cette colonie* (Paris, 1791), 1–5; Maclure Collection, vol. 757, #7. For the patriot version of events, see Crassous de Médeuil, *Rélation de ce qui s'est passé à la Martinique depuis le 1ᵉʳ septembre 1790, et Réponse au mémoire intitulé: Mémoire de M. Damas, gouverneur de la Martinique, sur les troubles de la Martinique, signé Damas, sans nom d'imprimeur* (Fort-Royal, 1791; repr. Fort-de-France: Société d'histoire de la Martinique, 1982), 1–15. See also: Dessalles, *Historique des troubles*, 253–71; Daney, 3: 64–72; Lémery, 97–9.

131 See Baron de Glandevès, Commandant at Toulon, to Minister of Marine, 29 October 1790, and Antoine-Jean-Marie Thévenard, Commandant at Lorient, to Minister of Marine, 3 November 1790, and Lieutenant de Boischâteau, commanding the brig *Épervier*, to Minister of Marine, 3 November 1790; Marine BB 4 / 3, 86, 89–93. See also *Mémoire de M. de Damas*, 5–6 and Crassous de Médeuil, *Rélation de ce qui s'est passé à la Martinique*, 24–5. Rebel troops prevented the departure of the naval sloop *Levrette* and kept it under guard in Fort-Royal's cul-de-sac until the arrival of the French fleet in March 1791; Marine BB 4 / 5, 94–5.

132 See: Damas, "Journal des troubles de la Martinique," Colonies C⁸ᴬ 93, 194–9; *Mémoire de M. de Damas*, 5–14; Crassous de Médeuil, *Rélation de ce qui s'est passé à la Martinique*, 17–66. See also Dessalles, *Historique des troubles*, 291–310. Regarding the volunteers from Guadeloupe, see also Lacour, 2: 34–9.

133 Donez (from Dominica) to Minister of Marine, 22 September 1790, Colonies C⁸ᴬ 95, 98.

134 Chevalier de Rivière, *Extrait du journal de ma station aux Îles du vent* (Fort-Royal, n.d.). See also the Minister of Marine's orders for Rivière, 5 September 1790; Marine BB 4 / 3, 229–37. For the captain's emphasis on legality, see Rivière to merchant captains at Saint-Pierre, and to the colonial assembly, 25 November and 4 December 1790; Marine BB 4 / 3, 244–7. For patriot accusations, see *Procès-verbal de la députation des capitaines de commerce, à bord du vaisseau du roi la Ferme, capitaine M. de*

Rivière (Saint-Pierre, n.d.), Marine BB 4 / 3, 241–5, and "Copie de la lettre écrite de Saint-Pierre, Martinique, le 11 décembre 1790, par MM. les commissaires du commerce à MM. les maires et députés de la chambre du commerce de Marseille," Colonies C⁸ᴬ 95, 138–9. Regarding the privateers and their threat to British colonies, see H.J.K. Jenkins, "Admiral Laforey and the St Pierre Raiders, 1790," *Mariner's Mirror* 71 (1985): 218–20.

135 See for example, *Journal exact de la situation dans laquelle était la Martinique, à l'époque du 18 octobre 1790* (Paris: Imprimerie du patriote François, place du théatre Italien, n.d.), Bordeaux C³ #10.

136 Adrien Queslin, "Rapport fait à l'assemblée nationale, au nom du comité des colonies, concernant les troubles arrivés à la Guadeloupe, 2 juillet 1792," AP, vol. 46, 50–1. See also Dubois, *A Colony of Citizens*, 96–7 and Lacour, 2: 27–34.

137 Baron de Clugny to Minister of Marine, 30 November 1790, Colonies C⁷ᴬ 44, 47–9. See also Lacour, 2: 26–34 and Pérotin-Dumon, *Être patriote sous les tropiques*, 141.

138 See also Baron de Clugny to Minister of Marine, 22 December 1790, Colonies C⁷ᴬ 44, 52–3.

4 "The Nation, the Law, the King"

1 Michael P. Fitzsimmons, *The Remaking of France: The National Assembly and the Constitution of 1791* (Cambridge: Cambridge University Press, 1994), esp. 33–68, 247–58.

2 Paul Cheney, *Revolutionary Commerce: Globalization and the French Monarchy,* (Cambridge, MA: Harvard University Press, 2010), 222–6.

3 "Délibérations: 30 juillet, 25, 27 novembre, 3 décembre 1789," AD Gironde C 4259, 39, 45–6. See also "Comité du commerce: 2, 26 novembre, 1 décembre," AD Gironde C 4438 [2], 8–10.

4 "Délibérations: 9, 16, 30 juillet 1789," AD Gironde C 4259, 37–9. See also "Comité du commerce: 11, 23 septembre 1789," AD Gironde C 4438, [2] 3–4.

5 Commissioners of Commerce of Saint-Pierre to Bordeaux Chamber of Commerce, 15 January 1790, in "Comité du commerce: 24 avril 1790," AD Gironde C 4438 [2], 22–3. See also AD Gironde C 4259, 52.

6 Commissioners of Commerce of Saint-Pierre to Bordeaux Chamber of Commerce, 18 April 1790, AD Gironde C 4438 [2], 26. See also Commissioners of Commerce of Saint-Pierre to Bordeaux Chamber of Commerce, 8 May 1790, AD Gironde C 4259, 55 and Foullon d'Écotier to Bordeaux Chamber of Commerce, 16 April 1790, AD Gironde C 4438 [2], 26.

7 Bordeaux Chamber of Commerce to Saint-Pierre's Deputies to the National Assembly, 13 August 1790 and to M. Thoumzaeau, Mayor of Saint-Pierre, 21 August 1790, AD Gironde C 4266, 188.

8 Bordeaux Chamber of Commerce to the Members of the National Assembly's Colonial Committee and Committee of Agriculture and Commerce, 31 August 1790, AD Gironde C 4266, 190.

9 "Délibérations, 18 novembre 1790," AD Gironde C 4259, 257.

10 Mayor and Municipal Officers of Marseille to Minister of Marine, 23 November 1790, Colonies C⁸ᴬ 96, 32. See also "Comité du commerce, 2 décembre 1790," AD Gironde C 4438 [2], 46–7. And see "Les proprietaires de biens aux colonies residents à Bordeaux, au roi, 17 décembre 1790," Colonies C⁸ᴬ 95, 141–2.

11 Barnave's Report on Martinique, 29 November 1791, AP, vol. 21, 125.

12 "Constitution votée le 28 mai 1790 par l'assemblée générale de la partie française siégeant à Saint-Marc," in 16 Pluviôse An II – Les colonies de la révolution, ed. Jean-Pierre Biondi and François Zuccarelli (Paris: Éditions Denoël, 1989), 53–5. With the backing of the assembly of the North, governor general the comte de Peynier sent troops to crush the Saint-Marc Assembly, but eighty-five deputies escaped aboard Le Léopard, a French ship of the line whose crew had mutinied against their captain and sailed to France. See: Abenon, Cauna, Chauleau, Antilles 1789, 129–32; Bénot, La révolution française et la fin des colonies, 53–4; David Patrick Geggus, Slavery, War, and Revolution: The British Occupation of Saint Domingue, 1793–1798, (Oxford: Clarendon Press, 1982), 33–6. Regarding the mutiny in Le Léopard, see Marquis de la Gallissonière to Minister of Marine, 2 August 1790, Marine BB⁴ 3, 119–28.

13 AP, vol. 21, 126.

14 AP, vol. 21, 127. See also "Décret suspendant l'assemblée coloniale de la Martinique et instituant des commissaires civils pour rétablir l'ordre dans les Îles du Vent," in Saintoyant, 1: 389–91.

15 "Loi relative à la situation de l'île de la Martinique et aux moyens de rétablir et d'assurer la tranquillité dans les colonies françaises des Antilles. Donné à Paris le 8 décembre 1790," AD Martinique B 18, 287.

16 Mémoire sur les colonies de l'Amérique méridionale, et sur la question du jour; par m. le comte de Béhague, Maréchal de Camps, ci-devant commandant en Amérique (Paris: Imprimerie de Vezard et le Normant, 1790). Regarding Béhague's background and his appointment, see Marquis de Valous, ed., Avec les "rouges" aux Îles du Vent: Souvenirs du chevalier de Valous (1790–1793) pendant la révolution française (Paris: Éditions Caribéenes, 1989), 58. See also Georges Six, Dictionnaire biographique des généraux et amiraux

français de la révolution et de l'empire, (1792–1814) (Paris: Georges Saffroy, 1934), 73–4.

17 Ordre du roi nommant en qualité d'"ordonnateur le sieur d'Eu de Montdenoix en remplacement du sieur Tascher à qui un congé a été accordé, 23 mai 1777," AD Martinique B 13, 201.

18 Lémery, 116–18.

19 "Mémoire du roi pour servir d'instructions aux sieurs de Lacoste, Magnytôt, de Montdenoix et Linger, commissaires de sa majesté pour l'exécution de la loi du 8 décembre 1790 relative aux troubles des Îles du Vent, 24 janvier 1791," Colonies C⁸ᴬ 98, 1–8.

20 Ibid.

21 Ibid.

22 *Mémoire de M. de Damas, gouverneur de la Martinique, sur les troubles de cette colonie* (Paris, 1791), 13.

23 Ibid., 14. See also Dessalles, *Historique des troubles*, 338.

24 Crassous de Médeuil, *Rélation de ce qui s'est passé à la Martinique depuis le 1ᵉʳ septembre 1790, et réponse au mémoire intitulé: Mémoire de M. Damas, gouverneur de la Martinique, sur les troubles de la Martinique, signé Damas, sans nom d'imprimeur* (Fort-Royal, 1791; repr., Fort-de-France: Société d'histoire de la Martinique, 1982), 59–64, 73–87. See also *Journal exact de la situation dans laquelle était la Martinique, à l'époque du 18 octobre 1790,* (Paris: Imprimerie du patriote François, place du théâtre Italie, n.d.), AM Bordeaux C³ [10].

25 Vicomte de Damas to Minister of Marine, 23 January 1791, Colonies C⁸ᴬ 98, 18.

26 Ibid., 19.

27 Ibid.; 19–20.

28 See the correspondence presented by Moreau de Saint-Méry to the National Assembly on 25 and 29 March 1791: "Au Gros-Morne-Martinique, le 23 janvier 1791" and "Extrait des délibérations de l'assemblée coloniale de Martinique, séante au Gros-Morne, le 24 janvier 1791," AP, vol. 24, 374–5, 455–6.

29 Crassous de Médeuil, *Rélation de ce qui passé à la Martinique*, 106.

30 Ibid., 111.

31 Vicomte de Damas to Minister of Marine, 24 February 1791; Colonies C⁸ᴬ 98, 24–5.

32 Monsieur de Girardin to Minister of Marine, 2 April 1791, Marine BB 4 / 5, 119. Regarding Girardin's orders, see "Mémoire du roi pour servir d'instruction particulière au S. de Girardin, chef de division des armées navales, commandant les forces navales de l'etat stationnée dans les colonies de l'Amérique. Paris, le 24 janvier 1791," Marine BB 4 / 5, 108–17.

33 King's Commissioners to Minister of Marine, 2 April 1791, Colonies C⁸ᴬ 97, 1.

34 "Proclamation, 13 mars 1791," Colonies C⁸ᴬ 98, 63.

35 "Les commissaires réunies de quatorze paroisses, les citoyens et garnisons de la ville du Fort-Royal et des forts Bourbon et Saint-Louis, à Monsieur de Béhague, gouverneur général, 13 mars 1791," Colonies C⁸ᴬ 98, 56–7.

36 See "De par le roi, fait à bord de l'Eole, le 14 mars 1791," and Comte de Béhague to Minister of Marine, 1 April 1791 [#1], Colonies C⁸ᴬ 98, 58, 54–5.

37 "Procès-verbal de la reddition du Fort-Bourbon, 14 mars 1791," Colonies C⁸ᴬ 98, 64–5.

38 Comte de Béhague to Minister of Marine, 1 April 1791 [#1], Colonies C⁸ᴬ 98, 55.

39 King's Commissioners to Minister of Marine, 2 April 1791, Colonies C⁸ᴬ 97, 2–3. After registering the commissions of the new governor general and the king's commissioners on 14 March, Martinique's Sovereign Council registered the National Assembly's decree of 29 November, the Law of 8 December, and the king's proclamation of 11 December 1790 at its extraordinary session of 1 April 1791, see AD Martinique B 18, 280–3, 287–9.

40 "Par le roi, au Fort-Royal, le 15 mars 1791," Colonies C⁸ᴬ 98, 67.

41 "Par le roi [n.d.]," Colonies C⁸ᴬ 98, 68.

42 Comte de Béhague to Minister of Marine, 1 April 1791 [#2], Colonies C⁸ᴬ 98, 59.

43 King's Commissioners to Minister of Marine, 2 April 1791, Colonies C⁸ᴬ 97, 3.

44 "Copie de la lettre du nommé Marais, caporal de la compagnie de Kergu, régiment de la Martinique, adressée au nommé Ardie, caporal du régiment de Forez au Fort-Bourbon. Du Fort-Royal ce 15 mars 1791," Colonies C⁸ᴬ 98, 66.

45 "Adresse du régiment de la Martinique aux battalions de la garnison du Fort-Bourbon. Fort-Royal ce 19 mars 1791," Colonies C⁸ᴬ 98, 66.

46 Commodore Girardin to Minister of Marine, 2 April 1791, Marine BB 4 / 5, 122.

47 Comte de Béhague to Minister of Marine, 2 April 1791 [#2], Colonies C⁸ᴬ 98, 59.

48 "Proclamation. Nous, lieutenant-général des armées du roi, gouverneur-générale des Îles du vent commandant les forces de terre et de mer, et nous commissaires du roi, Fort-Royal, 20 mars 1791," Colonies C⁸ᴬ 97, 7.

49 "Proclamation de gouverneur-général Béhague et des commissaires du roi, 22 mars 1791," AD Martinique B 18, 291. See also Colonies C⁸ᴬ 97, 8.

50 "Ordre aux imprimeurs. Lacoste, Magnytôt, Montdenoix, Linger. Fort-Royal, 21 mars 1791," Colonies C^{8A} 97, 11.

51 King's Commissioners to Minister of Marine, 2 April 1791, Colonies C^{8A} 97, 6.

52 Comte de Béhague to Minister of Marine, 2 April 1791 [#2], Colonies C^{8A} 98, 60.

53 "Proclamation du gouverneur-général Béhague et des quatre commissaires du roi: Lacoste, Magnytôt, Montdenoix, Linger; du 20 mars 1791," AD Martinique B 18, 291. See also Colonies C^{8A} 97, 8.

54 Comte de Béhague to Minister of Marine, 2 April 1791 [#2], Colonies C^{8A} 98, 61.

55 Linger to Minister of Marine, 24 April 1791; see also "Certificat aux volonatires de isles voisines à leur départ de la Martinique, 23 mars 1791," Colonies C^{8A} 97, 229–30.

56 King's Commissioners to Minister of Marine, 8 April 1791, Colonies C^{8A} 97, 14–15. See also Comte de Béhague to Minister of Marine, 1 April 1791 [#2], Colonies C^{8A} 98, 61–2.

57 King's Commissioners to Minister of Marine, 2 April 1791, Colonies C^{8A} 97, 4–5.

58 "Proclamation des MM. les commissaires du roi du 22 mars 1791," AD Martinique B 18, 291. See also Colonies C^{8A} 97, 9.

59 "Proclamation des MM. les commissaires du roi, du 29 mars 1791," AD Martinique B 18, 290–91. See also Colonies C^{8A} 97, 9–10.

60 King's Commissioners to Minister of Marine, 2 April 1791, Colonies C^{8A} 97, 4–5. See also King's Commissioners' response to Fort-Royal commissioners of commerce, 4 April 1791 and "Instructions de messieurs les commissaires du roi sur leur proclamation du 29 mars," Colonies C^{8A} 97, 44–5, 48–9.

61 See Saintoyant, 2: 39–46; Dubois and Garrigus, eds., *Slave Revolution in the Caribbean*, 21–2; and Abenon, Cauna, Chauleau, *Antilles 1789*, 133–4. For an examination of Blanchelande's dilemmas during this crisis, and throughout his tenure as governor general in Saint-Domingue, see Jeremy D. Popkin, "The French Revolution's Royal Governor: General Blanchelande and Saint-Domingue, 1790–92," *The William and Mary Quarterly* 71, no. 2 (April 2014): 203–28.

62 "Délibération, Fort-Royal, 3 avril 1791," and "Copie des propositions présentées par M. de Béhage aux commissaires du roi, 6 avril 1791," Colonies C^{8A} 97, 28–9, 30–1. See also Commodore Girardin's account of the deliberation of 3 April, his order to Du Chilleau, captain of the *Apollon*, 6

April, and his letter to the Minister of Marine, 29 April 1791, Marine BB 4 / 5, 128–9, 130, 131–3.

63 Comte de Béhague to Governor-General Blanchelande, 7 April 1791, Colonies C⁸ᴬ 98, 69–70.

64 King's Commissioners to Minister of Marine, 22 April 1791, Colonies C⁸ᴬ 97, 18–21.

65 "Proclamation adressée à la population par M. de Béhague et les commissaires du roi, 7 avril 1791," Colonies C⁸ᴬ 97, 32–3.

66 "Proclamation. Nous lieutenant-général et nous les commissaires du roi, 10 avril 1791," Colonies C⁸ᴬ 97, 34–5.

67 "Mesures prises entre MM. le général et commissaires du roi pour accélerer le repliement des troupes des différents postes notamment celui du Morne Rouge, le désarmement des esclaves et leur renvoi chez leurs maîtres dans les villes et dans les campagnes conformément aux proclamations des 7 et 10 avril," Colonies C⁸ᴬ 97, 36. The chevalier de Rivière had expelled the troops of the Normandy Regiment from the *Ferme* for insubordination, and their conduct at Prêcheur, where they received "incendiary writings" from Saint-Pierre, which led Béhague to deport them from the colony. See "Copie d'une lettre écrite à M. de Béhague par M. Desaulnois, capitaine commandant le détachement du régiment de Normandie, 20 avril 1791" and "Copie d'une lettre écrit à M. de Béhague par M. Drand, curé du Prêcheur, 20 avril 1791," Colonies C⁸ᴬ 98, 83–4. See also Commodore Girardin to Minister of Marine, 13 May 1791, Marine BB 4 / 5, 139–40.

68 "Proclamation. Nous lieutenant-général et nous commissaires du roi, 11 avril 1791," Colonies C⁸ᴬ 97, 37.

69 King's Commissioners to Minister of Marine, 22 April 1791, Colonies C⁸ᴬ 97, 22–3.

70 Comte de Béhague to Minister of Marine, 26 April 1791, Colonies C⁸ᴬ 98, 72.

71 "Proclamation. Nous lieutenant-général et nous commissaires du roi, 13 avril 1791," Colonies C⁸ᴬ 97, 39.

72 Comte de Béhague to Minister of Marine, 22 April 1791; see also Address Presented to Béhague by Dert, 15 April 1791, and his response in Colonies C⁸ᴬ 98, 72, 79–80, 81–2.

73 King's Commissioners to Commissioners of Commerce, 17 April 1791, Colonies C⁸ᴬ 97, 46–7.

74 King's Commissioners to Minister of Marine, 22 April 1791; see also "Copie d'une lettre des commissaires du commerce de Saint-Pierre aux commissaires du roi, 2 mai 1791," "Copie de la réponse des commissaires du roi, 4 mai 1791," "Copie d'une lettre adressé par les capitaines de

navires présents à Saint-Pierre aux commissaires du roi, 25 avril 1791," and "Copie de la réponse des commissaires du roi, 5 mai 1791" in Colonies C^{8A} 97, 23, 90–9.

75 "Copie d'une lettre des commissaires du roi aux commissaires des colons, 18 mai 1791," Colonies C^{8A} 97, 100–1.

76 King's Commissioners to Minister of Marine, 24 May 1791 [#2], Colonies C^{8A} 97, 63–6. The commissioners also found the colony's finances in dreadful shape and they believed that most colonists would be unable to pay the head tax for 1790 or 1791. Although they endeavoured to maintain a reserve to pay troops and keep up hospitals, they asked the minister to send funds for the security and administration of all the Windward Islands as soon as possible; King's Commissioners to Minister of Marine, 11 June 1791, Colonies C^{8A} 97, 102–3.

77 King's Commissioners to Minister of Marine, 24 May 1791 [#1], Colonies C^{8A} 97, 60–2. See also Comte de Béhague to Minister of Marine, 15 June 1791, Colonies C^{8A} 98, 85–6.

78 See "Requisition de MM. les commissaires du roi, 24 mai 1791," "Réponse de M. de Béhague, 24 mai 1791," "L'ordre de M. de Mallevault à M. de Lasseur, 24 mai 1791," and Declaration made by Lasseur and Dubrossai aboard *Calypso*, 26 May 1791, in Colonies C^{8A} 98, 90–3.

79 King's Commissioners to Comte de Béhague, 25 May 1791, Colonies C^{8A} 98, 96–7. See also Lagarde to King's Commissioners, 25 May 1791, M. Lemer to King's Commissioners, 24 May 1791, and Testimony of le Genti, Arnaud, Bogard, Pecheur, 24 May 1791, in Colonies C^{8A} 98, 93–6.

80 King's Commissioners to Comte de Béhague, 25 May 1791, Colonies C^{8A} 98, 96–7.

81 Comte de Béhague to King's Commissioners, 26 May 1791, Colonies C^{8A} 98, 97–8.

82 "Copie des pièces relatives à la croisière du vaisseau *L'Eole* avec deux frégates devant Saint-Pierre, Isle Martinique, à le fin de mai 1791," Marine BB 4 / 5, 147–55. See also Commodore Girardin to Minister of Marine, 17 June and 13 May 1791, Marine BB 4 / 5, 145–6, 139–40.

83 King's Commissioners to Comte de Béhague, 27 and 30 May 1791, Colonies C^{8A} 98, 99–100, 101.

84 Comte de Béhague to King's Commissioners, 31 May 1791, Colonies C^{8A} 98, 104.

85 Baron de Clugny to Minister of Marine, 19 March 1791, Colonies C^{7A} 45, 3–4.

86 Lacoste and Magnytôt to Minister of Marine, 20 November 1791, Colonies C^{7A} 45, 15–17.

87 Ibid.; Colonies C⁷ᴬ 45, 18–19. See also Saintoyant, 2: 204.
88 Baron de Clugny to Minister of Marine, 21 May 1791, Colonies C⁷ᴬ 45, 5–6.
89 "Extrait d'une lettre de M. de Clugny au Ministre, du 18 juillet 1791"
    and Lacoste and Magnytôt to Minister of Marine, 20 November 1791, in
    Colonies C⁷ᴬ 45, 11, 19–22. See also: Queslin, "Rapport … concernant les
    troubles arrivés à la Guadeloupe," AP, vol. 46, 52–3; Louis Dermigny and
    Gabriel Debien, eds., "La révolution aux Antilles: Journal maritime
    du commandeur de Villevielle, commandant de la frégate *La Didon*
    (septembre 1790–septembre 1792)," *Revue d'histoire de l'Amérique française*
    9 (1955): 65–6; Bangou, 46–47; Saintoyant, 2: 204–5; Lacour, 2: 67–9.
90 Lacoste and Magnytôt to Minister of Marine, 20 November 1791,
    Colonies C⁷ᴬ 45, 22–6. See also Lacour, 2: 70–1.
91 "Lettre de l'assemblée-coloniale aux commissaires du roi, écrite de la
    Pointe-à-Pitre, le 19 avril 1791," in *Détails de divers débats entre l'assemblée-
    coloniale de la Guadeloupe, et les commissaires du roi, envoyés aux îles du Vent
    pour l'exécution de la loi du huit Décembre 1790*, (Saint-Pierre: Imprimerie de
    P. Richard et Le Cadre, 1791), 29–30, Colonies C⁷ᴬ 44, 146.
92 "Réponse de commissaires du roi à l'assemblée coloniale, écrite du Fort-
    Royal, le 28 avril 1791," in *Détails de divers débats*, 30–1, Colonies C⁷ᴬ 44,
    146–7.
93 "Copie de la lettre de M. de Clugny aux commissaires du roi, en date
    du 9 mai 1791," Colonies C⁷ᴬ 45, 46–8.
94 "Copie de la réponse des commissaires du roi à M. de Clugny en datte
    du 15 mai 1791," Colonies C⁷ᴬ 45, 48–9.
95 "Lettre de l'assemblée-coloniale de la Guadeloupe aux commissaires
    du roi (n.d.)," in *Détails de divers débats*, 35–6, Colonies C⁷ᴬ 44, 149.
96 Ibid, 38–40, Colonies C⁷ᴬ 44, 150–1.
97 "Extrait des registres des délibérations de l'assemblée générale-coloniale
    de la Guadeloupe, séante à la Pointe-à-Pitre le 14 juillet 1791," in *Détails
    de divers débats*, 41–2, Colonies C⁷ᴬ 44, 152.
98 "Réponse des commissaires du roi à l'assemblée-coloniale, le 31 juillet
    1791," in *Détails de divers débats*, 46–52, Colonies C⁷ᴬ 44, 154–7.
99 Lacoste and Magnytôt to Minister of Marine, 20 November 1791,
    Colonies C⁷ᴬ 45, 25–8.
100 Queslin, "Rapport … concernant les troubles arrivés à la Guadeloupe,"
    AP, vol. 46, 54. See also Lacour, 2: 73–4 and Saintoyant, 2: 205–6.
101 "Fédérations particulières faites à Saint-Anne et à Basse-Terre. Exposé des
    commissaires," in *Détails de divers débats*, 8–15, Colonies C⁷ᴬ 44, 135–9.
102 Ibid.

103 Lacoste and Magnytôt to Minister of Marine, 20 November 1791, Colonies C⁷ᴬ 45, 30–2.

104 *Relation des événemens qui se sont passés le 15 septembre 1791, dans la ville de la Pointe-à-Pitre de l'île Guadeloupe, au sujet de l'insurrection de la compagnie de grenadiers du deuxième battalion du quatorzième régiment d'infanterie*, (Pointe-à-Pitre: Imprimerie de veuve Benard, 1791), Colonies C⁷ᴬ 45, 51–3. Despite this pamphlet's depiction of the heroic actions of "good citizens," the grenadiers did not fire a shot in resistance: Lacoste and Magnytôt to Minister of Marine, 20 November 1791, Colonies C⁷ᴬ 45, 32. Regarding the participation of the *Didon*'s officers in these events, see Dermigny and Debien, eds., "Journal maritime du commandeur de Villevielle," 69–72 and Valous, ed., *Avec les "rouges" aux Îles du Vent*, 83–8.

105 *Détails de divers débats*, 2–7, 21–8, Colonies C⁷ᴬ 44, 132–5, 142–5.

106 Lacoste and Magnytôt to Minister of Marine, 20 November 1791, Colonies C⁷ᴬ 45, 30. For the text of the colonial assembly's *arrêté* breaking Basse-Terre's municipality, see Bangou, 47–9. See also Queslin, "Rapport ... concernant les troubles arrivés à la Guadeloupe," AP, vol. 46, 53, 56.

107 "Arrêté de l'assemblée coloniale en date du 13 de ce mois, qui casse les officiers municipales de la Basse-Terre. Exposé des commissaires du roi, 22 septembre 1791," in *Détails de divers débats*, 16–18, Colonies C⁷ᴬ 44, 139–40.

108 "Réponse de l'assemblée coloniale," in *Détails de divers débats*, 18–20, Colonies C⁷ᴬ 44, 140–1.

109 The commissioners were forced to accept Masse's request for leave to return to France, the colonial assembly's hostility and obstruction having made it impossible for him to fulfill his duties. See *Détails de divers débats*, 67–8, Colonies C⁷ᴬ 44, 165. See also Masse to Minister of Marine, 13 August, 11 October 1791, Colonies C⁷ᴬ 45, 55–60.

110 "Proclamation de Lacoste, Magnytôt, Montdenoix, Linger à Basse-Terre, 29 septembre 1791," AP, vol. 46, 61–2.

111 Lacoste and Magnytôt to Minister of Marine, 20 November 1791, Colonies C⁷ᴬ 45, 35–7. See also Queslin, "Rapport ... concernant les troubles arrivés à la Guadeloupe,"AP, vol. 46, 56 and Saintoyant, 2: 208.

112 Lacoste and Magnytôt to Minister of Marine, 20 November 1791, Colonies C⁷ᴬ 45, 37–40. See also Queslin, "Rapport ... concernant les troubles arrivés à la Guadeloupe" and "Lettre de l'assemblée coloniale de la Guadeloupe aux commissaires du roi, 7 octobre 1791" and "Réponse des commissaires du roi à l'assemblée coloniale," AP, vol. 46, 56–7, 62–4. See also Saintoyant, 2: 209–10.

113 "Copie de la lettre écrite par MM. de Lacoste et Magnytôt, commissaires du roi, le 20 octobre 1791, à l'assemblée coloniale de la Guadeloupe," Colonies C⁸ᴬ 97, 189. Following the commissioners' departure, Guadeloupe's colonial assembly voted to send Romain Lacaze to France to counter the damning report Lacoste and Magnytôt would submit: "Extrait des régistres des délibérations de l'assemblée générale coloniale de la Guadeloupe séante à la Pointe-à-Pitre, le 21 octobre 1791" and "Séance du 23 octobre" and "Séance du 25 octobre," in Colonies C⁷ᴬ 45, 94–5.

114 "Extrait des déclarations faites par MM. de Lacoste et Magnytôt les 29 et 30 octobre, 2, 3 et 4 novembre dans leurs avis respectifs aux deux déliberations" and "Copie du procès-verbal de la délibération tenue chez M. de Béhague par les commissaires du roi, 30 octobre 1791," in Colonies C⁸ᴬ 97, 64–6, 182–4.

115 Lacoste and Magnytôt to Minister of Marine, 8 November 1791, Colonies C⁸ᴬ 97, 141.

116 See Montdenoix and Linger to Minister of Marine, 20 November 1791 [#2] and "Protestation de MM. de Montdenoix et Linger contre tous les actes et productions de piéces en France de la part de MM. de Lacoste et Magnytôt depuis leur rononciation à l'exercise de leurs fonctions, 20 novembre 1791," Montdenoix and Linger to Minister of Marine, 24 November 1791," "Note de M. Magnytôt au sujet de l'inventaire des papiers relatifs à l'activité des commissaires du roi depuis leur arrivée en Martinique, 16 novembre 1791," "Réponse de Montdenoix et Linger, 19 novembre 1791," "Note de Lacoste et Magnytôt, 18 novembre 1791," "Copie d'ordre donné à M. Duval, lieutenant de vaisseau, commandant la corvette *La Perdrix*, 24 novembre 1791," and "Procès-verbal dressé par MM. Lacoste et Magnytôt à bord du navire *Le Bienheureux*, 24 novembre 1791," in Colonies C⁸ᴬ 97, 177–81, 192–5, 223–5.

117 Lacoste and Magnytôt to Minister of Marine, 20 November 1791, Colonies C⁸ᴬ 97, 39–41.

118 Montdenoix and Linger to Minister of Marine, 9 November 1791, Colonies C⁷ᴬ 45, 142–4.

119 See Montdenoix and Linger to Minister of Marine, 20 November 1791 [#1] and "Observations remises par MM. de Montdenoix et Linger à M. Magnytôt sur le projet de proclamation relatif aux prétentions et entreprises de l'assemblée coloniale de Guadeloupe, 28 septembre 1791," in Colonies C⁸ᴬ 97, 167–76.

120 Comte de Béhague to Minister of Marine, 23 December 1791, Colonies C⁸ᴬ 98, 131–4.

121 Linger to Minister of Marine, 22 December 1791, Colonies C⁸ᴬ 97, 235–8.

122 Béhague blamed the disorder on the spread of letters claiming that the crews of the *Ferme* and the *Embuscade* were regarded as traitors and "aristocrats" in France: Comte de Béhague to Minister of Marine, 15 June 1791, Colonies C⁸ᴬ 98, 87. Behague had received a similar denunciation of the *Ferme* from the provincial assembly of the North in Saint-Domingue. See "Extrait des registres des délibérations de l'assemblée provinciale permanente du nord, séance du 8 janvier 1791" and "Observations faites par M. de Cambefort, commandant pour le roi dans la province du nord, en absence de M. de Vincent, à la séance du lundi 10 janvier 1791," in Colonies C⁸ᴬ 98, 102–4.

123 Chevalier de Rivière to Minister of Marine, 17 June 1791 and Commodore Girardin to Minister of Marine, 17 June 1791, in Marine BB 4 / 5, 68–9, 145–56. See also Dermigny and Debien, eds., "Journal maritime du commandeur de Villevielle," 65. Seeking to counter patriot propaganda, Montdenoix delivered a speech aboard the warships on 3 June 1791 that was intended to reassure the sailors of the patriotism and legitimacy of their past and present conduct: *Discours prononcé au nom de MM. les commissaires du roi par M. de Montdenoix, au gens de mer qui composent les équipages du vaisseau la Ferme, commandé par M. de Rivière chef de division, et la frégate l'Embuscade, commandé par M. D'Orléans* (Fort-Royal: Imprimerie de P. Richard et Le Cadre, au college St Victor, n.d.), in Marine BB 4 / 5, 70–1. For the manuscript version of this speech, and a similar one delivered to the Grenadiers of the Martinique and Sarre Regiments on 5 June 1791, see Colonies C⁸ᴬ 98, 105–7.

124 Declaration of Agathon de Pigache and Jean-Jacques Olivier in "Extrait des minutes du greffe de l'amirauté de l'isle Guadeloupe, 2 octobre 1791," Colonies C⁸ᴬ 97, 136–8.

125 "Extrait du procès-verbal des délibérations de l'équipage de *l'Embuscade*," AP, vol. 35, 318. See also Lémery, 327.

126 "Copie d'une lettre de M. d'Orléans, capitaine de la frégate *l'Embuscade*, en rade de l'île de Ré," AP, vol. 35, 316–18.

127 Montdenoix and Linger to Minister of Marine, 4 and 24 October 1791, Colonies C⁸ᴬ 97, 134–5, 139. See also Chevalier de Rivière to Minister of Marine, 9 November 1791, Marine BB 4 / 5, 86.

128 *Proclamation. Nous commissaires du roi envoyés aux Îles du Vent pour l'exécution de la loi du huit Décembre 1790* (Fort-Royal: Imprimerie de P. Richard et Le Cadre, 1791), in Colonies C⁸ᴬ 97, 140.

129 See Comte de Béhague to Minister of Marine, 2 November 1791, "Copie de la lettre écrites à M. de Béhague par M. de Blanchelande, 12 septembre

1791," and "Extrait des registres de l'assemblée générale de la partie française de Saint-Domingue, de la séance du 12 septembre 1791," in Colonies C⁸ᴬ 98, 122–4. Regarding the outbreak of slave revolt in Saint-Domingue, see Carolyn E. Fick, *The Making of Haiti: The Saint-Domingue Revolution from Below* (Knoxville: University of Tennessee Press, 1990), 91–117 and Laurent Dubois, *Avengers of the New World: The Story of the Haitian Revolution* (Cambridge, MA: The Belknap Press of Harvard University Press, 2004), 91–114. Béhague informed Blanchelande that he could spare no troops but would dispatch three warships carrying food and gunpowder. Commodore Girardin's flagship *Eole*, accompanied by the frigate *Didon* and the brig *Cerf*, sailed for Saint-Domingue on 8 November. See "Réponse de M. de Béhague à la lettre de M. de Blanchelande, 1 novembre 1791," Colonies C⁸ᴬ 98, 126–7. See also Dermigny and Debien, eds., "Journal maritime du commandeur de Villevielle," 250–8 and Valous, ed., *Avec les "rouges" aux Îles du Vent*, 91–119.

130 See King's Commissioners' postscript, dated 30 October, to Béhague's response to Blanchelande, 1 November 1791, giving approval for the dispatch of the *Eole* to Saint-Domingue; Colonies C⁸ᴬ 98, 126.

131 National Assembly, "Law on the Colonies, 1791," in *Slave Revolution in the Caribbean 1789–1804*, ed. Dubois and Garrigus, 84–5. See also Saintoyant, 1: 115–44, Bénot, *La révolution française et la fin des colonies*, 57–75 and Piquet, 71–96.

132 "Décret du 24 septembre 1791," in Saintoyant, 1: 398–9. See also Bénot, *La révolution française et la fin des colonies*, 75–87, Piquet, 97–126 and Quinney, 544–57.

133 Montdenoix and Linger to Minister of Marine, 1 December 1791 and "Proclamation. Nous commissaires du roi aux Îles du Vent pour l'exécution de la loi du 8 décembre," Colonies C⁸ᴬ 97, 196–200. Regarding the "concordat" signed by whites and free men of colour in Saint-Domingue, which recognized the decree of 15 May 1791, see Garrigus, *Before Haiti*, 260–3. See also Saintoyant, 2: 55–9, Bell, *Toussaint Louverture*, 31, and Abenon, Cauna, Chauleau, *Antilles 1789*, 138–41.

134 *Arrêté sur les gens de couleurs libres. Extrait des registres des délibérations de l'assemblée générale de la Guadeloupe, séante à la Pointe-à-Pitre, le 20 décembre 1791* (Pointe-à-Pitre: Imprimerie de veuve Benard, 1791), Colonies C⁷ᴬ 45, 86.

135 *Arrêté qui déclare que l'assemblée coloniale acutelle est constituante. Extrait des registres de délibérations de l'assemblée générale de la Guadeloupe, séante à la Pointe-à-Pitre, le 21 décembre 1791*, Colonies C⁷ᴬ 45, 88–91.

136 "Adresse de l'assemblée coloniale de la Guadeloupe au roi. Dattée de la Pointe-à-Pitre, le 22 décembre 1791," Colonies C⁷ᴬ 45, 96.
137 "Proclamation," Colonies C⁸ᴬ 97, 199–200.
138 "Procès-verbal de la délibération tenu par le gouverneur-général de Béhague et les commissaires du roi, au sujet de renvoi en France des sieurs Morel, Castendes, Querei, Terre, Duviquet et Salvador, 2 décembre 1791," Colonies C⁸ᴬ 97, 205–6.

5 Counter-Revolution

1 Lacoste and Magnytôt, from Richelieu, to Minister of Marine, 8 February 1792 [#1], Colonies C⁸ᴬ 100, 94–8.
2 AP, vol. 38, 107–8.
3 Decree of the National Assembly, 22 February 1792; see also Minister of Marine to President of National Assembly, 1 March 1792, Colonies C⁸ᴬ 100, 154–5.
4 Letter from Louis XVI announcing the nomination of Jean de Lacoste to replace Bertrand de Moleville as Minister of Marine, 16 March 1792; AP, vol. 40, 56. Regarding the circumstances surrounding Bertrand de Moleville's resignation and his assessment of his successor, see *Private Memoirs of A. Bertrand de Moleville, Minister of State, 1790–1791, Relative to the Last Year of the Reign of Louis the Sixteenth*, 2 vols., trans. R.C. Dallas (London, 1797; new ed., edited by G.K. Fortescue, Boston: J.B. Millet Company, 1909), 1: 242–3, 347–52, 357–8.
5 See Leigh Whaley, *Radicals: Politics and Republicanism in the French Revolution* (Sutton Publishing, 2000), 44–53 and M.J. Sydenham, *The Girondins* (London: Athlone Press, 1961), 99–106. See also Doyle, *Oxford History of the French Revolution*, 179–80, Sydenham, *French Revolution*, 93–8, and Furet, *Revolutionary France*, 105–8. France declared war on Austria on 20 April 1792, but the king dismissed the "Patriot Ministry" in June: Roland, Clavière and Joseph Servan on 13 June and Dumouriez on 15 June. Lacoste remained minister of marine, however, until 10 July when he resigned, stating that the powers of the executive had become inadequate to carry on government.
6 Kersaint, "Discussion of the Troubles in the Colonies, 28 March 1792," in *The French Revolution and Human Rights: A Brief Documentary History*, ed. Lynn Hunt (Boston, MA: St Martin's, 1996), 112–13. For discussions of the involvement of Brissot and his allies in the debates on free-coloured status preceding the Decree of 28 March 1792 and possible contradictions within

their arguments, see Bénot, *La révolution française et la fin des colonies*, 57–87 and Piquet, 127–56.

7 "Décret accordant les droits politiques aux hommes de couleur et noirs libres et prévoyant des envois de secours à Saint-Domingue, 28 mars 1792," in Saintoyant, 1: 407. See also "The National Assembly: Law of 4 April 1792," in *Slave Revolution in the Caribbean*, ed. Dubois and Garrigus, 115–16.

8 "Décret … 28 mars 1792," in Saintoyant, 1: 407–9.

9 AP, vol. 40, 544.

10 "Mémoire du roi pour servir d'instructions aux sieurs Leroi de Fontigny, Lamarre, et Girault, commissaires civils délégués aux Îles du Vent, pour l'exécution de la loi du 4 Avril dernier, relative aux colonies, 17 juin 1792," Colonies C^{8A} 99, 101–5.

11 See "Rapport fait à l'assemblée nationale, au nom due comité coloniale, sur les troubles de la Martinique, par P. Goyn, 2 May 1792," and "M. Queslin, au nom du comité colonial, donne lecture de la seconde partie du rapport sur les troubles de la Martinique et présente un projet de décret relatif à cet objet, 22 juin 1792," AP, vol. 42, 675–99 and vol. 45, 483–93.

12 "Rapport fait à l'assemblée nationale, au nom du comité des colonies, concernant les troubles arrivés à la Guadeloupe, par Adrien Queslin, député du département de la Manche, 2 juillet 1792," AP, vol. 46, 49–60.

13 "M. Queslin, au nom du comité colonial, présente un projet de décret concernant les troubles arrivés à la Guadeloupe, 2 juillet 1792," AP, vol. 46, 29–31. See also "Décret concernant les affaires des Îles du Vent et leur rendant applicable le décret du 15 juin 1792 (Décret additionel à la loi relative à l'envoi des commissaires civils à Saint-Domingue), 2 juillet 1792," in Saintoyant 1: 412–14.

14 "M. Queslin, au nom du comité colonial, présente un projet de décret pour mander à la barre de l'assemblée les sieurs Montendoix, commisaire civil aux isles-du-vent; Béhague, commandant général, Clugny, gouverneur de la Guadeloupe, et Darrot, commandant en second, 2 juillet 1792," AP, vol. 46, 31. See also "Décret concernant les affaires des Îles du Vent et leur rendant applicable le décret du 15 juin 1792, 2 juillet 1792", in Saintoyant, 1: 412–14.

15 "Compte rendu à l'assemblée nationale des mesures prises pour l'exécution de la loi du 4 avril 1792, 6 juillet 1792," Colonies C^{8A} 99, 4–8.

16 *Obéissance à la loi. Lettre de M. de Béhague, gouverneur-général des îles du vent, au comité intermédiaire de l'assemblée coloniale de la Martinique, 24 mai 1792* (Fort-Royal: Imprimerie de P. Richard et Le Cadre, 1792), Colonies C^{8A} 99, 72. Martinique's sovereign council registered the Law of 4 April during its session of 1 June 1792, AD Martinique 20, 19–20.

17 "Réponse du comité intermédiaire à M. de Béhague, 26 mai 1792," Colonies C⁸ᴬ 99, 72.

18 *Extrait des délibérations de l'assemblée coloniale de la Martinique, dans sa séance du 3 juin 1792* (Fort-Royal: Imprimerie de P. Richard et Le Cadre, 1792), Colonies C⁸ᴬ 100, 148.

19 "Copie d'une lettre de M.de Béhague au président de l'assemblée coloniale, 11 juin 1792," Colonies C⁸ᴬ 99, 75. See also AD Martinique B 20, 19.

20 "Observations du gouverneur-général sur l'opinion où l'assemblée coloniale paraît être," Colonies C⁸ᴬ 99, 75–6.

21 See "Deuxième observations du gouverneur-général sur l'arrêté de l'assemblée coloniale de la Martinique dans sa séance du 3 juin 1792" and "Réponse de M. de Béhague à l'arrêté de l'assemblée coloniale du 12 juin 1792, 14 juin 1792," Colonies C⁸ᴬ 99, 76–9.

22 "Extrait de la lettre de M. de Clugny, gouverneur de la Guadeloupe, à M. de Béhague, Pointe-à-Pitre, 27 mai 1792," Colonies C⁸ᴬ 99, 72.

23 Baron de Clugny to deputies of Guadeloupe's colonial assembly, 23 May 1792, Colonies C⁷ᴬ 45, 111.

24 Baron de Clugny to President of Guadeloupe's colonial assembly, 28 May 1792, Colonies C⁷ᴬ 45, 224.

25 *Instructions adressées par le gouverneur de la Guadeloupe à MM. les officiers municipaux des différentes paroisses du gouvernement, pour l'exécuion de la loi no. 1606, 4 juin 1792* (Pointe-à-Pitre: Imprimerie de la colonie, 1792), Colonies C⁷ᴬ 45, 225–6.

26 Baron de Clugny to Minister of Marine, 12 July 1792, Colonies C⁷ᴬ 45, 113.

27 "Mémoire remis au ministre par des colons des Îles du Vent protestant contre le décret du 28 mars qui ordonne l'envoi prochain d'une force armée aux Antilles (n.d.)," Colonies C⁸ᴬ 100, 189–92. See also "Lettre de sieur Romain Lacaze, député de la colonie de la Guadeloupe auprès du corps législatif et du roi ... 29 mars 1792," AP vol. 40, 680.

28 "Comité intermédiaire de la Martinique, Fort-Royal, à Dubuc-Deferret, 2 juillet 1792," Colonies C⁸ᴬ 100, 194.

29 See "Copie d'une circulaire de Béhague aux commandants de quartiers, 1 fevrier 1792," "M. de Venancourt, commandant au Carbet, à Béhague, 2 février 1792," "Letrre du curé de la Case-Piote, à M. Doens-Beaufond, commandant du quartier (n.d.)," "Lettre de M. de Soter, commandant au Gros-Morne, à M. de Béhague, 12 février 1792," and "Lettre de M. de Fressinaux, colonel du 37ᵉ Régiment, à M. de Béhague, 13 février 1792," in Colonies C⁸ᴬ 99, 53–5.

30 "Copie de la lettre écrite par Monsieur Astorg à Monsieur le gouverneur-général des Îles du Vent, au Fort-Royal, Martinique, à Saint-Pierre,

Martinique, le 31 mai 1792," Colonies C⁸ᴬ 100, 203–4. See also Dermigny and Debien, eds., "Journal maritime du commandeur de Villevielle," 261–3 and Valous, ed., *Avec les "rouges" aux Îles du Vent*, 132–6.

31 "Compte Rendu par M. de Fressinaux, Colonel du 37ᵐᵉ Régiment d'infanterie, ci-devant Maréchal de Turenne, commandant au Fort-Bourbon, depuis le 31 mai jusqu'au 14 juin 1792," Colonies C⁸ᴬ 100, 123–9.

32 "Lettre du commandant de Saint-Pierre à M. de Béhague, 17 août 1792," Colonies C⁸ᴬ 99, 79–80.

33 "Réponse du gouverneur-général au commandant de Saint-Pierre, 18 août 1792," Colonies C⁸ᴬ 99, 80.

34 "Lettre du commandant de Saint-Pierre au gouverneur-général, 20 août 1792," Colonies C⁸ᴬ 99, 81.

35 "Réponse du gouverneur-général au commandant de Saint-Pierre, 21 août 1792," Colonies C⁸ᴬ 99, 81.

36 "Lettre du gouverneur-général au comité intermédiaire … 21 août 1792," Colonies C⁸ᴬ 99, 82.

37 See "Extrait des pièces déposés aux archives de l'assemblée coloniale de la partie française de Saint-Domingue: Garrat, Député à l'Assemblée Coloniale … 29 août 1792," "Extrait du registre des declarations au Bureau surveillance de la municipalité de la ville et banlieu du Cap, 28 août 1792," and "Extrait des registres du greffe de la municipalité du Cap, 5 juillet 1792," Colonies C⁸ᴬ 99, 123–6.

38 Captain Eustache de Bruix, "Extrait de mon journal," Colonies C⁸ᴬ 100, 10–11.

39 "Copie du rapport de M. Gaillard, Lieutenant de Vaisseau, à bord de la frégate *La Sémillante*, 19 septembre 1792," Colonies C⁸ᴬ 100, 30.

40 See "Copie de la lettre adressé à MM. les commissaires civils délégués aux Îles du Vent par le comité intermédiaire de l'assemblée coloniale de la Martinique, 16 septembre 1792," "Copie de l'extrait des délibérations du comité intermédiaire de l'assemblée coloniale de la Martinique dans la séance du 16 septembre 1792," and Bruix, "Extrait de mon journal," in Colonies C⁸ᴬ 100, 65, 64, 11–13.

41 Béhague learned of the 20 April 1792 declaration of war on 5 July and announced subsequently that merchant shipping would be provided with naval escorts, even though neither Austria nor its Prussian ally possessed naval forces which could threaten the colonies. See Comte de Béhague to Minister of Marine, 9 July 1792 and "Copie d'une lettre écrite par M. de Béhague à MM. les capitaines de commerce en rade de Saint-Pierre, Isle Martinique, et à la Basse-Terre, Isle Guadeloupe, 9 juillet 1792," Colonies C⁸ᴬ 99, 37–8.

42 *Proclamation. Jean-Pierre-Antoine de Béhague, lieutenant-général des armées du roi, gouverneur-général des Îles du Vent, commandant en chef les forces de terre and de mer, 14 septembre 1792* (Fort-Royal: Imprimerie de P. Richard et Le Cadre, 1792), Colonies C⁸ᴬ 99, 89.

43 "Copie du rapport de M. Daucourt, aide de camp de M. Rochambeau, lieutenant-général et commandant général des Îles du Vent, envoyé par ce général pour remettre des lettres à M. Béhague, 20 septembre 1792," Colonies C⁸ᴬ 100, 31–3. See also General Rochambeau to Minister of Marine, 4 October 1792, Colonies C⁸ᴬ 99, 117–18.

44 See Bruix, "Extrait de mon journal," "Copie du procès-verbal dressé par MM. les officiers du bord du naivre *la Guianne*, 1 octobre 1792," "Copie du Procès-Verbal dressé par MM. des officiers des États Majors des batiments du commerce *L'Abeille* et *le Robuste*, 22 septembre 1792," "Copie du procès-verbal dressé par MM. les officiers majors et mariniers du naivre *le Chevalier d'Assas*, 22 septembre 1792," in Colonies C⁸ᴬ 100, 14–15, 46–7, 48–9, 52.

45 Bruix, "Extrait de mon journal," Colonies C⁸ᴬ 100, 15. See also General Rochambeau to Minister of Marine, 4 October 1792, Colonies C⁸ᴬ 99, 118.

46 "Copie de la lettre écrite par MM. les commissaires civils délégués aux Îles du Vent à M. le Président et aux MM. les députés composant l'assemblée coloniale de la Martinique, à bord de *la Bienvenue*, ce 17 septembre 1792," Colonies C⁸ᴬ 100, 36–7.

47 See "Précis de ce que m'a dit Mallevault, commandant la frégate *La Calypso* et des réponses que je lui ai faites. Le tout rapporté aussi littéralement qu ma mémoire m'a permis de le faire, 18 septembre 1792" and Bruix, "Extrait de mon journal," Colonies C⁸ᴬ 100, 33–6, 16–17. Observing Frenchmen, sailing under the same flag and equally paid by the state to maintain its laws, prepared to shed their brothers' blood, Bruix wrote: "I avow without shame that I felt my heart break."

48 The term *flûte* refers to a man of war, in *Bienvenue*'s case a frigate, which has had its cannon removed to serve as a transport. Unlike merchant ships chartered as transports, however, a *flûte* remained a ship of the French Navy commanded by a (often auxiliary) naval officer.

49 See "Copie de la réquisition de MM. les commissaires civils délégués aux Îles du Vent à M. Bruix, commandant la frégate *la Sémillante*, pour conduire le convoi à la Guadeloupe, 17 septembre 1792" and Bruix, "Extrait de mon journal," in Colonies C⁸ᴬ 100, 38–9, 17–21.

50 See "Copie de la réquisition de MM. les commissaires civils délégués aux Îles du Vent à M. Bruix, commandant la frégate *la Sémillante*, à l'effet de rallier le convoi, 18 septembre 1792," "Copie d'une lettre de M. Bruix où

il présente à MM. les commissaires civils les moyens qu'il emploie pour ralliés le convoi, 18 septembre 1792," "Copie de la demande de M. Collot, Gouverneur de la Guadeloupe, et de M. La Folie commandant en second, à MM. les commissaires civils, pour qu'ils veulent requerir M. Bruix de les conduire à la Guadeloupe, 18 septembre 1792," "Copie de la réponse de MM. les commissaires civils à la demande faite par MM. Collot et La Folie, 18 septembre 1792," "Copie d'une lettre de M. Bruix qui demande d'après l'impossibilité où il se trouve de ne pouvoir rallier le convoi d'aller faire de l'eau dans la Baie de Laignarde, Isle de Porto Rico, 20 septembre 1792," and "Copie de la reponse de MM. les commissaires civils à la demande de M. Bruix, 20 septembre 1792," in Colonies C⁸ᴬ 100, 39–43.

51 See "Copie d'une lettre de M. Bruix à MM. les commissaires civils par laquelle il expose la situation où se trouve son équipage, 23 septembre 1792," "Copie du procès-verbal dressé par MM. les officiers de l'État Major du bord de la frégate *La Sémillante*, 23 septembre 1792," "Copie de la reponse de MM. les commissaires civils à la lettre de M. Bruix, 23 septembre 1792," and Bruix, "Extrait de mon journal," in Colonies C⁸ᴬ 100, 44–6, 28–9. See also General Rochambeau to Minister of Marine, 4 October 1792, Colonies C⁸ᴬ 99, 119–120.

52 See "Copie du procès-verbal dressé par MM. les officiers du bord du naivre *La Guianne*, 1 octobre 1792" and "Copie du procès-verbal dressé par MM. des officiers des états majors des bâtiments du commerce *L'Abeille* et *le Robuste*, 22 septembre 1792," Colonies C⁸ᴬ 100, 47–52. One of the convoy's ships, the *Chevalier d'Assas*, actually arrived at Basse-Terre, Guadeloupe on 22 September, but men in a canoe told its officers that neither could anyone aboard land in the colony nor would the ship be given any water or supplies. Gunfire from a fortress forced the ship to leave and to sail for Cap Français. See "Copie du procès-verbal dressé par MM. les officiers majors et mariniers du naivre *le Chevalier d'Assas*, 22 septembre 1792," Colonies C⁸ᴬ 100, 52–5.

53 Lieutenant La Carrière to Minister of Marine, 27 September 1792 and "Compte au Ministre de la Marine rendu par le Sieur La Carrière, Lieutenant de Vaisseau, commandant la flûte de l'état *La Bienvenue*, 27 septembre 1792," Marine BB 4 / 12, 155, 156–9.

54 See Lieutenant La Carrière to Minister of Marine, 6 October and 3 November 1792, and La Carrière's *Procès-verbal*, signed also by the officers and mates of *Balthazar* and *St Nicolas*, 5 October 1792, in Marine BB 4 / 12, 169–71, 182–3, 174–6. For Mallevault's account of these events, see "Copie du journal de *la Calypso* du 29 septembre au 15 octobre 1792," Marine BB 4 / 12, 62–71. See also "Copie du procès-verbal de la prise de possession

de la gabarre *la Bienvenue*, 14 octobre 1792," "Lettre de deux capitaines du 44éme Régiment à M. de Béhague, 26 octobre 1792," and "Lettre du Chirurgien Major Ducaillé du bord de *la Bienvenue* à M. de Béhague (n.d.)," in Colonies C⁸ᴬ 100, 79–80.

55 See Lieutenant La Carrière to Minister of Marine, 22 October 1792 and "Traduction de la lettre de M. Laforey à M. de Rivière, 19 octobre 1792," "Réponse de M. de Rivière à Laforey, 28 octobre 1792," "Traduction de la lettre de S. Ex. M. Woodley à M. de Rivière, 13 octobre 1792," and "Réponse de M. de Rivière à S. Ex. M. Woodley, 28 octobre 1792," in Marine BB 4 / 12, 172, 42–6. See also H.J.K. Jenkins, "The Leeward Islands Command, French Royalism, and the *Bienvenue*, 1792–1793," *Mariner's Mirror* 71 (1985): 447–8.

56 "Déclaration faite par Jacques-Jérémie Paige, négociant à Saint-Pierre, aux MM. Étienne Polverel, Leger-Félicité Sonthonax et Jean-Antoine Ailhaud, commissaires civils délégués aux Îles sous le Vent, 15 octobre 1792," Colonies C⁸ᴬ 99, 127–8.

57 "Copie du rapport de M. Henry, 23 octobre 1792," Colonies C⁷ᴬ 45, 175–81. See also Lacour 2: 102–3, Saintoyant, 1: 211–12, and Bangou, 51.

58 "Copie du rapport de M. Henry, 23 octobre 1792," Colonies C⁷ᴬ 45, 177.

59 Ibid., Colonies C⁷ᴬ 45, 178–9. Henry left Guadeloupe in October and sailed to the Dutch colony of St Eustache. He visited nearby St Kitts and spoke with both *Bienvenue*'s first officer and a lieutenant colonel of the national guard who had been aboard the *flûte*. Their account was the basis of his report of the ship's capture. Regarding Marie-Galante's refusal to join Guadeloupe's counter-revolution, see Serane, Deputy of Marie-Galante to General Rochambeau and the Civil Commissioners, 23 September 1792, Colonies C⁷ᴬ 45, 191–2.

60 Leroi de Fontigny, Lamarre, Girault to Civil Commissioners for the Leeward Islands, 27 October 1792, Colonies C⁸ᴬ 99, 110–11.

61 Leroi de Fontigny, Lamarre, Girault to Civil Commissioners for the Leeward Islands, 28 October 1792, Colonies C⁸ᴬ 99, 112–13.

62 "Copie de l'adresse de l'assemblée coloniale de la Martinique au Roi, 8 octobre 1792," Colonies C⁸ᴬ 99, 114.

63 Ibid,, Colonies C⁸ᴬ 99, 115. Regarding the insurrection of 10 August 1792, see Rudé, 95–112 and Marcel Reinhard, *La chute de la royauté* (Paris: Gallimard, 1969), 389–410, 581–9. See also David Andress, *The Terror: Civil War in the French Revolution* (London: Little, Brown, 2005), 71–92 and Doyle, *Oxford History of the French Revolution*, 86–9.

64 "Copie de l'adresse de l'assemblée coloniale de la Martinique au Roi, 8 octobre 1792," Colonies C⁸ᴬ 99, 115. See also Daney, 3: 171–2.

65 "Copie du rapport de M. Henry, 23 octobre 1792," Colonies C⁷ᴬ 45, 177–8.

66 Letter by Romain Lacase, 4–12 September 1792 (no title) (Basse-Terre: Imprimerie de la colonie, 1792), Colonies C⁷ᴬ 45, 189–90. In his report to the National Convention on 26 January 1793, Guillermin quotes from a similar letter by another of Guadeloupe's emissaries, De Curt, dated 15 August 1792 from London. In this letter De Curt refers to the "horrible convulsion" in which France finds herself, and urges his fellow colonists to save their honour, families, and properties by rallying to the authority of the Bourbon monarchy. Guillermin states that the leaders of Guadeloupe's rebellion gained support by spreading such reports of imminent counter-revolution in France, AP, vol. 57, 694.

67 "Copie d'une lettre écrite par M. de La Villegégu au sieur Vasselin, négocian à Saint-Pierre, Paris, 15 août 1792," Colonies C⁸ᴬ 100, 80–4.

68 Comte de Béhague to Minister of Marine, 20 September 1792, Colonies C⁷ᴬ 45, 153–4.

69 Comte de Béhague and Petit de Viévigne to Minister of Marine, 23 September 1792, Colonies C⁸ᴬ 99, 25.

70 Comte de Béhague to Minister of Marine, 25 September 1792, Colonies C⁸ᴬ 99, 52.

71 "Copie de la lettre du comité intermédiaire de l'assemblée coloniale de la Martinique à MM. les armateurs et négociants des ports de France, 19 septembre 1792," Colonies C⁸ᴬ 100, 56–9.

72 Lettre de l'assemblée coloniale de la Guadeloupe à MM. les armateurs et négo-cians des ports de France. À la Guadeloupe, le 29 septembre 1792 (Basse-Terre: Imprimerie de la colonie, 1792), Colonies C⁷ᴬ 45, 233. See also Lacour, 2: 104–5.

73 "Déclaration de Jacques-Jérémie Paige, 19 octobre 1792," Colonies C⁸ᴬ 99, 131.

74 "Copie du rapport de M. Henry, 23 octobre 1792," Colonies C⁷ᴬ 45, 177.

75 Comte de Béhague to Baron de Constant, 20 September 1792, included in Béhague, "Réponse aux questions générales de la lettre de M. le comte de la Chapelle, Deuxième Partie (1798)," Colonies C⁸ᴬ 103, 55. Béhague does not clarify how he expected the princes to obtain ships or troops, given that only Austria and Prussia were then at war with France, or why he thought the British government would provide any guarantees under the Treaty of Pilnitz, which it had not signed.

76 Valous, ed., Avec le "rouges" aux Îles du Vent, 144.

77 Béhague, "Réponse à l'extrait de lettre communiqué au comte de Béhague par M. le comte de la Chapelle, et à la lettre de cet officier général,

Première Partie (1798)," Colonies C⁸ᴬ 103, 25. See also Lémery, 163–4 and Valous, ed., *Avec les "rouges" aux Îles du Vent*, 149–52.

78 Lémery, 168–9. See also Lacour, 2: 107–8.

79 Mallevault, "Copie du Journal de *la Calypso* du 22 septembre au 15 octobre 1792," Marine BB 4 / 12, 62–3.

80 *Mémoire pour le citoyen Louis-Charles-François Malleveault, détenu dans les prisons de la force, accusé d'avoir vendu à l'Espagne, étant en guerre avec la France, la frégate la Calipso qu'il commandait, et d'avoir livré la Martinique aux Anglais* (n.p., n.d.), Marine BB 4 / 26, 5–12.

81 Valous, ed., *Avec les "rouges" aux Îles du Vent*, pp. 72, 79, 88, 93–4, 119, 158.

82 Ibid., 127.

83 Dermigny and Debien, eds., "Journal maritime du commandeur de Villevielle," 266–7.

84 Duval's report to the National Convention, 5 November 1792, followed by discussion and the proposal of a decree of accusation against Fitzmaurice, D'Arrot, Mallevault, Béhague, Rivière and others, see AP, vol. 53, 314–16.

85 See Chevalier de Rivière to Minister of Marine, 8 August 1792 and attached *Procès-verbal* submitted by the *Didon*'s officers, Marine BB 4 / 12, 25–9. See also "Extrait du journal de la corvette de l'état *La Perdrix* commandée par M. Duval, lieutenant de Vaisseau, pendant son séjour à la Pointe-à-Pitre du 23 juillet au 31 du même mois 1792," Marine BB 4 / 12, 34–7.

86 Valous, ed., *Avec les "rouges" aux Îles du Vent*, pp. 137–43. See also Dermigny and Debien, eds., "Journal maritime du commandeur de Villevielle," 270–1.

87 "Rapport du lieuteneant Robert Rougemont, commandant l'aviso de la république *le Ballon*, armé de dix canons de trois de balle, sur les differents événements arrivé aux îles du vent depuis le 16 septembre jusques et compris le 3 décembre, jour de son évasion de ces colonies, 10 décembre 1792," Colonies C⁸ᴬ 100, 90–3. See also *Jugement du tribunal criminel et révolutionnaire … qui condamné à la peine de mort, Claude-Robert de Rougemont, Louis-Henri-Marie Montécler et Charles-Marie Keréon … 21 pluviôse l'an II*, reproduced in Philippe Henwood and Edmond Monage, *Brest: Un port en révolution, 1789–1799* (Rennes, 1989), 193.

88 See Charles-Joseph Mascarène, chevalier de Rivière, *Extrait du journal de ma station aux Îles du Vent*, (Fort-Royal, Martinique: Imprimerie de J.F. Bazille, n.d.), 1–2 and Comte de La Luzerne to President of the National Assembly, 17 September 1790, AP, vol. 19, 47. Regarding the mutiny of the fleet at Brest, see William S. Cormack, *Revolution and Political Conflict in the*

French Navy, 1789–1794 (Cambridge: Cambridge University Press, 1995), 85–97, 104–8.

89 Minister of Marine to Chevalier de Rivière, 5 September 1790, and "Mémoire du roi pour servir d'Instruction particulière au sieur Chevalier de Rivière, chef de division des armées navales, commandant la station des Isles sous le Vent," Marine BB 4 / 3, 229–37.

90 See for example *Jugement rendu par le conseil militaire assemblée à bord du vaisseau La Ferme, mouillé en rade du Fort-Royal, Isle Martinique, 4 janvier 1792* (Fort-Royal: Imprimerie de P. Richard et Le Cadre, n.d.) and *Jugement rendu par le conseil de guerre tenu à bord du vaisseau La Ferme* (Fort-Royal: Imprimerie de P. Richard et Le Cadre, n.d.), in Marine BB 4 / 12, 10, 47.

91 Chevalier de Rivière to Minister of Marine, 20 October 1792; Marine BB 4 / 12, 40.

92 Chevalier de Rivière to Minister of Marine, 19 November 1792; Marine BB 4 / 12, 41–50.

93 "Copie de l'ordre donné par M. de Rivière au citoyen Lacrosse, 28 décembre 1792," Marine BB 4 / 12, 50.

94 Minister of Marine to Captain Lacrosse, 29 and 30 September 1792, Marine BB 4 / 12, 99, 100. Lacrosse was born at Meilhan (Lot-et-Garonne) in 1760 and entered the navy as a member of the exclusively aristocratic *gardes de la marine* in 1778. He served in the American War in squadrons commanded by Guichen in the Caribbean and Suffren de Saint-Tropez in the Indian Ocean. He was promoted to *Lieutenant de Vaisseau* in 1786 and served in the *Cléopâtre* in the West Indies in 1790. See Etienne Taillemite, *Dictionnaire des marins français* (Paris: Éditions Maritimes et d'Outre-Mer, 1982), 187. See also Alfred Veilhon, *Le contre-amiral de Lacrosse: Gouverneur-général de la Guadeloupe, 1792–1793 and 1801–1802* (Agen: Imprimerie de l'Agenais, 1933), 13.

95 "Mémoire pour servir d'instructions particuliéres au citoyen Lacrosse, capitaine de vaisseau, commandant la frégate *La Félicité*, 3 octobre 1792," Marine BB 4 / 12, 101–2. These instructions also appear within "Pièce no. 14" following "Compte rendu à ses concitoyens par le capitaine Lacrosse, commandant la frégate de la république, *La Félicité*, de sa mission aux Isles-du-Vent de l'Amérique, pendant les années 1792 à 1793," AP, vol. 76, 521.

96 Captain Lacrosse to Minister of Marine, 26 September 1792, Marine BB 4 / 12, 107.

97 Captain Lacrosse to Minister of Marine, 5 and 8 October 1792, Marine BB 4 / 12, 108, 109.

98 Captain Lacrosse to _____ ("Mon camarade et ami"), 10 October 1792, Marine BB 4 / 12, 110–11.

99 Captain Lacrosse to Minister of Marine, 10 October 1792, Marine BB 4 / 12, 112.

100 "Pièce no. 3: Reseignements à prendre par l'officier qui ira à terre. Questions à faire," AP, vol. 76, 517.

101 Devers to Minister of Marine, 9 December 1792, Colonies C⁸ᴬ 100, 130–1. Regarding the murder of the patriot priest Father Macaire, allegedly by men of colour from Fort-Royal on the night of 9–10 October, see Daney, 3: 172–5.

102 "Pièce no. 4: Lettre écrite à mon arrivée devant la Martinique à Béhague, gouverneur général des Îles du Vent, 1 décembre 1792," AP vol. 76, 517.

103 Captain Lacrosse to Minister of Marine, 20 December 1792, Colonies C⁷ᴬ 45, 165. See also "Rapport du lieutenant Robert Rougemont … 10 décembre 1792" and Devers to Minister of Marine, 9 December 1792, Colonies C⁸ᴬ 100, 93, 132.

104 Captain Lacrosse to Minister of Marine, 20 December 1792, Colonies C⁷ᴬ 45, 166. See also Devers to Minister of Marine, 9 December 1792, Colonies C⁸ᴬ 100, 133.

105 "Pièce no. 7: Ma lettre au général Bruce, gouverneur de la Dominique, 3 décembre 1792" and "Pièce no. 8: Réponse de gouverneur Bruce, à ma lettre du 3 décembre 1792, 4 décembre 1792," AP vol. 76, 518.

106 "Compte rendu … Lacrosse," AP vol. 76, 509. See also Captain Lacrosse to Minister of Marine, 20 December 1792, Colonies C⁷ᴬ 45, 166.

107 *La dernier moyen de conciliation entre la mère patrie, et les colonies révoltées, adressé par le citoyen Lacrosse, capitaine de Vaisseaux de la république Française, commandant la frégate La Félicité, à tous les habitans, ses frères and ses amis* (À bord de la Frégate *la Félicité*, sur rade de Roseau, Dominique, le 4eme Décembre 1792), Colonies C⁸ᴬ 100, 5. See also "Piéce no. 6," AP vol. 76, 517–18.

108 Captain Lacrosse to Minister of Marine, 8 December 1792; Marine BB 4 / 12, 114–15.

109 *Le Dernier Moyen de conciliation*, Colonies C⁸ᴬ 100, 5.

110 *Précis des Nouvelles de la convention nationale et du succès des armes de la ré-publique Française, apportées par la frégate la Félicité, capitaine Lacrosse; depuis le 20 septembre 1792 jusqu'au 24 octobre, jour du départ de cette frégate de la rade de Brest*, Marine BB 4 / 12, 116–23.

111 Devers to Minister of Marine, 9 December 1792, Colonies C⁸ᴬ 100, 134.

112 Captain Lacrosse to Minister of Marine, 20 December 1792, Colonies C^{7A} 45, 166.

113 "Compte rendu … Lacrosse"; AP, vol. 76, 510. See also Devers to Minister of Marine, 19 December 1792, Colonies C^{8A} 100, 144.

114 See "Piéce no. 10: À Marguenat, gouverneur de Tobago, 12 décembre 1792" and "Piéce no. 11: Réponse de Marguenat, gouverneur de Tobago, à ma lettre, 16 décembre 1792," AP, vol. 76, 519–20.

115 "Pièce no. 9: Ma lettre au général Rochambeau, à Saint-Domingue, 16 décembre 1792," AP, vol. 76, 518–19.

116 "Pièce no. 12: Au commandant des forces de Mer de la Grande-Bretagne, en station aux Îles-du-Vent, 22 décembre 1792," AP, vol. 76, 520.

117 Captain Lacrosse to Minister of Marine, 20 December 1792, Colonies C^{7A} 45, 167.

118 *Proclamation. Jean-Pierre-Antoine de Béhague, lieutenant-général des armées du roi, gouverneur-général des Îles du Vent, commandant en chef des forces de terre et de mer, 13 décembre 1792* (Fort-Royal: Imprimerie de P. Richard et Le Cadre, 1792), Colonies C^{8A} 99, 91. See also Daney, 3: 178–80.

119 *Observations sur la proclamation de Béhague; adressées par le citoyen Lacrosse à tous ses concitoyens. Le 25 décembre 1792, l'an premier de la république fran- çaise* (Saint-Lucie: Imprimerie du patriote des Antilles-Françaises, 1792), Colonies C^{8A} 100, 8. See also "Pièce no. 14," AP, vol. 76, 520–2.

120 Devers to Minister of Marine, 14 December 1792, Colonies C^{8A} 100, 142–3.

121 *Réponse à l'arrêté du soi-disant comité intermédiaire de l'assemblée coloniale de la Guadeloupe, en date du 10 décembre 1792. Adressé à tous les français patriots* (Roseau, Dominque, le 19 décembre 1792), Colonies C^{8A} 100, 7.

122 *Extrait des procès-verbaux de l'assemblée coloniale de l'Isle Sainte-Lucie-la- Fidéle, l'an premier de la république. Séance du matin, 22 décembre 1792* (n.p., n.d.), Colonies C^{8A} 100, 152–3.

123 Captain Lacrosse to Minister of Marine, 20 December 1792, Colonies C^{7A} 45, 167–9.

124 Devers to Minister of Marine, 19 December 1792, Colonies C^{8A} 100, 145.

125 See "Réponse à l'extrait de lettre communiqué au comte de Béhague par M. le comte de La Chapelle, et à la lettre de cet officier général, Première Partie (1798)," Colonies C^{8A} 103, 14–15. See also Lémery, 170–2.

126 See "Extrait de la lettre du Cougnac-Myon, de Kingston, le 23 juillet 1793, au marquis de Castries," including Béhague's marginal notes, and "Réponse du comte de Béhague à la Proclamation, 29 janvier 1793" within Béhague's larger work of self-justification of 1798: "Réponse à l'extrait de lettre comminiqué au comte de Béhague par M. le comte de

La Chapelle, et à la lettre de cet officier général, Première Partie (1798)," Colonies C⁸ᴬ 103, 17–32.

127 Lémery, 174–80. See also Valous, ed., *Avec les "rouges"aux Îles du Vent*, 151–2.

128 Devers to Minister of Marine, 19 December 1792, Colonies C⁸ᴬ 100, 145–6.

129 "Copie d'une lettre écrite au citoyen Pierre Texier de Bordeaux par le citoyen Cadiot fils, de la Pointe-à-Pitre, 20 décembre 1792," Colonies C⁷ᴬ 45, 171–2.

130 "Copie d'une lettre écrite au citoyen Pierre Texier, négociant de Bordeaux, par le citoyen Cadiot fils, de la Pointe-à-Pitre, 23 décembre 1792," Colonies C⁷ᴬ 45, 173.

131 René-Marie d'Arrot to the comte de Béhague, 6 January 1793, in "Réponse à l'extrait de lettre communiqué au comte de Béhague," Colonies C⁸ᴬ 103, 21–2. For the perspective of Basse-Terre's patriots, see Chambert Ainé to an officer of the merchantman *Union de Bordeaux*, 29 December 1792, quoted in Bangou, 53–4. See also Valous, ed., *Avec les "rouges" aux Îles du Vent*, 157–65, Pérotin-Dumon, *Être patriote sous les tropiques*, 162–76 and Lacour, 2: 126–9.

132 "Pièce no. 15: Aux marins du commerce de France à la Pointe-à-Pitre, 30 décembre 1792," AP, vol. 76, 522.

133 "Compte rendu … Lacrosse," AP, vol. 76, 510. See also Lacour, 2: 131 and Saintoyant, 1: 219.

134 *Adresse des citoyens de couleur de la Martinique, à l'assemblée coloniale, séante au Lamentin, le 9 janvier 1793* (Martinique: Imprimerie de P. Richard et Le Cadre, 1793), Colonies C⁸ᴬ 102, 137–9. See also Élizabeth, "La république dans les Îles du Vent," 385. Regarding the reasons for free-coloured support of the republic in Martinique and Guadeloupe, and its implications, see Dubois, *Colony of Citizens*, 119–23.

135 "Proclamation de l'assemblée coloniale aux émigrés de la Martinique, 13 janvier 1793," Colonies C⁸ᴬ 102, 6–7. See also "Reponse du comte de Béhague à la Proclamation, 29 janvier 1793," Colonies C⁸ᴬ 103, 27–33. See also Daney, 3: 180–1.

136 Captain Lacrosse to Minister of Marine, 18 January 1793, Colonies C⁸ᴬ 102, 1–4. See also Valous, ed., *Avec les "rouges" aux Îles du Vent*, 166–8, and the Chevalier de Rivière to the Comte de Béhague, 20 February 1793, Colonies C⁸ᴬ 103, 57.

137 President of Martinique's Colonial Assembly to Captain Lacrosse, 13 January 1793, Colonies C⁸ᴬ 102, 5.

138 "Extrait de délibérations de l'assemblée coloniale de la Martinique en sa séance du 13 janvier 1793," Colonies C⁸ᴬ 102, 7–8. For a related statement

of the colony's new-found devotion to the republic, but with specific reference to administrative officers who loyally remained at their posts, see *ordonnateur* Petit de Viévigne to Minister of Marine, 20 January 1793, Colonies C^{8A} 99, 168.

6 The Slave-Holding Republic

1 Captain Lacrosse to Minister of Marine, 12 January 1793, Colonies C^{7A} 46, 169–70.

2 "Les citoyens du couleur de la Pointe-à-Pitre au citoyen Lacrosse, 8 janvier 1793," Colonies C^{7A} 46, 181.

3 Captain Lacrosse to Minister of Marine, 12 January 1793; see also *Précis du compte rendu par les députies de la ville Basse-Terre, auprès du citoyen Lacrosse, capitaine des vaisseaux de la république, commandant la frégate la Félicité, mouillé à la Pointe-à-Pitre; imprimé suivant la délibération prise le 11 janvier 1793 par les citoyens leurs constituans*, Colonies C^{7A} 46, 174, 182–5.

4 "Extrait de la délibération de l'assemblée coloniale de la Martinique dans sa séance du 9 janvier 1793," Colonies C^{8A} 102, 39.

5 Captain Lacrosse to Minister of Marine, 18 January 1793, Colonies C^{8A} 102, 1–4.

6 President of Martinique's Colonial Assembly to Captain Lacrosse, 13 January 1793 and "Extrait des délibérations de l'assemblée coloniale de la Martinique en sa séance du 13 janvier 1793," Colonies C^{8A} 102, 5–7.

7 *Proclamation de l'assemblée coloniale de la Martinique, aux émigrés de la Martinique, du 13 janvier 1793, l'an second de la république française* (Fort-Royal: Imprimerie de P. Richard, 1793), Colonies C^{8A} 102, 41.

8 Martinique's Executive Council to Minister of Marine, 18 January 1793, Colonies C^{8A} 102, 104–6. See also "Extrait du compte-rendu envoyé à la convention par l'assemblée coloniale de la Martinique, le 21 janvier 1793," Colonies C^{8A} 103, 35–6.

9 "Copie de la lettre du citoyen Lacrosse, aux citoyens députés de l'assemblée coloniale de la Martinique à Sainte-Lucie, 17 janvier 1793"; see also "Copie de la lettre du citoyen Lacrosse aux représentants de la Martinique, 16 janvier 1793," Colonies C^{8A} 102, 8–10.

10 Lacrosse, "Compte rendu," AP, vol. 76, 510.

11 Captain Lacrosse to Minister of Marine, 1 February 1793, Colonies C^{7A} 46, 175–6. See also "Pièce #17: Le citoyen Lacrosse aux citoyens habitants de la Guadeloupe (n.d.)," AP, vol. 76, 523–4 and Régent, 239–40 and Lacour, 2: 131–6.

12 "Pièce # 18: Extrait de la commission générale et extraordinaire de la Guadeloupe, séance du 24 janvier de l'an II de la république française," AP, vol. 76, 524.

13 Régent, 241–2.

14 See *Extrait des registres de la commission générale et extraordinaire de la Guadeloupe, séante à la Pointe-à-Pitre. Séance du 29 janvier, l'an 2 de la république française* (Pointe-à-Pitre: Imprimerie de la colonie, 1793) and *Extrait des registres de la commission générale et extraordinaire de la Guadeloupe, séante à la Pointe-à-Pitre. Séance du 31 janvier, l'an 2 de la république française* (Pointe-à-Pitre: Imprimerie de la colonie, 1793), Colonies C[7A] 46, 188, 189.

15 Captain Lacrosse to Minister of Marine, 1 February 1793, Colonies C[7A] 46, 179.

16 General Rochambeau to Minister of Marine, 10 February 1793, Colonies C[8A] 101, 43–4.

17 "Pièce # 20: Le ministre de la marine au citoyen Lacrosse, commandant la Félicité à Saint-Domingue, Paris, le 9 novembre 1793 l'an I de la république," AP, vol. 76, 524–5.

18 "Copie de la lettre du Lieutenant Général Rochambeau à l'assemblée coloniale de la Guadeloupe, à la Pointe-á-Pitre á bord de la Félicité, le 1er février 1793," Colonies C[8A] 101, 47.

19 "Copie des pouvoirs donnés au citoyen Lacrosse, par le citoyen Rochambeau, lieutenant général des armées de la République, commandant-générale des Îles du Vent, à la Pointe-à-Pitre, 1 février 1793," Colonies C[8A] 101, 111. See also Lacrosse, "Compte rendu" and "Pièce #21: Donatien Rochambeau, au nom de la république française, 1 février 1793," AP, vol. 76, 511, 525.

20 Captain Lacrosse to Minister of Marine, 13 February 1793, Colonies C[8A] 102, 12–13.

21 General Rochambeau to Minister of Marine, 10 February 1793, Colonies C[8A] 101, 45. See also Daney, 184 and Lémery, 209.

22 *Proclamation. Nous Donatien-Marie-Joseph Vimeur Rochambeau, lieutenant-général des armées de la république, gouverneur-général de la Martinique et commandant-général des Îles du Vent, à tous les homees libres de la colonie, 4 février 1793* (Fort-de-la-République: Imprimerie de P. Richard and Le Cadre, 1793), Colonies C[8A] 101, 148.

23 General Rochambeau to Minister of Marine, 10 February 1793, Colonies C[8A] 101, 45.

24 Commissioner of War Leborgne to Minister of Marine, 7 March 1793, Colonies C[8A] 102, 116. See also Captain Lacrosse to Minister of Marine,

13 February 1793, Colonies C^{8A} 102, 16. Regarding the formation of the clubs at Saint-Pierre and Fort-de-la-République, and their subsequent formal approval of Louis XVI's execution, see also Daney, 3: 185–6, 188 and Lémery, 214–15.

25 *Proclamation. Nous Donatien-Marie-Joseph Vimeur Rochambeau, lieutenant-général des armées de la république, gouverneur-général de la Martinique et commandant-général des Isles françaises du Vent, à tous les hommes libres de la colonie, 8 février 1793* (Fort-de-la-République: Imprimerie de P. Richard and Le Cadre, 1793), Colonies C^{8A} 101, 149.

26 General Rochambeau to Minister of Marine, 10 February 1793, Colonies C^{8A} 101, 46.

27 Commissioner of War Lebogne to Minister of Marine, 7 March 1793, Colonies C^{8A} 102, 114–17. Captain Lacrosse to Minister of Marine, 13 February 1793 places similar importance on support from white patriots and new citizens to preserve the colonies for France, Colonies C^{8A} 102, 15.

28 "Extrait de la lettre d'Aquart, habitant de la Point la Borgnese [Martinique], à son fils à la nouvelle angleterre, en date du 9 février 1793," Colonies C^{8A} 102, 20–1. See also "Pièce # 33: Extrait de la lettre d'Acquart, planteur de la Martinique, habitant du Marin, à son fils," AP, vol. 76, 530.

29 "Copie de la lettre circulaire écrite aux gouverneurs étrangers par le lieutenant-général Rochambeau en leur addressant les decrets de la Convention Nationale du 21 et 25 septembre 1792; au Fort-de-la-République ci-devant Fort-Royal de la Martinique, 9 février 1793," Colonies C^{8A} 101, 117. Rochambeau demanded that the governor of Trinidad return the French Navy's ships "seized and stolen" by Rivière: "Copie de la lettre écrite par le lieutenant-général Rochambeau au gouverneur de la Trinité Espagnole, au Fort-de-la-République, ci-devant Fort-Royal, de la Martinique, le 9 février 1793," Colonies C^{8A} 101, 116. He also restored the restrictions on trade benefiting French merchants: *Proclamation. Nous Donatien-Marie-Joseph Vimeur Rochambeau, lieutenant-général des armées de la république, gouverneur-général de la Martinique et commandant-général des Îles du Vent, à tous les hommes libres de la Martinique, 16 février 1793* (Saint-Pierre: J.B. Thounens, 1793), Colonies C^{8A} 101, 150.

30 Commissioner of War Leborgne to Minister of Marine, 7 March 1793, Colonies C^{8A} 102, 117. See also "Extrait des registres du contrôle de la Marine à la Martinique, 17 mars 1793," and *Proclamation. Nous Donatien-Marie-Joseph Vimeur Rochambeau, lieutenant-général des armées de la république, gouverneur-général de la Martinique et commandant-général des isles françaises du Vent de l'Amérique, 1 avril 1793* (Fort-de-la-République: F.J. Willox, 1793), Colonies C^{8A} 101, 163–4, 152.

31 *Proclamation. Nous Donatien-Marie-Joseph Vimeur Rochambeau, lieutenant-général des armées de la république, gouverneur-général de la Martinique et commandant-général des isles françaises du Vent de l'Amérique, 14 mars 1793* (Fort-de-la-République: F.J. Willox, 1793), Colonies C⁸ᴬ 101, 151.

32 "Extrait d'une lettre datée de St. François, le 15 mars 1793 et signée Desjardins de Saint-Pierre. Elle est addressée à Monsieur Mounier de Saint-Pierre à Roseau, Dominique," Colonies C⁸ᴬ 102, 33. See also "Pièce # 26: Extrait de la lettre de Mme de Saint-Pierre, à la Guadeloupe, à son mari, émigré, à la Dominique. Saint-François, ce 15 mars 1793," AP, vol. 76, 526.

33 See "Pièce # 22: Extrait du registre des délibérations du conseil générale de la commune de la ville de Basse-Terre, Guadeloupe, 4 février 1793" and "Pièce # 23; Ordre d'embarquement donné au général Collot par le général Rochambeau, fait au Cap, le 4 janvier 1793," AP, vol. 76, 525–6. See also "Copie de la lettre écrite par le citoyen Maire de la Basse-Terre, Guadeloupe, à la chambre administrative en date du 4 février 1793" and "Copie de la lettre écrite par le Général Collot à la chambre administrative, dattée de la Basse-Terre, le 4 février 1793," Colonies C⁸ᴬ 101, 112, 113.

34 "Copie de la lettre du citoyen Collot au Gouverneur provisoire des Isles Guadeloupe et dépendances addressée à la chambre administrative, à la Basse-Terre, Guadeloupe, le 24 février 1793," Colonies C⁸ᴬ 101, 118.

35 "Copie de la letter écrite de la Basse-Terre, île Guadeloupe, le 24 février 1793, par le citoyen Lacrosse au Général Rochambeau," Colonies C⁸ᴬ 101, 114.

36 "Copie de la lettre écrite par les membres de la chambre administrative de la Pointe-à-Pitre, Isle Guadeloupe, au citoyen gouverneur-général, du 25 février 1793," Colonies C⁸ᴬ 101, 120.

37 Lacrosse, "Compte rendu," AP, vol. 76, 512.

38 *Précis des Événemens qui se sont passés à la Guadeloupe pendant l'administration de George-Henry-Victor Collot, depuis le 20 mars 1793 jusqu'au 22 avril 1794. Présenté à la convention nationale* (Philadelphia, PA: Thomas Bradford, 1795), 4, Colonies C⁷ᴬ 46, 17.

39 "Copie de la lettre écrite au citoyen Lacrosse, commandant militaire de la Guadeloupe, [par Rochambeau] du Fort-de-la-République, le 26 février 1793," Colonies C⁸ᴬ 101, 121.

40 "Copie de la lettre écrite au citoyen Lacrosse, commandant militaire de la Guadeloupe, [par Rochambeau] du Fort-de-la-République, le 27 février 1793," Colonies C⁸ᴬ 101, 122.

41 "Copie de la lettre écrite au gouverneur-général des Îles du Vent par le capitaine Lacrosse, Basse-Terre, Guadeloupe, ce 2 mars 1793," Colonies C⁸ᴬ 101, 126.

42 "Copie de la lettre du citoyen Lacrosse, gouverneur provisoire des isles Guadeloupe, au citoyen président de la commission générale et extraordinaire de la Guadeloupe, à la Pointe-à-Pitre isle Guadeloupe, ce 10 mars 1793," Colonies C^{8A} 101, 131–2.

43 "Copie de la lettre du général Collot à la commission générale et extraordinaire séante à la Pointe-à-Pitre, daté de la Basse-Terre ce 4 mars 1793," Colonies C^{8A} 101, 127–8.

44 "Copie de la lettre du citoyen Collot, gouverneur de la Guadeloupe, au citoyen gouverneur-général des Îles du Vent, daté de la Basse-Terre, le 11 mars 1793" and "Extrait des registres de la commission général et extraordinaire de la Guadeloupe séante à la Pointe-à-Pitre, le 14 mars 1793," Colonies C^{8A} 101, 133–4. See also "Pièce # 24," AP, vol. 76, 526.

45 See "Copie de la lettre du citoyen Lacrosse, gouverneur provisoire de la Guadeloupe, au citoyen président de la commission générale et extraordinaire de la Guadeloupe, à la Pointe-à-Pitre isle Guadeloupe, le 14 mars 1793" and "Copie de la lettre écrite au citoyen Général Rochambeau, commandant général des Îles du Vent, [par Lacrosse] à la Pointe-à-Pitre isle Guadeloupe, ce 15 mars 1793," Colonies C^{8A} 101, 135, 136. See also "Pièce # 25," AP, vol. 76, 526.

46 "Copie de la lettre écrite au capitaine Lacrosse, du Fort-de-la-République, le 18 mars 1793, l'an 2 de la République française, par le Général Rochambeau," Colonies C^{8A} 101, 137.

47 "Pièce # 27: Extrait des registres de la commission général et extraordinaire de la Guadeloupe, séant à la Pointe-à-Pitre, le 20 mars 1793, l'an II de la République française," AP, vol. 76, 526–7. See also *Pièce justificative* #1 following Collot, *Précis des événemens*, 39; "Extrait de la lettre du citoyen Lacrosse, à la commission générale et extraordinaire, Basse-Terre, le 18 mars 1793," Colonies C^{7A} 46, 35.

48 See "Pièce # 29: Adresse des nouveaux citoyens de la Basse-Terre, au citoyen Lacrosse, gouverneur provisoire de la Guadeloupe, 3 mars 1793," "Piéce #30: Société des amis de la république française, séante à la Basse-Terre-Guadeloupe, le 25 mars, au citoyen Lacrosse," and "Adresse du conseil générale de la commune de la Basse-Terre, île de Guadeloupe, au citoyen Lacrosse, gouverneur de la dite île, du 4 mars 1793, l'an II de la république française," AP, vol. 76, 527–9.

49 "Extrait d'une letter écrite de la Pointe-à-Pitre, Guadeloupe, le 25 mars 1793, par le citoyen Caussade, habitant sucrier et officier municipale élu après la fuite des contre-révolutionnaires par le peuple légalement assemblée, adressée au citoyen Curieux Jeune, négociant à Bordeaux, son beau-frère, par le navire la Thérèsa de Nantes," Colonies C^{7A} 46, 215–17.

Pérotin-Dumon, *Être patriote sous les tropiques*,180 suggests that patriots who had returned from exile never accepted Lacrosse's replacement, while those who sought metropolitan pardon for having remained in Guadeloupe under the royalist government in 1792 recognized Collot as governor.

50 *Discours prononcé à la commission général et extraordinaire par le citoyen général Collot, séance du 23 mars 1793, l'an 2 de la république* (Pointe-à-Pitre: Imprimerie de la colonie, 1793), Colonies C⁷ᴬ 46, 50.

51 *Proclamation. Georges-Henri-Victor Collot, maréchal des camps et armées de la république française, à tous les citoyens libres de la Guadeloupe, le 23 mars 1793, l'an 2 de la république française* (Basse-Terre: Imprimerie républicaine de la veuve Bénard et Villette, 1793), Colonies C⁷ᴬ 46, 52.

52 General Collot to Minister of Marine, 25 March 1793, Colonies C⁷ᴬ 46, 57.

53 General Collot to Minister of Marine, 25 March 1793, Colonies C⁷ᴬ 46, 57–8.

54 Collot, *Précis des événemens*, 4–5, Colonies C⁷ᴬ 46, 17–18.

55 General Collot to Minister of Marine, 30 March 1793, Colonies C⁷ᴬ 46, 59–61.

56 *Lettre écrite par le citoyen gouverneur à la commission générale et extraordinaire, le 31 mars 1793, l'an second de la république française*; "Extrait du volume 6, no. 11, *Gazette nationale et politique*, mardi, 16 avril 1793, l'an 2e de la république française," Colonies C⁷ᴬ 46, 71. See also "Pièce #28," AP, vol. 76, 527.

57 "Nous commissaires délégués par la comission générale extraordinaire pour accompagner le citoyen gouverneur dans sa tournée, aux fins de constater l'état actuel de la colonie, 1 avril 1793," Colonies C⁷ᴬ 46, 75.

58 See *Lettre écrite par le citoyen gouverneur à la commission générale et extraordinaire de la Guadeloupe, Basse-Terre-Guadeloupe, le 5 avril 1793, l'an second de la république française* (Basse-Terre: Imprimerie républicaine de la veuve Bernard et d'Al. Villette, 1793) and General Collot to Minister of Marine, 10 April 1793, Colonies C⁷ᴬ 46, 78, 62.

59 *Lettre écrite par le citoyen gouverneur à la commission … 5 avril 1793*, Colonies C⁷ᴬ 46, 78.

60 General Collot to municipal officers, 5 April 1793, Colonies C⁷ᴬ 46, 79.

61 *Lettre écrit par le citoyen gouverneur à la commission générale et extraordinaire de la Guadeloupe. À la Basse-Terre, le 7 avril 1793, l'an second de la république française* (Basse-Terre-Guadeloupe: Imprimerie républicaine française de la veuve Benard et d'Al. Villette, 1793), Colonies C⁷ᴬ 46, 80.

62 *Mes principes sur la puissance militaire dans une république, pour détruire toutes les calomnies et les inquiétudes de quelques citoyens que l'on trompe. À la Basse-Terre, le 8 avril 1793, l'an second de la république française* (Basse-Terre: Imprimerie républicaine de la veuve Benard et d'Al. Villette, 1793), Colonies C⁷ᴬ 46, 81.

63 *Au nom de la république française. Nous Georges-Henri-Victor Collot, maréchal des camps et armées de la république française, gouverneur des îles Guadeoupe et dépendances, le 18 avril 1793, l'an 2e de la république française,* (Basse-Terre: Imprimerie républicaine de la veuve Benard et d'Al. Villette, 1793), Colonies C⁷ᴬ 46, 90.

64 Duffy, 16–31.

65 "Réponse du comte de Béhague à la proclamation [du 13 janvier 1793], de St-Vincent, le 29 janvier 1793," Colonies C⁸ᴬ 103, 31.

66 Chevalier de Rivière to Comte de Béhague, 20 February and 23 January 1793, Colonies C⁸ᴬ 103, 57.

67 R. Jourdan, from Saint-Pierre, Martinique, to Captain Lacrosse, 3 February 1793, Colonies C⁸ᴬ 102, 17–19. See also Valous, ed., *Avec les "rouges" aux Îles du Vent*, 169–78.

68 See Comte de Béhague to the chevalier de Rivière, 12 March 1793, and Béhague, "Compte Rendu: 2ème partie," Colonies C⁸ᴬ 103, 58–9, 60–1. See also Valous, ed., *Avec les "rouges" aux Îles du Vent*, 178–85.

69 The chevalier de Rivière, from Trinidad, to Comte de Béhague, 28 April 1793 and, from Puerto-Cabello, to the Princes, 11 September 1793, Colonies C⁸ᴬ 103, 64, 134–5. See also Valous, ed., *Avec les "rouges" aux Îles du Vent*, 185–7.

70 Lacrosse, "Compte rendu," AP, vol. 76, 513. See also Daney, 3: 192–9 and Lémery, 231–2.

71 "Dispositif de la proclamation du général Rochambeau du 17 avril 1793," Colonies C⁸ᴬ 102, 34. See also "Pièce #34: Dispositif de la proclamation du général Rochambeau contre les camps et attroupements des rebelles planteurs de la Martinique," AP, vol. 76, 530. Clerks also abandoned Martinique's administrative offices in Fort-de-la-République after 16 April, thus paralysing colonial administration: Ordonnateur d'Aigremont to Minister of Marine, 8 May 1793, Colonies C⁸ᴬ 101, 165.

72 Intermediate Committee of Martinique's Colonial Assembly, from Lamentin, to General Rochambeau, 23 April 1793, Colonies C⁸ᴬ 102, 35–36. See also "Pièce # 35," AP, vol. 76, 530–1.

73 "Journal du Blocus et du Siège de la Martinique [27 avril - 26 juin 1793] par Général Rochambeau," Colonies C⁸ᴬ 101, 55. See also Lacrosse, "Compte Rendu," AP, vol. 76, 513 and Daney, 3: 205–6 and Lémery, 233.

74 Chevalier de Rivière, "Extrait de mon journal renfermant simplement les faits qui ont eu lieu depuis mon départ de la Trinité Espagnol [1 mai–16 août 1793], 11 septembre 1793," Colonies C⁸ᴬ 103, 138.

75 See Béhague, "Compte Rendu: 2ème Partie," and Rivière, "Extrait de mon journal," Colonies C⁸ᴬ 103, 63–5, 137. See also Valous, ed., *Avec les "rouges" aux Îles du Vent*, 187–9.

76 Comte de Béhague to Major-General Bruce, 13 May 1793, Colonies C^{8A} 103, 65–7. See also Béhague, "Compte Rendu: 2ème Partie," Colonies C^{8A} 103, 68–72.

77 *Proclamation. Nous Donatien, Marie-Joseph, Vimeur Rochambeau, lieutenant-général des armée de la république, gouverneur-général de la Martinique, et commandant-général des îles Françaises du vent de l'Amérique, 2 mai 1793, l'an 2ème de la République Française* (Fort-de-la République, Isle Martinique: F.J. Willox, Imprimeur du Gouvernement, 1793), Colonies C^{8A} 101, 153.

78 Dubuc *fils* and Clairfontaine, from Roseau, Dominica, to "X" in London, 26 June–8 July 1793, Colonies C^{8A} 102, 149. According to Lémery, 233–4 the club *Amis de la Convention* declared on 2 May that, "les patriotes ne marcheraient en campagne que la torche d'une main et la Déclaration des Droits de l'Homme de l'autre," and that the governor would be asked to accord liberty provisionally to slaves who would fight under the national flag.

79 Rivière, "Extrait de mon journal," Colonies C^{8A} 103, 138–9. See also Rochambeau, "Journal du Blocus et du Siège de la Matinique," Colonies C^{8A} 101, 56.

80 Lacrosse, "Compte Rendu," AP, vol. 76, 513.

81 Rochambeau, "Journal du Blocus et du Siège de la Martinique," Colonies C^{8A} 101, 58–60.

82 Ibid, Colonies C^{8A} 101, 60–3. See also Lacrosse, "Compte Rendu," AP, vol. 76, 514 and Daney, 203–5.

83 Dubuc *fils* and Clairfontaine, from Roseau, Dominica, to "X" in London, 26 June–8 July 1793, Colonies C^{8A} 102, 148–9.

84 See Rochambeau, "Journal du Blocus et du Siège de la Martinique," Colonies C^{8A} 101, 63–5 and Béhague, "Compte Rendu: 2ème Partie," Colonies C^{8A} 103, 81–3 and Lacrosse, "Compte Rendu," AP, vol. 76, 514. See also Daney, 3: 208–12 and Lémery, 242–6. Rochambeau estimated that six to seven thousand *émigrés* departed Martinique both in the British fleet and in Rivière's ships: General Rochambeau to Minister of Marine, 10 July 1793, Colonies C^{8A} 101, 91.

85 Rivière, "Extrait de mon journal," Colonies C^{8A} 103, 142–3. After disembarking the refugees from Martinique at Port-of-Spain, and carrying out repairs to *Ferme*, in August Rivière sailed to Peurto Cabello on the Venezuelan coast where he was admitted into the Spanish navy.

86 Dubuc *fils* and Clairfontaine, from Roseau, Dominica, to "X" in London, 26 June–8 July 1793, Colonies C^{8A} 102, 152–9.

87 Duffy, 36–7.

88 General Rochambeau to Minister of Marine, 27 June 1793, Colonies C^{8A} 101, 76.

89 Surveillance and Police Committee of Saint-Pierre to National Convention, 2 July 1793, Colonies C^{8A} 102, 110–11. See also General Rochambeau to Minster of Marine, 29 June 1793 [#1], Colonies C^{8A} 101, 82–3.

90 General Rochambeau to Minister of Marine, 29 June 1793 [#1 and #2], Colonies C^{8A} 101, 82–3, 84.

91 *Proclamation. Nous Danatien, Marie-Joseph Vimeur Rochambeau, lieutenant-général des armées des la république, gouverneur-général de la Martinique, et commandant-général des îles Française du vent de l'Amérique, à tous les hommes libres de la colonie, le 2 juillet 1793, l'an 2éme de la république Française* (Fort-de-la-République: Chez F.J. Willox imprimeur du gouvernement, 1793), Colonies C^{8A} 101, 154.

92 General Rochambeau to Minister of Marine, 20 July 1793, Colonies C^{8A} 101, 93–4. Lémery, 250–3 suggests that the slaves' refusal to return to work reflected the escalation of revolutionary rhetoric in Martinique during the siege.

93 General Rochambeau to Minister of Marine, 3 *Pluviôse An II* (22 January 1794), Colonies C^{8A} 104, 1–2. For the promotions of coloured officers La Rochelle and La Corbière, see General Rochambeau to Minister of Marine, 5 July 1793, Colonies C^{8A} 101, 88. Leborgne insisted that in Saint-Domingue and the Windward Islands the "aristocratic prejudice of colour" was used as a pretext for counter-revolution, and that the bravery of citizens of colour had prevented royalists from delivering Martinique to England in June 1793: Commissioner of War Leborgne, from Lorient, to Minister of Marine, 15 Nivôse Year II [4 January 1794], Colonies C^{8A} 102, 118–19.

94 In the report he presented to the National Convention on 13 October 1793, Captain Lacrosse criticized Rochambeau for not having gone beyond appointing the surveillance committees to arrange the election of municipalities and a new colonial assembly: Lacrosse, "Compte Rendu," AP, vol. 76, 515.

95 General Rochambeau to Minister of Marine, 1 October 1793, Colonies C^{8A} 101, 96–7. See also the pamphlet Rochambeau circulated in Martinique when he convoked the primary assemblies, and the *procès-verbal* of the assembly's initial session: *Instruction pour la formation de la convention nationale. Extrait de la feuille villageoise, du 23 août 1792, no. 47* (Saint-Pierre: Imprimerie de J.B. Thounens, imprimeur du comité du surveillance et de la société patriotique, 1793) and "Première séance des représentants de la Martinique, 22 septembre 1793," Colonies C^{8A} 102, 123–4, 125–30. See also Daney, 3: 215–17.

96 Regarding the assembly's declaration that Martinique was a department and its provisional establishment of a departmental administration, see:

Extrait des registres des délibérations de l'assemblée représentative de la Martinique. Séance du 8 décembre 1793, l'an 2e de la République (Saint-Pierre: F.J. Willox, 1793), Colonies C⁸ᴬ 102, 97. Regarding municipalities, sequestered properties, and the census, see Colonies C⁸ᴬ 102, 45, 57, 58, 61, 75, 79, 80, 81, 83, 92.

97 "Extrait des registres des délibérations de l'assemblée représentative de la Martinique, séance du 25 septembre 1793," Colonies C⁸ᴬ 101, 100–1.

98 *Extrait des registres des délibérations de l'assemblée représentative de la Martinique. Séance du 20 octobre 1793, l'an 2e de la république* (Saint-Pierre: Imprimerie de J.B. Thounens, 1793), Colonies C⁸ᴬ 102, 64.

99 General Rochambeau to Minister of Marine, 25 October 1793, Colonies C⁸ᴬ 101, 98.

100 *Extrait des registres des délibérations de l'assemblée représentative de la Martinique. Séance du 9 octobre 1793, l'an 2e de la république,* [#2] (Saint-Pierre: F.J. Willox, 1793), Colonies C⁸ᴬ 102, 53.

101 *Extrait des registres des délibérations de l'assemblée représentative de la Martinique. Séance du 9 novembre 1793, l'an 2e de la république,* [#1] (Saint-Pierre: J.B. Thounens, 1793), Colonies C⁸ᴬ 102, 86.

102 *Extrait des registres des délibérations de l'assemblée représentative de la Martinique. Séance du 8 novembre 1793, l'an 2e de la république,* [#1] (Saint-Pierre: J.B. Thounens, 1793), Colonies C⁸ᴬ 102, 82.

103 A clear example of this influence can be seen in the assembly's declaration of 26 October that the popular societies in France were a "bulwark of the Revolution" and that anyone who threatened Martinique's clubs would be considered an enemy of the public welfare: *Extrait des registres des délibérations de l'assemblée représentative de la Martinique. Séance du 26 octobre 1793, l'an 2e de la république,* [#4] (Saint-Pierre: J.B. Tounens, 1793), Colonies C⁸ᴬ 102, 73.

104 *Extrait des registres des délibérations de l'assemblée représentative de la Martinique. Séance du 24 septembre 1793, l'an 2e de la république* (Saint-Pierre: J.B. Thounens, 1793), Colonies C⁸ᴬ 102, 42.

105 See *Extrait des registres des délibérations de l'assemblée représentative de la Martinique. Séance du 24 octobre 1793* [#1] and *Extrait des délibérations … Séance du 18 novembre 1793* [#1], Colonies C⁸ᴬ 102, 68, 88.

106 See *Extrait des registres des délibérations de l'assemblée représentative de la Martinique. Séance du 7 octobre 1793,* and *Extrait des délibérations … Séance du 9 octobre 1793,* [#1], Colonies C⁸ᴬ 102, 50, 52.

107 Quoted in Norman Hampson, *Danton* (Oxford: Basil Blackwell, 1978), 102. See also "Decree Providing for the Revolutionary Tribunal, 10 March 1793," in *A Documentary Survey of the French Revolution,* ed. Stewart,

409–12. Regarding the Revolutionary Tribunal's creation in Paris, see Doyle, *Oxford History of the French Revolution*, 226–8 and Andress, *The Terror*, 162–65, 213.

108 *Extrait des registres des délibérations de l'assemblée représentative de la Martinique. Séances des 28 septembre, 7, 10, 12, 17 et 18 octobre 1793, l'an 2e de la république*, (Saint-Pierre: J. B. Thounens, 1793), Colonies C⁸ᴬ 102, 59. For subsequent *arrêtés* regarding the Revolutionary Tribunal and how it would interrogate witnesses, see *Extrait des registres des délibérations … Séance[s des] 22 novembre, 11 décembre, 27 décembre 1793*, Colonies C⁸ᴬ 102, 91, 98, 103. According to Daney, 3: 223–4, the republicans erected a guillotine at Saint-Pierre but used it to execute only three people.

109 On 26 October, for example, the assembly ordered municipalities to post outside the colony's forts the names and descriptions of any prisoners they released: if these suspects attempted to enter, they were to be arrested. See *Extrait des registres des délibérations de l'assemblée représentative de la Martinique. Séance du 26 octobre 1793, l'an 2e de la république*, [#2] (Saint-Pierre: J.B. Tounens, 1793), Colonies C⁸ᴬ 102, 71.

110 *Extrait des registres des délibérations de l'assemblée représentative de la Martinique. Séance du 3 octobre 1793, l'an 2e de la république*, [#2] (Saint-Pierre: J.B. Thounens, 1793), Colonies C⁸ᴬ 102, 46.

111 *Extrait des registres des délibérations de l'assemblée représentative de la Martinique. Séance[s des] 5 [et] 6 octobre 1793, l'an 2e de la République*, (Saint-Pierre: J.B. Thounens, 1793), Colonies C⁸ᴬ 102, 48, 49.

112 "Decree for a Levy of 300,000 Men, 24 February 1793," in *Documentary Survey of the French Revolution*, ed. Stewart, 402–8.

113 *Extrait des registres des délibérations de l'assemblée représentative de la Martinique. Séance du 6 décembre 1793, l'an 2e de la république* (Saint-Pierre: F.J. Willox, 1793), Colonies C⁸ᴬ 102, 96.

114 "Addresse des amis de la république Française et de la convention séante au Fort-de-la-République, Isle Martinique, à Lacrosse (12 août 1793)," Colonies C⁸ᴬ 102, 37–8. See also "Pièce # 37," AP, vol. 76, 531–2.

115 General Rochambeau's order to Captain Lacrosse, 21 August 1793, Colonies C⁷ᴬ 46, 158. See also General Rochambeau to Minister of Marine, 21 August 1793, Colonies C⁸ᴬ 101, 139.

116 General Rochambeau to Minister of Marine, 16 October 1793, Colonies C⁸ᴬ 101, 140.

117 See Captain Lacrosse to the Citizens composing the Commercial Tribunal, Brest [n.d.] and Captain Lacrosse to Minister of Marine, 4 October 1793; Marine BB 4 / 23, 75–6, 84.

118 "Copie du procès verbal du départ de la frégate *la Félicité* du 27 août
1793, l'an 2 de la République"; Marine BB 4 / 23, 77–8.

119 "Copie du procès verbal fait par l'équipage de la frégate *la Félicité* lors
du départ pour la croisière, 27 août 1793," Marine BB 4 / 23, 79–82. While
Lacrosse makes no reference to the mutiny or to the circumstances of his
return to France in his report to the National Convention, he does echo
his crew's belief that colonial patriots had not overcome their racial
prejudice towards free men of colour: Lacrosse, "Compte rendu," AP,
vol. 76, 514.

120 General Rochambeau to Minister of Marine, 16 October 1793, Colonies
C^{8A} 101, 140.

121 General Rochambeau to Minister of Marine, 25 October 1793, Colonies
C^{8A} 101, 98.

122 General Rochambeau to Minister of Marine, 27 December 1793, Colonies
C^{8A} 101, 107. Rochambeau learned of the anticipated arrival of a British
fleet in part from a letter to the governor of Trinidad intercepted by a
French privateer: "Extrait de la lettre du gouverneur de la Trinité Espagnol,
Joseph-Marie Chacon, au Capitaine Lyndsey, son beaufrère dans le 55éme
régiment, à la trinité, 19 décembre 1793," Colonies C^{8A} 101, 108.

123 General Rochambeau to Minister of Marine, 3 *pluviôse an* II (22 January
1794). Five days later Rochambeau wrote that he was sending Dubouchet
to France with his dispatches and to press the minister to send ships, men
and money: General Rochambeau to Minister of Marine, 8 *Pluviôse An II*
(27 January 1794), Colonies C^{8A} 104, 1–2, 3–4.

124 *Journal républicain de la Guadeloupe*, (24 avril 1793), Colonies C^{7A} 47, 124,
quoted in Laurent Dubois, *Les esclaves de la république: L'histoire oubliée de
la première émancipation 1789–1794* (Paris: Calmann-Lévy, 1998), 116–18.

125 *Extrait des registres des délibérations de la commission générale et extraordinaire de la Guadeloupe, séante à la Basse-Terre, le 25 avril 1793,l'an 2e de
la république française*, (Basse-Terre: Imprimerie de la colonie, maison
Rannoué, 1793), Colonies C^{7A} 46, 94.

126 Dubois, *Colony of Citizens*, 130 explains this in terms of "the brilliance and
uniqueness of the Trois-Rivières insurgents" who "accused their masters
of treason and carried out the punishment, then presented the completed
act to the local officials." In contrast, Pérotin-Dumon, *Être patriote sous
les tropiques*, 182–5 places the acceptance of the insurgents' claims in
the wider context of a "plot psychosis" in which the isolated patriots of
Guadeloupe were becoming convinced that the slaves, the British, and
local aristocrats were all part of a general conspiracy.

127 *Rapport du comité de sûreté générale à la commission générale et extraordi-naire de la Guadeloupe, séance du 8 mai 1793, l'an 2 de la république française* (Basse-Terre: Imprimerie de la colonie, maison Rannoué, 1793), Colonies C[7A] 46, 218–29. Regarding the investigation of the revolt at Trois-Rivières, and particularly the committee's claim that it possessed intercepted correspondence suggesting the existence of a counter-revolutionary conspiracy, see also: "Rapport fait au citoyen ministre de la marine, par Marie, sur la Guadeloupe, août 1793," Colonies C[7A] 46, 211–13.

128 *Extrait des registres des délibérations de la commission générale et extraordi-naire de la Guadeloupe, séante à la Basse-Terre, le 8 mai 1793, l'an 2 de la république française,* (Basse-Terre: Imprimerie de la colonie, maison Rannoué, 1793), Colonies C[7A] 46, 115. Officers of the *sénéchaussées* of Basse-Terre and Pointe-à-Pitre would name members of the special tribunal, as well as a public prosecutor, whose powers were to conform to existing criminal ordinances: *Extrait des registres des délibérations de la commission générale et extraordinaire de la Guadeloupe, séante à la Basse-Terre, le 18 mai 1793, l'an 2 de la république française,* (Basse-Terre: Imprimerie de la colonie, maison Rannoué, 1793), Colonies C [7A] 46, 138. Regarding the formation of the special tribunal, and the judgments it rendered, see also Pérotin-Dumon, *Être patriote sous les tropiques,* 189.

129 General Collot to Minister of Marine, 10 May 1793, Colonies C[7A] 46, 116–18.

130 Collot, *Précis des événemens,* p. 7, Colonies C[7A] 46, 19.

131 *Réponse du citoyen gouverneur à la municipalité de la Capesterre, servant d'adresse à toutes les paroisses de l'île Guadeloupe et dépendances. À la Basse-Terre, le 2 mai 1793, l'an 2 de la République française* (Basse-Terre: Imprimerie de la veuve Benard et d'Al. Villette, 1793), Colonies C[7A] 46, 110.

132 *Proclamation. Georges-Henri-Victor Collot, maréchal des camps et armées de la République française, gouverneur général des îles Guadeloupe et dépendances. À tous les hommes libres de la colonie. Fait à la Basse-Terre, le 3 mai 1793, l'an 2 de la république française* (Basse-Terre: Imprimerie républicaine de la veuve Benard et d'Al. Villlette, 1793), Colonies C[7A] 46, 112.

133 General Collot to Minister of Marine, 5 June 1793, Colonies C[7A] 46, 118–20. Regarding the "spirit of proscription" that gripped Guadeloupe and the importance of arrest warrants to the factional conflict between radical and moderate republicans, see Pérotin-Dumon, *Être patriote sous les tropiques,* 194–9.

134 *Compte rendu au peuple de la Guadeloupe par le citoyen gouverneur Collot, dans la séance extraordinaire de la commission, du 15 mai 1793, l'an deuxième*

de la république française (Basse-Terre: Imprimerie républicaine de la veuve Benard et Villette, 1793), Colonies C⁷ᴬ 46, 232.

135 Régent, 254.

136 *Extrait des registres de la commission générale et extraordinaire de la Guadeloupe, séance extraordinaire du 15 mai 1793, l'an 2 de la République française* (Basse-Terre: Imprimerie de la colonie, maison Rannoué, 1793), Colonies C⁷ᴬ 46, 231.

137 See General Collot to Marie-Gallante's administrative chamber, 3 June 1793, and to Minister of Marine, 25 June 1793, Colonies C⁷ᴬ 46, 142–3, 120–1.

138 General Collot to Minister of Marine, 5 June 1793, Colonies C⁷ᴬ 46, 118–20.

139 General Collot to Minister of Marine, 5 July 1793, Colonies C⁷ᴬ 46, 128,

140 General Collot to Municipalities and Parish Commandants, 11 July 1793, Colonies C⁷ᴬ 46, 155. See also Régent, 254–6.

141 Collot, *Précis des événemens*, 9–10, Colonies C⁷ᴬ 46, 20.

142 Collot, *Précis des événemens*, 13, Colonies C⁷ᴬ 46, 22.

143 *Extrait des registres des délibérations de la commission générale et extraordinaire de la Guadeloupe, séante à la Basse-Terre, le 29 octobre, l'an 2e de la république française,* (Basse-Terre: Imprimerie de la colonie, maison Rannoué, 1793), Colonies C⁷ᴬ 46, 240–3. See also Pérotin-Dumon, *Être patriote sous les tropiques*, 199–201.

144 Régent, 261–2. See also Collot, *Précis des événemens*, 13, Colonies C⁷ᴬ 46, 22. Pointe-à-Pitre's popular society objected to Article 18 of the Constitutional Act which states: "Every man may contract his services or his time; but he may not sell himself or be sold; his person is not an alienable property. The law does not recognize the status of servant; only a blend of solicitude and acknowledgement may exist between the employee and his employer," see "The Constitution of 1793, 24 June 1793," in *A Documentary Survey of the French Revolution*, ed. Stewart, 454–68.

145 *Extrait des registres des délibérations du corps représentatif révolutionnaire de la Guadeloupe, séante à la Pointe-à-Pitre, le 21 décembre 1793, l'an 2e de la république française* (Basse-Terre: Imprimerie de Cabre, imprimeur de la société des amis de la république française, 1794), Colonies C⁷ᴬ 46, 245.

146 Collot, *Précis des événemens*, 14–17, Colonies C⁷ᴬ 46, 22–4.

147 *Comité du surêté générale and d'administration réunis, séante à la Pointe-à-Pitre, ce 26 décembre 1793, l'an 2 de la république française*, Colonies C⁷ᴬ 46, 246.

148 *Extrait des minutes du greffe du tribunal de district de la Basse-Terre, Guadeloupe, 2 janvier 1794*, Colonies C⁷ᴬ 46, 246–8.

149 Ibid, 248–9. See also Pérotin-Dumon, *Être patriote sous les tropiques*, 202.

150 Collot, *Précis des événemens*, 18. Regarding the insurrection at Basse-Terre, see 19–21, Colonies C^{7A} 46, 24–6.

151 See the discussion in Dubois, *Colony of Citizens*, 143–7 of Collot's decree, submitted to Guadeloupe's commission on 5 September 1793, which ordered that free people of colour no longer be referred to as "new citizens" or "citizens of colour" but simply as "citizens." See also Régent, 259–60.

152 Duffy, 41–64. Regarding the British intervention in Saint-Domingue, see Geggus, *Slavery, War and Revolution*, esp. 46–132.

153 Rochambeau, "Journal du siège de la Martinique entrepris les 4 et 5 février 1794, ou le 16 du 5e mois de l'an 2e de la république française une et indivisible, par le général Grey et le vice amiral Jervis," [10 January–21 March 1794], Colonies C^{8A} 104, 78.

154 General Charles Grey and Vice-Admiral John Jervis, "Declaration," 1 January 1794, Colonies C^{8A} 104, 107. See also AD Martinique B 20, 37–8, and Lieutenant-Colonel Bellegarde, from Trinité, to General Rochambeau, 18 *Pluviôse An II* [6 February 1794], Colonies C^{8A} 104, 106. Regarding the invasion strategy of Grey and Jervis, and the intelligence they had received from *émigrés*, see Duffy, 65–72.

155 Rochambeau, "Journal du siège de la Martinique," Colonies C^{8A} 104, 79–85. See also Duffy, 73–7, Lémery, 275–7 and Daney, 3: 229–31.

156 Rochambeau, "Journal du siège de la Martinique," Colonies C^{8A} 104, 84–5.

157 Ibid., 85–7. See also Duffy, 77–80.

158 General Charles Grey to General Rochambeau, 17 February 1794, Colonies C^{8A} 104, 110.

159 See Rochambeau, "Journal du siège de la Martinique," and General Rochambeau, from Fort-de-la-Convention, to General Grey, 1 *ventôse an II* [19 February 1794], Colonies C^{8A} 104, 87, 111.

160 General Grey to General Rochambeau, 21 February 1794; see also General Grey to General Rochambeau, 20 February 1794, and General Rochambeau, from Fort-de-la-Convention, 3 *Ventôse An II* [21 February 1794], Colonies C^{8A} 104, 112–14.

161 Rochambeau, "Journal du siège de la Martinique," Colonies C^{8A} 104, 88–9.

162 Officers of the garrison of Fort-de-la-Convention to General Rochambeau, 26 February 1794, Colonies C^{8A} 104, 115.

163 G. Sancé, captain of engineers in the British Army under the orders of Sir Charles Grey, to the municipality of Républiqueville, 27 February 1794, Colonies C^{8A} 104, 116.

164 Rochambeau, "Journal du siège de la Martinique," Colonies C^{8A} 104, 90.

165 General Rochambeau to the Executive Council of the Republic, *11 Ventôse An II* [1 March 1794], Colonies C⁸ᴬ 104, 6. In his journal Rochambeau quotes Jervis's letter of 3 March 1794, printed in *The Independent Chronicle and Universal Advertiser* of Boston, which describes the arrangements to send Bellegarde "and his suite" to Boston in an American schooner: "Journal du siège de la Martinique," Colonies C⁸ᴬ 104, 90. Duffy, 81 states that there is no record of a British bribe to Bellegarde. See also Lémery, 277–9 and Daney, 3: 232.

166 Rochambeau, "Journal du siège de la Martinique," Colonies C⁸ᴬ 104, 90–1.

167 General Rochambeau to the Executive Council of the Republic, *11 Ventôse An II* [1 March 1794], Colonies C⁸ᴬ 104, 6.

168 Rochambeau, "Journal du siège de la Martinique," Colonies C⁸ᴬ 104, 93–4. See also Duffy, 82–3.

169 "General Grey and Vice-Admiral Jervis, to Lieutenant-General Rochambeau, Governor-General of Martinique, and Commandant-General of the French Leeward Islands; the Mayor, Presidents of the Municipalities, and Citizens of Fort-Royal, 12 March 1794," Colonies C⁸ᴬ 104, 118.

170 General Rochambeau, at Fort-de-la-Convention, to General Grey and Vice Admiral Jervis, *22 Ventôse an II* [12 March 1794]," Colonies C⁸ᴬ 104, 119.

171 Rochambeau, "Journal du siège de la Martinique," Colonies C⁸ᴬ 104, 97. See also "État des batteries environnants le forts de la Martinique," Colonies C⁸ᴬ 104, 102. Regarding other prominent defenders who perished during the siege, see Daney, 3: 233–4.

172 See: "Extrait des minutes du Greffe de la maison commune de Républiqueville [20 March 1794]," Municipal Officers of Républiqueville to General Rochambeau, *30 Ventôse an II* [20 March 1794], and Petition Submitted to General Rochambeau by the Regular Troops of Fort-de-la-Convention; Petitions Submitted by National Guard Detachments from Trinité, Saint-Pierre, Sainte-Marie, Robert, and Case-Pilote in Garrison at Fort-de-la-Convention, 20 March 1794, in Colonies C⁸ᴬ 104, 126, 127, 128, 129–32. See also Duffy, 85–7 and Rochambeau, "Journal du siège de la Martinique," Colonies C⁸ᴬ 104, 100.

173 See General Rochambeau, in Fort-de-la-Convention, to General Grey, *30 ventôse an II* [20 March 1794] and General Grey and Vice-Admiral Jervis to General Rochambeau, 20 March 1794, Colonies C⁸ᴬ 104, 133, 134.

174 Terms of Surrender approved by General Grey, Vice-Admiral Jervis and General Rochambeau, 21–22 March 1794, Colonies C⁸ᴬ 104, 136–8.

175 Rochambeau, "Journal du siège de la Martinique," Colonies C^{8A} 104, 101.
176 General Rochambeau, from Newport, Rhode Island, to Minister of Marine, *29 Germinal an II* [18 April 1794], Colonies C^{8A} 104, 17–21. If he believed that metropolitan government had abandoned him, Rochambeau also believed that Martinique's free men of colour, Bellegarde in particular, had betrayed him. Learning that Bellegarde was in Philadelphia, Rochambeau demanded that Fauchet, the French minister plenipotentiary to the United States, arrest him as a traitor: "Copie de la lettre du général Rochambeau à Fauchet, ministre plénipotentiaire de la république française près des États Unis de l'amérique à Philadelphie, du Newport, 29 Germinal an II [18 April 1794]," Colonies C^{8A} 104, 15–16.
177 *Proclamation. Georges-Henri-Victor Collot, maréchal des camps et armées de la république française, gouverneur-général des îles Guadeloupe et dépendances, À tous les hommes libres de la colonie* (Basse-Terre: Imprimerie républicaine de la Veuve Benard et Villette, 1793), Colonies C^{7A} 46, 156.
178 "Lettre du commandant la Folie. Pointe-à-Pitre, le 2 jour du 6 mois, l'an 2 de la république française une et indivisible [20 February 1794]," Colonies C^{7A} 46, 35. See also the testimony of a privateer captain who claimed the committee of general security tried to silence his earlier warning that British forces were on their way to the Windward Islands, Colonies C^{7A} 46, 35.
179 Collot, *Précis des événemens*, 22–3, Colonies C^{7A} 46, 26–7. Dubois, *Colony of Citizens*, 149–52 suggests that initially Collot advocated arming slaves only "timidly" and that this was a "choice forced on him by the slaves' pro-Republican organizing." Yet Régent, 266 asserts that Collot decided to recruit slaves to defend the colony against imminent British attack, and that Guadeloupe's "sans-culottes" vigorously opposed this recruitment. See also Pérotin-Dumon, *Être patriote sous les tropiques*, 217.
180 Collot, *Précis des événemens*, 23–4, Colonies C^{7A} 46, 27. See also Régent, 265.
181 "Lettre du citoyen Dourneaux. Bisdary, le 8 Avril 1794, an 3e de la république française," Colonies C^{7A} 46, 36. See also Collot, *Précis des événemens*, 24–5, Colonies C^{7A} 46, 27–8.
182 Collot, *Précis des événemens*, 24, Colonies C^{7A} 46, 27. See also Régent, 267.
183 Duffy, 89–93.
184 Collot, *Précis des événemens*, 25, Colonies C^{7A} 46, 28. See also Duffy, 93–4.
185 See "Rapport des commandants La Folie et Fontenlliau, rapport du Poste du Boulogne du 16–17 Avril 1794" and "Lettre de la Pointe-Noire. Municipalité de la Pointe-Noire, le 15 avril 1794, l'an 3eme de la

république Française, une et indivisible," Colonies C⁷ᴬ 46, 36–7. See also Duffy, 94–5.

186 See "Lettre de Warrin, commandant au Parc. Houël, 17 Avril 1794" and "Lettre du Duval, commandant du Walkanard, ce 18 Avril 1794," Colonies C⁷ᴬ 46, 36. See also Collot, *Précis des événemens*, 27–8, Colonies C⁷ᴬ 46, 29.

187 "Délibérations des autorités constituées, pour la capitulation. Aujourd'hui, 29 Germinal an 2eme de la république Française, une et indivisible [18 April 1794]," Colonies C⁷ᴬ 46, 36.

188 "Lettre du commandant du Fort St Charles, le 29 Germinal, l'an 2eme de la république Française [18 April 1794]," Colonies C⁷ᴬ 46, 37.

189 "Délibérations des autorités constituées, pour la capitulation," Colonies C⁷ᴬ 46, 37. Regarding the motives for surrendering the colony, see Pérotin-Dumon, *Être patriote sous les tropiques*, 218.

190 See Collot, *Précis des événemens*, 29 and "Conseil de guerre, au sujet de l'incendie de la Basse-Terre," Colonies C⁷ᴬ 46, 30, 37.

191 See "Réquisition des autorités pour capituler" and "Délibération du Fort St Charles" [19 April 1794], Colonies C⁷ᴬ 46, 44–5.

192 "Sommation du général Grey, batterie Boudet, 20 Avril 1794," Colonies C⁷ᴬ 46, 38.

193 Colot, *Précis des événemens*, 31; see also "Articles de capitulation entre leurs excellences Sir Charles Grey, etc., et George Henry Victor Collot, Maréchal de Camp et Gouverneur de la Guadeloupe, etc., 20 Avril 1794," Colonies C⁷ᴬ 46, 31, 39.

194 Regarding Rochambeau's conflict with Fauchet, see Colonies C⁸ᴬ 104, 31–6. For Collot's quarrel with the Republic's representative to the United States, see Colonies C⁷ᴬ 46, 39–40.

195 Collot, *Précis des Événemens*, 32–3, Colonies C⁷ᴬ 46, 31–2.

7 Reign of Terror

1 Dubois, *A Colony of Citizens*, esp. 167, 172, 182.

2 Popkin, *You Are All Free*, 9, 16.

3 Regarding the conflict between Saint-Domingue's white patriots and the civil commissioners, from their arrival in September 1792 to June 1793, see Popkin, *You Are All Free*, 85–149. This conflict was implicit in the civil commissioners' instructions that authorized them to dissolve existing authorities in Saint-Domingue: "Décret additionnel à la loi relative à l'envoi des commissaires civils à Saint-Domingue (décret du 28 mars

1792), 15 juin 1792," in Saintoyant, 1: 410–12. Regarding Sonthonax's background and abolitionist sympathies, and the appointment of Sonthonax and Polverel as civil commissioners, see Robert Louis Stein, *Léger Félicité Sonthonax: The Lost Sentinel of the Republic* (London and Toronto: Associated University Presses, 1985), 15–25, 42–4 and Bénot, *La révolution française et la fin des colonies*, 125–33, 151–2.

4 For a contemporary account of the attack by Galbaud's forces, Sonthonax's promise of freedom to black insurgents who would fight for the republic, and the burning of Cap Français, see H.D. de Saint-Maurice, "Récit historique du malheureux événement qui a réduit en cendres la ville du Cap français, capitale de la province du nord, colonie de St Domingue," in *Facing Racial Revolution: Eyewitness Accounts of the Haitian Insurrection*, ed. Jeremy Popkin (Chicago and London: The University of Chicago Press, 2007), 184–208. See also Popkin, *You Are All Free*, 189–245, Stein, *Léger Félicité Sonthonax*, 69–77, and Dubois, *Avengers of the New World*, 154–9.

5 Léger Félicité Sonthonax, "Decree of General Liberty, August 29, 1793," in *Slave Revolution in the Caribbean 1789–1804*, ed. Dubois and Garrigus, 120–5. See also Popkin, *You Are All Free*, 246–77 and Stein, *Léger Félicité Sonthonax*, 78–90.

6 See Popkin, *You Are All Free*, 278–9, Stein, *Léger Félicité Sonthonax*, 95, and Dubois, *Avengers of the New World*, 168–70.

7 Doyle, *The Oxford History of the French Revolution*, 234–43. See also M.J. Sydenham, *The Girondins* (London, 1961; repr. Greenwood, CN: Greenwood Press, 1976), esp. 145–79, and Whaley, *Radicals*, esp. 151–67. Regarding the "Federalist Revolt," see: Paul R. Hanson, *The Jacobin Republic under Fire: The Federalist Revolt in the French Revolution* (University Park: Pennsylvania State University Press, 2003) esp. 59–98.

8 Regarding Page and Brulley's campaign in Paris against Sonthonax and Polverel, which culminated in the National Convention's decree of 16 July 1793, see Popkin, *You Are All Free*, 327–44. See also Stein, *Léger Félicité Sonthonax*, 107–9 and Piquet, 278–80. Colonists not only from Saint-Domingue but also from Martinique and Guadeloupe denounced Sonthonax and Polverel to the National Convention on 15 March 1793: *Moniteur* (17 mars 1793) 15, 716.

9 Popkin, *You Are All Free*, 351–2.

10 "Extracts from Saint-Just's *rapport* on *gouvernement révolutionnaire*, followed by the decree, 19 Vendémiaire an II – 10 October 1793," in John Hardman, ed., *The French Revolution Documents*, vol. 2, *1792–95* (Oxford: Basil Blackwell, 1973), 154–60. Regarding the circumstances surrounding the beginning of the Terror and the declaration of the Revolutionary

Government, see Doyle, *Oxford History of the French Revolution*, 247–52
and Andress, *The Terror*, 205–24. For an interpretation emphasizing the
role of ideology in the emergence of the Terror, see Dan Edelstein, "From
Constitutional to Permanent Revolution: 1649 and 1793," in *Scripting
Revolution*, ed. Baker and Edelstein, 118–30. See also François Furet,
"Terror" and "Revolutionary Government," in *A Critical Dictionary
of the French Revolution*, ed. Furet and Ozouf, 137–50, 548–59.

11 "Decree of the National Convention of February 4, 1794, Abolishing
Slavery in All the Colonies," in *The French Revolution and Human Rights*,
ed. Hunt, 115–16. Regarding the arrival and admission of Sonthonax's
delegation, and the impact of Dufay's speech to the National Convention
on 4 February 1794, see Popkin, *You Are All Free*, 352–63, Piquet, 333–56,
and Bénot, *La révolution française et la fin des colonies*, 181–3.

12 "Speech of Chaumette Celebrating the Abolition of Slavery, February 18,
1794," in *The French Revolution and Human Rights*, ed. Hunt, 116–18. See
also Piquet, 366–75.

13 F.V.A. Aulard, ed., *Recueil des actes du comité de salut public avec la correspondence officielle des représentants en mission et le registre du conseil exécutif
provisoire* (Paris: Imprimerie nationale, 1889–1951), 12: 532; see also the
committee's order of 22 Germinal an II (22 April 1794) for Lieutenant
Chambon, commanding the *Espérance*, to arrest Sonthonax and Polverel,
12: 511. Regarding the political machinations preceding the arrest of Page
and Brulley in Paris, and informing the decision not to rescind the indictment of Sonthoax and Polverel, see Piquet, 382–8.

14 Piquet, 388.

15 *Moniteur* (27 octobre 1792) 14, 299. See also Bangou, 69–70, Lacour, 2:
280–1, and Sainte-Croix de la Roncière, *Victor Hughes le conventionnel*
(Paris, 1932), 98–101.

16 Prior to his attempt to intercept the members of Sonthonax's delegation,
in June 1793 Hugues had secured the arrest of Philippe-Rose Roume de
Saint-Laurent, one of the first civil commissioners sent to Saint-Domingue;
Piquet, 274–81 322–6. See also Bénot, *La révolution française et la fin des
colonies*, 181.

17 Piquet, 389. See also Bénot, *La révolution française et la fin des colonies*, 185–6.

18 For the *arrêté* establishing the Revolutionary Tribunal at Rochefort on 29
October 1793, see Marine BB 3 / 38, 96. See also E.J. Fleury and J.T Viaud,
Histoire de la ville et du port de Rochefort (Rochefort: Honorine Fleury, 1845),
II, 330–8, and Lacour, 2: 274–82 who notes that the first suspect guillotined
at Rochefort as a result of Hugues's prosecution was a man of colour.

19 Cormack, *Revolution and Political Conflict in the French Navy*, 173–214.

20 Victor Hugues, *Acte d'accusation contre les complices de la trahison de Toulon. Rochefort, 29 Brumaire an II* (Rochefort: R.D. Jousseront, imprimeur du tribunal révolutionnaire, n.d.).

21 Léon Lévy-Schneider, *Le conventionnel Jeanbon Saint-André* (Paris: Félix Alcan, 1901), 2: 708–10 refers to Hugues as one of the *"hébertistes brestois,"* backed by Laignelot, whose fanaticism represented an obstacle to Jeanbon's efforts to impose order and to mobilize the fleet.

22 "Les représentants à Rochefort au comité de salut public, Rochefort, 7 floréal an II (26 avril 1794), réçu le 2 mai 1794," in *Recueil des actes du comité de salut public*, ed. Aulard, 13: 84. Regarding the suggestion that Chrétien disapproved of Hugues as a civil commissioner to implement the decree of 16 Pluviôse, see Bangou, 73. For examination of the request that Sijas be appointed as a third commissioner, and of Captain Maublanc's denunciation of Hugues, see Piquet, 390–1.

23 Régent, 271–2. See also Sainte-Croix de la Roncière, 96–7, 111–12.

24 Captain Leissègues to Military Commission of the Marine, 28 Prairial An II (16 June 1794) and Contre-Amiral Leissègues, "Conquête de la Guadeloupe sur les Anglais," (n.d.), Colonies C⁷ᴬ 47, 106, 107. See also "Le commissaire délégué par la convention nationale aux Isles-du-Vent [Victor Hugues] au comité de salut public, à la Pointe-à-Pitre, le 29 prairial l'an second de la république une et indivisible [17 June 1794]," in *Rapport fait au nom du comité de salut public, par Barère, sur les colonies Françaises Isles-du-Vent. Dans la séance du 19 thermidor l'an 2 de la république française une et indivisible* [6 August 1794] (Paris: Imprimerie nationale, 1794).

25 Duffy, 115.

26 Victor Hugues to Committee of Public Safety, 29 Prairial An II (17 June 1794), in *Rapport … par Barère … 19 thermidor l'an 2.*

27 Ibid. Regarding the assault on Fort Fleur-d'Épée and the French capture of Pointe-à-Pitre, see also Pierre Villegégu to Minister of Marine, 29 Prairial An II (17 June 1794) and Leissègues, "Conquête de la Guadeloupe sur les Anglais," Colonies C⁷ᴬ 47, 96–7, 107. See also Duffy, 116–18, Régent, 273, and Lacour, 2: 306–9.

28 *Proclamation des commissaires délégués par la convention nationale, aux Îles du Vent. Aux citoyens amis et défenseurs de la liberté et de l'égalité. À la Pointe-à-Pitre île Guadeloupe, le 19 prairial l'an II* [8 June 1794] (Pointe-à-Pitre: Imprimerie de la Pointe-à-Pitre, 1794), Colonies C⁷ᴬ 47, 7.

29 Pierre Chrétien and Victor Hugues, *Proclamation des commissaires délégués par la convention nationale aux Îles du Vent, aux citoyens de la Grande et Basse-Terre Guadeloupe, colonie de la république française, 19 prairial l'an 2* [8 June 1794] (Pointe-à-Pitre: Imprimerie de la Pointe-à-Pitre, 1794), Colonies C⁷ᴬ 47, 8.

30 Pierre Chrétien and Victor Hugues, *Proclamation. Nous commissaires délégués par la convention nationale aux Îles du Vent, à tous les citoyens de la Pointe-à-Pitre et autres communes adjacents, 20 prairial l'an 2* [9 June 1794] (Pointe-à-Pitre: Imprimerie de la Pointe-à-Pitre, 1794), Colonies C⁷ᴬ 47, 9.

31 Pierre Chrétien and Victor Hugues, *Au nom du peuple français. Proclamation. Les commissaires délégués par la convention nationale aux Îles du Vent. Aux habitans des campagnes de toutes les couleurs, le 25 pairial an II* [13 June 1794] (Pointe-à-Pitre: Imprimerie de la Pointe-à-Pitre, 1794), Colonies C⁷ᴬ 47, 10.

32 Victor Hugues, *Proclamation. Le commissaire délégué par la convention aux Îles du Vent. Aux citoyens noirs, à qui la convention nationale a accordée la liberté, par son décret du 16 pluviôse dernier, 30 prairial an II* [18 June 1794] (Pointe-à-Pitre: Imprimerie de la Pointe-à-Pitre, 1794), Colonies C⁷ᴬ 47, 14.

33 Victor Hugues to Committee of Public Safety, 29 Prairial An II [17 June 1794], Colonies C⁷ᴬ 47, 13. See also Dubois, *A Colony of Citizens*, 194–7.

34 Victor Hugues to Committee of Public Safety, 26 Prairial An II [14 June 1794] and Leissègues, "Conquête de la Guadeloupe," Colonies C⁷ᴬ 47, 11, 108. See also Duffy, 116–20.

35 Victor Hugues to Committee of Public Safety, 29 Prairial An II [17 June 1794]; see also Pierre Villegégu to Minister of Marine, 29 Prairial An II [17 June 1794], Colonies C⁷ᴬ 47, 12–13, 96–7. According to Sainte-Croix de la Roncière, 122, Hugues loaded a guillotine aboard the *Pique* before the frigate left Rochefort and set it up in Pointe-à-Pitre's main square.

36 Victor Hugues to Committee of Public Safety, 4 Thermidor An II [22 July 1794], Leissègues, "Conquête de la Guadeloupe," and Pierre Villegégu to Committee of Public Safety, 5 Thermidor An II [23 July 1794], Colonies C⁷ᴬ 47, 20–3, 108–9, 99–101. See also Duffy, 125–6, Régent, 273–4, and Lacour, 2: 310–21.

37 Victor Hugues to Committee of Public Safety, 5 Thermidor An II [23 July 1794] #1; Colonies C⁷ᴬ 47, 30. In his own dispatch Leissègues praised Hugues's leadership during the siege: Captain Leissègues to Military Commission of the Marine, 4 Thermidor An II [22 July 1794], Colonies C⁷ᴬ 47, 111–12.

38 Victor Huges, *Adresse aux républicains des armées de terre et de mer de la république, actuellement à la Guadeloupe, 20 thermidor an II* [20 July 1794] (Port-de-la-Liberté: Imprimerie du Port-de-la-Liberté, 1794), Colonies C⁷ᴬ 47, 18. See also Bangou, 83–5.

39 Victor Hugues, *Arrêté. Le commissaire délégué par la convention nationale aux Îles du Vent, 28 messidor an II* [16 July 1794] (Port-de-la-Liberté: Imprimerie du Port-de-la-Liberté, 1794; Colonies C⁷ᴬ 47, 15. The importance Hugues placed on republican symbolism can also be seen in his decision to adopt the uniform of a representative of the people, when in fact he was only

a commissioner rather than a deputy of the National Convention, and his request that thousands of tricolour cockades be sent for distribution among the new citizens: Victor Hugues to Committee of Public Safety, 5 Thermidor An II [23 July 1794] #2, Colonies C⁷ᴬ 47, 31.

40 Victor Hugues to the Committee of Public Safety, 4 Thermidor An II [22 July 1794], Colonies C⁷ᴬ 47, 24.

41 See also Victor Hugues, *Arrêté. Le commissaire délégué par la convention nationale aux Îles du Vent, 2 thermidor an II* [20 July 1794], Colonies C⁷ᴬ 47, 19.

42 Régent, 274. Regarding British casualties, see Duffy, 124–9.

43 "Le commissaire délégué par la convention nationale aux Isles-du-Vent [Victor Hugues], aux citoyens composant la comité de salut public. Quartier général, Basse-Terre-Guadeloupe, ce 26 frimaire, troisième année républicaine [16 Decmber 1794]," in Defermond, *Rapport fait au nom du comité de salut public, sur la Guadeloupe and autres Îles du Vent* (Paris: Imprimerie nationale, 1795), 8–12.

44 Régent, 275–6. Along with mobilizing the new armed force, Hugues's subordinates also worked to restore the hospitals and organize a civil administration in the weeks following the siege, see Pierre Villegégu to the Committee of Marine and Colonies, 5 Thermidor An II [23 July 1794], Colonies C⁷ᴬ 47, 102.

45 Victor Hugues to Committee of Public Safety, 4 Thermidor An II [22 July 1794], Colonies C⁷ᴬ 47, 24. See also Victor Hugues to Committee of Public Safety, 2 Frimaire An II [16 December 1794], in Defermond, *Rapport*, 8–12. Having named a French consul at Saint-Barthélemy, Hugues learned of the presence of patriot refugees there. He ordered them to return to Guadeloupe by 2 August or they would be declared *émigrés*: Victor Hugues, *Arrêté, 30 messidor an II* [18 July 1794], Colonies C⁷ᴬ 47, 17. Regarding Hugues's efforts to acquire supplies and his first use of corsairs, see also Lacour, 2: 327–8.

46 *Proclamation. Victor Hugues, commissaire délégué par la convention nationale aux Îles du Vent. Aux citoyens de l'Île Guadeloupe, 29 messidor an II* [17 July 1794] (Port-de-la-Liberté, 1794), Colonies C⁷ᴬ 47, 16.

47 For accounts of the siege of the Berville camp, and of the operations that preceded it, see Victor Hugues to Committee of Public Safety, 26 Frimaire An III [16 December 1794], in Defermond, *Rapport*, 9–11 and Leissègues, "Conquête de la Guadeloupe," Colonies C⁷ᴬ 47, 109. See also Duffy, 131–2, Bangou, 78–82, and Lacour, 2: 328–35.

48 Cooper Willyams, *An Account of the Campaign in the West Indies in the Year 1794*, (London, 1796; repr. Basse-Terre: Société d'histoire de la Guadeloupe, 1990), 137–8.

49 Donald Greer, *The Incidence of the Terror in the French Revolution* (Cambridge, MA: Harvard University Press, 1935), esp. 33–6. See also R.R. Palmer, *Twelve Who Ruled: The Year of the Terror in the French Revolution* (Princeton, NJ: Princeton University Press, 1941; repr. 1989), 153–76, 220–3; Doyle, *Oxford History of the French Revolution*, 253–8, and Furet, *Revolutionary France 1770–1880*, 137–40.

50 Victor Hugues to Committee of Public Safety, 26 Frimaire An III [16 December 1794], in Defermond, *Rapport*, 11. It is significant that Rear Admiral Leissègues, in his detailed account of the conquest of Guadeloupe that was written in 1797, three years after the Terror had been discredited in France, makes no reference to the mass executions. See Leissègues, "Conquête de la Guadeloupe," Colonies C⁷ᴬ 47, 107–10. See also Dubois, *A Colony of Citizens*, 201 and Lacour, 2: 335–8. Régent, 277–8 confirms that many of those executed after Graham's surrender were free men of colour whose attachment to the royalists reflected their refusal to accept the abolition of slavery and their loyalty to the masters who had freed them.

51 "The Ventôse Decrees, 3 March 1794 (13 Ventôse, Year II)," in *A Documentary Survey of the French Revolution*, ed. Stewart, 525–6. Regarding the context in which the decrees were passed, see Palmer, *Twelve Who Ruled*, 280–94 and Doyle, *Oxford History of the French Revolution*, 265–71.

52 Victor Hugues, *Arrêté, 1 frimaire an III* [21 November 1794], Colonies C⁷ᴬ 47, 36. According to Régent, 294–5, rich planters possessing many slaves were the most likely to emigrate and, therefore, a high proportion of the colony's large plantations were sequestered: republicans confiscated 78 per cent of Guadeloupe's sugar plantation (288 of 367) and 44 per cent of coffee plantations (285 of 652) by the end of 1794.

53 Victor Hugues to Committee of Public Safety, 26 Frimaire An III [16 December 1794], in Defermond, *Rapport*, 12. Hugues claimed that the British garrison of Fort Saint-Charles consisted of 860 soldiers, but Duffy, 133–4 states that General Prescott commanded only 400 men. For his account of the siege and of Prescott's evacuation, see Willyams, 138–47.

54 Victor Hugues, *Arrêté, 20 frimaire an III* [10 December 1794] (Port-de-la-Liberté: Imprimerie de la république, 1794) [published in both English and French], Colonies C⁷ᴬ 47, 38.

55 See "Lettre écrite aux délégués du convention nationale au Port-de-la-Liberté, le 12 Frimaire An III [2 December 1794]" and "Copie de la réponse du commissaire Hugues à la municipalité du Lamentin, 20 frimaire an III [10 December 1794]," in Colonies C⁷ᴬ 47, 119. See also Régent, 290–2.

56 Victor Hugues, *Arrêté, 1 nivôse an III* [21 December 1794] [#1] (Port-de-la-Liberté: Imprimerie de la république, 1794), Colonies C⁷ᴬ 47, 43.

57 Victor Hugues, Goyrand, Lebas, *Arrêté, 5 ventôse an III* [23 February 1795] (Port-de-la-Liberté: Imprimerie de la république, 1795), Colonies C⁷ᴬ 48, 7.
58 Victor Hugues, Goyrand, Lebas, *Arrêté, 23 ventôse an III* [13 March 1795] (Port-de-la-Liberté: Imprimerie de la république, 1795), Colonies C⁷ᴬ 48, 8.
59 Victor Hugues to Committee of Public Safety, 20 Pluviôse An III [8 February 1795], in Defermond, *Rapport*, 13–14.
60 Victor Hugues, at Port-de-la-Liberté, to his colleagues at sea, 14 Nivôse An III [3 January 1795], Colonies C⁷ᴬ 48, 4 or Marine BB 4 / 85, 86.
61 Victor Hugues to Committee of Public Safety, 20 Pluviôse An III [8 February 1795], in Defermond, *Rapport*, 13–14. Lebas to Committee of Public Safety, 20 Fructidor An III [6 September 1795], Colonies C⁷ᴬ 47, 5–6. See also William James, *The Naval History of Great Britain, from the Declaration of War by France in 1793 to the Accession of George IV* (London: Richard Bentley, 1859) 1: 308–13. Regarding the danger to French communications from British warships, see also "Extrait de la lettre du citoyen Villegégu, chef principal des bureaux civils de la marine aux Îles du Vent, dattée de la Guadeloupe, le 11 prairial an III [30 May 1795]," Marine BB 4 / 85, 97.
62 Victor Hugues and Lebas to Committee of Public Safety, 20 Prairial An III [8 June 1795]; in Defermond, *Rapport*, 5–7. See also David Barry Gaspar, "La Guerre des Bois: Revolution, War and Slavery in Saint Lucia, 1793– 1838," in *A Turbulent Time: The French Revolution and the Greater Caribbean*, ed. David Barry Gaspar and David Patrick Geggus, (Bloomington: Indiana University Press, 1997), 102–7, and Duffy, 142.
63 Victor Hugues and Lebas to Committee of Public Safety, 20 Prairial An III [8 June 1795], in Defermond, *Rapport*, 5–7.
64 Victor Hugues and Lebas to Committee of Public Safety, 20 Messidor An III [8 July 1795], Colonies C⁷ᴬ 48, 22–4. See also Gaspar, "La Guerre des Bois," 108–9, Dubois, *A Colony of Citizens*, 232–3, Duffy, 145, and Lacour, 2: 402–3.
65 Victor Hugues and Lebas to Committee of Public Safety, 20 Prairial An III [8 June 1795], in Defermond, *Rapport*, 5–7. See also Edward L. Cox, *Free Coloreds in the Slave Societies of St Kitts and Grenada, 1763–1833* (Knoxville: University of Tennessee Press, 1984), 76–8, 81–3 and Duffy, 143–4.
66 See Christopher Taylor, *The Black Carib Wars: Freedom, Survival, and the Making of the Garifuna* (Jackson: University Press of Mississippi, 2012), 51–8, 75–99. See also Michael Craton, "The Black Caribs of St Vincent: A Reevaluation," in *The Lesser Antilles in the Age of European Expansion*, ed. Robert L. Paquette and Stanley L. Engerman (Gainesville: University Press of Florida, 1996), 71–85.
67 Quoted in Taylor, 116–17.

68 Regarding the opening phase of the Carib revolt in St Vincent, and the British recapture of Dorcetshire Hill of 14 March 1795, see Charles Shephard, *An Historical Account of the Island of Saint Vincent* (London: W. Nichol, 1831), 56–74. See also Taylor, 117–22, Duffy, 142–4, and Lacour, 2: 404–6.

69 Victor Hugues and Lebas to Committee of Public Safety, 20 Prairial An III [8 June 1795], in Defermond, *Rapport*, 5–7. Regarding the Caribs' massacre of British planters and many of their slaves, see Taylor, 119–20 and Shephard, 64–8.

70 Quoted in Shephard, 55.

71 Victor Hugues and Lebas to Committee of Public Safety, 20 Prairial An III [8 June 1795], in Defermond, *Rapport*, 5–7.

72 Victor Hugues, *Arrêté, 11 germinal an III* [31 March 1795], Colonies C⁷ᴬ 48, 10. Hugues's order to show enemies accused of committing atrocities no mercy supports the argument that the Terror sprang not from the logic of war but from natural rights logic. See Dan Edelstein, "War and Terror: The Law of Nations from Grotius to the French Revolution," *French Historical Studies* 31, no. 2 (Spring 2008): 229–62.

73 Lebas to Committee of Public Safety, 20 Frimaire An III [6 September 1795], Colonies C⁷ᴬ 47, 6.

74 Victor Hugues and Lebas to Committee of Public Safety, 20 and 21 Prairial An III [8 and 9 June 1795], in Defermond, *Rapport*, 5–7 and Colonies C⁷ᴬ 48, 15.

75 Victor Hugues and Lebas to Committee of Public Safety, 20 Messidor An III [8 July 1795], Colonies C⁷ᴬ 48, 22–4.

76 Victor Hugues and Lebas to Committee of Public Safety, 21 Prairial An III [9 June 1795], Colonies C⁷ᴬ 48, 15. See also Victor Hugues and Lebas to President of the National Convention, 20 Prairial An III [8 June 1795], Marine BB 4 / 85, 87.

77 Victor Hugues and Lebas to Committee of Public Safety, 30 Brumaire An IV [21 November 1795], Colonies C⁷ᴬ 48, 39–40.

78 Victor Hugues and Lebas to Committee of Public Safety, 20 Prairial An III [8 June 1795], in Defermond, *Rapport*, 5–7.

79 In a letter dated 9 June 1795, they claimed that more than 150 English prizes had been taken: Victor Hugues and Lebas to the President of the National Convention, 21 Prairial An III [9 June 1795], Colonies C⁷ᴬ 48, 15.

80 Victor Hugues and Lebas to Rear Admiral Leissègues, 18 Floréal An III [7 May 1795], Colonies C⁷ᴬ 48, 12. See also the commissioners' orders for Lieutenant Faules, who was to patrol off St Thomas with three warships, and for Lieutenant David commanding the corvette *Brutus*, who was to

cruise one hundred leagues to windward of Antigua, Colonies C^{7A} 48, 13, 16.

81 Victor Hugues and Lebas to Committee of Public Safety, 20 Messidor An III [8 July 1795], Colonies C^{7A} 48, 22–4. Regarding Leissègues's success against a British convoy, see also Victor Hugues and Lebas to Étienne Lavaux, Governor General of Saint-Domingue, 19 Messidor An III [7 July 1795], Colonies C^{7A} 48, 7–18.

82 Rear Admiral Leissègues to Commission of Marine and Colonies, 24 Brumaire An IV [15 November 1795], Marine BB 4 / 85, 48–50.

83 See Thouluyre Mahé, "Coup d'oeil sur la Guadeloupe et dépendances en 1797 (vs), l'an 5 de la république," Colonies C^{7A} 49, 138–9. See also Saintoyant, 2: 253.

84 Rear Admiral Leissègues to Commission of Marine and Colonies, 20 Messidor An III [8 July 1795] and 24 Brumaire An IV [15 Novmeber 1795]. See also Lieutenant Lacouture to Commission of Marine and Colonies, 13 Messidor An III [3 July 1795], Marine BB 4 / 85, 46–50, 117.

85 "Département de la Guadeloupe. Jugemens du tribunal de commerce sur les prises, extraits de ses régistres, depuis le 23 vendémiaire an III [14 October 1794] de son etablissement inclusivement jusqu'au 7 brumaire an VII [28 October 1798]," Colonies C^{7A} 48, 79–157.

86 Régent, 305–8, 312–17. See also Dubois, *A Colony of Citizens*, 241–5.

87 Lacour, 2: 414–16. See also Sainte-Croix de la Roncière, 217–21.

88 Melvin H. Jackson, *Privateers in Charleston, 1793–1796: An Account of a French Palatinate in South Carolina* (Washington, DC: Smithsonian Institution Press, 1969).

89 Victor Hugues and Lebas, *Arrêté, 23 fructidor an III* [9 September 1795] (Port-de-la-Liberté: Imprimerie de la république, 1795), Colonies C^{7A} 48, 33.

90 Victor Hugues, *Arrêté* [n.d., but Response to Executive Directory's Arrêté of 14 Messidor An IV / 2 July 1796] (Port-de-la-Liberté: Imprimerie de la république), Colonies C^{7A} 48, 44–6. See also "Instructions et ordres donnés aux capitaines des bâtiments de la république par les commissaires, 5 vendémiaire – 9 thermidor an IV [27 September 1795–27 July 1796]," Marine BB 4 / 85, 72, 73, 76, 78.

91 "Instructions données par les agens du directoire exécutif aux Îles du Vent au citoyen Valteau, capitaine de vaisseau de la république, commandant la frégate la Pensée, 12 brumaire an V [2 November 1796]," Marine BB 4 / 108, 75–6. Regarding Hugues's accusations that American ships were aiding the British, see Victor Hugues and Lebas to Minister of Marine and Colonies, 21 Thermidor An IV [8 August 1796], Colonies C^{7A} 49, 27–8.

92 Régent, 308. See also Sainte-Croix de la Roncière, 222–5.
93 See Doyle, *The Oxford History of the French Revolution*, 272–96, Furet, *Revolutionary France*, 142–62, and Andress, *The Terror*, 332–60.
94 Victor Hugues and Lebas to Étienne Lavaux, Governor General of Saint-Domingue, 19 Messidor An III [7 July 1795], Colonies C⁷ᴬ 48, 17–18.
95 Victor Hugues and Lebas to the President of the National Convention, 20 Messidor An III [8 July 1795], Colonies C⁷ᴬ 48, 21.
96 *Proclamation. Les commissaires délégués par la convention nationale, aux citoyens des Îles du Vent, actuellement aux États-Unis de l'Amérique; 25 fructidor an III* [10 September 1795] (Port-de-la-Liberté: Imprimerie de la république, 1795), Colonies C⁷ᴬ 48, 34.
97 Victor Hugues and Lebas to the Committee of Public Safety or to the President of the Executive Directory, 7 Nivôse An IV [28 December 1795], Colonies C⁷ᴬ 48, 47–8.
98 See Doyle, *Oxford History of the French Revolution*, 295–6, 317–20 and Furet, *Revolutionary France*, 162–8 and Andress, *The Terror*, 365–7.
99 Victor Hugues and Lebas to the Committee of Public Safety or to the President of the Executive Directory, 7 Nivôse An IV [28 December 1795], Colonies C⁷ᴬ 48, 47–8.
100 Committee of Public Safety to the National Convention's delegates to the Windward Islands, 14 Fructidor An III [31 August 1795], Marine BB 4 / 85, 91.
101 Victor Hugues and Lebas to the Committee of Public Safety or to the President of the Executive Directory, 7 Nivôse An IV [28 December 1795], Colonies C⁷ᴬ 48, 47–8.
102 General Pelardy to Committee of Public Safety, 2 Floréal An III [21 April 1795], Colonies C⁷ᴬ 48, 50. See also the exchange of letters between Hugues and Pelardy on 27 Floréal An III [16 May 1795]: "Copie d'un extrait des registres des délibérations de la commune du Lamentin, Guadeloupe," Colonies C⁷ᴬ 47, 119–120.
103 General Pelardy, from Bordeaux, to the Committee of Public Safety, 19 Fructidor An III [5 September 1795], Colonies C⁷ᴬ 48, 52.
104 General Pelardy, at Bordeaux, to the Commission of Marine and Colonies, 15 Fructidor An III [1 September 1795], Marine BB 4 / 85, 94–5.
105 Régent, 235.
106 Janvier Littée to the Directory, 1 Ventôse IV [20 February 1796], Colonies C⁷ᴬ 49, 127.
107 Régent, 286–7, 298–306, 317–24.
108 See Victor Hugues and Lebas to Minister of Marine and Colonies, 26 Frimaire An V [16 December 1796] and "Extrait d'une lettre adressé

par le citoyen Victor Hugues, agent du directoire exécutif, au citoyen Fourniols, député de la Martinique; Guadeloupe, 26 frimaire an V [16 December 1796]," Colonies C⁷ᴬ 49, 64, 65.

109 Régent, 119.

110 Hapel de La Channie, at Bordeaux, to Citizen Fourcroy, 3 Messidor An III [21 June 1795], Colonies C⁷ᴬ 48, 69–70. See also his request to minister of marine for reimbursement to cover the cost of his voyage to Lorient, where he was not allowed to land, and his subsequent voyage to Bordeaux, 67–8. For a discussion of Victor Hugues's relationships with women, including Louise Jacquin whom he married in March 1797, see Sainte-Croix de la Roncière, 274–87.

111 "Observations présentées au comité de salut public sur la situation de la Guadeloupe, 22 Thermidor An III [9 August 1795]," Colonies C⁷ᴬ 48, 73–6.

112 Victor Hugues and Lebas to Committee of Public Safety, 27 Brumaire An IV [18 November 1795], Colonies C⁷ᴬ 48, 35.

113 Victor Hugues and Lebas to Committee of Public Safety, 29 Brumaire An IV [20 November 1795], Colonies C⁷ᴬ 48, 37–8.

114 "Observations présentées au comité de salut public sur la situation de la Guadeloupe, 22 thermidor an III [9 August 1795], Colonies C⁷ᴬ 48, 73–6.

115 Victor Hugues and Lebas to Committee of Public Safety or to the President of the Executive Directory, 4 Nivôse An IV [25 December 1795], Colonies C⁷ᴬ 48, 42–3.

116 Jeremy D. Popkin, "Thermidor, Slavery, and the '*Affaire des Colonies*,'" *French Historical Studies* 38, no. 1 (February 2015): 61–82.

117 Defermond, *Rapport fait, au nom du comité de salut public, sur la Guadeloupe et autres Îles du Vent* (Paris: Imprimerie Nationale, 1795).

118 Minister of Marine and Colonies to Victor Hugues, Goyrand and Lebas, 12 Nivôse An IV [2 January 1796], Colonies C⁷ᴬ 49, 155–6.

119 Colin Lucas, "The First Directory and the Rule of Law," *French Historical Studies* 10, no. 2 (Fall 1977): 231–60. See also Howard G. Brown, *Ending the French Revolution: Violence, Justice and Repression from the Terror to Napoleon* (Charlottesville: University of North Carolina Press, 2006), esp. 8–16, 21–6, 73–8, 350–8.

120 Minister of Marine and Colonies to Citizens Hugues, Goyrand and Lebas, Special Agents of the Directory at Guadeloupe, 16 Ventôse an IV [6 March 1796], Colonies C⁷ᴬ 49, 158–9.

121 Victor Hugues and Lebas to Minister of Marine and Colonies, 22 Thermidor An IV [9 August 1796], Colonies C⁷ᴬ 49, 43–4.

122 Victor Hugues and Lebas to Minister of Marine and Colonies, 21 Thermidor An IV [8 August 1796], Colonies C⁷ᴬ 49, 29–30.

123 Villegégu to Committee of Public Safety, 11 Prairial An III [30 May 1795], Colonies C⁷ᴬ 48, 54–5.

124 Victor Hugues and Lebas to Minister of Marine and Colonies, 20 Frimaire An V [10 December 1796], Colonies C⁷ᴬ 49, 61–3.

125 "Extrait d'une lettre adressé par le citoyen Victor Hugues, agent du directoire exécutif, au citoyen Fourniols, député de la Martinique, Guadeloupe, 26 frimaire an V [16 December 1796]," Colonies C⁷ᴬ 49, 65.

126 Dubois, *A Colony of Citizens*, 171–88.

127 Williams, 99–102, 139–58, 250–76.

128 Dubois, *A Colony of Citizens*, 198–200, 204–10.

129 Duffy, 159–221.

130 See "Copie de la soumation faite par les généraux angalises, à M. Goyrand, commissaire délégué, et à l'officier commandant les troupes de la nation française, à Sainte-Lucie, 27 avril 1796" and "Copie de la réponse de l'agent particulier du directoire exécutif, et être commandant général des forces républicaines à Sainte-Lucie, aux générals anglaise commandant les forces Britanniques de terre et de mer, 11 floréal an IV [30 April 1796]," Colonies C⁷ᴬ 49, 24, 25.

131 "Compte-rendu par citoyen Goyrand, ex-agent du directoire exécutif [n.d.]," Colonies C⁷ᴬ 49, 67–108. See also Duffy, 228–36.

132 Gaspar, "La guerre des bois," 110–22.

133 Victor Hugues and Lebas to Minister of Marine and Colonies, 24 Floréal An IV [13 May 1796], Colonies C⁷ᴬ 49, 12–13.

134 Duffy, 236–8.

135 See Craton, "The Black Caribs of St Vincent," 84–5, and Duffy, 257–63.

136 Victor Hugues and Lebas to Minister of Marine and Colonies, 16 Frimaire An V [6 December 1796], Colonies C⁷ᴬ 49, 58–60. Regarding the rebellion's defeat in Granada, see also Duffy, 236–40.

137 Minister of Marine and Colonies to Victor Hugues, Lebas and Goyrand, 13 Fructidor An IV [30 August 1796], Colonies C⁷ᴬ 49, 163.

138 See Victor Hugues and Lebas to Minister of Marine and Colonies, 6 Pluviôse An V [25 January 1797] and to the Commanders of His Catholic Majesty's Forces of Land and Sea at Trinidad, 9 Nivôse An V [29 December 1796], Colonies C⁷ᴬ 49, 181, 217–18 See also Victor Hugues and Lebas to Lieutenant Baudouin, 14 Fructidore An IV [31 August 1796], Marine BB 4 / 108, 87–90.

139 See Victor Hugues and Lebas to Captain Valteau Commanding *La Pensée* at Curaçao, 16 Fructidor An V [4 September 1796] and 12 Brumaire An V [2 November 1796], Marine BB 4 / 108, 78, 79. See also "Le conseil combiné de Curaçao au citoyen Valteau, capitaine de Vaisseau, commandant la frégate *La Pensée*, 23 novembre 1796," "Colonel et capitaine de Haut Bord commandant les forces navales de la république Batave à Curaçao,

au citoyen Valteau, capitaine de Vaisseau, commandant la division française à Curaçao, 22 novembre 1796," and "Le conseil militaire de Curaçao
à capitaine Valteau, 24 novembre 1796," in Marine BB 4 / 108, 81–2.

140 "Capitulation entre leur excellence Ralph Abercromby, chevalier de
l'ordre du bain, et Henry Harvey écuyer, commandans en chef des
forces de terre et de mer de sa majesté Britannique, et Don Jospeh-
Marie Chacon, gouverneur pour sa majesté Catholique de l'isle Trinité-
Espagnol," Colonies C^{7A} 49, 215–16. See also Duffy, 276–83.

141 Victor Hugues and Lebas to the Minister of Marine and Colonies,
17 Ventôse An V [7 March 1797], Colonies C^{7A} 49, 195.

142 Victor Hugues and Lebas to the Minister of Marine and Colonies,
20 Ventôse An V [10 March 1797], Colonies C^{7A} 49, 197–9.

143 "Thouluyre Mahé, ancien colon et habitant de la Guadeloupe, au citoyen
ministre des colonies, Port-de-la-Liberté, Guadeloupe, 2 ventôse an IV
[21 February 1796]," Colonies C^{7A} 49, 133.

144 "Thoulouyre Mahé, ancien colon et habitant de la Guadeloupe, au citoyen ministre des colonies, Port-de-la-Liberté (ci-devant Pointe-à-Pitre)
ce 4 prairial an IV [23 May 1796]," Colonies C^{7A} 49, 134.

145 "Extrait d'une lettre du citoyen Thoulouyre Mahé, dattée du Port-de-la-
Liberté, le 5 Frimaire An V [25 November 1796]," Colonies C^{7A} 49, 135–6.

146 "Copie de la lettre écrite de la Grande-Terre, Guadeloupe, des prisons de
la Pointe-à-Pitre, au ministre de la marine, en date du 22 frimaire an V
[12 December 1796]," Colonies C^{7A} 49, 137.

147 Thoulouyre Mahé, "Coup d'oeil sur la Guadeloupe et dépendances en
1797 (vs), l'an 5 de la république," Colonies C^{7A} 49, 138–43. Régent, 293–4
argues that the demographic decline of Guadeloupe's white population
was real but not as drastic as Mahé and other critics of Hugues claimed.

148 "Notes particulières sur la conduite et l'administration des agents par-
ticuliers du directoire exécutif au Îles du Vent," (no author, n.d.), Colonies
C^{7A} 48, 243–50.

149 Victor Hugues and Lebas to Minister of Marine and Colonies, 23 Nivôse
An VI [12 January 1798], Colonies C^{7A} 50, 4–11. See also Régent, 373–4.

150 Victor Hugues and Lebas to Minister of Marine and Colonies, 23 Nivôse
An VI [12 January 1798], C^{7A} 50, 4–11. Regarding the uprisings of black
cultivators in 1797, see also Dubois, *Colony of Citizens*, 308–14 and Régent,
354.

151 Colonies C^{7A} 50, 4–11. Regarding Hugues's distrust and hostility towards
former free men of colour, see Régent, 364–5.

152 Colonies C^{7A} 50, 4–11. Dubois, *Colony of Citizens*, 312 emphasizes that the
uprising at Lamentin was a conflict between two different groups of new

citizens. Régent, 355–6 notes that Guadeloupe's coloured army, which represented both an instrument of social promotion and apprenticeship in republican egalitarianism, intervened politically in 1797 and would again in 1799 and 1801.

153 Victor Hugues to Minister of Marine and Colonies, 23 Prairial An VI [11 June 1798], Colonies C^{7A} 50, 16–19. See also "Loi concernant l'organisation constitutionnelle des colonies, 12 nivôse an VI, 1er janvier 1798," in Saintoyant, 1: 445–50.

154 Regarding the decision to recall Hugues and to name General Desfourneaux as the directory's new agent in Guadeloupe, see Régent, 289 and 340, Lacour, 2: 472 and Sainte-Croix de la Roncière, 302–5. Regarding the Law of 4 Brumaire An VI, see Saintoyant, 1: 242–3.

155 Étienne Desfourneaux to Minister of Marine and Colonies, 29 Messidor An VI [17 July 1798], Colonies C^{7A} 50, 137. See also Sainte-Croix de la Roncière, 305–6.

156 Étienne Desfourneaux to President John Adams, 25 Frimaire An VII [15 December 1798] and Étienne Desfourneaux to Minister of Marine and Colonies, 25 Frimaire An VII [15 December 1798] [#2], Colonies C^{7A} 50, 149–50, 151–2. See also Ulane Bonnel, *La France, les États-Unis et la guerre de course (1798–1815)* (Paris: Nouvelle éditions Latines, 1961), 96–9. Regarding Desfourneaux's assessment of privateering at Guadeloupe as a "system of almost general piracy" upheld by the colony's tribunal of commerce, see: Étienne Desfourneaux to Minister of Marine and Colonies, 23 Frimaire An VII [13 December 1798], Colonies C^{7A} 50, 138–42.

157 Étienne Desfourneaux to Minister of Marine and Colonies, 25 Frimaire An VII [15 December 1798] [#1], Colonies C^{7A} 50, 143–7.

158 Ibid. See also Copy of Letter from Victor Hugues to General Desfourneaux, 16 Frimaire An VII [7 December 1798], Colonies C^{7A} 50, 28. Regarding Hugues's arrest and departure, see Dubois, *Colony of Citizens*, 327–33, Sainte-Croix de la Roncière, 307–9, and Saintoyant, 2: 257.

159 Pons-Martin to Minister of Marine and Colonies, 2 Frimaire An VII [22 November 1798], Colonies C^{7A} 50, 187–8.

8 Return of the Old Regime

1 General Sir Charles Grey and Vice Admiral John Jervis, "Declaration, 1 January 1794," Colonies C^{8A} 104, 107.

2 Sir Charles Grey, "Proclamation, 8 February 1794," AD Martinique B 20, 40.

3 *Proclamation concernant la police des cabarets. De par le colonel William Meyers, commandant par sa majesté Britannique, en la ville de Saint-Pierre*

et dépendances. À Saint-Pierre, Martinique, le 22 février 1794, Colonies C⁸ᴬ 104, 168.

4 Proclamation. De par le colonel William Meyers, commandant pour sa majesté Britannique, en la ville de Saint-Pierre et dépendances. Saint-Pierre, Martinique, le 25 février 1794, Colonies C⁸ᴬ 104, 169.

5 Sir Charles Grey to the Honourable Henry Dundas, Fort-Royal Martinique, 25 March 1794. French translation in The Martinico Gazette and General Advertiser 1, no. 12 (7 June 1794), Colonies C⁸ᴬ 104, 175.

6 Rochambeau, from Newport, Rhode Island, to Minister of Marine, 29 Germinal An II [18 April 1794], Colonies C⁸ᴬ 104, 17–21.

7 M. Berclery, "Abrégé historique des événements de la révolution à la Martinique, pour servir de renseignements et d'instruction au comité de salut public et autres qui en doivent connaître, 6 Nivôse An IV [26 December 1795]," Colonies C⁸ᴬ 104, 212–32.

8 Proclamation. By His Excellency Sir Charles Grey K.B. General of His Majesty's Army, and Commander-in-Chief of His Forces in the West Indies Etc. Fort-Royal, Martinique, 30 March 1794, Colonies C⁸ᴬ 104, 171.

9 Proclamation par Robert Prescott Ecuyer, lieutenant-général des armées de sa majesté, et gouverneur de cette Isle Martinique et dépendances. Saint-Pierre, Martinique, 12 Avril 1794, Colonies C⁸ᴬ 104, 174. This document also includes the text of the oath, "Serment de fidélité et allégeance."

10 "Séance extraordinaire du 24 avril 1794," AD Martinique B 20, 38.

11 AD Martinique B 20, 39.

12 "Adresse au général Prescott, rédigée par les conseillers De La Hante et Bence, 25 Avril 1794," AD Martinique B 20, 40.

13 Kiern Russell Kleczewski, Martinique and the British Occupation, 1794–1802 (PhD diss., Georgetown University, 1988), 153–4.

14 "Lettre du général en chef Charles Grey ... 16 mai 1794," AD Martinique B 20, 40.

15 "Séance extraordinaire du 17 mai 1794," AD Martinique B 20, 41–2.

16 "Commission provisoire d'administrateur général accordée à Louis-François Dubuc par Sir Charles Grey ... Fort-Royal, 24 mai 1794," AD Martinique B 20, 48–9.

17 "Séance du 7 Juillet 1794," AD Martinique B 20, 50. On 7 January 1795 the sovereign council registered Grey's order of 16 September 1794 that nullified the appointment of Benjamin Clifton as Martinique's treasurer and ordered him to turn over the tax records to Dubuc, 65. For evidence of tension between Clifton and Jervis, and of a colonist's enthusiasm for the appointment of Dubuc who it was assumed would give planters permission to ship their sugar, see: "Extrait d'une lettre du Fort-Royal, en date du 17 juin 1794," Colonies C⁸ᴬ 104, 183.

18 "Adresse du conseil souverain de la Martinique à sa majesté Britannique
 … 23 mai 1794," AD Martinique B 20, 47.

19 AD Martinique B 20, 39.

20 AD Martinique B 20, 44–5.

21 "Séance du 24 avril 1794," AD Martinique B 20, 39.

22 "Proclamation du général Prescott … 13 mai 1794," AD Martinique B 20, 44.

23 "Séance du 24 mai 1794," AD Martinique B 20, 48.

24 "Mémoire adressé à la commission permanente de la cour par M. Le
 Merle, commissionaire civil de Lamentin, n.d.," AD Martinique B 20, 45–6.

25 "Séance du 21 mai 1794," AD Martinique B 20, 46.

26 Duffy, 109.

27 Duffy, 106–14. See also Kleczewski, 152.

28 "Séance du 26 avril 1794," AD Martinique B 20, 40.

29 "Séance du 19 mai 1794," AD Martinique B 20, 42.

30 Ibid., 43.

31 Kleczewski, 148–9.

32 "Ordonnance de Sir Charles Grey concernant la régie des biens des
 personnes tuées, prisonnières pendant le siège de la colonie, déportée
 ou passée en France. À bord du Boyne, rade de Fort-Royal, 24 mai 1794,"
 AD Martinique B 20, 49–50.

33 Kleczewski, 285–6.

34 "Ordannance de Sir Charles Grey et vice admiral Jervis … À bord du
 Boyne, Gossier, Guadeloupe, 13 juin 1794," AD Martinique B 20, 51.

35 "Instruction pour l'administrateur général, traduction par le sieur
 Mendès, concernant les impositions. À bord du Boyne, rade de Fort-Royal,
 26 mai 1794," AD Martinique B 20, 51.

36 "Ordonnance rendue par sir Robert Prescott, lieutenant-général des forces
 de sa majestée, commandant en chef de cette île, et Dubuc, administrateur
 général, au sujet de l'imposition pour l'année en cours, 20 juillet 1794,"
 AD Martinique B 20, 55.

37 "Séance du 6 août 1794," AD Martinique B 20, 56.

38 "Séance du 4 septembre 1794," AD Martinique B 20, 57.

39 "Séance du 5 janvier 1795," AD Martinique B 20, 64.

40 Ibid., 65.

41 "Séance du 7 janvier 1795," AD Martinique B 20, 65–6.

42 "Lettre du Sir John Vaughan, 26 janvier 1795," AD Martinique B 20, 67.

43 "Séance du 20 mai 1794," AD Martinique B 20, 43.

44. "Proclamation de sir Charles Grey … à bord du Boyne, en rade du Fort-
 Royal, 23 mai 1794," AD Martinique B 20, 48.

45 *The Martinico Gazette and General Advertiser* 1 no. 12 (7 June 1794), Colonies
 C[8A] 104, 175–6.

46. "Extrait d'une lettre du Fort-Royal, en date du 17 juin 1794," Colonies C⁸ᴬ 104, 183.

47 "Séance du 6 août 1794," AD Martinique B 20, 55.

48 "Copie d'une lettre particulière, écrite du Fort-Royal par Grandprey, officier passé au service des Anglais, relative aux opérations militaires en Guadeloupe, 14 octobre 1794," Colonies C⁸ᴬ 104, 184–7.

49 "Séance du 3 novembre 1794," AD Martinique B 20, 60–1.

50 "Séance du 22 novembre 1794," AD Martinique B 20, 62.

51 "Copie d'une lettre de Frédéric Guillot, datée de Saint-Pierre, le 23 mars 1795, à un destinaire non dénommé, donnant un journal des événements survenus aux Îles du Vent depuis 26 février," Colonies C⁸ᴬ 104, 191–204.

52 Ibid., 194.

53 "Déclaration des commissaires délégués par la république de France aux commandants en chefs des forces Britanniques, Vaughan, Caldwell, Thompson, Stewart et Lindsey, 28 février 1795," Colonies C⁸ᴬ 104, 194–5.

54 "Copie d'une lettre de Frédéric Guillot ... le 23 mars 1795," Colonies C⁸ᴬ 104, 197.

55 Ibid.; Colonies C⁸ᴬ 104, 200.

56 *Proclamation. Les commissaires délégués par la convention nationale aux Îles du Vent, aux citoyens de la Martinique et autres Antilles. Basse-Terre, Guadeloupe, le 8 prairial, l'an 3 de la république française une et indivisible* [27 May 1795], Colonies C⁸ᴬ 104, 206.

57 "Copie de la lettre de son excellence Sir John Vaughan à MM. les commissaires des paroisses, en date du 1er avril 1795," AD Martinique, B 20, 74. See also "Copie d'une lettre de Frédéric Guillot ... 23 mars 1795," Colonies C⁸ᴬ 104, 200 and Kleczewski, 188–91.

58 "Séance du 5 Mai 1795," AD Martinique B 20, 73–4.

59 "Copie de nouveau serment prêté par les habitants de la Martinique au roi d'Angleterre, le 8 mai 1795," Colonies C⁸ᴬ 104, 205.

60 "Extrait de télégraph anglais. Du 3 juillet 1795," Colonies C⁸ᴬ 104, 207–10.

61 Kleczewski, 223–4. See also Chauleau, *Dans les Îles du Vent*, 191.

62 "Extrait de la déclaration des citoyens le Maître, capitaine, et maximin, commandant la Piroque des missions particulières, sur la situation à l'île Martinique, 29 grimaire an IV [20 December 1795]," Colonies C⁷ᴬ 49, 212–13.

63 "Extrait de la déclaration du capitaine Le Maître au citoyen Goyrand, commissaire délégué par la convention nationale aux Îles du Vent, sur la position de l'isle Martinique, 29 frimaire an IV [20 December 1795]," Colonies C⁷ᴬ 49, 214.

64 "Séance du 4 février 1796," AD Martinique B 20, 92.

65 Kleczewski, 192, 209.

66 "Séance du 6 juillet, 1795," AD Martinique B 20, 76–7.

67 Kleczewski, 256–69.

68 "Séance du 23 novembre 1795," AD Martinique B 20, 90–1. See also Kleczeswski, 271–2.

69 "Séance du 16 avril 1796." See also "Remise de la lettre du duc de Portland au gouverneur Milnes l'autorisant à revenir en Angleterre. Regrets exprimés par cour et passation de pouvoirs au Général Keppel," AD Martinique B 20, 94–5.

70 Kleczewski, 275–7.

71 "Séance du 2 novembre 1795," AD Martinique B 20, 88.

72 "Mémoire d'observations au roi, 10 novembre 1796," AD Martinique B 20, 101–3.

73 "Séance du 10 novembre 1796," AD Martinique B 20, 100.

74 "Séance du 3 juillet 1798," AD Martinique B 22, 46–7.

75 "Séance du 3 novembre 1800," AD Martinique B 22, 74–6.

76 "Séance du 6 septembre 1797," AD Martinique B 22, 36.

77 "Séance du 11 novembre 1798," AD Martinique B 22, 11.

78 Ibid.

79 "Séance du 2 mai 1797," AD Martinique B 22, 110–11.

80 "Seance du 29 décembre 1797," AD Martinique B 22, 3–4. The *procureur général* expressed similar concerns regarding the presence of prisoners of war on 6 September 1796: AD Martinique B 20, 98.

81 "Séance du 8 mars 1799," AD Martinique B 22, 24.

82 "Séance du 8 mai 1799," AD Martinique B 22, 27.

83 "Séance du 4 juillet 1799," AD Martinique B 22, 52–3.

84 "Séance du 4 janvier 1800," AD Martinique B 22, 65.

85 Kleczewski, 244–51. Regarding the effects of disease on troop mortality, and the British efforts to compensate by recruiting new black regiments in the West Indies, see also Duffy, 326–67.

86 Kleczewski, 333–5.

87 Geggus, "The Slaves and Free Coloreds of Martinique," 291.

88 "Lettre du conseil souverain au duc de Portland sur la révolte de Jean Kina, 5 janvier 1801," AD Martinique B 22, 81–2. See also Geggus, "Slaves and Free Coloreds of Martinique," 290–1 and Kleczewski, 335–6.

89 Quoted in Kleczewski, 337.

90 "Séance du 3 janvier 1801" and "Séance du 5 janvier 1801," AD Martinique B 22, 77, 81–2.

91 Geggus, "Slaves and Free Coloreds of Martinique," 292–4. See also Kleczewski, 338 and Chaleau, *Dans les Îles du Vent*, 197. Daney, 3: 240–1 argues that the revolt of Jean Kina demonstrated that England tried to ruin Martinique before returning it to France.

92 Regarding the Peace of Amiens, see Roger Knight, *Britain against Napoleon: The Organization of Victory 1793–1815* (London: Allen Lane, 2013), 215–16 and T.C.W. Blanning, *The French Revolutionary Wars 1787–1802* (London: Arnold, 1996), 256–61 and Doyle, *Oxford History of the French Revolution*, 374–81. Regarding Martinique specifically, see Kleczewski, 342–4 and Duffy, 388–9.

93 In November 1801 Bonaparte suggested to the Legislative Corps, one of two chambers created by the Constitution of the Year VIII, that he envisaged two contrasting policies regarding slavery in different French colonies: "Á Saint-Domingue, à la Guadeloupe, tout y est libre, tout y restera libre," whereas, "la Martinique a conservé l'esclavage, et l'esclavage y sera conservé," as quoted in Adélaïde-Merlande, 147.

94 "Séance du 20 janvier 1802" and "Séance du 21 janvier 1802," AD Martinique B 22, 97–9.

95 "Séance du 6 juillet 1802," AD Martinique B 22, 102–3.

96 "Réponse du gouverneur Keppel à l'adresse qui lui avait été envoyée. Saint-Pierre, 12 juillet 1802," AD Martinique B 22, 109–10.

97 "Séance du 15 juillet 1802," AD Martinique B 22, 110.

98 Kleczewski, 345.

99 AD Martinique B 22, 112–13. See also Kleczewski, 346 and Chaleau, *Dans les Îles du Vent*, 203.

Conclusion

1 Dubois, *A Colony of Citizens*, 328–42. See also Régent, 375–9 and Bangou, 111–12 and Lacour, 3: 39–48.

2 "Proclamation to the Citizens of Saint-Domingue (Decmber 25, 1799)," in *The French Revolution: A Document Collection*, ed. Laura Mason and Tracey Rizzo (Boston, MA: Houghton Mifflin, 1999), 348.

3 "The Constitution of the Year VIII, 13 December 1799 (22 Frimaire Year VIII)," in *A Documentary Survey of the French Revolution*, ed. Stewart, 767–9.

4 Dubois, *A Colony of Citizens*, 342–53. See also Yves Benot, *La démence coloniale sous Napoléon* (Paris: Éditions la Découverte, 1992), 38–9, 46–9.

5 The three civil commissioners who replaced Desfourneaux all had experience in the colonies: René-Gaston Baco was a former mayor of Nantes who, as civil commissioner to the Île-de-France in the Indian Ocean had

been expelled when he attempted to declare the decree of 16 *Pluviôse* in 1796; Étienne Laveaux had been governor-general in Saint-Domingue between 1793 and 1797; and Nicolas-Georges Jeannet-Oudin, Danton's nephew, had proclaimed the abolition of slavery in Guyana. See Benot, *La démence coloniale sous Napoléon*, 36–8 and Régent, 379–82 and Dubois, *A Colony of Citizens*, 343–5.

6 Régent, 395–6, 413–14. See also Bangou, 115–16, 123–4 and Dubois, *A Colony of Citizens*, 354–5.

7 Dubois, *A Colony of Citizens*, 353–62. See also Régent, 384–94 and Benot, *La démence colonial sous Napoléon*, 39–42 and Bangou, 113–17.

8 "Toussaint Louverture's Constitution, July 1801," in *The Haitian Revolution: A Documentary History*, ed. David Geggus (Indianapolis, IN: Hackett Publishing Company, 2014), 160–4.

9 "Notes to Serve as Instructions to Give to the Captain General Leclerc," in *Slave Revolution in the Caribbean*, ed. Dubois and Garrigus, 176–8.

10 Philippe R. Girard, "Napoleon Bonaparte and the Emancipation Issue in Saint-Domingue, 1799–1803," *French Historical Studies* 32, no. 4 (Fall 2009): 587–618. See also Benot, *La démence coloniale sous Napoléon*, 57–8.

11 Dubois, *A Colony of Citizens*, 367–9. See also Benot, *La démence coloniale sous Napoléon*, 45–6, 69. Regarding Bonaparte's formal decision that slavery would continue in Martinique, Sainte-Lucie, Tobago and the Île-de-France, see "To Consul Cambacérès (April 27, 1802)," in *The French Revolution*, ed. Mason and Rizzo, 349–50.

12 Louis Delgrès, "To the Entire Universe: The Last Cry of Innocence and Despair, 1802," in *Slave Revolution in the Caribbean*, ed. Dubois and Garrigus, 171–2.

13 Dubois, *A Colony of Citizens*, 389–400, 404–14. See also Bangou, 118–43, 147–51, Régent, 402–24, and Benot, *La démence coloniale sous Napoléon*, 69–74. For the account of one of Richepance's officers, see General Jean-François-Xavier de Ménard, "On the Final Stand of Delgrès, 1802," in *Slave Revolution in the Caribbean*, ed. Dubois and Garrigus, 173–5.

14 Regarding the influence of news from Guadeloupe on the situation in Saint-Domingue, see Dubois, *A Colony of Citizens*, 401–3 and Bangou, 162–3. For the betrayal and imprisonment of Toussaint Louverture, see Bell, *Toussaint Louverture*, esp. 230–84. On the transition from popular resistance to war of independence in 1802, see Fick, *The Making of Haiti*, 212–28 and Dubois, *Avengers of the New World*, 274–89 and Abenon, Cauna, Chauleau, *Antilles 1789*, 190–3.

15 "The Declaration of Independence, 1 January 1804," in *Haitian Revolution*, ed. Geggus, 179–80. Regarding Rochambeau's actions as commander in

Saint-Domingue, see Benot, *La démence coloniale sous Napoléon*, 83, Fick, 228–9, and Dubois, *Avengers of the New World*, 292–3. See also Popkin, ed., *Facing Racial Revolution*, 317–28.
16 Sainte-Croix de la Roncière, 310–20. See also Adélaïde-Merlande, 217–20.
17 Blackburn, *The Overthrow of Colonial Slavery*, 473–515.

Bibliography

Archival Sources

Archives des colonies

The central depot for these archives is the *Centre des Archives d'Outre-Mer* in Aix-en-Provence, but microfilm copies can also be consulted at the *Archives Nationales* in Paris.

Colonies C^{7A} 43 Guadeloupe, 1788–9
Colonies C^{7A} 44 Guadeloupe, 1790
Colonies C^{7A} 45 Guadeloupe, 1791–2
Colonies C^{7A} 46 Guadeloupe, 1793
Colonies C^{7A} 47 Guadeloupe, 1794
Colonies C^{7A} 48 Guadeloupe, 1795
Colonies C^{7A} 49 Guadeloupe, 1796–7
Colonies C^{7A} 50 Guadeloupe, 1798
Colonies C^{7A} 51 Guadeloupe, 1799
Colonies C^{8A} 89 Martinique, 1789
Colonies C^{8A} 90 Martinique, 1790
Colonies C^{8A} 93 Martinique, 1790
Colonies C^{8A} 94 Martinique, 1790
Colonies C^{8A} 95 Martinique, 1790
Colonies C^{8A} 96 Martinique, 1790
Colonies C^{8A} 97 Martinique, 1791
Colonies C^{8A} 98 Martinique, 1791
Colonies C^{8A} 99 Martinique, 1792
Colonies C^{8A} 100 Martinique, 1792
Colonies C^{8A} 101 Martinique, 1793

Colonies C^{8A} 102 Martinique, 1793
Colonies C^{8A} 103 Martinique, 1791–8
Colonies C^{8A} 104 Martinique, 1794–1801
Colonies C^{8B} 24 Martinique, 1790–1808
Colonies F^3 34 Martinique, 1790
Colonies F^3 35 Martinique, 1790
Colonies F^3 36 Martinique, 1790
Colonies F^3 37 Martinique, 1791

Archives de la marine

The central depot for these archives is the *Service historique de la marine* in
Vincennes.

Marine BB 4 / 3 1790
Marine BB 4 / 5 1791
Marine BB 4 / 12 1792
Marine BB 4 / 23 1793
Marine BB 4 / 26 1793
Marine BB 4 / 85 1795
Marine BB 4 / 108 1796

Archives départementales de la Martinique

FORT-DE-FRANCE, MARTINIQUE
Série B: Conseil souverain de la Martinique
B18 1787–91
B20 1791–7
B22 1797–1802

Archives départementales de la Guadeloupe

BASSE-TERRE, GUADELOUPE
Sous-série 2 Mi
4 Mi 21 *Affiches, annonces, et avis divers de l'île de Guadeloupe, 1789–1790*

Archives départementales de la Gironde

BORDEAUX
Série C fonds de la chambre du commerce de Guienne
C 4266 1785–91

Série J
8 J 422 *Fonds Bigot, 1714–1830*

Série L
3 L 177 *Demandes de passeports, 1790–An III (A–G)*
3 L 178 *Demandes de passeports, 1790–An III (H–Z)*

Archives Municipales de Bordeaux

Série C
C 3 *Publications diverses relatives aux colonies: 1789–90*
C 4 *Publications diverses relatives aux colonies: 1791–An 5*
C 15 *Affaires politiques: 1790*

Published Primary Sources

Archives parlementaires de 1787 à 1860. 95 vols. Paris: Libraire administrative
   de Paul Dupont [vols. 1–82], 1875–1913; C.N.R.S. [vols. 82bis-95], 1966–87.
Aulard, F.V.A., ed. *Recueil des actes du comité de salut public avec la correspondence*
   officielle des représentants en mission et le registre du conseil exécutif provisoire.
   25 vols. Paris: Imprimerie nationale, 1889–1951.
Barère, Bertrand. *Rapport fait au nom du comité de salut public, par Barère, sur*
   les colonies Françaises Îsles-du-Vent: Dans la séance du 19 thermidor, l'an 2 de
   la république française une et indivisible. Paris: Imprimerie nationale, n.d.
Bazoche, Claude-Hubert. *Rapport fait au nom du comité de division, par Claude-*
   Hubert Bazoche, député par le département de la Meuse à la convention nationale:
   Sur la validité de l'élection des députés de la Martinique et de la Guadeloupe.
   Paris: Imprimerie nationale, n.d.
Béhague, comte de. *Mémoire sur les colonies de l'Amérique méridionale, et sur*
   la question du jour. Paris: Imprimerie de Vezard et Le Normant, 1790.
Bertrand de Moleville, Antoine-François. *Private Memoirs of A.F. Bertrand*
   de Moleville, Minister of State, 1790–1791: Relative to the Last Year of the Reign
   of Louis the Sixteenth. 2 vols. Translated by R.C. Dallas. London, 1797.
   New edition edited by G.K. Fortescue. Boston: J.B. Millet Company, 1909.
Biondi, Jean-Pierre, and François Zuccarelli, eds. *16 pluviôse an II – Les colonies*
   de la révolution. Paris: Éditions Denoël, 1989.
Crassous de Médeuil. *Discours prononcés à la barre de l'assemblée nationale,*
   le 7 décembre 1791, par les députés de la ville de Saint-Pierre-Martinique.
   Paris: Imprimerie nationale, 1791.
– *Rélation de ce qui s'est passé à la Martinique depuis le 1ᵉʳ septembre 1790, et*
   réponse au mémoire intitulé: Mémoire de M. Damas, gouverneur de la Martinique,

sur les troubles de la Martinique, signé Damas, sans nom d'imprimeur. Fort-Royal, 1791. Reprint, Fort-de-France: Société d'histoire de la Martinique, 1982.

Damas, Charles-Claude, vicomte de. *Mémoire de M. de Damas, gouverneur de la Martinique, sur les troubles de cette colonie. 5 février 1791.*

Derfermond. *Rapport fait au nom du comité de salut public, sur la Guadeloupe et autres Îles du Vent*. Paris: Imprimerie nationale, an III.

Dermigny, Louis, and Gabriel Debien, eds. "La Révolution aux Antilles: Journal maritime du commandeur de Villevielle, commandant de la frégate La Didon (septembre 1790–septembre 1792)." *Revue d'histoire de l'Amérique française*, ix (1955): 55–73, 251–71.

Dessalles, Pierre-François-Régis. *Historique des troubles survenus à la Martinique pendant la révolution*. Edited by Henri de Frémont. Fort-de-France: Société d'histoire de la Martinique, 1982.

Dorigny, Marcel, and Bernard Gainot, eds. *La société des amis des noirs 1788–1799*. Paris: Éditions UNESCO, 1998.

Dubois, Laurent, and John D. Garrigus, eds. *Slave Revolution in the Caribbean 1789–1804: A Brief History with Documents*. Boston, MA: Bedford / St Martin's, 2006.

Dupuch, Élie-Louis. *Pétition à l'assemblée nationale, par M. Dupuch, député des paroisses de la Basseterre Guadeloupe, et de la municipalité de la même ville*. Paris: Imprimerie nationale, n.d.

– *Précis historique des troubles survenus à la Guadeloupe, depuis l'arrivée des commissaires du roi à la Martinique*. Paris: Imprimerie nationale, 1792.

État des décrets rendus sur les colonies, dans le cours de la législature actuelle, présenté par le comité colonial, en exécution du décret du 12 septembre 1792, l'an quatrième de la liberté, premier de l'égalité. Paris: Imprimerie nationale, 1792.

Geggus, David, ed. and trans. *The Haitian Revolution: A Documentary History*. Indianapolis: Hackett Publishing Company, 2014.

Hardman, John, ed. *French Revolution Documents: Vol. II 1792–95*. Oxford: Basil Blackwell, 1973.

Hardy, James D., John H. Jensen, and Martin Wolfe, eds. *The Maclure Collection of French Revolutionary Materials*. Philadelphia: University of Pennsylvania Press, 1966.

Hugues, Victor. *Acte d'accusation contre les complices de la trahison de Toulon. Rochefort: 29 brumaire an II*. Rochefort: R.D. Jousseront, imprimeur du tribunal révolutionnaire, n.d.

Hunt, Lynn, ed. *The French Revolution and Human Rights: A Brief Documentary History*. Boston, MA: Bedford / St Martin's, 1996.

Léotin, Marie-Hélène, ed. *La Martinique au temps de la révolution française 1789–1794*. Fort-de-France: Archives départementales del a Martinique, 1989.

Marec. *Rapport fait au nom de la commission chargée de l'examen d'une pétition des négocians de France intéressés au commerce de la Guadeloupe*. Paris: Imprimerie nationale, an V.

Mason, Laura, and Tracey Rizzo, eds. *The French Revolution: A Document Collection*. Boston, MA: Houghton Mifflin, 1999.

Merlet, Jean-François. *Opinion de Jean-François Merlet, député du département de Maine et Loire, sur la question de la représentation des colonies dans le corps legislative (Maclure Collection*, vol. 1008, no. 1).

Observations présentées à l'assemblée nationale, par les membres de la municipalité de la Basse-Terre-Guadeloupe, et par les citoyens de la même ville: Pour démontrer l'iniquité, l'incompétence et la nullité de divers arrêtés de l'assemblée coloniale de l'Îsle Guadeloupe. Paris: Imprimerie nationale, 1792.

Pautrizel. *Rapport sur les colonies par Pautrizel, (de la Guadeloupe), représentant du peuple*. Paris: Imprimerie nationale, an III.

Popkin, Jeremy D., ed. *Facing Racial Revolution: Eyewitness Accounts of the Haitian Insurrection*. Chicago, IL: The University of Chicago Press, 2007.

Précis sur les troubles de la Martinique (Maclure Collection, vol. 757, no. 9).

Réclamations pour les colonies des Antilles, adressées au roi et à l nation. Paris, 1789.

Réimpression de l'ancien moniteur depuis la réunion des états-généraux jusqu'au consulat (mai 1789–novembre 1799). 31 vols. Paris: Imprimerie d'A. René et cie, 1840–54.

Rivière, Charles-Joseph Mascarène, chevalier de. *Extrait du journal de ma station aux îsles du vent*. Fort-Royal, Martinique: Impimerie de J.F. Bazille, n.d.

Rouyer. *Projet de décret présenté par M. Rouyer, au nom des quatre comités réunis de commerce, de marine, colonial et diplomatique (Maclure Collection*, vol. 1136, no. 5).

Rudé, George, ed. *Robespierre*. Englewood Cliffs, NJ: Prentice Hall, 1967.

Stewart, John Hall, ed. *A Documentary Survey of the French Revolution*. Toronto: Macmillan, 1951.

Vissière, Isabelle, and Jean-Louis, eds. *La traite des noirs au siècle des lumières (témoignages de négriers)*. Paris: Éditions A.M. Métailié, 1982.

Valous, Marquis de, ed. *Avec les "rouges" aux Îles du Vent: Souvenirs du chevalier de Valous (1790–1793) pendant la révolution française*. Paris, 1930. Reprint, Paris: Éditions Caribéenes, 1989.

Willyams, Cooper. *An Account of the Campaign in the West Indies in the Year 1794*. London, 1796. Reprint, Basse-Terre: Société d'histoire de la Guadeloupe, 1990.

SECONDARY SOURCES

Abenon, Lucien, Jacques Cauna, and Liliane Chauleau. *Antilles 1789: La révolution aux Caraïbes*. Paris: Éditions Nathan, 1989.

Abenon, Lucien-René. *Petit histoire de la Guadeloupe*. Paris: Éditions l'Harmattan, 1992.

– "Les révoltes serviles à la Guadeloupe au début de la Réolution (1789–1793)." In *Esclavage, résistances et abolitions*, edited by Marcel Dorigny, 209–16. Paris: Éditions du CTHS, 1999.

Adélaïde-Merlande, Jacques. *La Caraïbe et la Guyane au temps de la révolution et de l'empire*. Paris: Éditions Karthala, 1992.

Andress, David. *The Terror: The Civil War in the French Revolution*. London: Little Brown, 2005.

Anduse, Roland. "L'histoire singulière du 1er bataillon de l'armée de la Guadeloupe: Loyalisme révolutionnaire et révoltes militaires." In *Mourir pour les Antilles: Indépendance nègre ou esclavage 1802–1804*, edited by Michel L. Martin and Alain Yacou, 57–62. Paris: Éditions Caribéennes, 1991.

Baczko, Bronislaw. *Ending the Terror: The French Revolution after Robespierre*. Translated by Michel Petheram. Cambridge: Cambridge University Press, 1994.

Baker, Keith Michael. *Inventing the French Revolution: Essays on French Political Culture in the Eighteenth Century*. Cambridge: Cambridge University Press, 1990.

Baker, Keith Michael, and Dan Edelstein, eds. *Scripting Revolution: A Historical Approach to the Comparative Study of Revolutions*. Stanford: Stanford University Press, 2015.

Banbuck, C.A. *Histoire politique, économique et sociale de la Martinique sous l'ancien régime (1635–1789)*. Paris, Marcel Rivière, 1935. Reprint, Fort-de-France, Martinique: Société de distribution et de culture, 1972.

Bangou, Henri. *La révolution et l'esclavage à la Guadeloupe 1789–1802*. Paris: Messidor / Éditions sociales, 1989.

Banks, Kenneth J. *Chasing Empire across the Sea: Communications and the State in the French Atlantic, 1713–1763*. Montreal and Kingston: McGill-Queen's University Press, 2002.

Batie, Robert C. "Why Sugar? Economic Cycles and the Changing of Staples on the English and French Antilles, 1624–54." *Journal of Caribbean History* 8–9 (1976): 1–41.

Bélénus, René. "Le pouvoir et l'agitation politique à la Guadeloupe de 1794 à 1802." In *Esclavage, résistances et abolitions*, edited by Marcel Dorigny, 217–22. Paris: Éditions du CTHS, 1999.

Bell, David A. "Questioning the Global Turn: The Case of the French Revolution." *French Historical Studies* 37, no. 1 (Winter 2014): 1–24.

Bell, Madison Smartt. *Toussaint Louverture: A Biography*. New York: Random House, 2007.

Benot, Yves. *La révolution française et la fin des colonies*. Paris: Éditions la découverte, 1987.

– *La démence coloniale sous napoléon*. Paris: Éditions la découverte, 1992.

Bérenger, Jean and Jean Meyer. *La France dans le monde au XVIIIe siècle*. Paris: Sedes, 1993.

Biondi, Carminella. "Le problème des gens de couleur aux colonies et en France dans le seconde moitié du XVIIIe siècle." *Cromohs* 8 (2003): 1–12.

Black, Jeremy. *Natural and Necessary Enemies: Anglo-French Relations in the Eighteenth Century*. Athens: University of Georgia Press, 1987.

Blackburn, Robin. *The Making of New World Slavery: From the Baroque to the Modern 1492–1800*. London: Verso, 1997.

– *The Overthrow of Colonial Slavery, 1776–1848*. London: Verso, 1988.

Blanning, T.C.W. *The French Revolutionary Wars 1787–1802*. London: Arnold, 1996.

Bonnel, Ulane. *La France, les États-Unis et la guerre de course (1789–1815)*. Paris: Nouvelles éditions latines, 1961.

Branda, Pierre, and Thierry Lentz. *Napoléon, l'esclavage et les colonies*. Paris: Fayard, 2006.

Brown, Howard G. *Ending the French Revolution: Violence, Justice, and Repression from the Terror to Napoleon*. Charlottesville: University of North Carolina Press, 2006.

Bruley, Georges. *Les Antilles pendant la révolution française: D'après la correspondance inédite de César-Dominique Duny, consul de France à Curaçao, né à tours le 22 juillet 1758*. 1890. Reprint, Paris: Éditions Caribéennes, 1989.

Butel, Paul. "France, the Antilles, and Europe in the Seventeenth and Eighteenth Centuries: Renewals of Trade." In *Caribbean Slavery in the Atlantic World: A Student Reader*, edited by Verne Shepherd and Hilary McD. Beckles, 194–205. Oxford: James Currey Publishers, 2000.

– *Histoire des Antilles françaises XVIIe – XXe siècle*. Paris: Perrin, 2002.

Censer, Jack Richard. *Prelude to Power: The Parisian Radical Press, 1789–1791*. Baltimore, MD: Johns Hopkins University Press, 1976.

Chauleau, Liliane. "Abolition de l'esclavage et déclaration des droits de l'homme sous la révolution française." In *Esclavage, résistances et abolitions*, edited by Marcel Dorigny, 151–64. Paris: Éditions du CTHS, 1999.

– *Conseil Souverain de la Martinique (Série B) 1712–1791: Inventaire analytique*. 2 vols. Fort-de-France: Archives départementales de la Martinique, 1985.

– *Dans les Îles du Vent: La Martinique XVIIe – XIXe siècle*. Paris: Éditions L'Harmattan, 1993.

– "La révolution Française à la Martinique." In *France in the New World: Proceedings of the 22nd Annual Meeting of the French Colonial Historical Society*, edited by David Buissert, 49–63. East Lansing: Michigan University Press, 1998.

Cheney, Paul. *Revolutionary Commerce: Globalization and the French Monarchy.* Cambridge, MA: Harvard University Press, 2010.

Conlin, Michael F. "The American Mission of Citizen Pierre-Auguste Adet: Revolutionary Chemistry and Diplomacy in the Early Republic." *The Pennsylvania Magazine of History and Biography* 124, no. 4 (October 2000): 489–520.

Cormack, William S. *Revolution and Political Conflict in the French Navy 1789–1794.* Cambridge: Cambridge University Press, 1995.

Cox, Edward L. *Free Coloreds in the Slave Societies of St Kitts and Grenada, 1763–1833.* Knoxville: University of Tennessee Press, 1984.

Craton, Michael. "The Black Caribs of St Vincent: A Reevaluation." In *The Lesser Antilles in the Age of European Expansion*, edited by Robert L. Paquette and Stanley L. Engerman, 71–85. Gainesville: University Press of Florida, 1996.

Crouse, Nellis M. *French Pioneers in the West Indies (1624–1664).* New York, 1940. Reprint, New York: Octagon Books, 1977.

Crouzet, François. "England and France in the Eighteenth Century: A Comparative Analysis of Two Economic Growths." In *Social Historians in Contemporary France: Essays from Annales*, edited by Marc Ferro, 59–86. New York: Harper and Row, 1972.

Daney, Sidney. *Histoire de la Martinique depuis la colonisation jusqu'en 1815.* 3 vols. Fort-Royal, 1846. Reprint, Fort-de-France: Société d'histoire de la Martinique, 1963.

Davis, David Biron. *The Problem of Slavery in the Age of Revolution, 1770–1823.* Ithaca, NY: Cornell University Press, 1975.

Davis, Ralph. *The Rise of the Atlantic Economies.* London: Weidenfeld and Nicolson, 1973.

Debien, Gabriel. *Les Colons de Saint-Domingue et la révolution: Essai sur le club massiac (août 1789–août 1792).* 2 vols. Paris: Colin, 1953.

– "Les engagés pour les Antilles (1634–1715)." *Revue d'histoire des colonies* 38 (1951): 5–274.

– *Les esclaves aux Antilles françaises aux XVIe et XVIIIe siècles.* Fort-de-France: Société d'histoire de la Martinique, 1974.

– "Le Marronage aux Antilles françaises au XVIIIe siècle," *Caribbean Studies* 6 (1966): 3–44.

Desan, Suzanne, Lynn Hunt, and William Max Nelson, eds. *The French Revolution in Global Perspective.* Ithaca, NY: Cornell University Press, 2013.

Doerflinger, T.M. "The Antilles Trade of the Old Regime." *Journal of Interdisciplinary History* 6 (1976): 397–415.

Doyle, William. *Origins of the French Revolution*. 3rd ed. Oxford: Oxford University Press, 1999.

– *The Oxford History of the French Revolution*. Oxford: Clarendon Press, 1989.

Dubois, Laurent. *Avengers of the New World: The Story of the Haitian Revolution*. Cambridge, MA: The Belknap Press of Harvard University Press, 2004.

– *A Colony of Citizens: Revolution and Slave Emancipation in the French Caribbean, 1787–1804*. Chapel Hill: University of North Carolina Press, 2004.

– *Les Esclaves de la république: L'histoire oubliée de la première émancipation 1789–1794*. Paris: Calmann-Lévy, 1998.

– "'The Price of Liberty': Victor Hugues and the Administration of Freedom in Guadeloupe, 1794–1798." *William and Mary Quarterly* 56, no. 2 (April 1999): 363–92.

Duffy, Michael. *Soldiers, Sugar, and Seapower: The British Expeditions to the West Indies and the War against Revolutionary France*. Oxford: Clarendon Press, 1987.

– "The French Revolution and British Attitudes to the West Indian Colonies." In *A Turbulent Time: The French Revolution and the Greater Caribbean*, edited by David Barry Gaspar and David Patrick Geggus, 78–101. Bloomington: Indiana University Press, 1997.

Dull, Jonathan R. *The French Navy and American Independence: A Study of Arms and Diplomacy, 1774–1787*. Princeton: Princeton University Press, 1975.

Dupuy, Roger, and François Lebrun, eds. *Les résistances à la révolution*. Paris: Éditions imago, 1987.

Eccles, W.J. *France in America*. Vancouver: Fitzhenry and Whiteside, 1972.

Edmonds, W.D. "'Federalism' and Urban Revolt in France in 1793." *Journal of Modern History*, 55 (March 1983): 22–53.

Ekman, Ernst. "St Barthélemy and the French Revolution." *Caribbean Studies* 3, no. 4 (1964): 17–29.

Élisabeth, Léo. "The French Antilles." In *Neither Slave nor Free: The Freedmen of African Descent in the Slave Societies of the New World*, edited by David W. Cohen and Jack P. Greene, 134–71. Baltimore, MD: Johns Hopkins University Press, 1972.

– "Gens de couleur et révolution dans les Îles du Vent (1789–Janvier 1793)." *Revue française d'histoire d'outre-mer* 76, no. 282–3 (1989): 75–95.

– "La république dans les Îles du Vent, décembre 1792–avril 1794." *Annales historiques de la révolution française* no. 3–4 (1993): 373–408.

– "Résistances des esclaves aux XVIIe et XVIIIe siècles dans les colonies françaises d'Amérique, principalement aux îles du Vent." In *Les abolitions de l'esclavage de L.F. Sonthanax à V. Schoelcher, 1793, 1794, 1848*, edited by Marcel Dorigny, 78–86. Paris: Presses universitaires de Vincennes, 1995.

Eltis, David. *The Rise of African Slavery in the Americas*. Cambridge: Cambridge University Press, 2000.

Engerman, Stanley L. "Europe, the Lesser Antilles, and Economic Expansion, 1600–1800." In *The Lesser Antilles in the Age of European Expansion*, edited by Robert L. Paquette and Stanley L. Engerman, 147–64. Gainesville: University Press of Florida, 1996.

Fick, Carolyn. "The Haitian Revolution in an Atlantic Context." In *Proceedings of the Nineteenth Meeting of the French Colonial Historical Society, Providence RI, May 1993*, edited by James Pritchard, 128–40. Bomanville, ON: Mothersill Printing, 1994.

– *The Making of Haiti: The Saint-Domingue Revolution from Below*. Knoxville: University of Tennessee Press, 1990.

Fitzsimmons, Michael P. *The Remaking of France: The National Assembly and the Constitution of 1791*. Cambridge: Cambridge University Press, 1994.

Fleury, E.J., and J.T. Viaud. *Histoire de la ville et du port de Rochefort*. Rochefort: Honorine Fleury, 1845.

Forrest, Alan. *Society and Politics in Revolutionary Bordeaux*. London: Oxford University Press, 1975.

Forster, Robert. "The French Revolution, people of color, and slavery." In *The Global Ramification of the French Revolution*, edited by Joseph Klaits and Michael H. Haltzel, 89–104. Washington, DC: Woodrow Wilson Centre Press, 1994.

Fouchard, Jean. *The Haitian Maroons: Liberty or Death*. Translated by A. Faulkner Watts. New York: E.W. Blyden Press, 1981.

Frostin, Charles. *Les révoltes blanches à Saint-Domingue aux XVIIe et XVIIIe siècle (Haïti avant 1789)*. Paris: L'École, 1975.

Furet, François. "Barnave," "Terror," and "Revolutionary Government." In *A Critical Dictionary of the French Revolution*, edited by François Furet and Mona Ozouf, 186–95, 137–50, 548–59. Translated by Arthur Goldhammer. Cambridge, MA: Harvard University Press, 1989.

– *Interpreting the French Revolution*. Translated by Elborg Forester. Cambridge: Cambridge University Press, 1981, Reprint, 1985.

– *Revolutionary France 1770–1880*. Translated by Antonia Nevill. Oxford: Blackwell Publishing, 1992. Reprint, 1995.

Garrigus, John D. *Before Haiti: Race and Citizenship in French Saint-Domingue*. New York: Palgrave Macmillan, 2006.

– "Blue and Brown: Contraband Indigo and the Rise of a Free Colored Planter Class in French Saint Domingue." *Americas* 50, no. 2 (October 1993): 233–63.

– "'Sons of the Same Father': Gender, Race, and Citizenship in French Saint-Domingue, 1760–1792." In *Visions and Revisions of Eighteenth-Century France*, edited by Christine Adams, Jack R. Censer, and Lisa Jane Graham, 137–54. University Park, PA: Pennsylvania State University Press, 1997.

Gaspar, David Barry. "La Guerre des Bois: Revolution, War and Slavery in Saint Lucia, 1793–1838." In *A Turbulent Time: The French Revolution and the Greater Caribbean*, edited by David Barry Gaspar and David Patrick Geggus, 102–30. Bloomington: Indiana University Press, 1997.

Gautier, Arlette. *Les soeurs de solitude: Femmes et esclavage aux Antilles du XVIIe au XIXe siècle*. Paris: Éditions Caribéennes, 1985.

Gay, Peter. *The Enlightenment: Vol. II The Science of Freedom*. New York: W.W. Norton and Company, 1969. Reprint, 1996.

Geggus, David Patrick. "The Haitian Revolution: New Approaches and Old," in *Proceedings of the Nineteenth Meeting of the French Colonial Historical Society, Providence, RI, May 1993*, edited by James Pritchard, 141–55. Bomanville, ON: Mothersill Printing, 1994.

– *The Impact of the Haitian Revolution in the Atlantic World*. Columbia: University of South Carolina Press, 2001.

– "Racial Equality, Slavery, and Colonial Secession during the Constituent Assembly." *American Historical Review* 94, no. 5 (Dec. 1989): 1290–1308.

– *Slavery, War and Revolution: The British Occupation of Saint Domingue, 1793–1798*. Oxford: Clarendon Press, 1982.

– "Slavery, War and Revolution in the Greater Caribbean, 1789–1815." In *A Turbulent Time: The French Revolution and the Greater Caribbean*, edited by David Barry Gaspar and David Patrick Geggus, 1–50. Bloomington: Indiana University Press, 1997.

– "The Slaves and Free Coloreds of Martinique during the Age of the French and Haitian Revolutions: Three Moments of Resistance." In *The Lesser Antilles in the Age of European Expansion*, edited by Robert L. Paquette and Stanley L. Engerman, 280–301. Gainesville: University Press of Florida, 1996.

Girard, Philippe R. "Napoleon Bonaparte and the Emancipation Issue in Saint-Domingue, 1799–1803." *French Historical Studies* 32, no. 4 (Fall 2009): 587–618.

Gisler, Antoine. *L'esclavage au Antilles françaises (XVIIe–XIXe siècle): Contribution au problème de l'esclavage*. Fribourg: Éditions universitaires Fribourg Suisse, 1965.

Godechot, Jacques. *The Counter-Revolution: Doctrine and Action, 1789–1799*. Translated by Salvator Attanasio. Princeton: Princeton University Press, 1971.

– *France and the Atlantic Revolution of the Eighteenth Century, 1770–1799*. Translated by Herbert H. Rowen. New York: Free Press, 1965.

Grant, William L. "Canada versus Guadeloupe: An Episode of the Seven Years' War." *American Historical Review* 17 (1912): 735–43.

Greer, Donald. *The Incidence of the Terror in the French Revolution*. Cambridge, MA: Harvard University Press, 1935.

Grimoüard, Vicomte Henri de. *L'amiral de Grimoüard au Port-au-Prince d'après sa correspondance et son journal de bord (Mars 1791–Juillet 1792)*. Paris: Société de l'histoire des colonies françaises et librairie larose, 1937.

Guerin, Léon. *Histoire maritime de France*. 6 vols. Paris: Dufour, Mulat et Boulanger, 1851–6.

Hampson, Norman. *Danton*. Oxford: Basil Blackwell, 1978.

– *Prelude to Terror: The Constituent Assembly and the Failure of Consensus, 1789–1792*. Oxford: Basil Blackwell, 1988.

Hanson, Paul. *The Jacobin Republic under Fire: The Federalist Revolt in the French Revolution*. University Park: Pennsylvania State University Press, 2003.

Hayot, Émile. *Les gens de couleur libres du Fort-Royal 1679–1823*. Paris: Société française d'histoire d'outre-mer, 1971.

Hochschild, Adam. *Bury the Chains: Prophets and Rebels in the Fight to Free an Empire's Slaves*. Boston, MA: Houghton Mifflin, 2005.

Jackson, Melvin H. *Privateers in Charleston, 1793–1796: An Account of a French Palatinate in South Carolina*. Washington: Smithsonian Institution Press, 1969.

James, C.L.R. *The Black Jacobins: Toussaint L'Ouverture and the San Domingo Revolution*. New York: Random House, 1963. Second edition, 1989.

James, William. *The Naval History of Great Britain, from the Declaration of War by France in 1793 to the Accession of George IV*. 6 vols. London: Richard Bentley, 1859.

Jenkins, H.J.K. "The Colonial Robespierre: Victor Hugues on Guadeloupe 1794–98." *History Today* 27, no. 11 (Nov. 1977): 734–40.

– "Controversial Legislation at Guadeloupe regarding Trade and Piracy, 1797." *Revue française d'histoire d'outre-mer* 76 no. 282–3 (1989): 97–106.

– "The Leeward Islands Command, French Royalism and the *Bienvenue*, 1792–1793," *Mariner's Mirror* 71 (1985): 477–8.

– "The Heyday of French Privateering from Guadeloupe, 1796–98," *Mariner's Mirror* 64 (1978): 245–50.

– "Guadeloupe, Martinique and Commerce Raiding: Two Colonies in Conflict, 1797–1798," *Revue française d'histoire d'outre-mer* 78, no. 293 (1991): 465–75.

– "Guadeloupe, Savagery and Emancipation: British Comment of 1794–1796," *Revue française d'histoire d'outre-mer* 65, no. 240 (1978): 325–31.

Kates, Gary, ed. *The French Revolution: Recent Debates & New Controversies*. London: Routledge, 1998.

King, Stewart R. *Blue Coat or Powdered Wig: Free People of Color in Pre-Revolutionary Saint Domingue*. Athens: The University of Georgia Press, 2001.

Kleczewski, Kieran Russell. "Martinique and the British Occupation, 1794–1802." PhD diss., Georgetown University, 1988.

Knight, Roger. *Britain against Napoleon: The Organization of Victory 1793–1815.* London: Allen Lane, 2013.

Lacour, M.A. *Histoire de la Guadeloupe.* 4 vols. Basse-Terre, 1855–60. Reprint, Paris: Édition et diffusion de la culture antillaise, 1976.

Lefebvre, Georges. *The Great Fear of 1789: Rural Panic in Revolutionary France.* Translated by Joan White. Princeton: Princeton University Press, 1973. Reprint, 1982.

Lémery, Henry. *La révolution Française à la Martinique.* Paris: Larose, 1936.

Lévy-Schneider, Léon. *Le conventionnel Jeanbon Saint-André.* 2 vols. Paris: Félix Alcan, 1901.

Liss, Peggy K. *Atlantic Empires: The Network of Trade and Revolution, 1713–1826.* Baltimore, MD: Johns Hopkins University Press, 1983.

Lucas, Colin. "The First Directory and the Rule of Law." *French Historical Studies* 10 no. 2 (Fall 1977), 231–60.

Marzagalli, Silvia. *Bordeaux et les États-Unis: Politique et stratégies négociantes dans la genèse d'un réseau commercial.* Geneva: Librairie Droz, 2015.

Meadows, R. Darrell. "Engineering Exile: Social Networks and the French Atlantic Community, 1789–1809." *French Historical Studies* 23, no. 1 (Winter 2000): 67–102.

Meyer, Jean. *L'armement nantais dans la deuxième moitié du XVIIIéme siécle.* Paris: SEVPEN, 1969.

Meyer, Jean, Jean Tarrade, and Annie Rey-Goldzeiguer. *Histoire de la France coloniale.* Vol. I *Des origines à 1914.* Paris: Armand Colin, 1991.

Mims, Stewart L. *Colbert's West India Policy.* New Haven, CT: Yale University Press, 1912.

Middleton, Richard. *The Bells of Victory: The Pitt-Newcastle Ministry and the Conduct of the Seven Years' War 1757–1762.* Cambridge: Cambridge University Press, 1985.

Moit, Bernard. "Slave Resistance in Guadeloupe and Martinique, 1791–1848." In *Caribbean Slavery in the Atlantic World,* edited by Verene A. Shepherd and Hilary McD. Beckles, 919–31. Oxford: James Currey Publishers, 2000.

Montmort, Comte de. *Antoine Charles du Houx, Baron de Vioménil: Lieutenant-General of the Armies of the King, Second in Command under Rochambeau.* Baltimore, MD: The Johns Hopkins Press, 1935.

Munford, Clarence J. *The Black Ordeal of Slavery and Slave Trading in the French West Indies, 1625–1715.* 3 vols. Lewiston, NY: Edwin Mellen, 1991.

Nègre, Docteur André. *La rébellion de la Guadeloupe: Guadeloupe contre consulat, 1801–1802.* Paris: Éditions caribéennes, 1987.

Oliver, Bette W. *Surviving the French Revolution: A Bridge across Time.* New York, NY: Lexington Books, 2013.

Outram, Dorinda. *The Enlightenment.* Cambridge: Cambridge University Press, 1995.

Palmer, R.R. *The Age of the Democratic Revolution: A Political History of Europe and America, 1760–1800.* 2 vols. Princeton, NJ: Princeton University Press, 1959. Reprint, 1974.

– *Twelve Who Ruled: The Year of the Terror in the French Revolution.* Princeton, NJ: Princeton University Press, 1941. Reprint, 1989.

Pares, Richard. *War and Trade in the West Indies 1739–1763.* London: F. Cass, 1963.

Parry, J.H. *Trade and Dominion: The European Overseas Empires in the Eighteenth Century.* London: Weidenfield and Nicolson, 1971.

Peabody, Sue. "'A Dangerous Zeal': Catholic Missions to Slaves in the French Antilles, 1635–1800." *French Historical Studies* 25 (2002): 53–90.

– *"There Are No Slaves in France": The Political Culture of Race and Slavery in the Ancien Régime.* New York, 1996.

Pérotin-Dumon, Anne. "Ambiguous Revolution in the Caribbean: The White Jacobins, 1789–1800," *Historical Reflections / Réflexions Historiques* 13, no. 2 and 3 (1986): 499–515.

– *Être patriote sous les tropiques: La Guadeloupe, la colonisation et la révolution.* Basse-Terre: Société d'Histoire de la Guadeloupe, 1985.

– "Free Coloreds and Slaves in Revolutionary Guadeloupe: Politics and Political Consciousness." In *The Lesser Antilles in the Age of European Expansion*, edited by Robert L. Paquette and Stanley L. Engerman, 259–79. Gainesville: University Press of Florida, 1996.

– "Guerre et révolution dans les Petites Antilles: Le prix du sucre ou de la liberté?." *Revue française d'histoire d'outre-mer* 76, no. 282–3 (1989): 239–45.

– "Les Jacobins des Antilles ou l'esprit de liberté dans les Îles-du-Vent." *Revue d'histoire moderne et contemporaine* 35 (1988): 275–304.

– *La ville aux Îles, la ville dans l'île: Basse-Terre et Pointe-à-Pitre, Guadeloupe, 1650–1820.* Paris: Éditions Karthala, 2000.

– "Révolutionnaires français et royalistes espagnols dans les Antilles." *Revue française d'histoire d'outre-mer* 76 no. 282–3 (1989): 125–58.

Petitjean Roget, Jacques. *La gaoulé, la révolte de la Martinique en 1717.* Fort-de-France: Société d'histoire de la Martinique: Librarie du Pont-Neuf, 1966.

Piquet, Jean-Daniel. *L'émancipation des noirs dans larRévolution française (1789–1795).* Paris: Éditions Karthala, 2002.

Popkin, Jeremy D. "The French Revolution's Royal Governor: General Blanchelande and Saint-Domingue, 1790–92." *The William and Mary Quarterly* 71, no. 2 (April 2014): 203–28.

– "Saint-Domingue, Slavery, and the Origins of the French Revolution." In *From Deficit to Deluge: The Origins of the French Revolution*, edited by Thomas E. Kaiser and Dale K. Van Kley, 220–48. Stanford: Stanford University Press, 2011.

– "Thermidor, Slavery, and the 'Affaire des Colonies.'" *French Historical Studies* 38, no. 1 (February 2015): 61–82.

– *You Are All Free: The Haitian Revolution and the Abolition of Slavery.* Cambridge: Cambridge University Press, 2010.

Pluchon, Pierre, ed. *Histoire des Antilles et de la Guyane.* Toulouse: Privat, 1982.

– *Le première empire coloniale: Des origines à la restauration.* Paris: Fayard, 1991.

Quinney, Valerie. "The Problem of Civil Rights for Free Men of Color in the Early French Revolution." *French Historical Studies* 7, no. 4 (Fall 1972): 544–57.

Regent, Frédéric. *Esclavage, métissage, liberté: La Révolution française en Guadeloupe 1789–1802.* Paris: Bernard Grasset, 2004.

Reinhardt, Catherine A. "Forgotten Claims to Liberty: Free Coloreds in St Domingue on the Eve of the First Abolition of Slavery." *Colonial Latin American Review* 10, no. 1 (2001): 105–24.

Resnick, Daniel P. "The Société des Amis des Noirs and the Abolition of Slavery." *French Historical Studies* 7, no. 4 (Fall 1972): 558–69.

Richardson, Patrick. *Empire and Slavery.* London: Longmans, 1968.

Rose, J. Holland. *Lord Hood and the Defence of Toulon.* Cambridge: Cambridge University Press, 1922.

Rose, R.B. *The Making of the Sans-Culottes: Democratic Ideas and Institutions in Paris, 1789–92.* Manchester: Manchester University Press, 1983.

Rudé, George. *The Crowd in the French Revolution.* Oxford: Oxford University Press, 1959. Reprint, 1972.

Ruggiero, Vincent di. "Le marronage en Guadeloupe à la veille de la révolution française de 1789." *Bulletin de la société d'histoire de la Guadeloupe* 116–18 (1998): 5–64.

Sainte-Croix de la Roncière, Georges comte de. *Victor Hugues le conventionnel.* Paris: Chez l'auteur, 1932.

Saintoyant, Jules-François. *La colonisation française pendant la révolution (1789–1799).* 2 vols. Paris: La Renaissance du Livre, 1930.

Scott, Julius C. "Crisscrossing Empires: Ships, Sailors, and Resistance in the Lesser Antilles in the Eighteenth Century." In *The Lesser Antilles in the Age of European Expansion*, edited by Robert L. Paquette and Stanley L. Engerman, 128–43. Gainesville: University Press of Florida, 1996.

Seeber, Edward Derbyshire. *Anti-Slavery Opinion in France during the Second Half of the Eighteenth Century.* Baltimore, 1937. Reprint, New York: Greenwood Press, 1969.

Shephard, Charles. *An Historical Account of the Island of Saint Vincent.* London: W. Nichol, 1831.

Sheridan, Richard. *The Development of the Plantations to 1750: An Era of West Indian Prosperity 1750–1775.* Kingston: Caribbean Universities Press, 1970.

– *Sugar and Slavery: An Economic History of the British West Indies, 1623–1775.* Baltimore, MD: Johns Hopkins University Press, 1974.

Six, Georges. *Dictionnaire biographique des généraux et admiraux français de la révolution et de l'empire, (1792–1814).* 2 vols. Paris: Georges Saffroy, 1934.

Steele, Ian K. *The English Atlantic, 1675–1740: An Exploration of Communication and Community.* Oxford: Oxford University Press, 1986.

Stein, Robert L. *The French Slave Trade in the Eighteenth Century: An Old Regime Business.* Madison: University of Wisconsin Press, 1979.

– *The French Sugar Business in the Eighteenth Century.* Baton Rouge: Louisiana State University Press, 1988.

– *Léger Félicité Sonthonax: The Lost Sentinel of the Republic.* London: Associated University Presses, 1985.

– "The Revolution of 1789 and the Abolition of Slavery." *Canadian Journal of History* 17 (1982): 447–68.

Sutherland, D.M.G. *France 1789–1815: Revolution and Counterrevolution.* London: Fontana, 1985.

Sydenham, Michael J. *The French Revolution.* London, 1965. Reprint, Westport, CT: Greenwood Press, 1985.

– *The Girondins.* London, 1961. Reprint, Westport, CT: Greenwood Press, 1976.

Taillemite, Étienne. *Dictionnaire des marins français.* Paris: Éditions maritimes et d'outre-mer, 1982.

– *L'Histoire ignorée de la marine française.* Paris: Librarie académique Perrin, 1988.

Tarrade, Jean. "Les colonies et les principes de 1789: Les assemblées révolutionnaire face au problème de l'esclavage." *Revue française d'histoire d'outre-mer* 76 no. 282–3 (1989): 9–34.

– *Le commerce coloniale de la France à la fin de l'ancien régime: L'évolution du régime de "l'exclusif" de 1763 à 1789.* 2 vols. Paris: Presses universitaires de France, 1972.

Taylor, Chrstopher. *The Black Carib Wars: Freedom, Survival, and the Making of the Garifuna.* Jackson: University Press of Mississippi, 2012.

Thibau, Jacques. *Le temps de Saint-Domingue: L'esclavage et la révolution française.* Paris: J. C. Lattès, 1989.

Tomich, Dale W. "Slavery in Martinique in the French Caribbean." In *Caribbean Slavery in the Atlantic World*, edited by Verne Shepherd and Hilary McD. Beckles, 413–34. Oxford: James Currey Publishers, 2000.

Veilhon, Alfred. *Le contre-amiral de Lacrosse, gouverneur-général de la Guadeloupe 1792–1793, 1801–1802*. Agen: L'imprimerie de l'agenais, 1933.

Viles, Perry. "The Slaving Interest in the Atlantic Ports, 1763–1792." *French Historical Studies* 7, no. 4 (Fall 1972): 529–43.

Whaley, Leigh. *Radicals: Politics and Republicanism in the French Revolution*. Stroud: Sutton Publishing, 2000.

Williams, David. *Condorcet and Modernity*. Cambridge: Cambridge University Press, 2004.

Index